APIL Guide to Accidents Abroad

CELEBRATING
150
YEARS

J O R D A N S

apil

APIL Guide to Accidents Abroad

General Editor

Sarah Crowther
3 Hare Court, London

Contributors

Asela Wijeyaratne

Katherine Deal

Pierre Janusz

Howard Stevens QC

Daniel Clarke

With assistance from

Alexander Halban

Helen Pugh

Patricia Londono

all of 3 Hare Court, London

JORDAI

Published by
Jordan Publishing Limited
21 St Thomas Street
Bristol BS1 6JS

British Library Cataloguing-in-Publication Data

A catalogue record for this book is available from the British Library.

ISBN 978 1 84661 332 6

Typeset by Letterpart Limited, Caterham on the Hill, Surrey CR3 5XL

Printed in Great Britain by CPI Antony Rowe, Chippenham and Eastbourne

FOREWORD

Suffering an injury at any time, let alone a catastrophic injury, is bad enough, but suffering it abroad adds to the difficulties. And that is just the injury.

Add into the mix decisions to be made and questions about: who can be sued for damages for losses as a result of the injury; which system of law governs the claim and limitation period; which system of law governs the assessment of damages; and in which jurisdiction can proceedings be brought, and one can see the need for immensely practical guidance, from experts in their field, to lead the injured person and their advisers through the maze.

This book provides that guidance, as well as other helpful advice for example about package travel, and rights to bring direct claims against insurers. It is also has specific chapters on air (or aviation) claims and sea (or maritime) claims. The book has been edited and part written by Sarah Crowther, who has coordinated (and exerted pressure on!) other writers including, in order of appearance in the book Asela Wijeyaratne, Katherine Deal, Pierre Janusz, Howard Stevens QC, Alexander Halban, Daniel Clarke, Helen Pugh and Patricia Londono.

All of these practitioners have very extensive practical experience of advising in this area, and representing parties in cases involving accidents overseas. It is a privilege to have been in Chambers with them at 3 Hare Court, and I hope you enjoy reading the book, and learning from it as much as I have done.

Hon Mr Justice Dingemans

ACKNOWLEDGEMENTS

This book has been a tremendous collaborative effort by various members of 3 Hare Court. I am grateful to all who have given their time, in particular those who have contributed chapters, but also other support from Hugh Mercer QC, Helen Pugh, Rowan Pennington-Benton, Mika Thom, Tony Hawitt and Patricia Londono. Thanks are also due to Cheryl Prophett for excellent editorial assistance.

I must also thank my husband, Alex Cooke, for his willingness to provide long additional hours of childcare and delicious meals.

The law is as it stands on 31 March 2013. Any mistakes are mine.

ASSOCIATION OF PERSONAL INJURY LAWYERS (APIL)

APIL is the UK's leading association of claimant personal injury lawyers, dedicated to protecting the rights of injured people.

Formed in 1990, APIL now represents around 5,000 solicitors, barristers, academics and students in the UK, Republic of Ireland and overseas.

APIL's objectives are:

- to promote full and just compensation for all types of personal injury;
- to promote and develop expertise in the practice of personal injury law;
- to promote wider redress for personal injury in the legal system;
- to campaign for improvements in personal injury law;
- to promote safety and alert the public to hazards;
- to provide a communication network for members.

APIL is a growing and influential forum pushing for law reform, and improvements, which will benefit injured people.

APIL has been running CPD training events, accredited by the Solicitors Regulation Authority and Bar Standards Board, for nearly 20 years and has a wealth of experience in developing the most practical up-to-date courses, delivered by eminent leading speakers, either publicly or in-house.

APIL training now runs almost 200 personal injury training events nationally each year, plus up to a further 100 meetings of our regional and special interest groups. Topics cover a wide range of subjects and are geared towards giving personal injury lawyers a thorough grounding in the core areas of personal injury law, whilst keeping lawyers thoroughly up to date in all subjects.

APIL is also an authoritative information source for personal injury lawyers, providing up-to-the-minute PI bulletins, regular newsletters and publications, information databases and online services.

For further information contact:

APIL
3 Alder Court
Rennie Hogg Road
Nottingham NG2 1RX
DX 716208 Nottingham 42
Tel 0115 9580585
Email mail@apil.org.uk
Website www.apil.org.uk

CONTENTS

TABLE OF CASES

References are to paragraph numbers.

TABLE OF STATUTES

References are to paragraph numbers.

TABLE OF STATUTORY INSTRUMENTS

References are to paragraph numbers.

TABLE OF EUROPEAN MATERIALS

References are to paragraph numbers.

TABLE OF INTERNATIONAL MATERIALS

References are to paragraph numbers.

CHAPTER 1

INTRODUCTION

'Remember what Bilbo used to say: It's a dangerous business, Frodo, going out your door. You step onto the road, and if you don't keep your feet, there's no knowing where you might be swept off to.' (JRR Tolkien)

1.1 INTRODUCTION

It is necessary to start by setting out briefly what this book is and is not about. This involves admitting that the title is, to some extent at least, misleading. First, the scope is not limited to merely 'accidents' in the traditional sense of slippers, trippers, colliding vehicles or skiers. In fact, the principles discussed extend to clinical negligence, illness claims, deliberate assaults and the other myriad circumstances in which personal injury can be sustained.

Secondly, it is not really a book just about events which occur 'abroad'. Although the majority of cases in which such issues will arise will involve a claimant who was outside England and Wales at the time he sustained injury, this book will also have relevance to those whose claims relate to events occurring in England and Wales to claimants who are habitually resident or domiciled elsewhere, or where the defendant is foreign. So, for example, where an Englishwoman is injured as a result of a road accident on the M25 for which a French registered lorry is at fault, questions of jurisdiction and applicable law still have a role to play.

Thirdly, the book does involve discussion of issues which are not related to a claim for personal injury damages, but which commonly arise in practice. For example, it is helpful to have some practical consideration of the principles which apply to the question of whether a defendant tour operator is entitled to join the local supplier in an additional claim, or whether co-defendants have rights of contribution. Such issues often have direct practical ramifications for the main action for personal injury damages.

On the other hand, it has been necessary to limit discussion to those aspects which relate directly to the personal injury element of accidents abroad. Whilst in practice the complainant traveller will often raise grievances such as regarding the quality of his accommodation, the misrepresentations in the brochure or made by the travel agent, the discrimination he suffered at the hands of airport staff or the horrendous delay to which his travel arrangements were subjected, these are topics which have had to be left for consideration elsewhere.

1.2   HOW TO USE THIS BOOK

Several aspects of the law which are addressed in this book are codified in some form or other. In an effort to avoid duplication, the key materials are appended to the text. Appendix 1 is the Package Travel Regulations 1992; Appendix 2 is EC Regulation 44/2001 ('Brussels I'); Appendix 3 is EC Regulation 864/2007 ('Rome II'); Appendix 4 is EC Regulation 593/2008 ('Rome I'); Appendix 5 is EC Regulation 392/2009 ('the 2002 Athens Convention') and Appendix 6 is the Montreal Convention 1999.

In addition, Chapter 10 sets out some short pleading precedents which address the main types of claim discussed in the narrative section of the book.

1.3   TERMINOLOGY IN THIS BOOK

It is an unfortunate truth of the law of conflicts that many of its concepts are pithily expressed in Latin tags. Whilst modernisers rightly complain that English law should not rely on a dead foreign language, the reality is that in conflicts cases Latin lives on. Some use of Latin has therefore been unavoidable. In any event, as the terms are widely used in other texts in this area, an officious attempt to eradicate Latin entirely is probably futile.

Some short explanation hopefully will assist. *Lex causae* is the law of the issue, or the substantive law. Its partner term is *lex fori*, which is the law of the forum where the dispute is being heard. *Lex loci delicti* is the law of the place of the tort and *lex contractus* is the law of the contract.

In cases where proceedings are pending, the Latin phrase used is *lis pendens*. Usually the context implies that there are proceedings pending in the courts of another country where the jurisdiction of the English court is challenged. Another basis of challenge to the English court is *forum non conveniens,* not as commonly assumed, meaning that the English court is not a convenient forum, but rather that there is another place where it is as or more appropriate for the claim or issue to be heard.

As if all that Latin were not enough, French also plays a part in conflicts terminology. *Renvoi* is a difficult concept in any language. It is an applicable law term which has the effect explained in Chapter 5 at **5.2.2.3**. Suffice it to say for introductory purposes that the *renvoi* is generally excluded from most choice of law regimes. This means that the 'applicable law' means all the rules of law of the country, but excluding that country's own rules of private international law.

Otherwise, where resort has been had to foreign language terminology, it is explained in the body of this work.

Another unhappy feature of conflicts of laws is the tendency for the same piece of legislation to be allocated several names. For example, EC Regulation 44/2001 is also variously known as the Judgments Regulation or Brussels I. Whilst consistency of use of these terms has not been achieved entirely, we hope that some overlap can be forgiven. The reader should be aware that other texts and legislation will use these terms interchangeably.

Finally, the expressions 'English' court and 'English' law are shorthand. No disrespect to the Welsh or Wales is intended.

1.4 PACKAGE TRAVEL

Where an individual has sustained injury or illness in the course of a temporary trip abroad, the Package Travel Regulations 1992[1] provide a first line of possible recourse. The vicarious liability imposed on the organiser or retailer of a package holiday in respect of services promised to the consumer is effective notwithstanding the fact that the actual supplier of the services is a third party independent of the 'tour operator'. This makes the Package Travel Regulations an important weapon in the armoury of the claimant.

It sidesteps complications of jurisdiction, applicable law and complications of agency, by imposing directly on the tour operator an obligation to meet the claimant's damages. It gives the real benefits to a claimant of litigating in his home country, using the language with which he is familiar and pursuant to his domestic procedure.

Chapter 2 addresses the question of which trips, for it is not just 'holidays', are within the scope of the Package Travel Regulations.[2] It also gives a detailed analysis of the considerable efforts undertaken by some parts of the travel industry to seek to avoid the effects of the Package Travel Regulations under the guise of 'dynamic packaging',[3] a concept well known to industry insiders but probably unheard of by the average consumer.

This chapter also tackles the sometimes tricky question of whether the consumer should pursue the travel agent, the traditional 'tour operator' or some other party to his travel arrangement contract.[4] New challenges are posed in respect of these issues where bookings are made through

---

[1]   SI 1992/3288.
[2]   At **2.2–2.4**.
[3]   See **2.4**.
[4]   See **2.6**.

websites or over the telephone.[5] Consideration is given to the practical effect of the law in this area and its likely impact on evidence.

The nature and extent of the tour operator's duty to his consumer is canvassed in detail in Chapter 3. The express and implied terms of the package travel contract are considered,[6] including in particular the vexed question of the impact of the 'local standards' pertaining in the place of the accident in determining whether the supplier's conduct was reasonable in all the circumstances.[7]

1.5   GASTRIC ILLNESS

Food and drink cases warrant special consideration, given that it has been successfully argued that a stricter standard of conduct applies. Chapter 3 details the cases for and against strict liability and examines the likely impact on the evidence.[8]

1.6   EXCURSIONS AND ACTIVITIES

Accidents which occur in the course of additional excursions or activities which do not fall within the scope of the prearranged services under the package contract often raise significant complications in practice. In Chapter 2 the circumstances in which the tour operator may still be liable for services outside the package are examined. Particular consideration is given to the nature and extent of any contractual or tortious duties owed by the tour operator to his customer in respect of excursions and activities sold and provided other than as part of the package.[9]

Where a tour operator is not in the frame, the claimant's representatives will need to assess whether there is potential for proceedings against a defendant not domiciled in England and Wales. In particular, there may well be jurisdiction in the English court to hear a claim against the insurer of a foreign provider of an activity, such as an aqua park, scuba diving excursion or skiing lessons. In such cases, the questions of jurisdiction and applicable law are studied in Chapter 6, Direct Rights Against Insurers.

More generally, where an action is brought against the local supplier, either by the tour operator joining the supplier as a third party to the claimant's proceedings[10] or where the claimant wishes to bring a claim

---

5   See **2.3.3–2.3.3.6**.
6   At **3.2**.
7   At **3.2.2.2–3.2.2.8**.
8   At **3.5**.
9   See **2.8**.
10   See **3.4**.

against a supplier of services domiciled outside England and Wales,[11] then questions of jurisdiction and applicable law arise.[12]

1.7 CRUISE HOLIDAYS

It is most likely that a cruise holiday will constitute a package.[13] However, it is also international carriage of a passenger by sea and, if properly incorporated into the package contract, such limitations and conditions of liability as are imposed by the Athens Convention regime will apply.[14] Special care is needed in the pleading and practice of carriage by sea cases as is addressed in Chapter 7.

1.8 AIR CARRIAGE CASES

Where a passenger is injured or suffers illness during carriage by air, special rules imposed by the international conventions under the Warsaw regime overlay the general English law. This codified regime brings its own complexities, with special rules on jurisdiction and a wholly exclusive liability code, with particular caps on liability and time limits. Chapter 8 addresses claims which are concerned with travel by air.

1.9 JURISDICTION

Jurisdiction is the question of whether there is power in the courts of England and Wales to hear a claim between the parties.

It is not only package travel which gives rise to claims in respect of accidents outside England and Wales. There are lots of practical benefits to a claimant in bringing a claim in the courts of his own domicile. His witnesses are more likely to be based in England and Wales, especially in respect of quantum issues such as medical evidence and consequential financial loss. He has a better chance of obtaining relevant evidence and has the convenience of instructing lawyers and dealing with the litigation in his own language.

Chapter 4 provides a comprehensive analysis of the rules of English law. It sets out which regime applies when seeking to establish jurisdiction[15] and considers what 'domicile' means for the purposes of jurisdiction issues.[16] It examines the general rule in cases which fall within the scope of Brussels I[17] of jurisdiction in favour of the courts of the defendant's

---

[11] Perhaps as a co-defendant see **4.4.4.4** in Brussels I cases and **4.6.2** in CPR, r 6.36 cases.
[12] Chapters 4 and 5.
[13] See **2.3.2.1**.
[14] See **2.7** and **3.2.3**.
[15] At **4.3.1**.
[16] At **4.4.3**.
[17] Which is referred to in Chapter 4 as simply 'the Regulation' to avoid repetition.

domicile and particularly those exceptions which are relevant in the context of accident or illness abroad.

For the purposes of jurisdiction and applicable law, Scotland and Northern Ireland are 'foreign' countries with foreign legal systems. Chapter 4 also canvasses the rules which apply where any choice is between different parts of the UK.[18]

Some of the specific additional jurisdiction enjoyed by the English court which is relevant to personal injury is:

(i)   where the foreign defendant is a co-defendant to a English domiciled defendant;[19]
(ii)   in third party claims;[20]
(iii) consumer contracts;[21] and
(iv)   individual contracts of employment.[22]

1.10   CONTRACT CASES WITH AN EXPRESS CHOICE OF JURISDICTION

The formal requirements of Brussels I with regard to valid jurisdiction agreements and the effect of such agreements is dealt with in Chapter 4.[23]

1.11   INDEPENDENT HOLIDAY LET CASES

A feature of the modern traveller is an increasing willingness to make independent holiday arrangements. The advent of website property rental agencies together with the recent trend for foreign buy-to-let ownership has led to a boom in private short-term letting arrangements.

Despite the obvious potential for conflicts of laws issues such as jurisdiction and applicable law disputes, many small scale landlords do not have express terms and conditions. Chapters 4 and 5 deal specifically with the issues which arise in such cases and the factors which will affect whether an injured tenant can claim against his holiday-let landlord[24] and whether the English courts can hear the claim.

---

[18]   At **4.5.**
[19]   At **4.4.4.4.**
[20]   At **4.4.4.5.**
[21]   At **4.4.4.8.**
[22]   At **4.4.4.9.**
[23]   See **4.4.4.11.**
[24]   At **4.4.4.10** and **5.3.2.5(c).**

1.12 *ODENBREIT* CLAIMS: DIRECT RIGHTS AGAINST INSURERS

The decision of the Court of Justice of the European Union (CJEU) in *FBTO v Odenbreit*[25] has opened the doors to increasing jurisdiction of the English courts to hear claims in respect of accidents abroad in circumstances where the claimant has a direct right of action against the insurer of the wrongdoer.

In road accidents, in respect of which within the EU at least there is a requirement for compulsory third party motor insurance, where a claimant is injured in a road accident abroad, his claim in tort will potentially be subject to the jurisdiction of the English courts, particularly if he enjoys a direct right of action against the insurer of the driver responsible and the insurer is domiciled in the EU.[26]

This can give claimants the benefit of generous foreign applicable law regimes regarding strict liability for traffic accidents.[27] It can also mean that heads of loss and the identity of potential secondary victims (either sufferers of psychiatric loss or in wrongful death claims) can be more widely construed than at English law.

Even in claims arising out of accidents outside the EU, the insurer can still potentially be exposed to the jurisdiction of the English courts.[28]

Further, there is nothing in the *Odenbreit* interpretation of Brussels I which limits the application of its principles to motor claims. In many civil jurisdictions the public liability insurers are generally exposed to direct action by the victims of the insured. Therefore proceedings can often be advanced against the insurer of the 'at fault' skier in collisions on the slopes. Increasingly cases against the insurers of occupiers of foreign premises, suppliers of professional services and activities, including medical provision are being considered for jurisdiction in England and Wales.

1.13 CHALLENGES TO THE JURISDICTION

Chapter 4 studies some of the other general rules which have practical import in personal injury litigation, including where proceedings are pending in more than one country in respect of the same or related actions,[29] particularly in view of the strict application of the 'first seised' principle under Brussels I.

---

[25] *(C-463/06)* [2007] ECR I-11321.
[26] See Chapter 6, Direct Rights Against Insurers, Chapter 4, Jurisdiction at **4.4.4.7**.
[27] See eg *Cox v Ergo Versicherung AG* [2012] EWCA Civ 854.
[28] See **4.6.2.1**.
[29] At **4.4.4.13**.

In respect of CPR, r 6.36 jurisdiction cases, the discretion of the English courts to decline jurisdiction or stay proceedings based on the principles of forum non conveniens (ie that the courts of another place are a more appropriate forum for the action) or lis alibi pendens (that the same action is proceeding elsewhere) are considered as these can act as a limit on the jurisdiction of the English court.[30]

1.14　APPLICABLE LAW

This is an area of law which has seen significant upheaval in recent times as a result of attempted harmonisation by the EU. The result is a state of flux. Many questions of both practice and principle will fall to be decided in respect of Rome II and Rome I in the future.

The scope and effect of the law applicable to a claim is of the utmost importance to the parties. Questions such as limitation;[31] assessment of damages;[32] the identity of the correct claimants and defendant are crucial.

Chapter 5 analyses the mechanisms by which the English courts decide which law applies to a tort claim.[33] Consideration is given to situations in which the English court will apply English law on the basis of public policy or where the rules of English law override the choice of law in a mandatory fashion.[34]

The law applicable to contribution claims between defendants is considered.[35]

Choice of law in contracts concluded after 17 December 2009 is also addressed,[36] including employment and consumer contracts.[37] For earlier contracts, the relevant provisions of the previous regime of the Rome Convention are also considered.[38]

1.15　DAMAGES

The court can only compensate personal injury in monetary form. Chapter 9 deals with the law and practicalities of both English law claims for loss and damage, such as where a package travel contract has been

---

[30]　At **4.7**.
[31]　At **5.2.2.10**(viii) and **5.2.5**.
[32]　Chapter 5 at **5.2.2.10**(iii), **5.2.3.6** and Chapter 9.
[33]　At **5.2.2.4–5.2.2.8** and **5.2.3**.
[34]　At **5.2.2.11** and **5.2.3.5**.
[35]　At **5.2.2.13** and **5.2.3.6**(iii).
[36]　At **5.3.2**.
[37]　At **5.3.2.10** and **5.3.2.9** respectively.
[38]　See **5.3.3.1**.

breached, but also tackles the difficult and unclear area of assessment of damage in cases where the English court is seeking to apply a foreign applicable law.

The tricky question of the scope of the applicable law in cases under Rome II is addressed,[39] together with potentially unanswered questions including, the meaning and effect of recital 33 to the preamble to Rome II[40] and whether periodical payments will be a feature of the landscape in such claims.[41] Comprehensive practical guidance supporting an approach to evidence gathering is discussed and special consideration is given to wrongful death claims[42] and interest.[43]

---

[39] At **9.3.2.1**.
[40] At **9.3.2.2**.
[41] See **9.3.2.3**.
[42] At **9.3.5.1**.
[43] At **9.3.7**.

CHAPTER 2

PACKAGE TRAVEL

Asela Wijeyaratne

2.1 INTRODUCTION

The Package Travel, Package Holidays and Package Tours Regulations 1992[1] ('the Regulations') came into force on 23 December 1992 and regulate 'packages' sold or offered for sale in the UK on or after 30 December 1992. The Regulations implement Council Directive 90/314/EEC ('the Package Travel Directive'). The preamble to the Package Travel Directive noted the 'many disparities' between the national laws of member states in the regulation of travel services sold in packages.

Prior to the adoption of the Package Travel Directive, only a few European countries had directly legislated in the field of travel contracts.[2] For instance Italy and Belgium had already ratified the International Convention on Travel Contracts which afforded comparable consumer protection to the Package Travel Directive with regard to the travel organiser's liability. However, in the UK, Austria, Denmark, Finland, Latvia and Poland (amongst other states), any consumer protection was left to the general rules and principles of contract law.

By Art 1 of the Package Travel Directive, its stated purpose is 'to approximate the laws, regulations and administrative provisions of the Member States relating to packages sold or offered for sale in the territory of the Community'.

2.2 THE DEFINITION OF PACKAGE

The phrase 'package holiday' evokes a certain kind of travel by individual or small groups of consumers solely for the purposes of tourism and leisure. Whilst it is undoubtedly true that consumer habits and industry practices have outgrown the Directive in the 20 years since its implementation, in fact, the reach of regulation for the travel services industry has always been far broader than the stereotypical family holiday.

---

[1] SI 1992/3288. See Appendix 1.
[2] See Prof Dr Hans Schulte-Nölke (ed) *EC Consumer Law Compendium – Comparative Analysis* prepared for the European Commission under Service Contract No 17.020100/04/389299 for detailed discussion.

All travel services sold or offered for sale in a 'package' are regulated. By reg 2(1), a 'package' is said to be:

'the pre-arranged combination of at least two of the following components when sold or offered for sale at an inclusive price and when the service covers a period of more than twenty-four hours or includes overnight accommodation:–
(a) transport;
(b) accommodation;
(c) other tourist services not ancillary to transport or accommodation and accounting for a significant proportion of the package, and
   (i)   the submission of separate accounts for different components shall not cause the arrangements to be other than a package;
   (ii) the fact that a combination is arranged at the request of the consumer and in accordance with his specific instructions (whether modified or not) shall not of itself cause it to be treated as other than pre-arranged.'

Accordingly, there are a number of elements of the definition, *all* of which must be satisfied in order for a package to be regulated:

(1) the package must comprise a combination of two or more of the qualifying components (transport, accommodation or 'other tourist services');
(2) the package must either extend for a period exceeding 24 hours, or include overnight accommodation;
(3) the combination of those qualifying components must have been pre-arranged; and
(4) the combination must be sold or offered for sale at an inclusive price.

The elements of this definition are considered in turn.

2.3   QUALIFYING COMPONENTS

2.3.1   Transport

There ought to be little difficulty with this aspect of the definition. Unlike with 'other tourist services', the Regulations do not provide for any de minimis rule with this component. As such, it would appear that the type and distance of transportation, and its significance in the context of the holiday, ought not to be relevant considerations for the court.

In practice however, such distinctions have been made. In the matter of *Keppel-Palmer v Exus Travel*,[3] the claimant had paid the sum of US$142,425 for a stay at a supposedly luxurious villa in the Bahamas over the millennium. The claimant and her husband had made their own arrangements (on Concorde) for their flight to the Bahamas. The

---

[3]   [2003] EWHC 3529 (QB).

claimant nevertheless argued, amongst other things, that the provision by the defendant of road transfers from the airport to the villa made the arrangements a package.

Whilst Gage J did not accept that the transport was pre-arranged at the time of booking and therefore could not be a component of any 'package', he also observed that:[4]

> 'I have great difficulty in accepting that the provision of transport to and from the airport, a journey of some 45 minutes' duration, can in the context of this case qualify as transport under the definition in Regulation 2. I accept that there is no quantitative definition of transport, but in my view in each case it must be a question of fact and degree as to what constitutes transport under the Regulation. Here, in my judgment, what was provided was so minimal that it can be disregarded.'

Gage J also found that the limousine service was 'ancillary' to the facilities of the luxury villa.[5] This finding is difficult to reconcile with his other finding that the limousine was pre-booked in a separate arrangement from the accommodation. However, in other cases it may well be that transport does not constitute a component in its own right. By way of example, a sprawling hotel complex may offer to convey a guest from its reception to her room on the other side of its grounds in an electric buggy.

Another potential issue is that of car hire. In the matter of *easyCar (UK) Ltd v Office of Fair Trading*,[6] the CJEU determined that car hire was included in the term 'transport services' used in the Distance Selling Directive,[7] on the basis that it involved making a means of transport available to a consumer. It is likely that a consistent interpretation would be adopted under the Package Travel Directive and the Regulations. As such, a fly-drive holiday comprising only a flight and car hire is unlikely to comprise a package, given that both components are for transport.

2.3.2   Accommodation

Similarly, in the vast majority of cases, whether something constitutes 'accommodation' is unlikely to give rise to much difficulty. The provision of a hotel room, self-catering apartment, youth hostel bed, villa or chalet is all within the ambit of the Regulations and would accordingly form one component of a package.

Difficulties may, however, arise with respect to accommodation which, from a common sense perspective, would be considered part and parcel of a long-distance or overnight transport service. Whilst no express

---

[4]   [2003] EWHC 3529 (QB) at [15].
[5]   [2003] EWHC 3529 (QB) at [16].
[6]   C-336/-03.
[7]   97/7/EC.

distinction is provided for in the Regulations, it is suggested that the accommodation element of such services should be sufficiently distinct from the transport in order to amount to a separate component such that package regulation applies. In each case, the question is likely to be one of fact and degree. The court is unlikely to construe the booking of a sleeping compartment on an overnight train or recliner seat on a coach to constitute a package. Similar considerations apply with respect to car and passenger ferry journeys.

On the other hand, a customer booking an Orient Express style 'experience holiday', which included overnight train travel in a luxury sleeper berth, may well legitimately expect that the booking ought to be considered as providing both transport and accommodation by the same medium. There is no reason in principle why the luxury sleeper berth cannot be considered a service for which the customer had paid, as distinct from, and in addition to, the transport from one train station to the next.

It may be that student and cultural exchange 'hosting' programmes enjoy a special exemption from the Directive and Regulations. In its decision in *AFS Intercultural Programs Finland ry*,[8] the CJEU held that a Finnish not-for-profit organisation was *not* liable under the Directive in respect of exchange students which it placed with host families in France because the essence of the hosting arrangement and the long-term duration of the stays were not of the character of 'accommodation' within the meaning of the Directive and accordingly the arrangements did not constitute 'packages'. This is a pragmatic decision based upon a purposive construction of the Directive and it is not entirely clear what special features of 'hosting' will be required to take an arrangement outside the meaning of 'accommodation'. It is suggested that where guests are treated as a member of the family or household, then it will no longer be appropriate to describe them as 'consumers' of 'accommodation'.

2.3.2.1   Cruises

Cruises are often sold with other services such as coach travel or flights to the port of departure and from the final port of call, together with hotel accommodation on the night before departure. Alternatively, the customer may have pre-booked certain shore excursions, which may themselves be considered 'other tourist services' within the meaning of reg 2(1). In each of these circumstances, there will often be little difficulty in identifying the booking as for a package.

Sometimes of course, all that is provided is the cruise itself, where the customers makes their own travel arrangements and accommodation arrangements for the night before departure. In such cases, it is likely that

---

[8]   Case C-237/97 [1999] ECR 1-00825.

the cruise alone will be considered a regulated package. The cruise is self-evidently transportation, even if the port of departure and the final port of call are one and the same, with no intermediate stops. However, it also provides accommodation which is more than merely a facility of the transport. Indeed, on any sensible view, it is artificial to consider a cruise to be anything other than the provision of transport and accommodation services.

2.3.3 Other tourist services not ancillary to transport or accommodation which account for a significant proportion of the package

The term 'tourist' as deployed in reg 2(1) is not a defined term of art. Although the main dictionary definitions[9] link 'tourism' with travel for pleasure, Saggerson[10] suggests that the term is not limited to a leisure traveller 'but merely one who tours'. Grant and Mason[11] also suggest that:

> 'People who travel on business and for educational purposes, or as pilgrims (the original tourists) would all qualify as tourists.'

Any narrower a construction of the term would on the face of it seem to conflict with the full title of the Regulations, and the Package Travel Directive's broadly stated purpose of consumer protection.

The other service must, however, be more than merely 'ancillary to' transport or accommodation before qualifying as a component. The pointing out of sights or landmarks by the driver over the tannoy of a coach transfer from the airport to the hotel is unlikely to be considered anything more than ancillary to transport. Similarly, the provision of refreshments or stewarding services in the course of transport is unlikely to be considered sufficiently free-standing.

Equally in the case of accommodation, there are a number of 'services' which are incapable of being regarded as independent of the customer's stay. These may include, by way of example, currency exchange, laundry, lobby shops and swimming pools. There is of course no exhaustive list of all provisions not considered ancillary. Each will turn on its own facts and will be a question of degree. It may be a fine question for instance whether a courtesy shuttle bus to the beach, provided by a hotel, amounts to a service which is separate from the hotel accommodation.

Further, what constitutes a 'significant proportion' of a package is not limited in either quantitative or qualitative terms by the Regulations but

---

[9] Oxford English Dictionary, Collins.
[10] *Travel Law and Litigation* (XPL, 4th edn, 2008) p 38.
[11] *Holiday Law: The Law Relating to Travel and Tourism* (Sweet & Maxwell, 5th edn, 2012).

ought to be assessed by reference to both. For instance, an introductory meeting by the tour operator's representative at the hotel, where a brief guide to local attractions is provided, is probably not ancillary to the accommodation, but is unlikely to be considered sufficiently significant to constitute a separate qualifying component of the package itself. By contrast, the provision of an expert and fluent Egyptologist, for a tour of ancient Egyptian tombs, is likely to be considered sufficiently significant in the context of the consumer's expectation as to the content of his booking.

Examples of such services commonly encountered in practice which it is suggested generally will amount to separate components of a package include: specialist tuition such as skiing, sailing or paragliding lessons; ski and snow equipment hire; Sherpa or guiding services on walking trips; scuba diving tours; shore-based excursions on cruise holidays; and lectures and readings on educational or historical tours.

2.3.3.1   *Pre-arranged combination*

The combination of the components has to take place prior to the sale or offer to sell to the consumer. This definition clearly encompasses the typical scenario of a consumer who purchases an entire holiday (comprised of two or more qualifying components) from a brochure. Such 'off the shelf' holidays are arranged in advance of the point of sale and offered as advertised in the brochure without revision.

Even where revisions are made by the offeror, or indeed where a bespoke arrangement is tailored to the consumer's request, the Regulations make explicit, (whereas the Package Travel Directive is silent), that the combination of the components of the holiday 'at the request of the consumer and in accordance with his specific instructions' shall not of itself cause the package to be treated 'as other than pre-arranged'.

Given the silence of the Package Travel Directive on this issue, its interpretation was considered in the case of *Club-Tour Viagens e Turismo SA v Garrido*.[12] There the ECJ found that the term package used in Art 2(1) must be interpreted so as to include holidays organised by travel agents, at the request of and in accordance with the specifications of a consumer or a limited group of consumers. It also found that the term 'pre-arranged combination' must be interpreted so as to include combinations of services put together at the time when the contract is concluded between the travel agency and the consumer.

---

[12]   C-400/00.

2.3.3.2   Excursions and extras

It is worth noting, however, that post-contractual arrangements made between a consumer and the provider of his package holiday will not fall within the scope of the package and are unregulated. A common example in practice arises in the case of cruise holidays where shore-based excursions are booked after the cruise but prior to departure. Nor do locally booked excursions or activities purchased from a tour operator's representative in resort qualify for the benefit of the Regulations.[13]

2.3.3.3   Combination sold or offered for sale at an inclusive price

This element of the definition has received the most judicial attention, and can now properly be described as the touchstone test. The first occasion on which it was considered was in the Administrative Court in the matter of *R (the Association of British Travel Agents Ltd) v Civil Aviation Authority (CAA)*[14] ('*ABTA v CAA*'). At issue were the circumstances in which a travel agent was obliged to have an Air Travel Organiser's Licence (ATOL), which scheme the CAA administered. The dispute centred on the CAA's interpretation of the meaning of 'package' for the purposes of the Civil Aviation (Air Travel Organisers' Licensing) Regulations 1995.[15] ABTA's complaint was with a guidance note issued by the CAA, which set out how it intended to 'help travel organisers and travel agents decide what parts of their business needed ATOL protection'.

The CAA expressed the view in its guidance note, under the heading 'inclusive price' that:

> 'This term refers to the price of the package. It does not matter if the cost of a package is made up of separate sums relating to the value of each element (travel, accommodation, other ancillary tourist services). In these circumstances, the whole arrangement can still be sold at an inclusive price.'

In the High Court, Goldring J found as follows with respect to this aspect of the definition:

> '156 ... the words "inclusive price" should be given their ordinary and natural meaning. The ordinary and natural meaning of the word "inclusive" connotes more than a mere arithmetical total of the component parts of a price. If the substance of a transaction is the sale by the travel agent of separate and discrete components of (for example) a holiday, with no one part being connected with or dependent upon any other part (other than that they are sold together), to call the resulting price "inclusive" is in my view to stretch the ordinary and natural meaning of that word. It is in reality no more an "inclusive price" than is the total price of goods at the check out

---

[13]   For such cases, see **2.8**.
[14]   [2006] EWHC 13 (Admin); [2006] ACD 49.
[15]   SI 1995/1054.

of a supermarket. For the sale of a package at an inclusive price the relationship between the component parts of that package must be such as to mean that the consumer is buying and paying for them as a whole: that the sale of one component part is in some way connected with or dependent on the sale or offer for sale or others.'

Goldring J accordingly decided that the guidance note was unlawful and quashed it. The decision was upheld by the Court of Appeal,[16] where, Chadwick LJ went on to elaborate upon Goldring J's finding, by applying it to a number of instructive holiday scenarios.

The typical scenario is where the price of the components, when combined, is different (and in most cases cheaper) than the cost of each component when offered for sale individually. Such a situation is common, given that some components cannot be purchased in isolation (for instance a courtesy airport transfer) or because package holidays are competitively and more cheaply priced. In these cases, Chadwick LJ found that 'there is unlikely to be difficulty in reaching the conclusion, on the facts, that the components ... are being sold as a pre-arranged combination at an inclusive price' and therefore as a package within the meaning of the Regulations.

The more difficult scenario, for interpretative purposes, is where the price of the holiday is equal to the aggregate of the prices for which the components would have been sold or offered for sale separately. In such instances, the price is only inclusive if the services are being sold or offered for sale as components of a combination, rather than as separate components simply sold at the same time. It is the combination of the services which renders the price inclusive, notwithstanding the fact that the package price is equal to the aggregate price of the individual components.

Chadwick LJ went on to provide some useful examples to illustrate the latter scenario more neatly. In the first example, a customer in London makes enquiries with a travel agent with a view to spending a week in a named hotel in Rome. The travel agent ascertains that the cost of the return flights will be £X, the cost of the accommodation will be £Y, that the cost of the transfers will be £Z. Without disclosing the cost of each component, the travel agent informs the customer that the cost of the holiday is £X+Y+Z. In these circumstances, 'there would be little doubt – as seems to me – that the services were sold as a pre-arranged combination and at an inclusive price'.

By contrast, if the travel agent informed the customer of the cost of each of the components, and explained that he could purchase any one or more of those components as he chooses, without the need to purchase others,

---

[16]   [2006] EWCA Civ 1356, [2007] All ER (Comm) 898, [2007] 2 Lloyd's Rep 249, (2006) 150 SJLB 1430.

or purchase alternatives, what was sold or offered for sale was patently not a package. Such example is tantamount to Goldring J's supermarket customer.

What is critical therefore is the need for combination between the components which are sold or offered for sale, rather than merely forming a basket of services which are purchased at the same time. It is the inclusivity of the price paid which evidences this combination. Whilst the examples provided by Chadwick LJ are helpful, and are typically considered by the courts by way of analogy, the Court of Appeal was clear that the question is one of fact, to be determined on a case–by–case basis.

2.3.3.4   *Website bookings*

Where website holiday services are in issue, the decision in the criminal case of *Civil Aviation Authority v Travel Republic Limited*[17] is of some assistance. Once on Travel Republic's website, consumers were offered a choice of flights, hotels and apartments, car hire and other related services. On appeal, the High Court noted, with respect to the booking process that:

> 'Some web links specifically refer to what are described as "tailor made holidays". The various components which make up a holiday are ostensibly all sold separately but can be linked together by a customer to provide all the necessary elements of a holiday, and indeed the system consciously facilitates their ability to do this. The total cost of the combined services will be the same as the aggregate cost of each of the components priced separately. In other words there is no price discount for booking more than one element of the holiday.'

The High Court found that those facts fell squarely within the scope of Chadwick LJ's example in *ABTA v CAA* as to when a package was not sold, namely where individual components were purchased at the same time as a basket of goods, but not as part of a pre-arranged combination for an inclusive price.

2.3.3.5   *Telephone bookings*

Very many holidays are now purchased by consumers over the telephone. The overwhelming majority of consumers will be unaware of the *ABTA v CAA* decision. On the other hand a significant minority of tour industry operators are keen to limit the application of the Regulations to their business. Such operators seek to exploit the uncertainty generated by the requirement for detailed factual analysis of an interaction which neither consumer nor booking clerk has real cause to remember several years

---

[17]   [2010] EWHC 1151 (Admin).

after the event, to deter consumers from seeking remedy often after clear failures to provide contracted services and even where the consequences have been profound.

Travel Republic also sold services by way of telephone bookings. Its operatives used a script which was supposed to emphasise that it acted as an agent for the providers of each component; that it did not provide package holidays itself; and that each component is provided separately. The trial judge found on the evidence that 'telephone operatives dealt with the customer in different ways and the script is not always adopted'. Nevertheless, on the basis of the information which had been laid, the trial judge was entitled to find that no packages had been sold.

Of particular importance with respect to telephone bookings, the High Court found that:

> '... the distinction between cases caught by the regulations and those falling outside it can on the particular facts be a fine one; to the extent that each transaction is fact sensitive. So the regulation will almost certainly bite in a case where the customer specifically tells the agent that he wishes to buy a holiday and the component services are either offered or suggested to him as part of a proposed single holiday package. The combination is then put together by the agent, for the customer. Whilst that may well have happened on occasions with this agent, particularly where holidays were booked by telephone, this is not the typical situation which we are required to address in this test case.'

The High Court accordingly tacitly recognised that it was far easier for a travel agent operating a model such as that used by Travel Republic to unwittingly sell (or offer for sale) a package by telephone, than through a website. Websites lend themselves to being travel supermarkets. The customer may be taken to pages where individually priced components are chosen, such that it is abundantly clear that they may each be substituted, or purchased without another. Further still, websites may also easily facilitate the coordination of components, to provide all the necessary elements of a holiday in a basket of goods, without inextricably linking them to form a package. Even if at the time an individual consumer does not subjectively appreciate that she is supermarket shopping, the website itself provides a full written record of the transaction.

From the travel agent's perspective, it is much harder to construct the neat division between components when a customer books over the telephone. Not having the legal niceties of the Regulations in mind, there is broad scope for the customer to simply seek to purchase 'a holiday' in respect of which he is offered services for which he is quoted a single price by the telephone operative, who may even be using the travel agent's own website to do so. It is likely that what is sold is a package, whether it was intended to be or not.

This was precisely what happened in *Titshall v Querty Travel Ltd.*[18] Here, Mr Titshall and his partner booked a holiday to Corfu, during which he suffered serious injuries as a result of glass patio door shattering.

The booking of the holiday took place during a telephone call lasting no more than 10 or 12 minutes. The trial judge found that Mr Titshall had wished to purchase a last-minute holiday advertised on Teletext, departing the following day. He rang the number shown on the advert and spoke to Querty's sales representative. It was found that the sales representative had provided Mr Titshall with 'an elementary and simple breakdown' of the cost of the components, before 'arriving at the bottom line, which was all that interested Mr Titshall' who duly booked the holiday. Mr Titshall was also told that Querty were acting as agent of identified suppliers of the flights and accommodation.

After the litigation had been intimated, Querty also provided a record of the booking, which had not (and was not supposed to have been) given to Mr Titshall at the time of booking. The document showed that three separate charges, entitled 'Service Fee', had been added to the price of Mr Titshall's booking. Querty was unable to inform the court exactly as to what these charges related to.

The Court of Appeal found that whilst 'the transaction had the potential to develop into an offer for sale and a sale of separate services, it did not develop that way'. First, it was relevant that Mr Titshall was never told that the flights or the accommodation were available for separate purchase, the one without the other (and by analogy that the components were capable of being substituted). Secondly, it was found that the 'service cost … must in some way have been presented as in part the price for putting together the package'.

The first part of the Court of Appeal's reasoning is consistent with Chadwick LJ's examples in *ABTA v CAA* and the trap identified in *CAA v Travel Republic*. However, when placed in the factual framework of *Titshall*, the requirements on the part of the travel agent to avoid the Regulations are brought into sharp relief. Despite the fact that Mr Titshall was told of the cost of each component, and of the identity of the suppliers of those components, he was still required to be told that each component could be purchased without the other, or could be substituted for another. This is despite the fact that Mr Titshall had informed the sales representative of the holiday (as fully constituted) which he wanted to book, the flight for which was departing the very next day.

This second part of the Court of Appeal's reasoning is consistent with Goldring J's dicta in *ABTA v CAA*. Whilst he posited that the required nexus between components may be evidenced by a discount on their

---

[18]   [2011] EWCA Civ 1569, [2012] 2 All ER 627, [2012] 2 All ER (Comm) 347.

aggregate value once combined, it is equally true the nexus may be evidenced by an additional cost for the price of putting together the package.

2.3.3.6   Evidence

Despite the number of occasions on which the question has been considered, given the fact sensitive nature of the issue, the question of whether the combination was offered for sale at an inclusive price is likely to arise time and again in litigation. When in issue, the first port of call is the substance of the interaction between parties at the time when the holiday was booked. In respect of website bookings, disclosure of screenshots to evidence the booking process is often required. With respect to telephone bookings, any scripts used by the operator are likely to be of strong evidential value.

The Court of Appeal has shown tendency to place primary weight on the understanding of the consumer at the time of booking. In circumstances where the consumer believed she was paying an inclusive price for 'a holiday', cogent evidence will have to be produced by the defendant to demonstrate that it had in fact simply sold more than one service at the same time without any nexus between them.

2.4   'DYNAMIC PACKAGING'

'Dynamic packaging' is a term presently in vogue for holidays sold by tour operators and travel agents purporting not to be packages, despite their resemblance to them. Any 'dynamism' in fact achieved by such sales is largely for the sole benefit of the seller, given that non-regulated arrangements do not attract ATOL bonding or liability for the negligence of local subcontractors and suppliers under the Regulations.

Ordinarily, such holidays sold include flights, accommodation and transfers, as with a traditional package. However, the components are sold such as to provide the appearance of a separate contract in respect of each, with a breakdown of the cost and named supplier of each component. The object of this, which is sometimes also referred to as 'contract splitting', is to avoid the appearance that the components were 'arranged' or sold at an 'inclusive price' within the meaning of the Regulations. Some travel agents go so far as to describe themselves as 'booking platforms' or 'intermediaries' in the hope of avoiding common law or statutory terms of art altogether.

It is impossible to provide any broad statements of principle with respect to such schemes. Rather, they must be judged on the merits. The first step is to identify whether, notwithstanding the operator's protestations to the contrary, the holiday purchased by the consumer was a package after all.

It ought to be remembered that the submission of separate accounts for different components 'shall not cause the arrangements to be other than a package' under reg 2(1). Neither will the fact that the combination is arranged at the request of the consumer and in accordance with her instructions.

Operators purporting to sell dynamic packages often rely upon documentation purporting to show separate contracts entered into by the consumer in respect of separate components, often with named suppliers shown on such documents. However, documentation provided to the consumer after the execution of the contract, which is ordinarily construed to be the time of booking, is likely to be of limited relevance in determining whether the contract was for a package. As appears from *ABTA v CAA* and *Titshall v Querty Travel*, the principle consideration for the court will be what the consumer understood, and was told, at the time of booking.

As explained above (**2.3.3.3–2.3.3.5**), dynamic packaging is most likely to succeed where the sole interactions between the consumer and the operator are through a website, however, this dynamism has much potential to breakdown where the interactions between the consumer and the operator are over the telephone. When all the consumer wishes to do is purchase 'a holiday', he must be told that the components need not be purchased together and can be discarded or swapped, and should be made aware of the price of each component, in order for the operator to avoid selling a package.

Where it is possible to show that the arrangement was for a package, it will ordinarily also be possible to show that the operator selling the package was 'the other party to the contract'. The names of the suppliers of each of the components will often be disclosed to the consumer at the time of booking, in an attempt to demonstrate that the operator is acting only as agent of those suppliers. However, if the holiday is found to have been a package, then it would follow that the operator is 'the other party to the contract' given that the named suppliers only provided individual components.

2.5   PERSONS PROTECTED BY THE REGULATIONS

The civil liabilities imposed by the Regulations are in favour of the 'consumer', defined in reg 2(2) as:

> '... the person who takes or agrees to take the package ("the principal contractor") and elsewhere in these Regulations "consumer" means, as the context requires, the principal contractor, any person on whose behalf the principal contractor agrees to purchase the package ("the other beneficiaries") or any person to whom the principal contractor or any of the other beneficiaries transfers the package ("the transferee").'

In general terms the Directive and the Regulations look to the substance rather than the form in relation to the identification of a 'consumer'. The express reference to context invites the court to adopt a flexible and purposive approach with a view to giving protection to those for whose benefit the package contract was concluded.

2.5.1   The principal contractor

The 'principal contractor' is the person who 'takes or agrees to take' the package, with the focus being on the party who agrees the contract. The principal contractor may therefore also be the purchaser of the package, but not necessarily so, given that the purchase monies may have come from someone else.

Nor is there any requirement for the principal contractor to actually go on the package holiday. The principal contractor who in fact also goes on the package will also be a 'consumer', but if the contract was entered into solely for the benefit of another, he may be a consumer for some, but not all of the rights in the Regulations.

It is accordingly suggested that legal as well as natural persons are capable of being the principal contractor. Such circumstances could include packages purchased by employers for their employees or schools for their pupils. In the personal injury context such entitlement is likely to be of limited relevance, given that the injured party will have standing to bring the claim, whether as a beneficiary or a transferee.

2.5.2   Other beneficiaries

'Other beneficiaries' include 'any person on whose behalf the principal contractor agrees to purchase the package'. The definition is accordingly limited by the need for there to be a principal contractor, and the need for that principal contractor to have agreed the contract for the holiday.

The protection of other beneficiaries in the Regulations is significantly broader than the common law. Under the common law, the party to the contract is required to be a party to the claim, albeit that she may claim damages for the loss suffered by those persons she intended to benefit from the contract (*Jackson v Horizon Holidays Ltd*).[19] Under the Regulations however, the beneficiary may now bring proceedings himself, without need to persuade the contracting party to do so on his behalf.

It should be noted, however, that the contractual analysis has not now been made entirely redundant. Whilst a beneficiary is entitled to sue for his own losses under the Regulations, it is unclear whether he is entitled to claim for the damages suffered by other beneficiaries. Take the example of

---

[19]   [1975] WLR 1468.

a wife as the principal contractor to a package booked for herself, her husband, her mother-in-law and son. If the husband suffers injury as a result of the improper performance of the contract, it is likely to be the case that the entire family will have suffered a loss of enjoyment of the holiday. The wife, assuming that she paid for the package, may well also have a claim for her loss of bargain. Under the common law, the wife may bring proceedings in her sole name not only for her own loss, but also for her husband's losses, and the loss of enjoyment suffered by them all. There is no authority as to whether, under the Regulations, the husband in the given situation may bring proceedings in his sole name for the loss of enjoyment suffered by the family in addition to his own losses. In practice the point is rarely taken by tour operators when faced with claims by beneficiaries for the loss of enjoyment of other beneficiaries and loss of bargain by the principal contractor. If the issue is raised in the defence or counterschedule, then generally a straightforward answer will be to add the principal contractor to the action as a claimant, because it is suggested that the principal contractor, in line with the previous common law, is entitled to recover damages for and on behalf of any member of the party. For further discussion of damages issues in package claims see Chapter 9, Remedies.

2.5.3 Transferees

Regulation 10 governs the situations in which a consumer may assign her rights pursuant to a package contract to a third party. A consumer may therefore also be the person to whom a package is transferred under reg 10. In certain limited circumstances, either the principal or the beneficiary is entitled to make a transfer of his rights under the package contract to a third party. After such transfer takes place, the transferee acquires the same legal rights under the Regulations as both of the other two categories of consumer. It is notable that the Regulations do not appear to envisage the possibility of a transferee making an onward transfer. These provisions appear to be little known to consumers and seldom used.

2.6 PERSONS SUBJECT TO OBLIGATIONS UNDER THE REGULATIONS

The Regulations variously impose liabilities upon 'the other party to the contract', the 'organiser' and the 'retailer'. These potential defendants to a claim for breach of a regulated contract will be examined in turn.

2.6.1 Organiser

By reg 2(1):

> '"Organiser" means the person who, otherwise than occasionally, organises packages and sells or offers them for sale, whether directly or through a retailer.'

This definition, despite being somewhat circular, can be readily understood as referring to someone who, otherwise than occasionally, arranges or combines the component parts of a package. This clearly includes conventional tour operators who sell packages in the course of their business. However, the definition extends well beyond the typical tour operator.

Travel agents for example arrange package holidays on a frequent basis. Where a travel agent combines the individual components of a package, it will invariably be the organiser. Beyond tour operators and travel agents, a number of other persons may fall within the definition of organiser. Schools which organise school trips, employers and charities organising trips or missions for its members may fall within the ambit of the Regulations. It should be noted that an organiser need not be acting for commercial gain. Not–for–profit organisations and even individuals organising travel for friends or colleagues potentially fall within the definition.

There is no reported authority on the question of the meaning of 'otherwise than occasionally'. In the unreported decision of HHJ Mackay in *Gill v Plessington Catholic High School*,[20] it was held that because a school in the usual or foreseeable course of events did organise trips for its students that it was doing so 'otherwise than occasionally', regardless of any detailed factual analysis of frequency or regularity of actual trips organised.

2.6.2   Retailer

By reg 2(1):

> '"Retailer" means the person who sells or offers for sale the package put together by the organiser.'

Travel agents largely fall squarely within the definition of retailer. Retailers are subject to certain obligations concerning the information to be provided to consumers in brochures (reg 5) and incur a civil liability for loss caused to the consumer by the provision of misleading information.

The other organisations or individuals listed in **2.6.1** are all capable of acting as a retailer, depending upon the facts of the case. Further likely candidates that may find themselves being considered a retailer are newspapers, websites and television shows providing holiday promotions.

---

[20]   Liverpool County Court, 24 June 2008.

Detailed factual and legal consideration may be necessary in some circumstances to determine whether an intermediary is in fact a principal contractor acting on behalf of a beneficiary or rather a retailer of a package organised by another. The example of school trips given at **2.6.1** illustrates this point: is the school selling its pupils places on a package tour put together by an operator or is the school agreeing to purchase a package from the operator on its pupil's behalf? Such questions fall to be determined in accordance with the law of agency.[21]

2.6.3   The other party to the contract

The 'other party to the contract' is defined by reg 2(1) as 'the party, other than the consumer, to the contract, that is, the organiser, the retailer, or both, as the case may be'. 'Contract' is in turn defined as 'the agreement linking the consumer to the organiser or to the retailer, or to both, as the case may be'.

The use of the word 'linking' has received considerable academic attention. It has been suggested by some[22] that given that 'linking' is not a term of art in English contract law, it is possible for a party with whom the principal contractor has no contract to nevertheless be considered 'the other party to the contract' within the meaning of the Regulations.

However, this interpretation ignores the word 'agreement' in reg 2(1). It is clear from the definition of contract that there must be an agreement which links the consumer to the organiser, or the retailer, or both. In the absence of an agreement, the mere presence of a 'link' to the consumer is insufficient. In every case therefore, 'the other party to the contract' must be the principal contractor's counterparty to the contract for the package holiday. The enumeration of 'organiser' and 'retailer' only serves to particularise the closed list of two entities which that counterparty is capable of being.

In *ABTA v CAA*, Goldring J put it thus:

> '161 ... the PTR do not exclude the application of the English law of contract. There is continual reference to "the" contract and "the other party to the contract:" see paragraphs 2, 6(3), 7(1), 8(1) and 9(1). In my view, whether the agreement links the consumer to the organiser or retailer or both depends upon the application of the English law of contract, in particular the law of agency. So too do decisions as to whether the organiser or retailer or both are parties to the contract or whether under Regulation 15, the organiser or retailer or both are liable under it. If by application of the English law of contract the retailer is liable under the contract between him and the consumer, he cannot escape his liability by

---

[21]   A detailed treatment of the principles of agency falls outside the scope of this work. See *Bowstead on Agency* (Sweet & Maxwell, 19th edn, 2012).

[22]   David Grant and Stephen Mason *Holiday Law: The Law Relating to Travel and Tourism* (XPL, 5th edn, 2012) pp 56–62.

blaming the lack of proper performance of the obligations under it on someone else ... In short, that there may be such an additional obligation upon the retailer does not mean that the normal English law of contract has no relevance. It means that in the case of the sale of a package, the retailer cannot escape liability by pointing to someone else's failure: that he must provide sufficient bonding to give that obligation value.'

A tour operator which organises packages may be the 'other party to the contract' in a number of ways. It may have a contract with the consumer as a result of having directly supplied the package to him. In such a case, the tour operator will be both the organiser and the retailer. Alternatively, it could have supplied the package through the agency of a retailer, such as a travel agent. Where that agency was disclosed, it will be the tour operator, as organiser, that is the 'other party to the contract', and not the retailer. A travel agent that acts as an agent of tour operator which is disclosed will not therefore be 'the other party to the contract'.

Such a travel agent may unwittingly be considered 'the other party to the contract', or have a liability which is consummate with it, where its principal is not disclosed to the consumer. Such a scenario occurred in *Hone v Going Places Leisure Travel Limited*.[23] There, it was found that in the circumstances, the defendant travel agent was the other party to the contract given it has not disclosed to the consumer that it was acting on behalf of a principal, a tour operator which had become insolvent by the time of trial.

It is also otherwise possible for 'the other party to the contract' to be a retailer but not also an organiser. A travel agent acting solely as a retailer may enter into direct contractual relations with the consumer, selling packages organised by a tour operator which acts as its supplier, rather than as its principal. In such a scenario it will be the travel agent, as retailer, that is 'the other party to the contract', and not the organising tour operator.

It is beyond doubt that the Regulations impose on 'the other party to the contract' a duty which is more extensive than the common law rules on privity and vicarious liability allow. However, the Regulations do nothing to abrogate the English contract and agency law when determining the *identity* of the 'other party to the contract'. It is those rules, on privity, offer and acceptance, and agency, which are relevant to the analysis.

2.7 RELATIONSHIP WITH INTERNATIONAL CARRIAGE CONVENTIONS

Whilst not the detailed subject to this chapter,[24] it is worth noting here that some claims will be the subject of international conventions for the

---

[23] [2001] EWCA Civ 947.
[24] See Chapter 7, Accidents at Sea and Chapter 8, Travel by Air.

carriage of passengers. Accordingly, it will be important in any such claim for the relationship between such conventions and the Regulations to be understood because it has practical implications for limitation and pleading.

2.7.1 The Montreal Convention

The Montreal Convention of 1999 has been given effect in English law by the Carriage by Air Acts (Implementation of the Montreal Convention 1999) Order 2002 and applies to international carriage of persons, baggage and cargo performed by air. Article 17(1) of the Montreal Convention 1999 provides for a liability on the part of 'the carrier' for:

> '... damage sustained in the case of death or bodily injury of a passenger upon condition only that the accident which caused the death or injury took place on board the aircraft or in the course of any of the operations of embarking or disembarking.'

Where the package includes a flight on a tour operator's charter, it is likely that the tour operator will also be carrier for the purposes of the Montreal Convention. However, the Montreal Convention provides for an exclusive liability regime (art 29). As such, any injury occurring in the course of international carriage by air to which the convention is subject must be brought subject to the conditions and limits set out in the convention.

In many cases, the carrier will not be the tour operator, but one of the tour operator's suppliers within the meaning of the Regulations. In such cases, it is ordinarily possible to bring a claim against the tour operator for the failure on the part of the carrier to perform the contract properly. It is very common, however, for tour operators to seek to incorporate the conditions and limitations of the Montreal Convention into their booking conditions with the consumer with respect to losses sustained in the course of carriage, which is expressly permitted by reg 15(3).[25]

2.7.2 The Athens Convention

The Athens Convention of 1974 has been given effect in the UK by s 193 of the Merchant Shipping Act 1995 and applies to the international carriage of passengers and luggage by sea. Like the Montreal Convention, the Athens Convention also provides for an exclusive liability regime. As such, the convention applies to the exclusion of the Regulations, even where the carrier is also 'the other party to the contract' within the meaning of the Regulations, as in *Norfolk v My Travel Tour Operations*

---

[25] For an example of case in which such incorporation failed: see *Akehurst v Thomson Holidays Ltd & Britannia Airways Ltd*, Cardiff County Court, 6 May 2003, per HHJ Graham Jones.

Limited.[26] There, the claim was time-barred because it had not been brought within the 2-year time-limit provided for by the Convention.

Article 3(1) of the Athens Convention provides that:

> 'The carrier shall be liable for the damage suffered as a result of the death or personal injury to a passenger and the loss or damage to luggage if the incident which caused the damage so suffered occurred in the course of carriage and was due to the fault or neglect of the carrier or his servants or agents ...'

If the injury to the passenger did not occur in the course of carriage, there is no reason in principle why the claim cannot be pursued under the Regulations in the usual manner. Tour operators providing cruises often also provide other services, such as shuttle bus services from ports of call to sights and attractions, and guided tours at such sites. An accident occurring whilst boarding a shuttle bus laid on by the tour operator at the port will not have occurred 'in the course of carriage' and will not therefore be subject to the conditions and limitations set out in the convention.

2.8   EXCURSIONS AND EXTRAS

Personal injury which occurs in the course of an excursion can create unique difficulties for claimants, with respect to the identifying the proper defendant, establishing the duty and standard of care, and founding the jurisdiction of the courts of England and Wales. Much will depend upon the time and the manner by which the excursion was booked. Examples of the most commonly encountered type of excursion are considered below. Similar considerations apply in the case of additional services such as ski or equipment hire. Other common examples are where additional services are purchased by the consumer from the hotel, including meals in the hotel restaurant, not included in the board arrangement under the package contract, or the recent trend for holidaymakers, including small children, to have so-called 'henna tattoos' applied by poolside artisans.

2.8.1   Pre-booked excursions

2.8.1.1   *Inclusive excursions*

Many excursions are booked with the tour operator prior to departure. Despite being described as an excursion, it may well form one of the components of the package, if the entire holiday is inclusively priced. Such arrangements are sometimes described as a twin-centre or multi-centre trip, depending upon the length and substance of the excursion.

---

[26]   [2004] 1 Lloyd's Rep 106.

For instance, a consumer seeking an all-inclusive holiday to Luxor, Egypt, may wish to undertake a one-day sightseeing trip to Cairo during the holiday. If the holiday, including the one-day trip to Cairo, is priced inclusively, then this 'excursion' is likely to form a component of the package. In such circumstances, there ought to be little difficulty in bringing proceedings against the other party to the contract in the same manner as with any other regulated package.

2.8.1.2   *Collateral excursions*

A pre-booked excursion will not form a component of the package if it is not inclusively priced. In the above example, the consumer may be quoted £1,500 for the all-inclusive trip to Luxor, with an additional price of £750 for the one-day excursion to Cairo. In such circumstances, the fact that the price of the excursion is additional, and the remainder of the holiday can be taken without the excursion, is likely to indicate that the excursion does not form part of the package.

Pre-booked excursions which do not form part of the package will be the subject of a collateral contract with the consumer. In many cases the tour operator's standard terms and conditions apply to the excursion also. One example is *Moore v Hotelplan Limited t/a Inghams Travel*,[27] which concerned a skidoo excursion booked whilst on holiday. The tour operator's terms and conditions provided, under a section headed 'Our Liability' as follows:

> 'We promise to make sure that all parts of the holiday we have agreed to arrange as part of our contract are provided to a reasonable standard and in accordance with the contract. We also accept responsibility for what our employees, agents and suppliers do or do not do ...'

It was found that the skidoo excursion was the subject of a collateral contract between the claimant and the tour operator. It was also found, however, that '[t]he holiday contract provided the context within which [the excursion contract] was entered into'. Given that it would be 'wholly artificial' to view the excursion contract in isolation from the holiday contract, the court found that the skidoo excursion was subject to the 'Our Liability' clause in the booking conditions.

Unless the relevant liability clause in the booking condition is expressly limited to the provision of the package, or expressly excludes excursions, it is likely that any assumption of liability for proper performance of the holiday arrangements, or for the negligence of suppliers and subcontractors, is likely to apply equally to collateral excursions.

---

27   [2010] EWHC 276 (Ch).

2.8.1.3   A 'package in a package'

Some collateral excursions will be capable of being construed as a
separate package, which attracts the protection of the Regulations. Again,
such arrangements may sometimes be referred to as 'twin-centre' or
'multi-centre' holidays. The principal differences with inclusive excursions
are that a separate priced is charged, and the excursion itself constitutes
two or more qualifying components within the meaning of reg 2(1).

By way of example, a consumer booking an all-inclusive holiday to
Colombo, Sri Lanka, may wish to take an excursion to the Maldives. An
inclusive sum of £2,000 is quoted to him for a flight from London
Heathrow to Colombo, and accommodation in Colombo for 12 nights. A
further sum of £800 is quoted for a boat trip from Colombo to Malé, in
the Maldives, a 2-night stay in a hotel there, and a flight home from Malé
to Heathrow.

The 2-night excursion to the Maldives in the above example will itself
form a package, or a 'package within a package' given that it constitutes
two or more qualifying components sold to the consumer at an inclusive
price. It is a separate package to that booked for the principal destination
of the holiday. Bringing a claim in respect of personal injury sustained
during such an excursion will be no different in practice to any other
claim in respect of a regulated agreement.

2.8.2   Excursions and extras booked locally

Most excursions and extras, properly so described, are booked after
arrival at the holiday destination. Such excursions or extras do not form
part of the package for the holiday itself, given that they were not, by
necessity, sold or offered for sale at an inclusive price, together with the
other components of the holiday such as flights and accommodation.

2.8.2.1   Claims in contract against the tour operator

The first step with such excursions or extras is to identify the party with
whom the holidaymaker has contracted. If the contracting party is in fact
the tour operator, the claim may be pursued in contract. The proper
identity of the party providing the additional services will often be the
subject of dispute. Whilst excursions and extras are usually promoted by a
local representative of the tour operator, it commonly alleged that the
tour operator is only acting as an agent of a local supplier, for the
negligence of whom it has no liability.

The factual circumstances relating to the booking of the excursion must
accordingly be analysed on a case–by–case basis to determine whether the
contract for the additional services was with the tour operator, or whether

the tour operator was acting as an agent for an undisclosed[28] supplier. In either case, the tour operator will be the proper defendant to the claim.

The courts have had cause to consider such arguments on a number of occasions of late. In *Moran v First Choice Holidays and Flights Limited*,[29] the claimant and her husband had booked a holiday to the Dominican Republic with First Choice, the defendant tour operator. After arriving at the hotel, the claimant was given a 'Welcome Pack' by the defendant's representative which stated that First Choice:

> '... offer an exciting selection of trips to suit everybody ... All our excursions are fully insured and regularly checked to ensure that they meet our safety standards. First Choice cannot be held responsible for any excursion not supplied by First Choice as they probably will not meet our stringent insurance and safety requirements, at First Choice you safety and enjoyment are our first priority.'

The claimant was also provided with a booking form in respect of the various trips on offer, which stated that:

> 'There are several "Pirate" companies operating excursions in the Dominican Republic, these companies are not used by British tour operators because they do not reach the qualify, safety and hygiene standards that we as your tour operator demand. We cannot accept any responsibility for illness, injury or death caused as a result of participating in a pirate excursion.'

The court found that both documents were written in precisely the same spirit, namely 'book for tours operated by First Choice and it will provide safe tours for which they will accept responsibility in the event of a tour not meeting its rigorous standards and injury resulting'. The claimant and her husband booked a quad bike tour, in the course of which she was injured when she was thrown from the bike as a result of a defect with it.

At trial First Choice denied that it was the principal to the excursion contract. It argued that it acted as an agent for a local supplier of the excursion. The High Court found that given the contents of the welcome pack and the booking form, the claimant and her husband were left 'with the justifiable impression that the excursion contract was being made with the tour operator', and that there was no reference to the name of the local supplier. Indeed, the excursion was promoted in a manner designed to prevent holidaymakers from booking with local suppliers, or 'pirate companies' as they were unflatteringly termed. The High Court accordingly found that First Choice had failed to disclose that it was

---

[28] Care must be taken not to confuse this situation with the one in which the consumer is well aware that additional services will be provided by a party other than the tour operator, although the precise identity of the supplier is not known to the consumer. In this situation, the proper defendant is the unidentified supplier.

[29] [2005] EWHC 2478 (QB).

acting as agent, and that it was liable to the claimant as if it were the principal contracting party, for the failure to regularly and competently maintain the hire bike.

In *Moore v Hotelplan Limited*, the skidoo excursion was also one which was offered by a representative of the tour operator, as advertised in the tour operator's welcome pack. The claimant asked the tour operator's representative to arrange the excursion, and paid her in cash. The receipt provided to the claimant displayed the tour operator's logo. The tour operator's representative also admitted in evidence that she would ordinarily have asked the claimant to sign its own disclaimer of liability. As with the claimant in *Moran*, the claimant in *Moore* had no reason to believe or suspect that the excursion was being provided by anyone other than the tour operator. The High Court accordingly found the tour operator liable for breach of the excursion contract. It might be said that these cases demonstrate a conflation of the concepts of the 'undisclosed principal' with that of the 'unidentified principal' given that one might expect a consumer to realise that excursions such as skidoo or quad bike trips would be provided by a local supplier rather than by the tour operator itself.

Often the evidence will be far more ambiguous than in the cases of *Moran* and *Moore*. It may be for instance that the injured person was told, in the course of a promotional welcome meeting, that the tour operator provided excursions which were of the highest standard, unlike those that could be booked with suppliers across the street from the hotel. However, the booking form for the excursion might bear the logo of a local supplier, and indicate that the tour operator is only acting as agent.

It is to be noted, however, that documentary evidence will not necessarily be conclusive in such cases. If, as in *Moran*, the injured party was led to believe that there was a material distinction in price, quality and safety of excursions offered by the tour operator compared to those offered by local providers, it will be a difficult argument for the tour operator to make that the liability for the accident rests with a local supplier after all.

If the excursion is found to have been booked with a disclosed local supplier, the tour operator may nevertheless have assumed a duty of care in tort (to which see below). Alternatively, if the excursion was in an EU member state, the injured person may have a cause of action in the courts of England and Wales against the supplier's public liability insurer (to which see Chapter 6, Direct Actions Against Insurers). Further still, the injured party may seek to avail himself of the option of redress against the local supplier in the local courts.

2.8.2.2 *Claims in tort against the tour operator*

Where the excursion contract is between the injured person and the tour operator, or where the tour operator acts as an agent of an undisclosed principal, the existence of an accompanying common law duty of care is likely to add little. However, in cases where there is no contract between the tour operator and the injured person, the facts may nevertheless evidence the assumption of a free-standing tortious duty of care.

The Court of Appeal's decision in *Parker v TUI UK Limited*,[30] found such a duty, albeit obiter, in an excursion context. There, the claimant, her husband and their two sons booked a skiing holiday (which was a package) with TUI, the defendant tour operator. Whilst on holiday, the party booked a tobogganing event organised by a local supplier. The claimant suffered an accident whilst on the toboggan run.

The Court of Appeal found that 'it was not easy to determine, on the exiguous evidence before the judge, whether [the claimant] had a contract with TUI in relation to the toboggan run'. However, TUI's representatives had accompanied the group who booked the excursion through them on the run, and indeed had carried out a risk assessment in respect of it. Whilst counsel for the tour operator 'bravely argued that TUI had no duty of care and could leave their customers to the tender mercies of the elements, and the icy terrain at night without a qualm', this submission was not supported by the evidence. Rather, the evidence indicated that TUI's representatives had assumed a common law duty of care by accompanying those booking on the trip. On the facts of the case however, that duty was found to have been performed.

As such, in circumstances where the tour operator was not a party to the excursion contract, or where it was acting as an agent for a disclosed local supplier, its representatives may nevertheless have assumed a tortious duty of care to the injured party. If those representatives accompanied the trip, or provided instructions or safety warnings, or supervised the excursion in some other way, that may be sufficient for the duty to be established. If that duty was breached, the tour operator will be vicariously liable for the negligence of its employees.

It is, however, fundamental to the success of such argument that the persons assuming the duty of care to the injured person were employees of the tour operator, rather than independent subcontractors. If only those persons employed by the local supplier accompanied the trip, the tour operator will not be vicariously liable for any negligence.

This was recently emphasised by the Court of Appeal in *Harrison v Jagged Globe (Alpine) Limited*.[31] There, the defendant agreed to provide a

---

[30]   [2009] EWCA Civ 1261.
[31]   [2012] EWCA Civ 835.

self-led mountaineering expedition to Sir Ranulph Fiennes and the claimant to Ecuador. The defendant also arranged local guides and a cameraman to film the expedition. The guides were independent contractors. In the course of the trip, Sir Ranulph Fiennes decided to organise the filming of various stunts, which the trial judge concluded formed no part of the package provided by the defendant, or contemplated by the contract.

The stunts involved the claimant pretending to fall into a crevasse whilst attempting to jump over it, and later fall whilst climbing. The claimant alleged she was injured during both stunts. The Court of Appeal rejected the trial judge's finding that the defendant was liable for the negligence of the guides with respect to the stunts. It noted however, that the position would have been different if the guides had been negligent with respect to the subject matter of the package, such as 'training and climbing at altitude', given that in such circumstances, the tour operator would be responsible for the improper performance of the package by its suppliers.

It is suggested that the facts in *Parker* are relatively unusual and the circumstances in practice in which the tour operator will be found to have assumed a relevant duty of care in respect of the provision of a service which is the subject of a contract between the consumer and a third party supplier are limited. Even where such duty has been assumed, its scope is likely to be narrow.

2.9   NON-REGULATED AGREEMENTS

Where it cannot be established that the holiday sold was a package, whether as a result of successful dynamic packaging or otherwise, the first port of call must be the express terms of the contract. Tour operators' terms often mirror reg 15(1), even where only accommodation is provided. If the tour operator has undertaken a responsibility for the negligence of its suppliers and subcontractors, it will make little difference to the injured party that the contract was not for a package.

Further still, where the contract is for the provision of a single component, the operator may nevertheless be found to have an implied contractual obligation to provide the service with reasonable care and skill. In *Wong Mee Wan v Kwan Kin Travel Services Ltd*,[32] the defendant tour operator's brochure suggested that it would be responsible for providing each of the items on a tour itinerary. The Privy Council found that the defendant had 'undertook to provide and not merely arrange all the services in the programme, even if some activities were to be carried out by others'. Given the undertaking to *provide* the services, there was an implied term that this would be done with reasonable care and skill.

---

[32]   [1996] 1 WLR 38.

Where the holiday sold is not regulated, the literature provided to the customer from the relevant provider of the service will have to be closely scrutinised to determine whether the customer was left with the impression that the tour operator had undertook to actually provide rather than arrange the service. Similarly, discussions between the customer and the tour operator's representative or travel agent will also have to be considered.

The duty of care found in *Wong Mee Wan* was as extensive as that of tour operators selling packages pursuant to the Regulations. As such, it is suggested that it is likely to be relatively rare for a tour operator to knowingly undertake such an extensive duty in its literature, where the express booking conditions do not so provide. For those operators purporting to sell dynamic packages, there will have been a conscious effort to avoid any literature to this effect.

As in *Parker v TUI*, any assumption of duty may have been in tort, even if there has been no such agreement in contract. Where the contract is only for the arrangement of accommodation abroad, there may be nothing in the pre-contractual documentation comparable to that found in *Wong Mee Wan*. Nevertheless, if the accommodation provider routinely demands health and safety audits from its hotels, and sends its own representatives to those hotels to check safety and hygiene measures implemented, it is arguable that a common law duty of care has been assumed. Disclosure of the accommodation provider's dealings with the hotel, including of any audits and inspections, is essential when seeking to determine whether such duty exists.

Where there has been no assumption of such a duty to provide the service, the duty will be limited to arranging the service. In such circumstances, the contract between the parties is likely to be the subject to an implied term that the operator exercise reasonable skill and care in selecting those who provide the service. In practice, most unregulated agreements are likely to be the subject of this narrow duty. In *Wilson v Best Travel Ltd*,[33] the Court of Appeal did not consider a tour operator to be obliged to boycott any hotel, unless the absence of some safety feature there 'might lead to a reasonable holidaymaker to decline to take a holiday at the hotel in question'.

In this typical situation then, the party with whom the customer contracts for the arrangement of a service abroad is unlikely in most instances to bear any liability for the negligent acts or omissions of the local provider. In the first instance, the duty was only to *arrange* rather than to *provide*. Secondly, and in any event, given that the local provider was a supplier or subcontractor, the tour operator will not have any vicarious liability for negligence.

---

[33] [1993] 1 All ER 353.

2.10   REFORM OF THE REGULATIONS

It is beyond doubt that the popularity of the traditional package holiday has waned. On the one hand, there has been a movement towards greater independence by consumers in making travel arrangements. Low-cost airlines have made booking other components of a holiday with different providers a cost-effective and attractive option. Holidays beyond the traditional Mediterranean basin have also become more popular. On the other hand, there has been an impetus by travel agents and tour operators to sell holidays resembling packages, but which do not attract the protection of the Regulations, under the guise of 'dynamic packaging'. In the UK it is estimated that fewer than 50% of passengers on leisure flights are now protected by the Regulations, whereas in 1997 around 98% were.

It is therefore beyond doubt that the extent of consumer protection offered by the Regulations is far narrower now than when first implemented. The sister domestic ATOL scheme has undergone significant reform of late with the protection of 'flight-plus' arrangements.[34] A flight-plus holiday is created whenever a flight out of the UK is sold with accommodation and/or car hire outside of the UK, under the same contract as, or in connection with the fight. Unlike with the definition of a package within the meaning of the Regulations, there is no requirement for the flight-plus components to be combined, or sold at an inclusive price. The flight-plus category therefore, by and large, reflects the reality of modern dynamic travel arrangements.

These changes have not gone unnoticed by the European Commission. In 2007 the Commission published a working document which attempted to distil the principal regulatory problems and to consult stakeholders. In November 2009, the Commission launched a public consultation on the revision of the Package Travel Directive. Following the close of the consultation, the Commission had intended to present its revision proposals at the beginning of 2011. That deadline was missed, and a new draft directive is still awaited.

It is likely that any changes to the Package Travel Directive would reflect the changes to the ATOL scheme, by the introduction of a protected category of flight-plus arrangements. In its summary of the responses to the consultation, the Commission recognised that:

> 'There was broad agreement across all stakeholder groups for revising the current definition of a package ... Consumers and consumer organisations, as well as Member States, indicated that they were in favour of extending the definition of a package and, thereon, the scope of the Directive to provide protection for a wider range of so-called "dynamic packages" ... More than half of both industry associations and individual companies responding to the consultation were also in favour of extending scope on this way.'

---

[34]   The Civil Aviation (Air Travel Organisers' Licensing) Regulations 2012, SI 2012/1017.

Given both industry demands for a level playing field between traditional tour operators and other travel component providers on the one hand and consumer requirements for clarity on the other, it seems likely that any modernisation of the scope of the Directive will be to widen, rather than reduce its effects.

CHAPTER 3

PACKAGE TRAVEL II – THE LIABILITY OF THE TOUR OPERATOR TO THE CONSUMER AND THE TOUR OPERATOR'S RIGHTS AGAINST HIS SUPPLIERS

Katherine Deal

3.1 INTRODUCTION

This chapter explores in detail the nature of the tour operator's liability to his consumer in respect of loss and damage caused by personal injury as a result of the Package Travel Regulations. It considers the scope and nature of the duty owed, the relevant evidential issues and also specific statutory and common law defences available to the tour operator. In many claims brought against tour operators, the claimant's real complaint is that the local supplier did not meet their obligations and therefore increasingly additional claims against foreign domiciled suppliers are a feature of this type of litigation. Issues which commonly arise in these third party claims are addressed. The final section looks at one common type of tour operator claim which raises specific issues; gastric illness claims.

3.2 SCOPE OF THE CONTRACT

A claim arising out of an incident during the course of a regulated package holiday should be brought in contract. The Regulations themselves do not establish a free-standing statutory duty. What they do is set out various things that will be deemed to be included in the contract between the consumer and the other party to that contract. It is worth noting that, remote as the prospect may be in practice, terms which are implied as a result of the Regulations apply notwithstanding the fact that the law applicable to the contract might be the law of a country other than England and Wales.[1] Depending on the law governing that contract, additional terms may be implied into the holiday contract if they are not otherwise set out expressly.

The most common basis for a claim is one brought by reference to reg 15 on the basis that the accident or illness was caused 'by a failure to perform

---

[1]   Regulation 28 and see Chapter 5, Applicable Law.

the contract or the improper performance of the contract'. Accordingly, it is always necessary to examine the precise scope of the contract in order to assess whether there has been improper performance.

The first step will therefore be to consider the contract itself. The overwhelming majority of package holidays sold in England and Wales are sold by tour operators – often the same outfit trading under a variety of different names. For example, Thomas Cook, Airtours and Direct Holidays are just some of the many current trading names in the Thomas Cook group. Although every brand name may have its own booking conditions (generally the only basis on which the main tour operators will contract), the basics are likely to be remarkably similar.

It is overwhelmingly likely that the booking conditions for the major tour operators will already include (sometimes word for word) the various provisions of the Regulations. However, it can quite often be the case that the booking conditions actually provide rather more extensive rights than the Regulations themselves dictate.

In *Jay v TUI*,[2] for example, the defendant tour operator had voluntarily extended its liability to include liability for the contractors of the defendant's suppliers, as opposed to those who were simply employed by the suppliers, as is more usual. This could have extended the chain of those for whom the tour operator accepted responsibility beyond those for whom it was vicariously liable. In the event, the judge found for a more conservative construction, effectively conflating contractors with servants and agents. However, the potential for expansion of duties owed beyond those provided for under the Regulations was not doubted.

3.2.1 Express terms

As always, the first port of call must be the contract. What do the booking conditions say the tour operator agrees to do or agrees to provide? This will also be relevant in determining whether the event giving rise to the claim falls within the scope of the holiday contract or whether, as with most excursions, it falls outside.

Almost certainly they provide that the tour operator accepts responsibility for the proper performance of the holiday contract, frequently mirroring in exact terms the wording of reg 15(1). Generally they will state that reasonable skill and care will be exercised. Usually there will be a reference to the relevance of local standards. All of these will be discussed below.

In addition, the following issues may be relevant:

---

[2]   Bristol County Court, 23 November 2006, Adrian Palmer QC (QBD), Lawtel 17 June 2007.

- What are the descriptions of the hotel in the brochure? Does it refer to a swimming pool, air conditioning, a holiday club for children, sea views, nightlife and so on? If specific features and facilities are specified then their existence and availability are likely to amount to contractual obligations, which give rise to an absolute obligation to provide.
- Are there any promises of quality? Is the hotel '5 star' or 'luxury' or 'budget'? Is food 'gourmet'?
- What has the tour operator promised to do as regards monitoring or supervising the accommodation it offers? Does it say it has taken care to select only 'the best, most luxurious, finest' hotels? Does it guarantee that its local service providers run 'reputable, efficient, responsible' businesses?

If the combination of the booking conditions and the brochure are sufficient to show that the tour operator has accepted an absolute obligation, the liability will be strict. Thus, if a swimming pool is promised but when the customer arrives it emerges that the pool is out of order then, subject to being able to rely on any of the statutory defences, the tour operator is likely to be liable because there has been a failure in the performance of that contractual obligation.

Three points may, on occasion, be of relevance:

- to what extent are the promises in the brochure properly to be regarded absolute obligations, as opposed to mere hyperbolic puff;
- is the tour operator able to retreat from an absolute obligation by its own booking conditions; and
- does the consumer have any recourse under reg 4?

3.2.1.1 Promises vs puff

It is sometimes suggested by claimants that the lyrical descriptions in the brochure concerning the opulence and luxury of the hotel, for example, can be taken at face value and thereby place an absolute obligation on the tour operator if that standard is not met.

It is certainly the case that, under reg 6, particulars in the brochure constitute implied warranties.[3] Thus on one construction, the tour operator might be deemed to have warranted that the often florid language of advertising (or the impressively wide-angled lens used for the photograph of the room) would be reflected in the realities of a stay at the hotel. It is worth bearing in mind that reg 6 extends to 'any contract to which the particulars relate' and could therefore bite on contracts where the consumer never even saw the brochure.

---

3   Regulation 6(1).

However, such a construction is unlikely to appeal to the majority of judges. It is probably more realistic to suggest that, where the obligation that is sought to be relied on is essentially subjective ('opulent', 'luxurious', 'tranquil', for example) the court is unlikely to accept that the tour operator accepted an absolute obligation to provide. What to one man is luxury may be slumming it to another, after all. Whilst the effusive language may touch on what is reasonable, or rather on the extent to which the fault-based obligation of reasonableness has been breached, it does not amount to an express obligation.

But if the obligation is objective ('swimming pool', 'kids' club'), it will be far easier to construe that as an absolute promise or warranty.

3.2.1.2   *Retreat from absolute obligations*

Tour operators generally include a clause in the small print at the back of the brochure reminding would-be customers that the brochure may have been printed many months previously and situations can change. This is sometimes used as a defence against a breach of what would be an absolute obligation such as the provision of a swimming pool. Under reg 6, such arguments are hopeless because the tour operator can only escape the consequences of a breach of warranty if the relevant changes in the brochure are communicated to the customer either before the contract is concluded,[4] or the parties agree that they should not form part of the contract after the contract has been made.[5]

So if the swimming pool has been filled in, the tour operator must either tell the customer before the contract is made, or inform the customer later on and hope that the customer does not challenge this under reg 12 as breach of an essential term. If it does not, there is unlikely to be any defence to the charge that there was improper performance of the absolute obligation to provide a swimming pool.

3.2.1.3   *Regulation 4*

Regulation 4 provides that the organiser or retailer is liable to compensate the consumer for loss suffered in consequence of the supply of misleading information in any descriptive matter concerning a package. This is considered in more detail below (at **3.3.1**), but is worth bearing in mind when considering the effusive descriptions of the hotel in the brochure to see whether the contrast between advertising and reality is sufficient to give rise to an argument that the information in the brochure was misleading.

---

[4]   Regulation 6(2)(b).
[5]   Regulation 6(3).

3.2.2 Implied terms

Generally, where a package contract is offered for sale in England and Wales, the contract will be governed expressly or by implication by English law.[6] If the holiday contract is governed by English law, then normal English principles of construction apply. So any holiday contract will be subject to terms being implied, where necessary, under the relevant provisions of the Sale of Goods Act 1979 or the Supply of Goods and Services Act 1982.

Unless a higher standard is expressly undertaken (eg by express reference to the existence of a swimming pool), it is likely that the obligations under the holiday contract will demand no more and no less than that the other party to the contract, by itself and its suppliers, will exercise reasonable care and skill. As the Court of Appeal confirmed in *Hone v Going Places*:[7]

> 'In the absence of any contrary intention, the normal implication will be that the service contracted for will be rendered with reasonable care and skill.'

This is not invariable. In *Eldridge v TUI*,[8] a case about cryptosporidium infections in the Balearics, HHJ Worster accepted that there was no reason why a term that imposed an absolute obligation could not be implied,[9] where the evidence led to that conclusion. This was so, even where the statutory implied term at English law would only have required the exercise of reasonable skill and care. In that case, the obligation was to keep a swimming pool free from the cryptosporidium pathogen.

Accordingly, under English law at least, a tour operator accepts and is deemed to accept fault-based liability, rather than strict liability, unless it says otherwise.

In the context of a personal injury claim this will result in the following obligations:

- There may be an absolute obligation to provide a swimming pool if it is promised in the brochure. However, the pool itself need only be reasonably safe for guests to use.
- The provision of a courtesy bus may be an absolute obligation. However, the driver is required to drive with reasonable skill and care and neither he nor the tour operator warrant passengers' safety.

---

[6] References to 'English law' mean the law of England and Wales. For further discussion of applicable law issues with reference to package travel contracts see Chapter 5, Applicable Law at **5.3.2.9** Consumer contracts and **5.3.3.1** Rome Convention, Certain consumer contracts.

[7] [2001] EWCA Civ 947.

[8] Birmingham County Court, 16 December 2010, HHJ Worster.

[9] The proper law of the contract in this case was English law.

- Flight attendants will exercise reasonable skill and care in assisting passengers during an emergency evacuation.[10]
- The tour operator will assess the safety of the lagoon around a Maldive atoll with reasonable skill and care but does not warrant that guests will be safe using it.[11]
- The hotel will be reasonably safe for customers to stay in.

3.2.2.1 Food and drink cases

One exception to this concerns the provision by the foreign hotel of food and drink to the tour operator's customers. This will be discussed later on, but in essence, the quality and fitness for purpose requirements of s 14 of the Sale of Goods Act 1979 or s 4 of the Supply of Goods and Services Act 1982 will apply. Food contaminated with bacteria in sufficient quantity to cause illness is not 'fit for purpose' or of 'satisfactory quality'. Accordingly, if the consumer can establish that his gastric illness was caused by consumption of contaminated food and drink, the tour operator is likely to find itself liable even if that contamination was not because of any failure on the part of the tour operator or even the supplier to exercise reasonable skill and care.

This approach is, in any event, possibly more consistent with the original wording and purpose of the directive on which the Regulations are based. Although an argument for the Supreme Court or indeed the Court of Justice of the European Union (CJEU) if anywhere, it is often said, at least at academic level, that the Court of Appeal in *Hone* appeared to ignore the guidance provided by the CJEU[12] that those provisions of national law which implement an EU directive should be interpreted in the light of the wording and purpose of the directive to achieve the intended result. An implied term merely to exercise reasonable skill and care with regard to the provision of facilities or services does not, arguably, provide the protection to the consumer which the directive intended. This is for two reasons. First, because reg 15 itself provides for specific defences, suggesting that there is no scope for a general defence of exercising all reasonable skill and care.[13] Secondly, because the legislative aim of reg 15 is to put the consumer in a position to treat the tour operator as if it had promised to supply the package services itself.

This second point is even stronger where the local law of the place where the improper performance is said to have occurred would provide a higher duty of care. Thus if the local law provided for the reversal of the burden of proof, or for strict liability, it could be argued that this more onerous standard is the standard of care that ought to be implied into the holiday

---

[10]   *Hone v Going Places* [2001] EWCA Civ 947.
[11]   *Jones v Sunworld* [2003] EWHC 591 (QB).
[12]   In the case of *Faccini Dori v Recreb Srl* (Case C-91/92). See also *Marleasing* Case C-106/89 [1990] ECR I-4135 at para 8.
[13]   The specific defences are dealt with in detail at **3.3.4.4**.

contract. Whether it should also mean that a lower standard in that foreign country ought then to be ignored in favour of the English 'reasonableness' test is open to question.

3.2.2.2   How to determine 'reasonableness'

Where the claimant contends that the tour operator was itself negligent (ie breached the implied or express obligation to exercise reasonable skill and care), there will be no difficulty in assessing this by reference to ordinary English principles.

So if it is said that the tour operator's representatives did not assist the claimant; or the tour operator's health and safety auditors did not perform a satisfactory audit of the hotel; or the tour operator did not live up to its contractual promise to ensure that only 'reputable local businesses' were used, the court will be in no different a situation than if the incident giving rise to the claim had happened in London.

For most package holiday claims, however, the claimant is in reality taking advantage of his right to pursue the tour operator on the holiday contract even though the tour operator itself did nothing wrong. The real complaint is with the local supplier. In such cases the perennial issue is, against what standard of reasonableness should that suppliers be judged.

In the majority of cases, tour operators will spell out the standard by which they agree the acts or omissions of their local suppliers should be judged in their booking conditions. Generally, it will be specified that standards of services and facilities provided by local suppliers are judged against the standards applicable in the country in which the accident happened at that time. If this is not stated, it will be implied. It will not avail a claimant to complain that the marble floor in the Greek hotel reception area was not sufficiently non-slip and that this would fall foul of British standards if in fact it complies with all relevant Greek standards. The Court of Appeal confirmed this prior to the entry into force of the Regulations in *Wilson v Best Travel*[14] and then again afterwards in *Codd v Thomson Tour Operations Ltd*.[15]

This is of course quite unsurprising – a Greek hotel may accommodate guests from a wide range of countries over the course of the summer season and it would be a nonsense if it had to adhere to different standards applied depending on the guest's country of origin.

The two routes claimants might have round this, considered in more detail below, are:

- uniform international regulations; and

---

[14]   [1993] 1 All ER 353.
[15]   *The Times*, 20 October 2000.

- where the local standards are so low that they might lead a
  reasonable holidaymaker to decline to take a holiday at that hotel,
  both of which were raised as hypotheses in *Wilson v Best Travel*.

So far so uncontroversial. But what local standards, and how must they be
evidenced?

3.2.2.3   *What local standards?*

In the early days of the Regulations, the emphasis was to a large extent on
applicable local regulations and safety standards. So the discussion in
Wilson (admittedly pre-Regulations) was about established requirements
for toughened glass in Britain which simply did not exist in Greece; and in
Codd on British safety standards concerning lift doors which again did
not apply in Spain.

As the number of cases in this area started to increase, so the arguments
became more refined. Where there is an established standard, there is
unlikely to be much dispute that the hotel must adhere to it. So the tiling
surrounding a Portuguese swimming pool must adhere to Portuguese
regulations which regulate precisely such matters, as in *Healy v
Cosmosair.*[16]

But personal injury actions in this jurisdiction, particularly outside the
workplace, are seldom dependent on set standards and regulations. Where
what is essentially being alleged is that the conduct of the hotel's agents
was negligent, how is the court to determine whether there was improper
performance of the contract without any clear standard?

3.2.2.4   *Holden v First Choice*

In *First Choice Holidays & Flights Ltd v Holden*,[17] the claimant slipped on
liquid on a staircase in a Tunisian hotel. The recorder at first instance
found that the hotel had fallen short of the requisite standard because
someone ought to have checked the stairs whenever anyone came into the
restaurant with an open container. Reliance was placed on factors such as
the high standard of medical care received by the claimant after the
accident as showing that Tunisia expected a high standard of attention to
potential spills. Goldring J allowed the tour operator's appeal. The hotel
was not negligent even by English standards of reasonableness. The
claimant had not adduced any actual evidence of Tunisian standards (as
opposed to the material from which the recorder had inferred the relevant
standards) and, he said:

> 'It is for the Claimant to prove that the Defendant fell short of the standards
> applicable in Tunisia.'

---

[16]   [2005] EWHC 1657 (QB), [2005] All ER (D) 432 (Jul).

[17]   Lawtel document number AC0111823 (unreported) 22 May 2006, Goldring J.

This led to a brief 'golden period' for defendant tour operators when the majority of claims failed because claimants simply did not have evidence that the offending act or omission was regarded as blameworthy in the local jurisdiction. Judges in the county court frequently complained that they felt constrained to dismiss claims where the claimant had injured himself in circumstances which in this country would have given rise not unfairly to the presumption that they spoke for themselves, purely because the claimant had not proved that similar criteria applied in the locale of the accident. It also arguably lulled tour operators into a false sense of security, leading some to assert, plainly incorrectly, that a claim had to fail unless a claimant could point to an established local regulation or standard which had been breached.

In 2008, the Court of Appeal had cause to consider the issue of local standards in *Evans v Kosmar Villa Holidays Ltd.*[18] The claimant was rendered paraplegic diving into a pool. He complained that the tour operator breached a duty to warn him not to do this. There was no specific evidence as to standards in Greece (although a failure to adhere to the same was pleaded in short form). The Court of Appeal considered (in the context of considering an appeal not precisely on this issue) that it was still open to a claimant to pursue a claim on basis of that most general duty to take reasonable care. Compliance with local standards is not necessarily sufficient to fulfil that duty.

This decision is often relied on by claimants as support for the proposition that expert evidence is not needed to make good an allegation of breach of local standards because the court can simply determine whether there has been a failure to take reasonable care. However, if the complaint is that the staircase at the Greek hotel should have had a handrail, but Greek regulations did not impose such a requirement, it is most unlikely, barring exceptional circumstances, that *Evans* could be used to establish breach on the part of the hotel for which the tour operator is liable. Whilst a tour operator may owe a general duty of reasonable care and skill, it surely is not the case that this can be used to circumvent or override an obligation on the part of the hotel to comply with local structural requirements, and no more.

Most recently the Court of Appeal revisited the issue of local standards in *Gouldbourn v Balkan Holidays.*[19] The claimant was injured whilst skiing in Bulgaria. The issue was whether the instructor was negligent in his instruction. The judge found as a fact that the instructor's choice of piste was suitable. The Court of Appeal upheld the judge's conclusion that the conduct of the instructor had to be judged against relevant local standards. The FIS Rules[20] on which the claimant relied only laid down

---

[18]   [2008] 1 WLR 297.
[19]   [2010] EWCA Civ 372.
[20]   *Fédération Internationale de Ski*: www.fis-ski.com.

the framework duty and how that was applied might vary from country to country. The claimant had adduced no evidence in that regard and so the claim was rightly dismissed.

3.2.2.5 *'Negligence' allegations and local standards*

So the question remains, to what extent must the court have regard to the location of the accident or injury in determining whether there has been negligence on the part of the supplier? Swinton Thomas LJ said in *Codd* that:

> '... the law of this country [England and Wales] is applied to the case as to the establishing of negligence, but there is no requirement that a hotel for example in Majorca is obliged to comply with British Safety Standards.'

It is often suggested by litigants that this passage, particularly coupled with *Evans*, indicates that whilst facilities must comply with local standards, when considering whether there has been negligence in the provision of services, the court can approach it on English principles of reasonableness. It is suggested that this is not so. The principles of the English law of negligence apply in that a claimant must establish loss caused by a failure on the part of the supplier to exercise (in the absence of a higher contractual standard) reasonable care and skill.

But one cannot conclude that negligence has been established under English law unless there has been a breakdown in the standard of services the holidaymaker could reasonably have expected in that location. The behaviour must be set against the standards of the location – what was it reasonable to expect *that* hotelier in *that* location to provide. Thus the failure on the part of an English hotelier to mop up water on the front step might be negligent, but the self-same failure on the part of a Greek hotelier, accustomed to spills drying in minutes in the heat of the sun, might very well not be. For further discussion of the evidence likely to be necessary in such claims see **3.3.4.1** to **3.3.4.3**.

3.2.2.6 *National or regional 'local' standards?*

One final question emerges which has, as yet, not been the subject of precise judicial consideration. How 'local' should the standards be? An example: a Greek regulation could hypothetically provide that outdoor staircases with more than 10 steps need a handrail. The hotel in question is on one of the Ionian islands, and did not provide such a handrail. The witnesses from the hotel all assert (credibly and with photos) that numerous other hotels in the area also offer staircases without handrails, and all of the hotels were signed off and are properly licensed by the relevant local authorities. The expert local architect witness confirms that it is unusual for handrails to be provided on that island. It might be thought that the claimant got no less from that Ionian hotel than he could reasonably have expected from any other hotel in the area. Is there not an argument that 'local' in that context should properly refer to the island? Whilst tempting, it is suggested that this is not the right approach. The ramifications could be enormous – one could end up arguing that different standards should apply to a county, or a specific city, irrespective of the legal position. There could be interesting questions about an English court effectively sanctioning a flouting by the hotel of the foreign regulation (or conversely, about the English court effectively ruling that a hotel is non-compliant when the relevant architect and authorities are content that it is). The safe option is likely to be that a Ionian hotel's performance is judged against the regulation that applies to it. If it, and any other hotel, choose to ignore that, they should probably be regarded as doing so at their own risk, not at the claimant's.

3.2.2.7 *Uniform international regulations*

In *Wilson v Best Travel* Phillips J identified that, save where 'uniform international regulations' applied, one had to look to the relevant local standard to determine whether the supplier (and therefore the tour operator) is in breach. He did not attempt to identify what those regulations might be. Subsequent attempts by claimants to establish certain international guidance as 'uniform' have generally stalled on the basis that such rules tend to be too general for specific application to the facts of a particular claim:

- Claimants will often assert that hazard analysis and critical control points (HACCP) or ISO 220000, which are recognised systematic preventative approaches to food safety, are just such uniform international regulations. Many countries do indeed provide for their implementation. The way in which the seven principles of HACCP are applied may well differ from country to country, however.
- The Court of Appeal in *Gouldbourn* similarly confirmed that the FIS Rules merely set down general principles, rather than regulating how that duty is to be performed in every country which has adopted them.
- The Court of Appeal in *Evans v Kosmar* confirmed that neither does the guidance issued by the Federation of Tour Operators amount to uniform international regulations.
- However, because there are standardised European guidelines relevant to the control and prevention of legionella (albeit in conjunction with national laws) there might be more prospect of establishing that these are closer to uniform standards not requiring additional evidence as to local standards.

3.2.2.8   Standards so low no reasonable holidaymaker would go there

Although with the benefit of hindsight many claimants will say that they would never have gone there 'if they'd known', judges are unlikely to conclude, save in the face of evidence of the most appallingly low standards, that a claimant would have declined to go. In the modern world where everything is available at the click of a mouse, the lower the standards in the destination country, the more likely it must surely be that the claimant would have known something of what to expect in advance of booking.

3.2.3   Incorporation of Convention defences

It is very common, given that tour operators often sell packages which include transport components where the provider of that component can rely on international travel conventions, for tour operators to seek via their booking conditions to imply into the holiday contract the booking conditions of their supplier.

In *Akehurst v Thomson Holidays Ltd & Britannia Airways Ltd*[21] the claimants were all passengers whose package holiday with Thomson included a flight from Cardiff to Gerona on a Britannia plane. The plane crashed on landing and the claimants sustained primarily psychological injuries for which, pursuant to the relevant terms of the Warsaw Convention, they were unable to recover damages as against the airline. Thomson's standard terms and conditions provided inter alia: 'When you travel by air ... the transport company's "Conditions of Carriage" will apply to your journey.'

Thomson argued, unsuccessfully, that this clause incorporated the airline's terms and conditions, reliant on the Warsaw Convention, into its own standard terms. HHJ Graham Jones concluded that the wording was too ambiguous for Thomson to rely on an attempt to qualify its otherwise clear acceptance of liability for injuries caused by the fault of a service provider. As a result, passengers were not able to rely on the strict liability provisions in the Convention and had to prove fault in the usual way, but were able to claim damages for their psychological injuries to the extent that they were able to establish fault.

By contrast, the flight attendants on the same flight, whose claims were not based on their employer's conditions of carriage nor on the Regulations, were able to maintain a claim for psychological damage against the airline that employed them.

---

[21]   HHJ Graham Jones in Cardiff County Court, 6 May 2003.

In *Lee v Airtours*[22] the tour operator failed to incorporate the limitations on damages in the Athens Convention on which the supplier of the cruise could rely, apparently on the basis that contractual terms attempting to incorporate them were not produced until after the contract was made.

However, in *Norfolk v My Travel*,[23] the claimant, who had an accident on board a cruise ship in the course of a package holiday, was held to be statute barred when she commenced her claim against the tour operator outside the 2-year limitation period provided by the Athens Convention. There, it was accepted that the defendant was the contracting carrier for the purposes of the Convention (unlike Thomson in the *Akehurst* case) as well as being the other party to the contract within the Regulations. The court held that the Convention applied without the need for express reference, and there was no conflict between the Convention and the Regulations.

3.3 LIABILITY OF THE OTHER PARTY TO THE CONTRACT

The two primary routes by which a claimant will generally seek to claim damages for an accident or illness on holiday are those provided by regs 4 and 15 (as reflected in any case in the relevant booking conditions).

3.3.1 Regulation 4

Regulation 4 provides:

> '4(1)   No organiser or retailer shall supply to a consumer any descriptive matter concerning a package, the price of a package or any other conditions applying to the contract which contains any misleading information.
>
> 4(2)   If an organiser or retailer is in breach of paragraph (1) he shall be liable to compensate the consumer for any loss which the consumer suffers in consequence.'

'Any descriptive matter concerning a package' is, no doubt deliberately, extremely wide ranging. Virtually anything in a brochure or on the tour operator's website is likely to be covered, whether photographs, written descriptions, pictograms or any other material relevant to any aspect of the package.

Regulation 4 covers the supply of misleading information. 'Misleading' is a sufficiently wide term to capture some information which would not be considered to be a misrepresentation at English law. It almost certainly covers a situation where the information is literally true (the view from the

22   Central London County Court, October 2002.
23   [2004] 1 Lloyd's Rep 106.

restaurant is over rolling meadows) but gives rise to a false impression that the hotel is rural and peaceful whereas in fact it borders a major highway; or where the tour operator has provided information which commits the sin of omission (such as emphasising the proximity to the beach, but omitting reference to an adjoining sewage outfall which makes bathing if not hazardous, at least undesirable).

In *Mawdsley v Cosmosair plc*,[24] the claimant booked a holiday at a hotel in Turkey which boasted both a 'lift (in main building)' and its suitability 'for parents with young children'. The claimant discovered on arrival that the restaurant in the main building was in the mezzanine and accessible only by a flight of some 39 steps. In attempting to negotiate the stairs with young children and a pushchair she fell and injured herself.

The Court of Appeal upheld her contention that she suffered loss in consequence on the supply of misleading information – the statement about the lift in the main building implied that the lift would give access to all floors in the main building and this was misleading because it did not. The statement about the hotel's suitability for parents with young children was not misleading because the need to negotiate steps to the restaurant was but one factor in making a value judgment about its suitability.

In *Jones v Sunworld*,[25] the claimant and her husband travelled to an island in the Maldives for their honeymoon. Mr Jones drowned in the lagoon. The brochure contained a statement that the island had two neighbouring islands 'which you can reach at low tide'. The claimant submitted that this gave rise to the misleading impression that it was safe to wade anywhere in the lagoon. This was rejected. It denoted no more than that guests could walk to the islands at low tide, a statement which was probably true but which did not in any event cause Mr Jones's death.

3.3.2   Regulation 15

Far and away the majority of personal injury actions arising out of accidents in the course of package holidays will be based on reg 15, or rather the term of the holiday contract which mirrors reg 15.

Under reg 15(1):

> 'The other party to the contract is liable to the consumer for the proper performance of the obligations under the contract, irrespective of whether such obligations are to be performed by that other party or by other suppliers of services but this shall not affect any remedy or right of action which that other party may have against those other suppliers of services.'

---

[24]   [2002] EWCA Civ 587.
[25]   [2003] EWHC 591 (QB).

Subject to the statutory defences, the other party to the contract (usually the tour operator) is liable to the consumer if there has been a failure or improper performance of the holiday contract. It does not matter if the tour operator itself did everything right and the problem was caused by the hotel. If the problem amounted to improper performance of the contract to which the tour operator and the consumer are parties, the tour operator cannot avoid liability. In effect, therefore, reg 15 imposes a form of qualified vicarious liability on the tour operator for breaches of the holiday contract.

3.3.3   Obligations under the contract

Improper performance can only be determined by reference to what obligations were owed under the holiday contract. These have been considered above (**3.2.1–3.2.2.1**) but in summary, are likely to fall into the following categories:

- Strict obligations, such as the promised availability of a courtesy bus.
- Fault-based obligations, such as the requirement for reasonable care and skill to be exercised by the driver of the courtesy bus.

In the context of a personal injury claim (apart from, possibly, food poisoning cases, which are dealt with separately at **3.5**), it is considerably more likely that reliance will be placed on express or implied fault-based obligations. Although not impossible (it is conceivable, for example, that a claimant could suffer a foreseeable exacerbation of asthma because a promised courtesy bus was not available), it will be a rare occasion when injury will be caused by a failure on the part of the tour operator to comply with a strict obligation.

More frequently the claimant will be seeking to show that there was a failure or improper performance of the holiday contract because the local suppliers failed to exercise reasonable care and skill in some particular area and this failure caused the accident or illness.

3.3.4   Establishing improper performance

It is therefore suggested that improper performance can be considered in the following ways:

(1) The standard to which the tour operator is expected to adhere is likely to be the normal English standard of reasonable skill and care, assessed by reference to normal English principles of negligence. This is so even if the failing is said to be that of the representative on site.

(2) The standard to which the local supplier is expected to adhere is the applicable local standard.

(a)   Where there are relevant regulations which lay down the requisite standard, the hotel must adhere to them.

(b)   Where there are no relevant regulations, the hotel must exercise reasonable skill and care. This standard is informed by the fact that the accident happened overseas and not in England.

Where the accident arises because of something structural (the presence of a handrail on stairs; an unmarked drop; the requirement for slip resistant flooring; applicable minimum lighting; the statutory minimum number of fire doors; and so on), it is suggested that it is likely that there will be some statutory or regulatory requirements. Expert evidence will therefore be essential. A claimant who arrives at trial asserting that she fell on the stairs of a Turkish hotel because there was no handrail armed with nothing more than her belief that a handrail would have been sensible is likely to lose.

Where the accident happened because of a temporary breakdown in the standard of services provided (a spill on the stairs, a broken light, a cable left trailing across the lobby, overgrown grass covering a pothole in the gardens, and so on) it is probably as likely that there is an established regulatory framework against which to assess negligence in the country where the accident happened as if the accident happened in England (ie highly unlikely). So, on the fairly safe assumption that the tour operator will plead a local standards defence, how can a claimant get over the hurdle of establishing that the hotel fell short of the expected standard?

The sort of evidence may be one or more of the following:

•   expert evidence from a local lawyer;
•   expert evidence in another discipline;
•   documentary evidence;
•   witness evidence.

3.3.4.1   *Expert evidence*

It is often said that there is no scope for foreign law in a package holiday claim. The contract is governed by English law and it is a matter of irrelevance, so it is said, how that law would be applied as against the foreign supplier. Were it otherwise, the tour operator could conceivably pray in aid foreign limitation periods, for example, and thereby defend the claim on the basis that any claim against the local supplier would be guaranteed to fail and so it would not be open to the English court to conclude that the supplier fell short of the standard expected of it.

In fact, the relevance of local law is probably rather more nuanced. Questions of limitation in the foreign country are almost certainly irrelevant. If the claimant chooses to take advantage of a right to claim against the tour operator rather than the supplier, the establishing of a legal right against that supplier is surely not pertinent. This would otherwise require an English claimant suing an English defendant on an English contract to obtain evidence simultaneously of limitation periods in a foreign country, which would surely undermine the consumer protection which underlines the Directive on which the Regulations are based. Similarly, where the local law provides for the reversal of the burden of proof, it is unlikely to assist the claimants as against the tour operator.

But whether there is a viable claim against the supplier under the local law may not be irrelevant. If the local law provides (as does the law in many if not most jurisdictions) for liability for one's negligence, and local case law shows that, for example, Greek courts tend to find negligence where spills go uncleaned, why should a claimant not be entitled to rely on that evidence, obtained no doubt from a local lawyer, in support of the assertion that the hotel did not act with the reasonable skill and care expected of it locally? And in many cases the court will agree at case management stage, leaving it to the trial judge to determine whether that standard was met.

Where claimants must take care is ensuring that the lawyer does not descend into the arena and seek to give his opinion on whether the local supplier would be found liable in a local court. Such evidence is likely to be held to be inadmissible, and irrelevant.[26] What can properly be set out are the relevant principles, with the application of those principles a matter for trial.

Expert evidence might also come from other disciplines. Whilst a civil engineer is likely to be needed for the structural-type breaches referred to above, it is conceivable that an expert could assist in a services claim as well. The writer has been involved in a case, for example, where a District Judge provided (admittedly in the face of bilateral opposition) for the single joint instruction of an expert from the local association of hoteliers to consider what standard of cleaning was regarded locally as sufficient. Sometimes it may pay to think a little outside the box.

3.3.4.2 *Documentary evidence*

As to documentary evidence, a claimant will largely be dependent on what is disclosed by the tour operator – which will in its turn be dependent on what is provided by its supplier. But the documentation can be critical. If a hotel has a documented policy of putting out warning signs when the floor is wet, but its cleaner omitted to do so on the occasion when the claimant slipped, the claimant should have few difficulties convincing the

---

[26] For a more detailed treatment of expert evidence of foreign law see *Dicey, Morris & Collins on the Conflict of Laws* (Sweet & Maxwell, 15th edn, 2012).

court that the hotel did not act with reasonable skill and care. Its own policies may well be relied on as evidence of what it accepts is reasonable.

This should not be confused with those policies being treated as though they set the standard for the local area. Clearly they do nothing of the kind. Goldring J was clear in *Holden* that a hotel's individual policies are unlikely to be reliable evidence of relevant local standards. However, it is suggested that the claimant need not go that far. He is entitled to proper performance of the obligations under the contract. The hotel in which he was accommodated took it on itself to hold itself to a certain standard. If it fell short (and often hotel managers will accept in cross-examination that 'something went wrong'), it would be perplexing if the tour operator could defend successfully on the basis that the standard to which the hotel had to adhere was not the standard to which it held itself, but rather to another unidentified standard, for the absence of proof of which the claim should fail.

Such a scenario arises extremely commonly in slipping cases. If the accident happened in England, there is no doubt the court will proceed on the basis of the principles stated in *Ward v Tesco Stores*.[27] In that case Megaw LJ confirmed:

> 'It is for the plaintiff to show that there has occurred an event which was unusual and which in the absence of explanation is more consistent with fault on the part of the defendants than absence of fault.'

Once he does so – and generally people do not slip unless there is something under their feet to reduce the natural co-efficient:

> '... the defendants can still escape from liability if they could show that the accident must have happened, or even on balance of probability would have been likely to have happened, even if there had been in existence a proper and adequate system in relation to the circumstances to provide for the safety of customers. But if the defendants wish to put forward such a case it is for them to show that on the balance of probability either by evidence or by inference from the evidence that is given or is not given this accident would have been at least equally likely to have happened despite a proper system designed to give reasonable protection to customers.'

This is still routinely adopted by judges as the relevant test even where the claimant slips in a foreign hotel (and indeed expressly approved as the relevant test on board a foreign-registered cruise ship in international waters in *Dawkins v Carnival plc*).[28] Accordingly, even if the hotel's policies are not to be regarded as indicative of the relevant local standard, it is unlikely that the tour operator will succeed in proving that there was nonetheless in place a proper system designed to give reasonable protection to customers where they have not been adhered to.

---

27   [1976] 1 WLR 810.
28   [2011] EWCA Civ 1237.

Other documentation which may turn out to be critical could include:

- the claimant's accident report form (including the tour operator's own copy, which may well provide for the hotel's input, which the claimant would not ordinarily get to see);
- maintenance and repair logs;
- the hotel's completed cleaning logs;
- the hotel's complaints book;
- the tour operator's audits, health and safety checklists and any other assessments;
- photographs or videos – taken by both sides. It is not unknown for photos taken of the same offending feature to look very different depending on the angle at which they are taken, for example.

3.3.4.3 *Witness evidence*

Whilst it is unlikely, for the reasons given, that a claimant will choose to run to trial relying only on his evidence as to the relevant local standards, nonetheless there certainly have been cases where judges have been prepared to rely on such evidence. In *Phillips v Kosmar Villas plc*,[29] for example, the judge accepted the evidence given by the claimant's husband as to the way in which courtesy buses had been driven on their previous holidays in Greece as the benchmark against which to find wanting the standard of driving to which the claimant was subjected on that occasion.

By contrast, tour operators can quite properly adduce evidence from their representatives, many of whom will cover more than one hotel, as to what happens in similar situations at other hotels in the area.

Finally, it may be thought that there are some circumstances which are so obvious that the only possible conclusion is that the supplier did not exercise reasonable skill and care. If the driver of the courtesy bus is on the wrong side of the road when the accident happens, could it really be said by the tour operator that the claim should fail because there was no expert evidence to confirm that this is contrary to accepted standards in that country? In *Kempson v First Choice Holidays & Flights Ltd*,[30] the judge raised, obiter, the possibility of a claimant in such circumstances making a Part 18 request for further information from a defendant raising a local standards defence to inquire whether it is asserted that such conduct is acceptable by local standards. In practice, such a request is likely to be met (overriding objective notwithstanding) with a curt assertion that proof of local standards is for the claimant and not the defendant.

For something as ostensibly cut and dried as driving on the wrong side of the road, it is likely that any attempt to rely on *Holden* will meet with

---

[29] Birmingham County Court, 12 December 2007, HHJ Charles Harris QC.
[30] Birmingham County Court, 7 June 2007, HHJ Stephen Davies.

extremely short shrift from the judge. However, the scenarios in which a claimant could take this tack are probably fairly few and far between. Perhaps it could be said that if a claimant could legitimately rely on the doctrine of res ipsa loquitur had the accident happened in this country (ie the facts of the accident speak for themselves as evidence of negligence), he might be safe leaving it to the defendant to justify what appears to be negligence as acceptable practice from that local supplier.

Examples of the sort of accident where lack of expert or other evidence might not prove to be a fatal omission for the claimant could include:

- the driver of courtesy bus on the wrong side of the road;
- the water in the shower almost boiling and sufficient to cause severe burns;
- a complete absence of lighting at night in an area of the hotel which includes unguarded drops;[31]
- a wardrobe collapsing onto the claimant when opened;[32]
- the reasonableness of evening entertainment in which volunteers were encouraged to participate.[33]

It is, though, probably a rare set of facts and a bold claimant that will end up at trial relying on nothing more than a statement of the obvious, particularly in the light of the Court of Appeal's judgment in *Gouldbourn*. Just as it may be an optimistic defendant that pleads a local standards defence and then disputes either the need for the claimant to obtain expert evidence, or the cost of obtaining the same.

3.3.4.4 *Statutory defences*

Even if the claimant can establish that there was a failure or improper performance of the holiday contract causative of the illness or injury, the other party to the contract may still be able to avoid liability if it can rely on one of the statutory defences set out at reg 15(2), which provides:

> 'The other party to the contract is liable to the consumer for any damage caused to him by the failure to perform the contract or the improper performance of the contract unless the failure or improper performance is due neither to any fault of that other party nor to that of another supplier of services, because –
> (a)   the failures which occur in the performance of the contract are attributable to the consumer;
> (b)   such failures are attributable to a third party unconnected with the provision of the services contracted for, and are unforeseeable or unavoidable; or

---

[31]   As was the case in *Deacon v TUI*, Colchester County Court, 4 December 2009, HHJ Collender QC.

[32]   As in *Ross v TUI*, Bow County Court, 21 June 2007, HHJ Roberts.

[33]   As was the case in *Sullivan v TUI*, Northampton County Court, 20 August 2008, HHJ Hampton.

(c) such failures are due to –
    (i) Unusual or unforeseeable circumstances beyond the control of the party by whom this exception is pleaded, the consequences of which could not have been avoided even if all due care had been exercised; or
    (ii) An event which the other party to the contract or the supplier of services, even with all due care, could not foresee or forestall.'

(1) Attributable to the consumer: reg 15(2)(a)

This is not the equivalent of a defence based on contributory negligence (which has long since ceased to be a complete defence under English law anyway).[34] It only assists the tour operator where there is a failure in the performance of the holiday contract, but this is due solely to the acts or omissions of the customer. Thus, if the hotel fails to provide the promised courtesy bus, there is improper performance. But if the failure is because the claimant himself put the bus out of action by letting its tyres down, it perhaps scarcely needs a specific provision to rule out the tour operator being liable for the consequences of the failure to provide the bus (and generally under English law such claims would fail on causation anyway). Whether there might be a separate allegation regarding the failure to make alternative arrangements is another matter.

The defendant can, however, run an argument of contributory negligence as well in appropriate circumstances. In *Forsikringsakitieselkapet Vesta v Butcher*,[35] it was held that this is only if the breach of contract that is alleged is coextensive with liability in negligence. That would appear to rule out a contribution where the basis of the claim is a strict obligation. This could have repercussions in gastric illness claims, which are considered separately below.

(2) Attributable to a third party: reg 15(2)(b)

This defence needs to be analysed under three separate heads. The defendant can only rely on it if all three of the following limbs are met:

- the failure in the performance of the holiday contract is attributable to a third party;
- where that third party is unconnected with the provision of services contracted for; and
- the failure in performance was unforeseeable *or* unavoidable.

The most common use of this defence is in the context of criminal activity. If the claimant is shot by armed robbers in his Caribbean hotel the tour operator might fairly contend that the robbers are unconnected – that they only targeted the hotel because of the prevalence of 'wealthy'

---

[34] Law Reform (Contributory Negligence) Act 1945.
[35] [1986] 2 All ER 488.

Western tourists is probably not enough to 'connect' them with the hotel (although it might well be different if there was some evidence to suggest that hotel staff were connected, even tangentially).

The defendant must also establish that the failure in performance was either unforeseeable or unavoidable. Whilst the Caribbean robbers may have been unconnected, their presence was hardly unforeseeable and proper security systems at the hotel might well have avoided the incident.

The Regulations do not qualify the steps the parties delivering the services contracted for need to take in order to render a failure unforeseeable or unavoidable, no doubt leaving that to the national courts. There is no reported authority on the correct interpretation under English law. However, a literal interpretation of these words would make this defence extremely narrow. Steps can almost always be taken to avoid even the smallest risk – need they be taken if this would be unreasonable and disproportionate? It is suggested that the failure will be 'unavoidable' if it could not be avoided by the taking of reasonable steps when the nature and consequences of the risk to the customer are weighed against the cost and practicality of the measures needed to avoid it are weighed in the balance. So if the hotel has a history of intrusions from armed robbers and yet has not increased its security arrangements, the tour operator is unlikely to make good its defence. However, it is arguable that this interpretation leaves the 'unforeseeable' or 'unavoidable' limb devoid of any real meaning in light of the fact that the claimant has in any event to prove that the hotel was in breach of the duty to make its accommodation reasonably safe from intruders.[36]

(3)   Unusual or unforeseeable circumstances: reg 15(2)(c)(i)

This is generally regarded as the defence most closely approximating 'force majeure' or 'act of God'.

The availability of this defence depends on the defendant establishing each of the following limbs:

- unusual circumstances,
- which are also unforeseeable,
- which are beyond the defendant's control,
- the consequences of which could not have been avoided,
- even if all due care had been exercised.

A Western tourist raped in the Dominican Republic may be statistically unusual but clearly foreseeable. The 2004 tsunami might be said to be foreseeable, in the broad sense that tsunamis are known to occur from time to time, but since it was not in fact foreseen or forecast by local

---

[36]   See **3.2.2** regarding the implied terms.

governments or scientists, could it really be said that it was foreseeable by the tour operator pleading this defence?

It is suggested that if the circumstances are both unusual and unforeseeable, in the sense of being unforeseen by a defendant taking all reasonable care to avail itself of any relevant information, it ought to be able to establish limbs (1), (2) and (3).

More important, in the context of this statutory defence, is the fourth limb. This focuses on the consequences of the unusual circumstances, and not the circumstances themselves. So a claimant raped in the Dominican Republic might well be able to say that her psychiatric distress would have been avoided if she had been immediately repatriated by the tour operator as she requested and not left on her own for several days undergoing scrutiny and disbelief from those around her. And any tour operator could potentially avoid at least some of the consequences of a natural disaster by having in place contingency plans just in case.

Finally, the defendant must show that that the exercise of all due care would have made no difference. Gastrointestinal illness is so commonplace for travellers to Egypt or India that it might well be said, and has been said successfully on various occasions in unreported county court cases, that the risk of contracting it could not be avoided due to prevailing local standards of hygiene and deficiencies in the local infrastructure (although it might be said that this is more a question of the claimant not establishing improper performance in the first place rather than the defendant needing to rely on a statutory defence).

(4) Unforeseeable event: reg 15(2)(c)(ii)

This final statutory defence applies where the defendant can establish:

- an event,
- which the other party *or* the supplier,
- even with all due care,
- could not foresee or forestall.

This is potentially of far wider significance to defendants as it provides so many alternatives. On its face it would appear to suggest that if the hotel was able to foresee or forestall the rape of the claimant by an ex-employee sacked following the victim's complaints of theft, but the tour operator was not, the tour operator would nonetheless be able to rely on this defence. It is most unlikely that the courts would accept this construction, undermining so completely as it does the imposition of vicarious liability on a tour operator for its supplier's defaults under reg 15(1).

As to the first element, it has been held at circuit judge level that 'event' can comprise a chain or series of separate events as well as each separate event itself, *Bensusan v Airtours*.[37] Each one may be foreseeable or forestallable but their combination may not. In that case, a number of separate misfortunes led to the claimants missing their connection with a cruise. However, because the tour operator had not taken all due care to forestall the cruise's departure, it was not in fact able to rely on the defence.

A hurricane or other natural disaster may be plainly foreseeable and even foreseen, but with the best will in the world is unlikely to be forestalled by a tour operator no matter how diligent. The hotel might with hindsight have been able to foresee that the ex-employee might take his revenge on the customer but in the absence of some indication that he planned the rape, it might fairly argue that it could not have foreseen or forestalled the actual event. And the collapse of a boat's mast during a boat excursion due to an inbuilt defect could not have been predicted or avoided by the tour operator or its suppliers.[38]

3.3.5   Other common law defences

The statutory defences are, in the form in which the Directive was implemented in the various member states, common to all member states. However, there is nothing to prevent an English tour operator from relying on any other defence available to it under English law.[39]

An example might be that which is still commonly referred to as 'volenti', most frequently relied on perhaps in the context of adrenaline activities. In *Wooldridge v Sumner*,[40] Diplock LJ identified the issue thus:

> 'The consent that is relevant is not consent to the risk of injury but consent to the lack of reasonable care that may produce that risk ... and requires on the part of the plaintiff at the time at which he gives his consent full knowledge of the nature and extent of the risk that he ran.'

The scope is therefore extremely limited. A participant in a camel trek might well have consented to the risk inherent in such an activity, such as falling off. However, he is most unlikely to have consented to those who ran the trek failing to provide a saddle when one ought to have been provided and thereby rendering the risk of falling a certainty.

---

[37]   Brentwood County Court, 8 August 2001.
[38]   As in *Jay v TUI UK Ltd*, Bristol County Court, 23 November 2006, Adrian Palmer QC (QBD), Lawtel 17 June 2007.
[39]   Although, note that reg 15(3) and (4) prevent tour operators from limiting liability for personal injury in their contractual terms, and only, in respect of other damage, as is in accordance with international conventions in relation to the carriage of passengers, see Chapters 7 and 8 in relation to carriage by sea and air.
[40]   [1963] 2 QB 43 at 69.

3.4 THIRD PARTY CLAIMS AGAINST SUPPLIERS

Tour operators often find themselves, courtesy of the Regulations, in a position of potential or actual liability towards their customers through no fault of their own. They may be struggling to obtain documents from the local supplier, or the commercial arrangements may have broken down leaving the tour operator with little bargaining power. Or the claim may have settled and the tour operator is simply looking to recoup its outlay. In any case, the tour operator may find itself in a position before, during or after the main claim is resolved when it wishes to join the local supplier as third party.

3.4.1 Jurisdiction

The jurisdiction of the English courts where the local supplier is domiciled in a member state is governed by the Judgments Regulation:[41]

- jurisdiction may be conferred either pursuant to a jurisdictional clause in the accommodation contract (given effect by Art 23 of the Judgments Regulation); or
- pursuant to Art 6(2) of the Judgments Regulation in any other third party proceedings, in the court seised of the original proceedings, unless these were instituted solely with the object of removing him from the jurisdiction of the court which would be competent in his case.

Where the local supplier is domiciled outside the EU, jurisdiction is dependent on obtaining permission to serve, see CPR, r 6.37ff.

3.4.1.1 *Contractual jurisdiction clauses*

Accommodation contracts between the tour operator and the hotelier will often contain a jurisdiction clause, ie 'the parties submit to the non-exclusive jurisdiction of the English Courts'.

By Art 23(1) of the Judgments Regulation, the English courts will have jurisdiction to settle any disputes in connection with the accommodation contract if the parties have so agreed. The English courts will have exclusive jurisdiction unless the parties have agreed otherwise (which they will have done in the example above). By Art 23(1)(a), an agreement conferring jurisdiction must be in writing or be evidenced in writing.

Sometimes the contract will provide for two jurisdiction clauses (generally coupled with choice of law clauses), one covering the right to an indemnity and the other covering the rest. This can present problems for the tour operator in anything other than straightforward cases. If the

---

[41] EC 44/2001.

hotel maintains that the contract is invalid for one reason or another, or the name of the contracting party is wrong, there may well be arguments that these are matters that fall first to be determined by the competing jurisdiction (and governing law) rather than by the English court.

3.4.1.2 Pursuant to Art 6(2) of the Judgments Regulation

Article 6(2) of the Judgments Regulation provides that:

> 'A person domiciled in a Member State *may also be sued as a third party in an action* on a warranty or a guarantee or in any other third party proceedings, *in the court seised of the original proceedings*, unless these were instituted solely with the object of removing him from the jurisdiction of the court which would be competent in his case.' (emphasis added)

As such, where proceedings have been commenced in the English courts by a claimant against a tour operator, the court should have jurisdiction in respect of any additional claim pursued by the tour operator against the hotel in the same proceedings as long as:

- the third party claim is a legitimate third party claim, ie there is a main claim to which it can be attached;[42]
- the object of the third party claim was not the removal of the hotel from its own jurisdiction.

Article 6(2) may be relied upon even where:

(a) the accommodation contract (or written evidence of it) cannot be produced;
(b) the accommodation contract does not contain a jurisdictional clause;
(c) the accommodation contract provides for the non-exclusive jurisdiction of a foreign court.

Unusually the court does have discretion to refuse jurisdiction,[43] and depending on the stage of proceedings it may exercise its discretion to refuse to permit the third party claim to be brought, or to refuse to allow the third party to participate in the main claim or even direct that the third party will not be bound by any judgment or decision made in the main claim.[44]

Although tactically many tour operators prefer to leave the hotels out of proceedings until late in the day, opting instead for amicable attempts to obtain documents and keep commercial arrangements on a solid footing,

---

[42] *Barton v Golden Sun Holidays Ltd (In Liquidation) and Avilda Hotels Ltd* [2007] IL Pr 57.
[43] *Kongress Agentur Hagen GmbH v Zeehaghe BV* [1990] ECR 1-1845.
[44] See the comprehensive powers in CPR, r 20.13 and PD 20, section 5.

there can be no doubt that the later an application is left, the more likely it is that the court may decline jurisdiction or refuse to permit the claim to be brought or tried at the same time, leaving the tour operator to any standalone remedy it may have in this jurisdiction, or any other remedy it may have in the hotel's local court.

3.4.2 Causes of action

3.4.2.1 *Contractual indemnity clause*

Accommodation contracts will commonly contain an indemnity clause for the benefit of the tour operator in respect of claims made by holidaymakers. For example in *Healy v Cosmosair plc and another*,[45] the indemnity clause (of relatively common wording) was as follows:

> 'The Hotelier shall indemnify and keep indemnified Cosmos against all losses, liabilities, claims or expenses for or in respect of injury … loss or damage to persons … which may arise from any cause whatsoever arising out of or in connection with the supply of services to Cosmos (excluding the negligence or default of Cosmos …).'

3.4.2.2 *Potential pitfalls*
- The contractual indemnity must be provided by the legal owner or operator of the hotel. For instance, a purported accommodation contract for Ells Bells hotel between 'X Travel Limited' and 'Ells Bells Hotel' will not assist if the legal owner and operator of the hotel is in fact 'Dodgy SA' (unless it can be established that the former is merely the trading name for the latter).
- The contractual indemnity must be provided to the defendant in proceedings. If the defendant to proceedings is 'X Travel Limited' a contractual indemnity provided by the hotel to 'X Holidays Limited' or 'X Travel (Operations) Limited' will not assist (unless it can be established that the contracting party did so as agent for X Travel Limited).
- The indemnity clause must, on proper construction, provide an indemnity in respect of the loss suffered by the claimant. The clause will be construed in favour of the hotel. In *Cosmos Holidays plc v Dhanjal Investments Ltd*,[46] the hotelier operated a hotel and an off-site elephant sanctuary. If the indemnity clause had been worded to cover only 'loss in connection with the supply of services at the hotel', the clause may not have covered any claim arising from the provision of the elephant sanctuary. Whilst the hotel will be given the benefit of any uncertainty, the indemnity clause must be construed to give business efficacy to the agreement or arrive at a sensible result (*Healy v Cosmosair plc*).

---

[45] [2005] EWHC 1657.
[46] [2009] EWCA Civ 316.

3.4.2.3 *Civil Liability (Contribution) Act 1978*

- A claim for an indemnity or contribution may also be brought under s 1(1) of the Civil Liability (Contribution) Act 1978:

    '... any person in respect of any damage suffered by another person may recover contribution from any other person liable in respect of the same damage (whether jointly with him or otherwise).'

- Proof of wrongdoing by the hotelier is a prerequisite to the success of the claimant's action – ie inadequate system of inspection and cleaning; failure to comply with local building regulations; insufficient lighting etc. As such, if the claimant is successful against the tour operator, the hotelier will usually be 'liable in respect of the same damage'.
- The potential liability of the hotel to the claimant for the same damage may be determined by a different governing law to that which applies as between claimant and defendant.
- There may be nice arguments where the claimant succeeds in separate allegations against the tour operator on its own behalf, and those where it is liable by virtue of reg 15!

3.4.3 Type of proceedings

3.4.3.1 *Additional claims*

Where the claim against the hotel is brought solely pursuant to the Civil Liability (Contribution) Act 1978, it may only be brought by way of additional (Part 20) claim and no standalone action can be brought relying on it. Jurisdiction will therefore only be established if the hotel is a third party to a claim in which the court is already seised.

If the additional claim is brought when the defence is filed, the court's permission will not be needed. The additional claim should in any event be brought before the claimant's claim has substantially concluded, in order to avoid any argument by the hotel that the claim was brought with the purpose of depriving its local court of competent jurisdiction (see *Barton v Golden Sun Holidays Ltd and Avilda Hotel Ltd*).

3.4.3.2 *Separate Part 7 proceedings*

Where there is an accommodation contract which provides for an indemnity clause and the jurisdiction of the English courts, proceedings may be commenced by way of separate Part 7 proceedings (for instance if the holidaymaker's claim against the tour operator has already concluded).

3.4.4 Insurance considerations

The hotel is very likely to have public liability insurance in place – usually it will be a precondition of any agreement by a (responsible) tour operator to send customers to that hotel. Indeed, many accommodation contracts limit a tour operator's liability to a certain level of insurance cover (which may be negotiated locally without knowledge of the levels of costs than can accrue in English proceedings, and which may be wholly inadequate to meet any third party claim).

Some public liability (PL) policies exclude any liability under contract which is greater than the liability the assured would have without the contract. So where a hotel is obliged to indemnify the tour operator pursuant to an indemnity clause, but would only have been liable for an 80% contribution under the Civil Liability (Contribution) Act 1978, there may be no insurance cover for the difference.

Some PL policies exclude cover for any liability under contract. As such, the hotel's liability pursuant to a contractual indemnity may not be covered at all.

3.4.4.1 'Clawback' provisions

Certain accommodation contracts contain 'clawback' provisions where any loss incurred by the tour operator in one season is offset against the consideration paid by the tour operator to the hotel for accommodation in the next season.

Whereas local suppliers will be insured against Part 20 claims, most insurance policies are unlikely to cover losses incurred pursuant to clawback provisions. As such, it may not be advisable to rely solely upon any such provision where there may be issues as to enforcement, or ongoing commercial relations with the hotel are sought to be maintained by the tour operator.

3.5 GASTRIC ILLNESS CLAIMS

Given their increasing number, gastric illness claims warrant a section of their own. Claims of this kind are not for the unwary: they involve numerous issues which simply do not arise in other package holiday claims.

3.5.1 Strict liability or reasonable skill and care?

Although the basis of the claim is exactly the same as any other package claim, so a claimant needs to establish improper performance of the holiday contract causative of illness, the way it is approached is rather different.

As explored above, ordinarily, in the absence of any express acceptance of a more onerous standard, the court will imply a term of reasonable skill and care.

This implied term originates in the Supply of Goods and Services Act 1982 where under s 13, in a contract for the supply of a service where the supplier is acting in the course of a business there is an implied term to that effect.

In addition, by s 4, it is provided that there is an implied condition that the goods supplied under the contract are of satisfactory quality. Goods are regarded as being of satisfactory quality under s 4(2A) if they 'meet the standard that a reasonable person would regard as satisfactory, taking account of any description of the goods, the price (if relevant) and all the other relevant circumstances'.

In *Kempson v First Choice Holidays & Flights Ltd*,[47] the judge considered that this amounted to a strict duty on the supplier (the tour operator) to provide food that was fit for consumption because food that was not so fit would not be regarded as being of satisfactory quality. So if the claimant was able to establish that he fell ill as a result of consuming food contaminated with bacterial pathogens in sufficient number to cause illness, there was no defence that both the hotel and the tour operator may have taken reasonable steps to ensure that this did not happen. So it would not assist a tour operator to show zero other reported illnesses, ordinarily indicative of a well-run hotel, if in fact the claimant contracted salmonella poisoning through the consumption of a single dish of incompletely scrambled eggs.

Kempson was also relevant because the tour operator initially pleaded the standard *Holden* defence.[48] The judge considered that local standards were essentially irrelevant. Whether the food provided was of satisfactory quality is a matter of fact. If someone eats it and falls ill as a result, it is not satisfactory, which is a breach of the English holiday contract. It does not matter, on this construction, if in fact the hotel adhered to all relevant local standards (although it is probably a rare country which expressly permits its hoteliers to serve up contaminated food, even if that is what may happen not infrequently in practice).

---

[47] Birmingham County Court, 7 June 2007, HHJ Stephen Davies.
[48] As to which see **3.2.2.4**.

This decision has since been considered in two cases.

In *Eldridge v TUI*,[49] the claimants suffered gastric illness not as a result of eating contaminated food but as a result of consuming pool water containing cryptosporidium in a Balearic hotel. Expert evidence adduced by the claimants (unchallenged prior to trial by the tour operator) indicated that under the local law there was a positive obligation on the hotel to ensure that swimming pools were at all times free of pathogens including cryptosporidium (regardless of the quality of the system for cleaning pools and regardless of how little time there was between the oocysts getting into the pool and them being ingested by another bather). In other words, the local law provided for what was essentially zero tolerance on the part of the local supplier. The judge accepted that this was the local standard to which the hotel had to adhere, and the tour operator was liable for improper performance when that standard was breached.

In *Antcliffe v Thomas Cook*,[50] the Judge revisited the issue and again concluded that s 4 of the 1982 Act renders a tour operator strictly liable if its customers contract food poisoning from food or drink served by a local supplier. He did, however, find against the claimants on the allegation that there had been improper performance of the contract under reg 15, concluding that the provision of food and drink did involve a transfer of goods from the hotel to the consumer in respect of which in accordance with s 4 of the Supply of Goods and Services Act 1982. Accordingly it was the food and drink which had to be of satisfactory quality, not merely the level of care taken in the preparation, storage or selection of that food and drink. Food which is contaminated with a pathogen which causes illness in humans is not of a satisfactory quality. He also indicated that such food would not be fit for its purpose.[51]

It is suggested that the combined effect of these various decisions, albeit at county court level, is hard to ignore. If a claimant can establish on the balance of probabilities that he fell ill as a result of consuming food or drink or from contact with swimming pool water provided as part of the holiday contract which was contaminated by bacterial or protozoan organisms in sufficient quantities to cause illness, he is strongly likely to succeed. The real issue in the majority of cases will therefore be likely to be causation of illness.

3.5.2 Causation

How then is a claimant to establish (or a defendant to challenge) causation of illness? The following issues may require consideration in any individual case:

---

[49]   Unreported, Birmingham County Court, 16 December 2010, HHJ Worster.
[50]   Birmingham County Court, 4 July 2012, HHJ Worster.
[51]   In reliance on *Frost v The Aylesbury Dairy Company* [1905] 2 KB 605.

- What was provided as part of the package, ie full board, all inclusive, bed and breakfast or self catering? Tour operators are well used to claimants on half board packages denying that a morsel of food ever passed their lips between breakfast and supper. Others will assert that they only ate lunch at the hotel. This latter should not assist them because meals provided by the hotel for payment on site are provided outside the package for which the tour operator is liable. In the real world however, the more meals provided under the holiday contract, the more likely it will be that the court will conclude that the offending item was provided under the package rather than outside it.

- Is there a diagnosis of illness such as salmonella or campylobacter? A clear diagnosis of illness caused by bacterial pathogens will greatly increase the claimant's prospects of success. However, as Mrs Kempson found, not having a clear diagnosis is not fatal. There, the fact that her daughter had a diagnosis of salmonella permitted the judge to infer that she had contracted the same infection. It might have been different if no one in her party had a confirmed diagnosis and the tour operator could more easily suggest a viral infection. However, even the absence of any confirmed diagnoses may not assist the tour operator where the court accepts the claimants' evidence as to whether they fell ill and where there is insufficient evidence to cause the court to conclude that it was as a result of a viral infection.

- Is there more information available than merely 'salmonella' (or whatever)? Some phage types are more common to different areas of the world. A claimant who contracted salmonella phage type 13 is (apparently) far more likely to have contracted that from eggs originating from the US rather than in the UK. So an English claimant who fell ill shortly after his arrival in Puerto Rico is probably more likely to have contracted it as a result of something eaten on holiday rather than at home.

- What is the likely and possible incubation period for the relevant illness? A microbiologist may well be able to say that a certain illness commencing early in the holiday is more likely than not to have resulted from something consumed prior to departure from the UK.

- Does the claimant have any idea what the offending item was? Sometimes they may be able to identify an undercooked bit of chicken (inviting the obvious question as to why they ate it). More often though the claimant will only have a variety of inevitably subjective observations as to general food hygiene practices said to have been observed during the holiday from which to invite the court to infer that it must have been something the hotel did (or did not do). Tour operators to whose representatives illness was reported on holiday can usefully ask for food diaries at the time (as cruise ships usually do admittedly with the benefit of a captive audience) – such a request is unlikely however to assist anyone if made 3 years down the line.

- When was the diagnosis made? A claimant whose illness was identified a few weeks after his return home may find it harder to establish that it resulted from food eaten on holiday. On the other hand, in the absence of any evidence to suggest late onset of illness, a tour operator should not place too much reliance on a belated diagnosis, particularly where there is evidence that the claimant did in fact fall ill on holiday.
- Was the illness reported on holiday? This may be relevant to causation particularly where no clear diagnosis is given. It may also be relevant to credibility in multi party claims, which are considered separately below.
- Is there any extraneous evidence available? So a tour operator that is able to show high levels of illness in neighbouring hotels may have a better chance at establishing that the claimant contracted a virus rather than a bacterial infection.
- What is the surrounding area like? If the hotel is situated in the middle of a bustling town with numerous bars, restaurants and other dining establishments, it may be far harder for claimants to persuade the court that they never set foot outside the hotel.
- Many tour operators sell excursions with local suppliers. Leaving aside questions of when the tour operator may itself be liable for failings in the way the excursion was run, which are considered elsewhere, a lot of these excursions will feature food and drink: a beach barbecue, sangria and paella under the stars and so on. The more excursions on offer, and the more the claimants or members of their family booked, the higher the likelihood may be that they contracted illness outside the hotel.

3.5.2.1 *Viruses*

In cases where there is no clear bacterial or protozoan cause, it may be open to the tour operator to assert a viral cause such as the infamous norovirus.[52] A tour operator is not strictly liable when its customers contract viral illness and fault must be established. The nature of a viral infection is that it arises without warning, is likely to be extremely contagious and passed from person to person very easily, particularly if personal hygiene standards are not scrupulously maintained. So claimants who fell ill after contracting a viral infection may (and arguably should) struggle to establish liability.

This only applies, however, to the onset of the virus. No tour operator (or hotel) can guard against the development and initial transmission. However, there may come a time where a claimant can properly assert that something ought to have been done to stop the spread of the infection. In this regard, evidence will be needed as to numbers of illness, particularly when set against the population of the hotel (or cruise ship). Generally a

---

[52] Known colloquially as the 'winter vomiting bug'.

tour operator will have internal policies as to the critical mass of illness which will wave red flags and trigger further measures. A tour operator (aided or hindered by the hotel) which fails to pick up on increased levels of illness, at that hotel or arguably in the local area, may struggle to show that it acted reasonably.

Once the critical point has been reached, a tour operator will need to disclose its policies and the regime implemented by the hotel for the prevention of the spread of infection (POSI). Doing nothing when a virus is in full flow is almost guaranteed to give rise to a finding of liability from the time that critical point was reached.

If those measures are, on their face, reasonable (and most tour operators will have very similar policies) there may then be a period when claimants again fail to establish a want of reasonable skill and care on the part of the tour operator. If, however, the measures do not suffice to bring numbers of those ill down, this may again be regarded as placing an onus on the tour operator and hotel to take further measures, and a failure to respond could again result in liability.

Thus where a claim involves numerous claimants ill at various stages over a season where the likely cause is viral, a tour operator may find itself able to defend some and others – on paper at least. In reality, the risks that some may win and some may lose are probably more likely (given the nature of the typical multi-party claim) to play into the level of an overall settlement than into separate awards for some and not for others.

3.5.2.2   *Contributory negligence*

As explored above, contributory negligence is only a defence to a claim in contract where the breach of contract that is alleged is coextensive with liability in negligence, *Forsikringsakitieselkapet Vesta v Butcher.*[53] Although there is as yet no authority to this effect, this may suggest that there is no defence of contributory negligence open to a tour operator where its customers are able to assert strict liability for illness caused by the consumption of contaminated food, drink or water.

There may however be the extremely rare case where a tour operator could plead that a claimant voluntarily consented to the risk that the hotel or other local supplier was supplying contaminated food or drink (the 'volenti' defence considered above). A claimant who goes on a Bedouin excursion where the main dish is killed and cooked before their eyes may conceivably be one of those rarest of claimants whose knowing acceptance of the risk means the defendant can avoid responsibility if that risk eventuates.

---

[53]   [1986] 2 All ER 488.

3.5.3 Multi-party claims

The nature of gastric illness caused by consumption of contaminated food, drink or water, or indeed caused by viral infection, means that isolated incidents of illness are relatively unusual. If there was a breakdown in the hotel's systems of health and hygiene sufficient to lead to one contracting campylobacter, often there will be others. And conversely, if there are no others, this might lend weight to the tour operator's assertion that the illness must have been contracted other than at the hotel.

Accordingly, it is rather more common to have numerous claimants involved in a single claim arising out of complaints at one hotel. This brings with some very particular issues which may need to be considered:

- who can claim;
- consolidation or management together;
- is a group litigation order appropriate;
- trial by lead case;
- case management;
- costs management;
- expert and lay evidence;
- arrangements for trial; and
- settlement.

3.5.3.1 Who can claim

Very often a single claim will encompass a period of a few months and cover an entire season at the same hotel. So there might be claimants who travelled in April and others in October. With big hotels, it is not uncommon to have numbers of claimants reaching into the high hundreds.

The advantages are (or at least should be) savings of costs and time; and avoidance of inconsistent judgments: if the same issues are to be litigated, within a tight nexus of time and place, there is every reason why they should be considered at the same time.

The disadvantages, for tour operators at least, are that the judge may incorrectly draw adverse inferences about standards at the hotel if numerous people seem to have fallen ill over a prolonged period, all with similar complaints. Additionally, whilst audits may have been good at the beginning of the season, giving the tour operator confidence that it could defend the claims of those who travelled in April, the audits later in the season may be worse. But the April claimants will get to see the September audits which they might well not have done had the April claims been litigated separately. This is a legitimate concern, but unlikely to sway the judge into dividing up the claims and thereby causing costs to proliferate.

Where numerous claimants are joined into one action, it is inevitable that the particulars of claim will be largely generic, without specific particulars from individual claimants as to which complaints they adopt, and without specific details of each illness.

Finally, it is worth highlighting that a claimant who falls ill is not entitled to claim for the loss of enjoyment or diminution in value of family member's holidays (save to the extent that his own enjoyment was affected by witnessing their disappointment). Nor, of course, do family members have their own claims for loss of enjoyment and diminution in value merely because another member was ill: these are claims in contract and there is no breach of the contract with X merely because Y fell ill. Put another way, the tour operator did not owe X a duty not to injure Y.[54] However, where (as is frequently the case) X can say that there was a breach of his contract because there were too many flies, the swimming pool was filthy (even if no illness resulted) and the staff were rude, that will sound in damages and he should be named as a claimant in his own right.

3.5.3.2 *Consolidation or management together*

It is not unusual for claimants to approach different solicitors following holidays at the same hotel. So there may end up being three or more claims against one tour operator (or even against numerous tour operators) all arising out of allegedly substandard holidays at the Ells Bells Hotel in summer 2009.

Consolidation means, in effect, that these three claims become one. So one firm of solicitors will act for all claimants and one for all defendants – hence their lack of attraction to claimants, who may say they should not be obliged to instruct solicitors other than their first choice. However, consolidation almost guarantees costs savings because, for example, there will only be one exercise in disclosure. Accordingly it may be worth consideration at the allocation stage.

More frequently, the courts simply order that the claims should be tried together. This can raise slight problems particularly where some are in the county court and some in the High Court – one court cannot order another court to transfer its claim, for example – although these are seldom insurmountable.

---

[54] For further discussion on the protected persons in package travel claims see Chapter 2, Package Travel at **2.5**.

3.5.3.3 Group litigation order

It may be worth considering whether a group litigation order (GLO) under CPR Part 19 is appropriate in the larger claims. A GLO is said to 'provide for the case management of claims which give rise to common or related issues of fact or law' (CPR, r 19.10).

Although this writer is unaware of any gastric illness claim where a GLO has in fact been made, there may be advantages on all sides if the court agrees to make one. For claimants, there are the guarantees on several liability for costs and costs sharing under CPR, r 48.6A. For defendants, there is the certainty that all claims arising from one season, for example, will be determined at once, with judgment binding on all who are on the group register, and potentially all who are subsequently entered on the register, and perhaps an increased prospect of obtaining a costs capping order.

However, the reality is that many of the features of a GLO that would render it attractive can be ordered by the court as part of its inherent case management powers, and many courts (particularly those with a lot of experience in managing multi-party illness claims) may consider that there is no tangible benefit to making such an order.

3.5.3.4 Trial by lead case

Trial by lead case is almost certain to be the most proportionate approach to sizeable multi party claims. This means that the court will give directions limited to the lead cases and will determine the claims of the lead claimants at trial. However, unless the parties agree specifically that the lead cases are to be representative of other claimants, judgment on the lead cases is not necessarily binding on the others.

So, even if the court finds for claimant A (a lead case), this does not necessarily mean that claimant B (a non-lead case) is entitled to damages, even if they were staying at the same hotel at the same time. There may be separate arguments particularly on causation available to the tour operator as against B.

However, selection of lead cases should, if conducted sensibly, result in the court having an appropriate spread of claimants before it. Thus, where the claimants span an entire season, it might be wise to have some from the beginning, middle and end of the season; some who were ill and some who were not; some with a confirmed diagnosis and some without; some who have ongoing symptoms; some where the evidence suggests they travelled outside the hotel, and so on.

The number of lead cases obviously depends on the number of claimants. Where there are less than 50, for example, four or six lead cases might be appropriate. Even in the largest cases, though, 20 lead cases is about the maximum that can be managed proportionately.

As to selection, the general rule is that each side should have an equal pick. Usually claimants will nominate their selection first, followed by the defendant, to minimise the risk of duplication and then having to repeat the process. Ordinarily an order will then provide for a short period in which the parties can attempt to negotiate settlement of those lead cases and, if settlement is reached, additional lead cases are then selected. But after this first period it is generally uncommon, even where settlement is reached, then to add in further lead cases.

For claimants, selection of lead cases is usually fairly simple. Solicitors will no doubt already have received their clients' medical records and will be able to work out who the strongest claimants are likely to be.

For the tour operator it may well be trickier. There are rare cases, of course, where claimant A is well known because he went around the hotel urging people to contact the press and to report illness. However, selection of lead cases is generally done, for obvious reasons, early in the case management process and often before much if anything in the way of disclosure has been given (pre-action protocols notwithstanding). Not infrequently the defendant will not even have seen GP records.

There are various ways in which the selection process can be handled. Some or all of the following may be appropriate:

- The court may direct that the claimants should answer what are commonly referred to as 'sickness questionnaires', but which essentially ask what and where the claimant ate before falling ill; what symptoms they had; whether it was reported in resort or to the GP; whether there was a confirmed diagnosis, and so on. Some judges consider such an approach to be proportionate (particularly where disclosure of medical records has not been forthcoming), not least because they should ordinarily be completed by the claimant without solicitors' input; others doubt their jurisdiction to make such an order, at least in advance of witness statements.
- The tour operator may want disclosure, at least of certain categories of documents such as complaint forms, GP records, holiday photos and videos, before selection.
- The tour operator may simply ask for an order that it should specify in advance of selection whose GP reports they wish to see. Since medico-legal reports will have been served with proceedings, it should be possible to identify at least some of the claimants where this might assist.

- On occasion the court may consider that the tour operator should be permitted to ask for witness statements of selected claimants up front in order to assist the selection process. This is likely to be unusual.

3.5.3.5 *Case management*

Case management of multi-party claims, even with lead cases, is seldom straightforward. Many matters of case management are relevant in respect of costs management, which is considered separately below. Issues that may need to be considered include:

- Case management with other claims.
- Which track is appropriate. Usually the multitrack will be inevitable, but if the claimants are few in number, their illnesses are all short lived and there is a realistic prospect that the claimants will receive less than £1,000 by way of general damages, it may be one of those rare cases where the small claims track is more proportionate.
- Time scales. Tour operators are dependent to a large extent on the co-operation of their suppliers, many of whom (even if contractually obliged to assist) will be slow in responding over the prime holiday period, which could delay disclosure and exchange of witness statements of fact.
- Selection and management of experts. This may involve consideration of whether there should be single joint experts in any discipline; whether the costs recoverable should be limited; whether expert evidence should be considered at the first opportunity or more piecemeal; should it be simultaneous exchange or sequential; who can give oral evidence at trial and on what issues, and so on.
- Control of evidence. It may be appropriate for the court to direct that witness evidence of fact may only be adduced by the lead claimants, for example. This could avoid the risk that 40 witness statements are served, all saying much the same thing. The court may want direct that a party should identify within 14 days of receipt of the other side's statements which statements will be actively disputed. In a multi party claim, it may be perfectly appropriate for the tour operator to challenge the evidence of the lead claimants but not to require their supporting witnesses to attend for cross-examination on the basis that the same challenge should be deemed to be directed to those statements.
- Building in time for settlement discussions.
- Duration of trial. A trial involving five lead cases may be capable of being dealt with in 5 days. A larger case could easily last 10 days.
- Is the case of sufficient complexity and value to warrant a transfer to the High Court?
- Where there are, or there are proposed Part 20 proceedings against the local supplier, does the tour operator propose that these should

be considered at the same time as the main trial? Should the local supplier be permitted to take part in the main trial anyway, as in *Tantera v Moore*?[55]

- Is there any reason to direct the parties to give the court updates outside of hearings? It has been known for judges to direct, where there has been significant delay and a trial looming, that the parties should send in updates to the court as to their progress with reasons for any delays as soon as the deadline for compliance with any direction has passed. This can be surprisingly effective, if a drain on court resources.

3.5.3.6 Costs management

Costs are often the real battleground in such claims. The individual claims may be worth less than £1,000 but, given the number of issues that may fall to be determined, as well as the usual complexities of multi-party actions, the costs per claimant can turn out to be many times this. Accordingly, courts are increasingly anxious about maximising their case management powers to reduce costs.

Much of this section will fall away (for claims issued after 1 April 2013 at least) in the light of the Jackson costs reforms and the amendments to the Costs Rules. However, since the old Rules and law will continue to govern costs incurred in current cases for a considerable time, they are considered here. More detailed consideration of the Jackson reforms and their implications for personal injury litigation generally is given in the Special Supplement to the 2013 White Book.

The sort of issues that may need to be considered (in pre-1 April 2013 claims) include:

- Costs capping orders. These are considered separately below.
- Costs budgets. Here, the court may set an overall budget for the steps that remain to be taken as part of its inherent powers of case management. This is likely to err on side of generosity to both sides because the aim is not to render otiose or otherwise inhibit subsequent detailed assessment, but simply to give the parties some boundaries on the information then available to the court. The budget should not be regarded as a target to aim for. Court-approved budgets under a costs management order (CMO) post-1 April will carry far more weight.
- Undertakings. In essence both sides undertake to the court and to each other not to exceed a certain figure. These are again likely to err on the side of caution in the favour of the incurring party. *In Barr & ors v Biffa Waste Services Ltd (No 2)*,[56] the claimants agreed to limit

---

[55] [2009] EWCA Civ 1393. For more on joinder of local suppliers as third parties and/or defendants to claims against tour operators.
[56] [2009] EWHC 2444 (TCC).

future expenditure to the estimate provided to the court. In principle there is no good reason why both sides should not be happy to limit themselves to their estimates, subject as ever to the proviso that they can apply to the court in the event that circumstances change.

- Regular filing and exchange of Form H costs estimates. The court can order estimates at any time under CPR 43 PD para 6.3 (pre-1 April 2013). The court has an obvious interest in knowing from time to time what costs have been incurred, not least so it can refer back to previous estimates to get a feel for the case. The parties have an interest in seeing accurate estimates, which can be used in negotiation and, if needs be, as reference points under CPR PD 43, para 6.5A(1) (pre-1 April 2013) if final bills exceed estimates by more than 20%.
- Caps on individual disbursements. This will be particularly applicable to experts' fees. There is nothing inherently inequitable in limiting the amount a party can recover for a simple gastroenterological report, for example, as long as there is nothing to suggest that the limit would effectively prevent that party from obtaining expert evidence which would otherwise be reasonably required.
- Case management issues regarding control of evidence and so on – considered earlier in this section.

3.5.3.7 *Costs capping orders*

These were made on a fairly regular basis in multi-party actions until the Rules were changed by way of the Civil Procedure Rules[57] with effect from 6 April 2009. The changes themselves were apparently opposed by some of the judges with most experience of multi-party gastric illness litigation, however, suggestions that such claims should fall outside the amended Rules fell on deaf ears. Since they came into force the writer is unaware of a single successful application for a costs cap (as opposed to a costs budget) in a multi-party gastric illness claim.

Accordingly the test for a costs capping order (CCO) is that set out in CPR, rr 44.18 and 44.19 together with section 23A of the Costs Practice Direction (pre-1 April 2013) and CPR Part 3 Section III at 3.19 and 3.20 (post-1 April).

CPR, r 44.18 provides that:

'(1)   A costs capping order is an order limiting the amount of *future costs* (including disbursements) which a party may recover pursuant to an order for costs subsequently made.

(2)   In this rule, "future costs" means costs incurred in respect of *work done after the date of the costs capping order* but *excluding the amount of any additional liability*.

---

[57]   Amendment (No 2) Rules 2009, SI 2009/3390.

...

(5)   The court may *at any stage of proceedings* make a costs capping order against all or any of the parties, if –

(a)   it is *in the interests of justice* to do so;

(b)   there is a *substantial risk* that without such an order costs will be *disproportionately incurred*; and

(c)   it is *not satisfied that the risk in sub-paragraph (b) can be adequately controlled* by –
      (i)   case management directions or orders made under Part 3; and
      (ii)   detailed assessment of costs.

(6)   In considering whether to exercise its discretion under this rule, the court will consider all the circumstances of the case, including –

(a)   whether there is a *substantial imbalance* between the financial position of the parties;

(b)   *whether the costs of determining the amount of the cap are likely to be proportionate to the overall costs of the litigation*;

(c)   the *stage* which the proceedings have reached; and

(d)   the *costs* which have been incurred to date and the future costs.'

(emphases added)

The principles have been considered in various authorities and can be summarised as follows:

- There is no possibility whatsoever of arguing for a retrospective cap. Any cap will only be from the date of the order.
- A CCO can only be made if all three conditions in CPR, r 44.18(5) are satisfied – and then there is discretion.
- The court cannot cap additional liabilities. In all likelihood the prospect of the uplift and ATE premiums should be disregarded when considering proportionality – *Barr & ors v Biffa Waste Services Ltd (No 2)*.[58]
- However, funding arrangements may be of some relevance if there is insufficient ATE cover etc – *Barr*.[59]
- The exceptionality principle is a high threshold.
- Timing is important. Some case management should have taken place, ie so the court determining the application can identify what steps have been taken, what the costs of those steps were, what is left to do etc – *Eli Lilly & Co Ltd v James*.[60]
- There needs to be some evidence to underpin assumptions that costs are being disproportionately incurred – *Eli Lilly*.
- 'It is not sufficient that there should be a risk that, without a CCO, costs will be disproportionately incurred' – *Eweida v British Airways plc*.[61]

---

[58]   [2009] EWHC 2444 (TCC) at [46].
[59]   [2009] EWHC 2444 (TCC) at [15(c)].
[60]   [2009] EWHC 198 (QB).
[61]   [2009] EWCA Civ 1025 at [33].

- 'The sanction, and the protection for the paying party, lies in the power of the costs judge to assess the costs at a reasonable level and to disallow excessive expenditure, not as between solicitor and client, but as between opposing parties' – *Eweida*.[62]
- Excessive levels of past costs may not entitle the court to presume that such profligacy will continue. 'Of course, the fact that such a large sum has been incurred is largely irrelevant for the purposes of any costs capping exercise because that can relate to prospective costs only' – *Barr*.[63]
- Costs are not necessarily disproportionate just because they exceed the value of the claims – *Barr*.[64]
- The court should be capable of controlling disproportionate expenditure through case management and detailed assessment – *Barr*.[65]

Since the new Rules repeat the wording of the old Rules, there is no reason to suppose that applications will be any more successful. Defendants will, however, be entitled to expect rather more protection against exorbitant costs by virtue of CMOs and the changes to the Rules relating to assessment.

3.5.3.8 Evidence

Lay evidence

Some of the steps the court may seek to take to narrow the issues and control costs have been considered earlier. In particular, thought will need to be given to choice of witnesses. There is not necessarily strength in numbers – having six witnesses saying the same thing may well not be regarded as six times more likely to persuade the judge (especially if they are part of the same family group), and could well be penalised in costs later on.

Generally speaking, and save where the court has given directions limiting witnesses to the lead claimants only (as may well be the case), lay evidence from each of the lay claimants, no more than one witness in support on liability and no more than one in support of quantum should prove ample.

Expert evidence

Where all aspects of liability and quantum are in dispute in a big multi-party claim, and notwithstanding the probably modest value of the individual claims, it is not uncommon for the parties to have (or at least to

---

[62]   [2009] EWCA Civ 1025 at [44].
[63]   [2009] EWHC 2444 (TCC) at [24].
[64]   [2009] EWHC 2444 (TCC) at [43].
[65]   [2009] EWHC 2444 (TCC) at [50].

seek permission for), on each side, expert evidence in the fields of
gastroenterology; microbiology; food hygiene standards; swimming pool
management; virology; and local standards; as well as any other medical
discipline indicated by the individual claimants' symptoms.

Issues that ordinarily ought to be considered in respect of expert evidence
include:

- Are all disciplines needed at the outset? Ordinarily a microbiologist
  will be critical from the beginning, because his job will be to
  consider, inter alia, likely causes of any illness (salmonella,
  campylobacter, viral infection etc); incubation periods; and probable
  cause of infection (food, swimming pool water etc). But there is
  seldom any need for a virologist at the outset unless all parties agree
  that the claim concerns a viral outbreak.
- Are all disciplines needed at all? Given the preponderance of the
  case-law concerning strict liability, it may be questionable whether
  local standards and health and hygiene evidence will be needed in the
  future save in exceptional cases, but this will largely depend on
  whether the tour operator concedes the point before the court is
  asked to decide on nomination of experts.
- Would it be appropriate for the claimants to serve their evidence in
  any given discipline first? This may be an effective way of limiting
  costs as the tour operator may be content to put its case in questions
  but not obtain its own report. On the other hand, this could put the
  claimants at a disadvantage if they have to 'show their hand' before
  the tour operator does.
- Is any discipline suited to a single joint expert? Almost certainly not
  microbiology, since the parties will want to have open but privileged
  discussions on what are likely to be the central issues. But there may
  well be scope for single joint instruction of a local lawyer (if needed
  at all) or a medical expert to consider symptoms beyond
  gastroenterological ones.
- Should an agenda be prepared for the experts prior to their
  discussions? Does the court need to have any input into the contents
  of the agenda if one is to be provided?
- Should the scope of oral evidence be limited to issues that remain in
  dispute following discussions? Almost certainly yes.
- Should the costs of an expert's report be limited upfront? This may
  appeal particularly for some of the 'lesser' disciplines which are
  unlikely to be determinative of the claim. Both sides should take care
  to have details at case management hearings of their likely experts,
  time scales for preparation of reports and costs of the same so that
  the court can take a view.

3.5.3.9 *Arrangements for trial*

Multi-party claims may potentially end up with over 30 lay witnesses and more than 10 experts. A trial timetable that: (a) sets aside enough time for judicial reading and last minute applications; and (b) allocates witnesses to agreed days is likely to be critical. Since an expert may charge several thousand pounds for a day's attendance at trial, it would be nonsensical to end up in a position, barring the unforeseen, where two microbiologists end up waiting at court for 3 days before finally giving evidence.

Video link facilities

Particular attention needs to be given to video link facilities. Although the desire for witnesses to give evidence by video link is not limited to gastric illness claims but is common to many claims arising out of overseas accidents and incidents, it can be especially important where so many other witnesses and experts are waiting until the video link evidence is completed before giving their evidence.

The guidance for video link evidence are set out in CPR PD 32, Annex 3. Factors to be considered may include:

(1) Checking in advance whether video evidence is permitted under the law of that foreign country or whether it is only permitted in circumstances where the local Court has made the arrangements.
(2) Ensuring foreign witnesses have a trial bundle or at least an agreed and paginated core bundle (with translations where necessary); and that the court has an identical bundle.
(3) Checking the connection before the court day starts.
(4) Ensuring foreign witnesses have seen any documents prepared by them or by other local witnesses such as illness report forms.
(5) Emphasising to foreign witnesses the need to ensure that only the witness (with or without a translator) is in the room. Foreign hotels may and often do try to insist that the company lawyer or managing director should sit in. If this is the case:

(a) everyone in the English court needs to know who they are and why they are there;
(b) they should be instructed not to speak or communicate with the witness; and
(c) if any concerns arise during the witness's evidence, the other person should be asked to sit where they can be seen by the camera.

(6) Ensuring that a translator is available, even where the witness's English is competent. Thought will need to be given as to whether the translator should be in the foreign country or in the court.

(7)   Ensuring that the witness has available whatever Holy book is needed if they prefer to swear rather than affirm.

3.5.3.10   *Settlement*

Settlement is of course to be encouraged in all claims and not just multi-party gastric illness claims. Some issues arise more frequently in these claims, however, which may need to be considered in the context of any given case.

(1)   Would a global offer in respect of damages and costs be acceptable to either side (even if not Part 36-compliant)?

(2)   Where a global offer is made in respect of all claimants' damages (as is frequently the case, the tour operator having little interest in what sums each claimant receives and little knowledge about those claimants who were not lead cases), who is taking the risk on minors' approval?

    (a)   Should any settlement identify what sums are to be allocated to each child and proposed for court approval?

    (b)   Should any settlement provide for the claimants' solicitors to undertake not to put forward for approval for any child any sum lower than that which counsel has advised is appropriate?

    (c)   Should the tour operator attend the approval hearings, which it would not ordinarily do?

(3)   Is a confidentiality clause appropriate? In what terms?

(4)   Will it present possible difficulties down the line for the tour operator recouping its outlay from the local supplier if the settlement is by way of Tomlin order and not by way of a court order? In this regard, it should be noted that the mandatory recognition and enforcement of English judgments in other member states under Chapter III of Council Regulation 44/2001 only applies to 'judgments', and not to out of court settlements.

CHAPTER 4

JURISDICTION

Pierre Janusz

4.1 IS THERE A NEED TO SUE A DEFENDANT DOMICILED ABROAD?

This chapter is concerned with identifying those cases where the courts of England and Wales can exercise the power to hear and determine cases which relate to events or parties outside England and Wales. There are strong practical reasons why a victim of an accident abroad, or of illness sustained abroad, who lives in England and Wales would wish to avoid bringing proceedings in a court outside England and Wales. These include practical issues traditional to the question of convenience of the forum, such as availability of evidence, including witnesses, the need to apply a law other than that of England and Wales, increased cost and delay and possible difficulties of enforcement.

Even if it is the case that the person directly responsible for the claimant's losses and against whom a claim would lie is domiciled abroad, it does not always follow that redress can be obtained only from that person. In relation to most claims arising out of package tours it will be possible to bring an equally valid claim against a tour operator or other person domiciled in England and Wales under reg 15 of the Package Travel, Package Holidays and Package Tours Regulations 1992.[1] Accordingly, the question of jurisdiction is not generally important in package tour related claims. It is however, more likely to be an issue in relation to road traffic accident and non-tour operator claims.

4.2 WHAT IS 'JURISDICTION'?

The word jurisdiction can be used in a number of different senses in a legal context,[2] but here we are dealing with the question of the competence or power of a court in England and Wales to hear and determine a claim which a claimant wishes to make against one or more defendants. An English court[3] does not have jurisdiction to entertain

---

[1] SI 1992/3288. See Appendix 1.
[2] For example whether the case should be heard by the High Court or county court or some other specialist domestic tribunal.
[3] In this chapter reference to 'English court' and 'English law' means a court in and the law of England and Wales.

every sort of claim against every possible defendant in the world. This is an issue of international private law. This chapter is concerned with establishing which claims in respect of accidents abroad can legitimately be heard by an English court.

4.2.1   Jurisdiction and applicable law

Jurisdiction is an entirely different concept from that of applicable law. The applicable law determines which set of legal rules a court will apply when deciding substantive or procedural issues which arise between litigants and is not generally relevant to the question of whether a court has the competence to determine the claim.[4] It is, however, surprising how often practitioners (and even sometimes courts) allow the two concepts to become confused and question the jurisdiction of an English court to hear a matter by reference to the foreign location of the relevant events or the involvement of a foreign system of law in deciding the relevant issues.

4.2.2   Jurisdiction is determined at the time of proceedings

The rules discussed below relating to the question of whether an English court will have jurisdiction are those which are in force at the time of writing. It is not considered necessary to give any account of the various rules which have been applicable in the past, because it is the situation which obtains at the point in time when proceedings are issued (or in some cases when they are served) which is relevant to the question of jurisdiction. As we are concerned only with the possibility of bringing claims before an English court and because there is a very limited period of time in which any challenge to the jurisdiction of the court can be made,[5] cases in which the older regimes may be relevant are now very unlikely to arise in practice. As to the future, see n 7 with regard to changes which are at present known to come into effect as from 10 January 2015. It should also be borne in mind that the discussion below is concerned with claims which do not fall within the scope of the liability regimes created by international conventions relating to specific forms of international carriage, ie carriage by air (Warsaw and Montreal Conventions), carriage by sea (Athens Convention) and carriage by rail (COTIF). Each of these Conventions has its own special jurisdiction rules which override the general rules discussed below, and reference should be made to Chapters 7 and 8 where the scope of these Conventions and their jurisdictional rules are explained.

---

[4]   Chapter 5 addresses applicable law issues relevant to accidents abroad.

[5]   See CPR Part 11, r 11.1(4) requires an application to be made within 14 days after filing an acknowledgement of service. Although an extension of this period is possible, lengthy extensions are extremely unlikely to be granted.

4.3 JURISDICTION REGIMES – RELEVANCE OF DEFENDANT'S DOMICILE

The question of whether an English court has jurisdiction to decide a matter arises, so far as claims of the type with which this work is concerned, because, given the foreign location of the relevant events, there is a high likelihood that there may be a defendant who is not domiciled in England and Wales.[6] Leaving aside for the moment the special situation of a defendant who is domiciled in Scotland or Northern Ireland (which is dealt with separately at **4.5**), there are in principle two sets of rules for determining whether an English court can have jurisdiction over the matter: on the one hand the rules under Council Regulation (EC) 44/2001 ('the Regulation')[7] and the Lugano Convention ('the Convention'),[8] the relevant provisions of which are in identical terms mutatis mutandis[9] and on the other hand the rules of domestic English procedural law with regard to jurisdiction.

The main difference with regard to procedure between the Regulation or Convention and domestic procedural regimes is the need for permission to serve proceedings outside England and Wales. If the substantive jurisdictional rules[10] of the Regulation or the Convention are applicable and they allow an English court to exercise jurisdiction in the matter, a claimant can bring and prosecute proceedings as of right in the English

---

[6]   As will be seen below, in general an English court will have jurisdiction over a defendant domiciled in England and Wales.

[7]   This Regulation will be replaced as from 10 January 2015 by Regulation (EU) No 1215/2012, which was enacted on 12 December 2012 and entered into force on 9 January 2013, but by a combination of Arts 66(1) and 81 its substantive provisions will apply only from 10 January 2015 and then only in respect of legal proceedings instituted on or after 10 January 2015. There are differences between its provisions as to jurisdiction and those in Regulation (EC) No 44/2001, but in substance the differences are confined to section 9 (lis pendens and related actions), where refinements to the rather blunt scheme of the original Regulation are introduced, but there are also some changes of significance in section 7 (prorogation of jurisdiction). The changes also mean that the numbering of the Articles relating to jurisdiction will change, so unless a correspondingly amended Lugano Convention is negotiated and brought into force, there will be not only some differences between the Regulation and Convention regimes but also an absence of correspondence between the numbers of the Articles dealing with specific matters. A further matter to be noted is that recital 41 records that Denmark is not taking part in the adoption of the new Regulation, so there is the possibility that Regulation (EC) 44/2001 will continue to apply as between the other member states and Denmark.

[8]   This is the 'new' Lugano Convention which came into force between all EU member states and Norway on 1 January 2010, between all EU member states and Switzerland on 1 January 2011 and between all EU member states and Iceland on 1 May 2011.

[9]   As the Articles of the Regulation and of the Convention are in essentially identical terms, references below to a numbered Article of the Regulation should be taken as a reference also to the equivalent numbered Article of the Convention.

[10] This means all of the provisions in Arts 2 to 30 except for the provisions in Art 4 which allow a court to apply its own jurisdictional rules in relation to a defendant not domiciled in a Regulation or Convention state.

courts[11] and if it is necessary to serve the proceedings outside England and Wales he requires no permission to do so. If the substantive jurisdictional rules of the Regulation or the Convention do not apply, then, if it is necessary to serve the proceedings outside England and Wales,[12] permission to do so is required. Permission can be granted only if one or more of the grounds referred to in CPR, r 6.36 apply. The court has a discretion whether to grant permission and will need to be satisfied both that there is a serious issue to be tried and that it is the appropriate forum for the dispute between the parties before it grants permission.[13]

4.3.1 Which regime applies?

It is the defendant's domicile which generally is relevant in order to determine which regime applies. If the defendant is domiciled (or deemed to be domiciled)[14] in any of the member states of the European Union[15] ('a Regulation state') or any of the states outside the European Union which are party to the Convention[16] ('a Convention state'), then in relation to the classes of actions with which the Regulation and the Convention are concerned, ie civil and commercial matters not within any of the express exceptions specified in Art 1(1) and (2),[17] an English court will have jurisdiction only if the provisions of the Regulation or the Convention permit. In a case within the scope of either the Regulation or the Convention their provisions will also determine if an English court can exercise jurisdiction, irrespective of the domicile of the defendant, if (i) the proceedings are ones specified by Art 22, which, subject to one exception,[18] confers exclusive jurisdiction on the courts of one Regulation or Convention state for certain types of proceedings or (ii) they are caught by the provisions of Art 23 relating to jurisdiction agreements.

CPR, r 6.36 determines if the court can exercise jurisdiction, if the claim falls outside the scope of the Regulation or the Convention, (even where the defendant is domiciled in a Regulation or Convention state), or the defendant is domiciled neither in a Regulation state nor in a Convention state (and the proceedings are not caught by Arts 22 or 23) and it is

---

[11] Subject only to the lis alibi pendens and related actions provisions in section 9 of Chapter/Title II of the Regulation and the Convention.

[12] This will not be necessary if it is possible to serve the defendant while he is present in England and Wales; see **4.6.1**.

[13] It will, however, still be open to a defendant who is served pursuant to permission granted under CPR, r 6.36 (or served solely on the basis of being while present in England and Wales) to seek a stay of proceedings on the grounds of forum non conveniens, something which is not possible under the Regulation or the Convention regime: *Owusu v Jackson* [2005] QB 801.

[14] As under e g Art 9(2).

[15] Although Art 1(3) of the Regulation defines 'member state' as meaning member states with the exception of Denmark, Denmark has been subject to the Regulation regime as from 1 July 2007 by virtue of a parallel agreement ([2006] OJ L120/22).

[16] Norway, Switzerland or Iceland.

[17] Discussed at **4.4.1–4.4.2**.

[18] See **4.4.4.10** (exception for certain short-term residential tenancies).

necessary to serve the proceedings outside England and Wales. It is worth noting that if in either of these cases it is not necessary to serve the proceedings outside England and Wales, because, for example, the defendant can be served while he is physically present in England and Wales, the English court will have jurisdiction if he is so served.

Note, however, that under both regimes jurisdiction can be exercised by an English court if the defendant submits to the jurisdiction,[19] even if there is no other basis on which it could do so, although in cases which are within the scope of the Regulation or Convention this cannot happen if the proceedings are ones which are within the exclusive jurisdiction of the courts of one member state or Convention state pursuant to Art 22. Submission to the jurisdiction is dealt with in more detail at **4.4.4.12**.

4.4 DOES THE CLAIM FALL WITHIN THE SCOPE OF THE REGULATION OR THE CONVENTION?

As noted above, the Regulation and the Convention apply only to 'civil and commercial matters', but their application to such matters is not affected by the nature of the tribunal before which they are brought (Art 1(1)). Partial definition of what is meant by 'civil and commercial matters' is also to be found in Art 1(1) which states in each case that the scope does not extend to revenue, customs or administrative matters. By way of further clarification of, or express exclusion from, the scope of their application, Art 1(2) then identifies other classes of matters to which they do not apply, of which the only potentially relevant one for the purposes of this work is 'social security' (Art 1(2)(c)).

In the vast majority of cases arising out of accidents abroad there will be no doubt but that the claim is a civil or commercial matter within Art 1. However, questions can arise as to whether it is such a matter if a public body is involved, as claims by and against a public body arising out of the exercise by it of its public functions do not fall within the rubric of 'civil and commercial matters'.[20]

In *Summers v Stubbs*,[21] the defendant in a road traffic accident claim sought a contribution from the Comune Di Milano ('Milan') on the basis that it had allowed a dangerous alteration to the layout of a pavement. Milan argued that the English court had no jurisdiction over it pursuant to the Brussels Convention (the precursor to the Regulation) because the claim against it was concerned with the exercise of its public functions. The court, however, held that the duty relied on (not to injure others) was

---

[19] Although the concept of submission to the jurisdiction is referred to here, it should be noted that under the Regulation and Convention regime the conduct by the defendant which allows the English court to exercise jurisdiction is entering an appearance other than for the purposes of contesting the court's jurisdiction.

[20] *LTU GmbH v Eurocontrol* (C-29/76) [1976] ECR 1541.

[21] [2002] EWHC 3213 (QB).

in the sphere of private law so that the claim was not concerned with public law functions and accordingly the court had jurisdiction.[22]

In claims arising out of accidents abroad involving uninsured or untraced drivers it has been argued that proceedings brought against the equivalent in other member states of the Motor Insurers' Bureau (MIB) fall outside the scope of the Regulation because they are performing public functions on behalf of the state when meeting claims arising out of such accidents. There is no reported decision on this point, but although it raises an interesting question about the nature of the functions which such bodies perform, having to deal with it can now be avoided in most such cases by relying on the Motor Vehicles (Compulsory Insurance) (Information Centre and Compensation Body) Regulations,[23] highlighted by the case of *Jacobs v Motor Insurers Bureau*.[24] These Regulations will enable a claim arising in such circumstances after they came into force on 19 January 2003 to be made in England against the MIB as long as the required steps specified in the Regulations are taken.

4.4.1   Social security

Social security was expressly excluded from the scope of the regime because it was not uniformly treated in countries which were the original six parties to the Brussels Convention. It was a matter of public law in some of them, but in others it was on the borderline between public and private law, and there were also differences as to the courts which possessed jurisdiction in relation to it.[25] Its exclusion is relevant to claims arising out of accidents abroad because there is an argument that certain types of claims by an employee against an employer which arise out of accidents at work are to be properly categorised as social security claims. In principle what falls within the concept of social security for the purposes of European Union law is determined by the matters which are covered by Council Regulation (EEC) 1408/71 ('Reg 1408/71'),[26] and this is the meaning which it has for the purposes of the Regulation and Convention. Reg 1408/71 applies to all legislation concerning a number of branches of social security, including 'benefits in respect of accidents at work and occupational diseases'[27] and also applies to all general and special social security schemes and to 'schemes concerning the liability of an employer ... in respect of' the benefits specified in Art 4(1)(e) of Reg 1408/71. In the case of a scheme relating to an employer's liability in

---

[22]   See also Case C-172/91 *Sonntag* [1993] ECR I-1963, a fatal accident involving a school child where the allegation of fault was against a state-employed teacher.

[23]   SI 2003/37.

[24]   [2010] EWCA Civ 1208; [2011] 1 WLR. 2609. See Chapter 6, Direct Actions Against Insurers for discussion on claims against the MIB.

[25]   As explained at p 12 in the report of Mr P Jenard on the Brussels Convention and the 1971 Protocol OJ C 59, 5.3.1979.

[26]   Which was concerned with the application of social security rules to employed persons and their families moving between the member states.

[27]   Reg 1408/71, Art 4(1)(e).

respect of those benefits, both the employer and the insurer involved are 'competent institutions'.[28] The argument is that where there is a statutory liability[29] on an employer or his insurers to compensate an employee in respect of losses he has sustained as a result of a workplace accident, that compensation constitutes 'benefits in respect of accidents at work' and the claim is therefore a social security one. There are no reported decisions dealing with this argument, but it is considered that it is not correct to equate compensation, the quantum of which is determined by the actual losses suffered by the employee, with social security benefits paid out under legislation.

4.4.2   What is a defendant's domicile?

The meaning of the term 'domicile' for the purposes of jurisdiction is quite different from that of the common law concept of domicile for individuals (a status one acquires at birth and which, subject to change by adoption, remains fixed until changed by choice by a combination of residence in another country and an intention to reside there permanently or indefinitely). For these purposes 'domicile' for individuals is closer to, but not identical with, the concepts of habitual or ordinary residence. In all cases it is necessary to refer to the specific definitions of domicile for both natural and legal persons in order to determine the domicile of any proposed defendant. One matter which should be noted is that, unlike under the common law principles, it is possible for an individual to have more than one domicile.

In claims which are within the scope of the Regulation or the Convention, ie civil or commercial matters as explained above, a party's domicile is determined in accordance with the schemes prescribed by those instruments, which are identical mutatis mutandis.

Under Art 59(1) of each instrument, if an English court is seised of a matter the first stage is to determine whether the party is domiciled in the UK, and that question is answered by reference to the law of the forum, ie English law. If the party is not domiciled in the state where the forum is located, then the second stage (under Art 59(2)) is to determine whether the party is domiciled in another Regulation or Convention state, and that question is answered by reference to the law of that other state.

---

[28]   Reg 1408/71, Art 1(o)(iv).
[29]   The need for it to be statutory derives from the reference to legislation in Art 4(1). In principle there will be a statutory basis for liability in all countries which have codified laws. The argument would not appear to depend on whether the liability is fault based or not.

Different rules apply for determining a party's domicile according to whether one is concerned on the one hand with 'a company or other legal person or association of natural or legal persons'[30] or, on the other hand, an individual.

In the former case, Art 60(1) provides that such a party is domiciled at the place where it has its statutory seat, central administration or its principal place of business, and for the purposes of the UK and Ireland 'statutory seat' is defined as the registered office, or if there is none, the place of incorporation, or if none, the place under the law of which formation took place. As a company may be incorporated in one country, have its central administration in another country and have its principal place of business in a third country it is possible for a company to be domiciled in all three of those countries, and the same could apply to other legal persons or associations of natural or legal persons. Because both the Regulation and the Convention have direct effect in English law, Art 60 is both the law of the forum for the purposes of Art 59(1) and the law of the Regulation or Convention state for the purposes of Art 59(2). This means that as an English lawyer one can have the competence to decide whether a party which is a company, other legal person or association of natural or legal persons is domiciled in the UK, in another Regulation or Convention state or elsewhere.

For the purposes of jurisdiction as between the constituent parts of the UK (ie England and Wales, Scotland and Northern Ireland) in relation to claims such as those arising out of accidents abroad, the question of whether a company or association is domiciled in one of those parts is determined by s 42 of the Civil Jurisdiction and Judgments Act 1982, by reference to the 'seat' of the company or association. Its seat can only be in one of the constituent parts of the UK if:

(1)   its seat is in the UK; and
(2)   it:

    (a)   has its registered office or some other official address in that part;
    (b)   its central management and control is exercised in that part; or
    (c)   it has a place of business[31] in that part of the UK.

In the case of a party who is an individual the questions of whether he is domiciled in the UK, and if so in which one of its constituent parts, or whether he is domiciled in a non-Regulation or non-Convention state are answered by reference to the rules in the Civil Jurisdiction and Judgments Order 2001[32] (in the case of the Regulation) and in s 41A of the Civil

---

[30]   Article 60(1); in *Phillips v Symes* [2002] 1 WLR 753 this expression was held to include an English partnership.
[31]   Defined in s 42(4).
[32]   SI 2001/3929, Sch 1, para 9.

Jurisdiction and Judgments Act 1982 (in the case of the Convention), the terms of which are identical mutatis mutandis. These rules provide as follows:

(1) An individual is domiciled in the UK if, and only if, he is resident[33] in the UK and the nature and circumstances of his residence indicate that he has a substantial connection with the UK.[34]

(2) He will be domiciled in one of the constituent parts of the UK if, and only if, he is resident in that part and the nature and circumstances of his residence indicate that he has a substantial connection with that part,[35] but if he is domiciled in the UK he will be treated as domiciled in the part in which he is resident even if the requirement of an indication of a substantial connection with that part is not satisfied.[36]

(3) In relation to both domicile in the UK and in one of its constituent parts there is a rebuttable presumption that the requirement of an indication of a substantial connection with the UK or the relevant constituent part (as the case may be) is fulfilled if the individual has been resident there for the last 3 months or more.[37]

(4) An individual is domiciled in a state other than a Regulation or Convention state if, and only if, he is resident in that state and the nature and circumstances of his residence indicate that he has a substantial connection with that state.[38][39]

The question of whether a party who is an individual is domiciled in a Regulation or Convention state other than the UK is determined by the law of that other Regulation or Convention state,[40] and because there is no equivalent to Art 60 in relation to individuals this means that there is no generally applicable rule and that it is therefore necessary to obtain expert local law advice from a relevantly qualified lawyer if it considered necessary to ascertain if an individual is domiciled in such a state.

4.4.3 Claims within the scope of the Regulation or the Convention where the defendant is domiciled in a Regulation or Convention state: the general rule

The general rule established by Art 2 is that a defendant domiciled in a Regulation or Convention state shall, whatever his nationality, be sued in the courts of that state. However, one should not forget the possibility of

---

[33] What is meant by 'resident' and 'residence' is not defined, but the words connote a degree of permanence or continuity.

[34] Paragraph 9(2); s 41A(2).

[35] Paragraph 9(3); s 41A(3).

[36] Paragraph 9(5); s 41A(5).

[37] Paragraph 9(6); s 41A(6).

[38] Paragraph 9(7); s 41A(7).

[39] Note that there is no equivalent of the rebuttable presumption based on residence of 3 months or more.

[40] Article 59(2).

a defendant being domiciled in more than one state (see above), and if that is the case then under the general rule he can be sued in any of the Regulation or Convention states in which he is domiciled. By virtue of Art 3 this general rule is subject to a number of exceptions and qualifications which can either (i) allow persons domiciled in a Regulation or Convention state also to be sued in the courts of another Regulation or Convention state or (ii) provide that the courts of a Regulation or Convention state other than those of the defendant's domicile have exclusive jurisdiction over a matter. These exceptions and qualifications are exhaustively stated in the rules set out in Arts 5 to 24, and therefore, unless one of them is applicable, jurisdiction cannot be exercised over a defendant domiciled in another Regulation or Convention state who is not also domiciled in the UK, even if it is possible to serve him within England and Wales.[41]

This general rule and the exceptions and qualifications to it do not apply to a defendant who is neither domiciled in a Regulation or Convention state nor deemed to be so domiciled by, for example, Art 5(5), and the jurisdiction of the courts of a Regulation or Convention state over such a defendant will, subject only to the provisions of Art 22[42] and 23,[43] be determined by the law of that state (Art 4(1)). It is this provision which means that questions of jurisdiction over defendants not domiciled in a Regulation or Convention state are generally decided by the English domestic rules (principally, but not exclusively, CPR, r 6.36; see **4.6**) even in relation to matters which fall within the material scope of the Regulation or Convention.

4.4.4   The exceptions and qualifications

Because many of the exceptions and qualifications under Arts 5 to 24 either cannot or are extremely unlikely in practice to be relevant in claims arising out of accidents abroad the following treatment is far from exhaustive. It is proposed to deal only with the exceptions and qualifications which are likely to be material to such claims. Before looking at the relevant ones individually, it is important to note that as they represent derogations from the general and fundamental principle that jurisdiction is to be based on the domicile of the defendant they are to be interpreted narrowly rather than generously, as stated in a number of decisions of the CJEU, such as *Reisch Montage* AG v *Kiesel Baumaschinen Handels GmbH*.[44] It should also be noted that the need to rely on many of the exceptions to the general rule has been greatly

---

[41]   Eg in the case of a company, under CPR, r 6.9 at a place of business of the company in England and Wales or on the person authorised to accept service of process under ss 1139–1142 of the Companies Act 2006.

[42]   This Article specifies matters over which the courts of a particular Regulation or Convention state shall have exclusive jurisdiction.

[43]   This Article deals with jurisdiction agreements involving at least one party who is domiciled in a Regulation or Convention state.

[44]   [2003] ECR I-6827.

reduced by the decision of the CJEU in *FBTO v Odenbreit*,[45] which concerns a claim by a claimant domiciled in England and Wales against a potential defendant who has relevant liability insurance with an insurer domiciled in a Regulation or Convention state and there is a direct claim available to a victim against the insurer.[46] As explained below, in these cases the English court will have jurisdiction over the insurer irrespective of whether there can be jurisdiction over the wrongdoer himself, whom, in practice, it will only be necessary to sue (assuming he is able to meet any judgment) if the insurer might have effective grounds for repudiating liability or there is a material limit to the indemnity under the policy.

4.4.4.1 *Matters relating to a contract – Art 5(1)*

Under Art 5(1)(a), in matters relating to a contract an English court will have jurisdiction over a defendant domiciled in a Regulation or Convention state other than the UK if the place of performance of the obligation in question was in England and Wales.

Cases in which jurisdiction can be established in respect of a claim arising out of an accident abroad only under this exception will be fairly rare, and it is mentioned more for the purposes of contrast with the other exceptions, discussed below, in respect of consumer and employment contracts. However, such cases can conceivably occur, for example, if one suffered injury abroad as a result of a defect amounting to a breach of contract in a product bought direct from a supplier in another Regulation or Convention state. Article 5(1)(b) and (c) define 'the place of performance of the obligation in question' with the effect inter alia that in the case of a sale of goods the place of performance of the obligation in question is the place in a Regulation or Convention state where the goods were delivered under the contract. So if one bought a pair of skis from a supplier domiciled in Austria which were delivered under the contract to a place in England and Wales in circumstances where one would not be found to have been dealing as a consumer (and therefore unable to take advantage of a basis of jurisdiction which could be available under Arts 15 and 16) and suffered an injury (whether in the UK or elsewhere) because they were defective, the English court would have jurisdiction over the Austrian supplier.

4.4.4.2 *Matters relating to tort – Art 5(3)*

Under Art 5(3), in matters relating to tort, delict or quasi-delict an English court will have jurisdiction over a defendant domiciled in another Regulation or Convention state if the harmful event occurred in England and Wales.

---

[45] (C-463/06) [2007] ECR I-11321. See Chapter 6, Direct Actions Against Insurers for a detailed treatment of such claims.

[46] There will always be a direct claim in relation to claims arising out of a road traffic accident, and in many states there is a direct cause of action in other situations as well.

The term 'tort, delict or quasi-delict' is an autonomous concept for the purposes of the Regulation and Convention and has been held by the CJEU to comprise all bases for liability which cannot be classified as relating to a contract.[47] The concepts of 'matters relating to a contract' and 'matters relating to tort, delict or quasi-delict' are mutually exclusive, and it follows from this that in cases where there is a contract between the parties such that as a matter of English law there would be concurrent duties in contract and tort and a claimant could rely on either or both bases for his claim, for the purposes of jurisdiction a claimant cannot use the Art 5(3) exception; see *Source v TUV Rheinland Holding AG*.[48] This would appear to mean that in cases where an employee wishes to bring a claim arising out an accident abroad against his employer, jurisdiction will be determined by the rules for matters relating to contracts, and specifically those relating to individual contracts of employment (dealt with at **4.4.4.10**) rather than Art 5(1).

The 'harmful event' will have occurred in England and Wales if either the event giving rise to the damage occurred there or the resulting damage was sustained there.[49] Without qualification this might suggest that if a claimant suffers an injury in an accident abroad and then returns to England where he continues to experience pain and suffering, incurs medical expenses or suffers loss of income, jurisdiction of the English courts will be established. However, (in contrast with the equivalent basis of jurisdiction in cases under CPR r.6.36) this is not the case, as decisions of the CJEU have made it clear that (certainly in the case of personal injury) it is the place where the physical damage is sustained and not the place where the consequences (economic or otherwise) of that physical damage may be suffered.

4.4.4.3   Disputes arising out of a branch, agency or other establishment – Art 5(5)

Under Art 5(5) an English court will have jurisdiction over a defendant domiciled in another Regulation or Convention state if the defendant has a branch, agency or other establishment in England and Wales and the dispute arises out of the operations of that branch, agency or other establishment.

The concept of 'a branch, agency or other establishment' is an autonomous Regulation and Convention concept and the CJEU has required that there must be an appearance of permanency for there to be a branch, agency or other establishment.[50] It has to have a management

---

[47] *Kalfelis v Bankhaus Schröder, Münchmeyer, Hengst Und Co* (C-189/87) [1988] ECR 5565.
[48] [1988] QB 54 (CA).
[49] *Handelskwekerij GJ Bier BV v Mines de Potasse d'Alsace SA* (C-21/76) [1976] ECR 1735; [1978] 1 QB 708.
[50] *Somafer SA v Sarr-Ferngas AG* (C-33/78) [1978] ECR 2183; so it would seem that attendance at e g a trade fair would not engage this exception.

and be materially equipped to negotiate business with third parties.[51] It is also an essential requirement that the parent body exercises direction and control, so an independent commercial agent or exclusive distributor is not a branch, agency or other establishment.[52]

There must also be a link between the activities of the branch etc and the dispute in question, but it is not necessary in relation to a contract concluded by the branch that the contract is to be performed in the state where the branch is established [53] Therefore if an English branch of a German domiciled company sells a cruise in the Mediterranean, the English courts will have jurisdiction in relation to disputes arising out of the cruise.[54]

4.4.4.4   Co-defendants – Art 6(1)

Under Art 6(1) an English court will have jurisdiction over a defendant domiciled in another Regulation or Convention state (D2) if there is a defendant domiciled in England and Wales (D1), provided that the claims against D1 and D2 are so closely connected that it is expedient to hear and determine them together to avoid the risk of irreconcilable judgments resulting from separate proceedings. More than one additional defendant domiciled in another Regulation or Convention state may be joined under this provision, but in relation to each such defendant the proviso must be satisfied with regard to the claim against *him* and D1.

Until the possibility of exercising jurisdiction over liability insurers domiciled in another Regulation or Convention state was clarified by the CJEU decision in *Odenbreit*[55] this exception to the general rule provided the only clear basis for making a claim against a defendant domiciled in another Regulation or Convention state in at least two types of regularly encountered situations arising out of accidents abroad. First, in a package tour claim one might, in addition to suing the English-domiciled tour operator, wish to sue the person actually responsible for the accident, such as the hotel or excursion provider (eg in a case where there was doubt as to the applicability of the Package Travel, Package Holidays and Package Tours Regulations 1992). Secondly, in a road traffic claim where one

---

[51]   *Mahamdia v People's Democratic Republic of Algeria* (C-154/11) [2012] IL Pr 41, para H7.

[52]   *De Bloos Sprl v Bouyer SA* (C-14/76) [1976] ECR 1497; *Blanckaert & Willems PVBA v Trost* (C-139/80) [1981] ECR 819.

[53]   *Lloyd's Register of Shipping v Société Campenon Bernard* (C-439/93) [1995] ECR 961.

[54]   As a contract for a cruise is one which provides for a combination of travel and accommodation for an inclusive price there would also be jurisdiction under the consumer contracts section (Arts 15 to 17, see below). This additional ground of jurisdiction would not be available if the German company had sold just a coach journey (see Art 15(3)). For further consideration of jurisdiction issues claims pursuant to the Athens Convention (Carriage of Passengers and their Luggage by Sea) see Chapter 7.

[55]   (C-463/06) [2007] ECR I-11321.

defendant was domiciled in England (because eg the claimant was the passenger in a hire care driven by a holiday companion) one might also wish to sue a local driver involved in the accident because of the risk of the English domiciled driver being found not to blame. Joining such additional defendants may still be necessary in those types of case (for example if there is no effective liability insurance),[56] but there are, of course, also other situations where a claimant may wish to take advantage of this exception.

As a result of obiter dicta at para 50 in the judgment of the CJEU in *Réunion Européenne SA v Spliethoff's Bevrachtingskantoor BV*,[57] it was for several years thought that the first part of the proviso in Art 6(1) meant that the scope for its application was substantially limited. The CJEU appeared to say that claims could not demonstrate the necessary close connection if they were based on different causes of action, for example, one arising out of a contract and the other being tortious. It seemed that the causes of action had to be either all contractual or all tortious. It has, however, been made clear by the more recent decision of the CJEU in *Freeport plc v Olle Arnoldsson*[58] that there is no such limitation on its applicability; at para 47 of its judgment it says:

> 'Article 6(1) of Regulation No 44/2001 is to be interpreted as meaning that the fact that claims brought against a number of defendants have different legal bases does not preclude application of that provision.'

The *Freeport* decision now makes it clear that there is no fundamental problem in a package tour case in seeking to use Art 6(1) to sue a foreign-domiciled hotel on the basis of an allegation of negligence on its part when the claim against the English-domiciled tour operator is founded on contract.[59]

There is, however, some doubt as to the need for the claim against the English-domiciled defendant to be viable in order for Art 6(1) to be invoked. The English courts have imposed a requirement in cases where reliance is placed on Art 6(1) that there has to be a real claim against the defendant domiciled in England. If that claim is unsustainable as a matter of law then the foreign defendant will be able to challenge jurisdiction successfully; *The Rewia*.[60] In *FKI Engineering Ltd v De Wind*

---

[56]   Although in many road traffic cases where there is no insurance it will be possible to bring a claim against the MIB (see Chapter 6, Direct Actions Against Insurers).

[57]   Case C-51/97 [2000] QB 690.

[58]   (C-98/06) [2007] ECR I-839; [2008] QB 634.

[59]   This was essentially the situation in *Watson v First Choice Holidays and Flights Ltd* [2001] EWCA Civ 972 [2001] 2 Lloyd's Rep 339, where because of concerns arising from the CJEU's obiter dicta in *Réunion Européenne*, the Court of Appeal made a reference to the CJEU on the point. The case was, however, settled before the CJEU heard the reference.

[60]   [1991] 2 Lloyd's Rep 325.

Holdings Ltd,[61] it was common ground between the parties that the anchor claim had to have real prospects of success (see para 18), and the Court of Appeal therefore considered the merits of that claim not exclusively on a legal viability basis. It would seem that had it found there were no real prospects of success it would have upheld the challenge to jurisdiction. Logically, this principle would extend further to a case where the factual basis was demonstrably unsustainable or being advanced purely tactically, such as where (pre-*Odenbreit*) a passenger sued an English-domiciled driver who was really not considered to be liable in order to sue a driver domiciled in another Regulation or Convention state as an additional defendant.

However, the extent to which this additional requirement under English law is legitimate is uncertain.[62] In *Reisch Montage AG v Kiesel Baumaschinen Handels GmbH*,[63] the CJEU ruled that Art 6(1) can be relied on even if the claim against the anchor defendant was unsustainable for procedural reasons from the outset[64] and was dismissed on those grounds. The claim against the other defendant, domiciled in another Regulation state (Germany) and only subject to the jurisdiction of the Austrian court if Art 6(1) was applicable, could proceed. It did emphasise, however, at para 32 that Art 6(1):

> '... cannot be interpreted in such a way as to allow a plaintiff to make a claim against a number of defendants for the sole purpose of removing one of them from the jurisdiction of the Courts of the Member State in which that defendant is domiciled.'

This would indicate that if there had been a conscious decision to bring a claim against one defendant which was known to be unsustainable just in order to be able to sue another defendant domiciled in another Regulation or Convention state the outcome would have been different. But the messages coming from the CJEU on this point are possibly inconsistent as it subsequently expressly said at para 54 in *Freeport*, in answer to the second question referred to it, that Art 6(1) was applicable:

> '... without there being any further need to establish that the claims were not brought with the sole object of ousting the jurisdiction of the Courts of the member state where one of the defendants is domiciled.'

It went on perhaps to compound the uncertainty by then expressly declining to answer the third question referred to it, namely:

---

61   [2008] EWCA Civ 316; [2009] All ER (Comm) 118.
62   Even if it is not legitimate to introduce it as a prerequisite in its own right, it may nevertheless be a valid consideration when determining if there is a risk of irreconcilable judgments. Without such a risk the proviso in Art 6(1) cannot be satisfied.
63   (C-103/05) [2006] ECR I-6827.
64   The anchor defendant had been declared bankrupt before the commencement of the proceedings, and Austrian law did not permit a claim to be brought against him once that had occurred.

'... should the likelihood of success of an action against a party before the Courts of the state where he is domiciled otherwise be taken into account in the determination of whether there is a risk of irreconcilable judgments for the purposes of article 6(1)?'

The ability to invoke Art 6(1) is dependent on the court being properly able to exercise jurisdiction over the English-domiciled defendant, so that if there is an agreement between the claimant and the English-domiciled defendant that the courts of another Regulation or Convention state shall have exclusive jurisdiction in relation to relevant disputes between them, the claimant cannot use Art 6(1) to sue another defendant domiciled in another Regulation or Convention state. Similarly, if there was such an agreement between the claimant and the additional defendant, Art 23 would override Art 6(1) and the claimant would be restricted to suing the additional defendant in the courts specified in the agreement.[65]

4.4.4.5   *Third party claims – Art 6(2)*

Article 6(2) allows a person domiciled in another Regulation or Convention state to be sued in an English court as a third party in an action on a warranty or guarantee, or in any other third party proceedings, unless the proceedings were instituted solely with the purpose of removing him from the jurisdiction of the court which would be competent in his case. Self-evidently this is not a basis of jurisdiction which will concern claimants in cases arising out of accidents abroad, but it is of great value to defendants in such cases, for example in package tour claims where the tour operator wishes to obtain an indemnity or contribution from one of its suppliers who was responsible for the claimant's accident.[66] It is to be noted that this exception in relation to third party claims can in principle be relied on in all cases where there is a valid basis of jurisdiction over the defendant. There is no requirement, as there is under Art 6(1), that there be an anchor defendant domiciled in England and Wales.

It has been held by the CJEU in *Groupement d'intérêt économique (GIE) Réunion Européenne v Zurich España*[67] that it is the third party proceedings rather than the original proceedings which must not have been instituted with the forbidden purpose. If, as will usually be the case where this basis of jurisdiction is relied on, there is a genuine claim made against the defendant and also an arguable claim by the defendant against the third party for an indemnity or a contribution in respect of the claim made against it, it is difficult to see what scope there could be for a challenge based on the contention that the third party proceedings have been instituted with the forbidden purpose. However, it would seem to be

---

[65]   *Hough v P & O Containers Ltd* [1999] QB 834 (a case involving Art 6(2)).
[66]   For more on the practicalities of such third party claims see Chapter 3, Package Travel II at **3.4**.
[67]   (C-77/04) [2005] ECR 4509.

the case that if the third party proceedings had been commenced as a result of the claimant and the defendant colluding in the bringing of the original proceedings because it provided a springboard for bringing the third party before an English court when there was no other means of achieving that end, that would mean that the third party proceedings had been brought with the forbidden purpose.

It has been suggested by some commentators that the third party claims which can be brought under this exception are restricted to those which are in the nature of claims for an indemnity or contribution in respect of the defendant's liability to the claimant. Such a restriction would mean that a defendant to a claim arising out of a road traffic accident abroad could claim an indemnity or contribution from another driver domiciled in another Regulation or Convention state, but could not make a claim under this exception in respect of his own losses, even though that would be something he could do under English procedural provisions relating to third party claims.[68] This interpretation would also be inconsistent with the principles stated in recital 15 to the Regulation that 'it is necessary to minimise the possibility of concurrent proceedings and to ensure that irreconcilable judgments will not be given in two Member States', which even though stated in the context of lis alibi pendens and related actions, should be seen as guiding principles where not excluded by express words or necessary implication. There is nothing in the words of Art 6(1) or any of the official commentaries[69] to justify this narrow reading, and it is considered that a court would not construe Art 6(1) so restrictively. It is accepted that there must be a connection between the main proceedings and the third party claims, but whether the connection is sufficient is to be determined by reference to the requirement that the third party proceedings were not instituted solely with the purpose of removing the third party from the jurisdiction of the court which would be competent in his case.

There are decisions by English courts[70] which hold that a third party claim brought after the conclusion of the main proceedings does not constitute 'any other third party proceedings' for the purposes of Art 6(2), even if it may satisfy the applicable English procedural rules as to a claim which can be the subject matter of a third party claim (now an 'additional claim' under CPR Part 20). Insofar as these decisions purport to restrict the interpretation of the phrase 'any other third party proceedings' there is no support at European Court level for such a restriction. At any rate, these decisions are based to a significant extent on the fact that once the main proceedings have been determined the opportunity for efficiency

---

[68] He could, however, achieve this end by suing the driver's insurers, invoking the *Odenbreit* jurisdiction under the section of the Regulation or Convention dealing with insurance matters.

[69] Ie the commentaries on the Brussels Convention such as the Jenard (1968) 90/C 189/07 and Schlosser (1979) C 59/72 Reports.

[70] *Waterford Wedgwood plc v David Nagli Ltd* [1999] IL Pr 9; *Barton v Golden Sun Holidays Ltd* EWHC 136(QB), [2007] IL Pr 57.

which can be achieved by the claims being dealt with together has been lost and that the risk of irreconcilable judgments is not necessarily increased by requiring the defendant to sue the third party in the state of his domicile. They emphasise the need to consider whether there are grounds for a claim against a third party at an early stage and to take prompt steps to bring it into the action.[71]

Unusually in relation to bases of jurisdiction under the Regulation and the Convention, the CJEU has ruled that national courts possess a procedural discretion as to whether jurisdiction over the third party should be exercised. In *Kongress Agentur Hagen GmbH v Zeehaghe BV*,[72] it said that a Dutch court could apply its own procedural rules to determine whether a third party claim should be allowed to proceed. The Dutch court had determined that the main action would be delayed and complicated by the third party proceedings, and on that ground refused to allow a German company to be joined as a third party. This refusal was upheld by the CJEU, although it said that national procedural rules could not be allowed to impair the effectiveness of the Brussels Convention (that being the legislation in force at the time), so that it would be impermissible to refuse to allow the third party proceedings solely on the ground that delay would be caused by the fact that the proposed third party was domiciled in another Regulation or Convention state.

A third party domiciled in another Regulation or Convention state who is joined under Art 6(2) becomes a party generally in the action for procedural purposes.[73] However, this principle does not extend to questions of jurisdiction. For example, he cannot, without more, be joined as a second defendant to the main claim. The court's jurisdiction over him by virtue of Art 6(2) is limited to the matters properly within the third party proceedings, so if he is to be made a second defendant there must be a separate basis of jurisdiction over him for that purpose.

It is also the case here, as in relation to Art 6(1), that the exceptional jurisdiction is overridden by Art 23, so that if there is a valid jurisdiction agreement between the defendant and the third party which provides for the courts of a different Regulation or Convention state to have exclusive jurisdiction over the relevant matters between them, the English court cannot exercise jurisdiction pursuant to Art 6(2).[74]

---

[71] A point which is reinforced by CPR Part 20 pursuant to which permission of the court to issue an additional claim form in a third party claim is not required if it is issued at the same time as the defendant serves his defence.

[72] (C-365/88) [1990] ECR I-1845.

[73] See CPR, r 20.10.

[74] *Hough v P & O Containers Ltd* [1999] QB 834.

4.4.4.6 Counterclaims – Art 6(3)

Article 6(3) allows the English court to exercise jurisdiction over a person domiciled in another Regulation or Convention state in respect of a counterclaim against him arising out of the same contract or facts on which the original claim was based.

The decision of the House of Lords in *Jordan Grand Prix Ltd v Baltic Insurance Group*[75] (which was concerned with the meaning of counterclaim in what is now Art 12(2) of the Regulation and the Convention in the section dealing with 'matters relating to insurance') indicates that English courts will confine this basis of jurisdiction to claims against the claimant in the original claim and will not allow it to be used to join any other person as an additional defendant to a counterclaim. However, in a case where the more natural way of pursuing a claim against such a person would be to make them an additional defendant to a counterclaim but this option is not available because of the narrow interpretation which is likely to be given to Art 6(3) in the light of the *Jordan Grand Prix* case, it is considered that it will in most cases be possible to join that person as a third party pursuant to Art 6(2). This was not possible in the *Jordan Grand Prix* case because the defendant, being an insurer, was limited by the terms of the equivalent of Art 12(1) as to where it could bring proceedings against such a person.

4.4.4.7 Insurance – Arts 8 to 14

In respect of matters relating to insurance, save that Arts 4 and 5(5) continue to be of effect in relation to them, questions of jurisdiction are to be determined only in accordance with the provisions of Arts 8 to 14 (as is made absolutely clear by the words of Art 8). The general rule under Art 2 and the exceptions to it under Art 5 (apart from the one under Art 5(5) relating to disputes arising out of branches etc in a Regulation or Convention state) and Art 6 do not apply, although jurisdiction can be conferred by a submission to the jurisdiction under Art 24. It is to be noted, however, that this special regime does not apply to reinsurance matters.[76]

(a) Article 9

Under Art 9(1) an insurer domiciled in a Regulation or Convention state may be sued (a) in the courts of the state in which he is domiciled, (b) in another Regulation or Convention state in the courts for the place where the claimant is domiciled if the action is one brought by the policyholder, the insured or a beneficiary and (c) if he is a co-insurer, in the courts of another Regulation or Convention state in which proceedings are brought

---

[75] [1999] 2 AC 127.
[76] *Universal General Insurance Co (UGIC) v Group Josi Reinsurance Co SA* (C-412/98) [2000] ECR I-5925; *Agnew v Länsförsäkringsbolaget AB* [2001] 1 AC 223.

against the leading insurer. Article 9(2) provides that an insurer domiciled elsewhere than in a Regulation or Convention state will be deemed to be domiciled in a Regulation or Convention state in which it has a branch, agency or other establishment in relation to disputes arising out of the operation of that branch, agency other establishment.

(b)   Article 10

Article 10 applies to liability insurance and insurance of immovable property, and allows the insurer in such cases in addition to be sued in the courts for the place where the harmful event occurred. The term 'the harmful event' has the same meaning as it has under Art 5(3) (see **4.4.4.2**), and therefore in the context of accidents abroad this Article will not be of any relevance.

(c)   Article 11(1)

Article 11(1) applies also to liability insurance (but not to insurance of immovable property) and allows a liability insurer to be joined in proceedings which the injured party has brought against the insured if the law of the forum permits. To the untutored eye this might seem to say that, subject to the law of the forum permitting such joinder, an injured party could join the wrongdoer's non-English-domiciled liability insurer as an additional defendant to proceedings which he has brought against the wrongdoer. This is not, however, what is meant by Art 11(1). All it does is permit the *insured* to join his insurer as a third party to proceedings which the injured party has brought against *him*. This interpretation is based on the *Jenard* report[77] (at p 32) and was accepted by Morland J in *Patterson v Carden*.[78]

(d)   Article 11(2) and FBTO v Odenbreit

However, as a consequence of the CJEU's decision in *FBTO v Odenbreit*,[79] an injured party domiciled in England and Wales has a much more powerful ground for jurisdiction against an insurer domiciled in another Regulation or Convention state in cases involving accidents abroad under Art 11(2) read in conjunction with Art 9(1)(b). Article 11(2) states that Arts 8, 9 and 10 shall apply to actions brought by the injured party directly against the insurer, where such direct actions are permitted by the national law. The CJEU ruled that the effect of this provision was

---

[77]   Dealing, of course, with the Brussels Convention, the precursor to the Regulation and Convention, but still possessing the same authority in relation to the later instruments.

[78]   Unreported, judgment given on 14 September 2000. It is submitted that the obiter views of Moore-Bick LJ at para 21 in *Maher v Groupama* [2010] 1 WLR 1564 were confined to the question of whether the insured could be joined as an additional defendant under Art 11(3) (as to which see **4.4.4.7**), and do not cast doubt on the correctness of the decision of Morland J on the question of what form of joinder is permitted under Art 11(1).

[79]   (C-463/06) [2007] ECR I-11321.

to add the injured party who has a direct cause of action to the list of plaintiffs specified in Art 9(1)(b), so that he too may bring a claim in the courts for the place where he is domiciled against an insurer domiciled in another Regulation state. This interpretation will be of equal application to the Convention.[80]

Although this decision was made in the context of a road traffic accident and the court appears to have been influenced by a recital in the Fourth Motor Insurance Directive,[81] there is nothing in the language of the Regulation which suggests that the ruling is limited to road traffic cases. It is worth noting that many civil law systems widely recognise direct rights of action in favour of victims of personal injury against the wrongdoer's insurer, not necessarily limited to causes of action arising in tort or delict. Such rights arise in many contexts, not just road traffic accidents.

It needs to be recalled that the Regulation and Convention rules may give the courts of the UK jurisdiction, but this does not necessarily mean the English court. Where, for example, a Scottish-domiciled victim has a direct right of action against a French insurer, the Civil Jurisdiction and Judgments Act 1982 will then determine the courts of which *part* of the UK can hear the claim, in this instance, the Scottish courts, see **4.5**.

It was fundamental to the decision in *Odenbreit* that the claimant was the weaker party, as is demonstrated by the later decision of the CJEU in *Vorarlberger Gebietskrankenkasse v WGV-Schwäbische Allgemeine Versicherungs AG*.[82] The claimant was an Austrian social security institution which had paid benefits to the victim of a road traffic accident which had occurred in Germany. Under Austrian law it was the statutory assignee of the victim's rights to claim compensation from a third party insofar as it had to provide benefits to the victim. It brought an action in an Austrian court seeking recovery of the benefits it had paid from the German-domiciled insurer of the person liable for the accident, relying on the *Odenbreit* decision. The CJEU ruled that the court did not have jurisdiction over the German-domiciled insurer. The special rules as to jurisdiction in relation to insurance matters were to be interpreted in the light of recital 13, which states that in relation to inter alia insurance the weaker party should be protected by rules more favourable to his interests than the general rules. The claimant was not an economically weaker party than the insurer and therefore the provisions should not be interpreted to allow it to bring a claim in the courts of its member state against an insurer domiciled in another member state.

---

[80] The ramifications and practicalities of the decision in *Odenbreit* are discussed in detail in Chapter 6, Direct Actions Against Insurers.

[81] Recital 16a: 'Under Article 11(2) read in conjunction with Article 9(1)(b) of [the Regulation] injured parties may bring legal proceedings against the civil liability insurance provider in the Member State in which they are domiciled.' Interestingly, this recital did not feature in the 4th Directive (adopted in 2000) until May 2005 when it was added by amendment by means of the 5th Directive.

[82] (C-347/08) [2009] ECR I-8661.

This could have practical consequences in the context of subrogated claims which an insurer may wish to bring to obtain reimbursement of monies it has paid out under a victim's insurance policy. For example, repatriation costs or the cost of medical treatment. Under English law, an insurer obtains such reimbursement by means of a claim brought in the insured's name, or it can require the insured to include such claims within any claim he brings. It is no defence to the claim made by or in the name of the victim or insured that the loss has already been met by the insurance policy. However, in some civil law systems such a defence is available to the wrongdoer. Instead, title to recover the loss and damage passes to the insurer itself, which is entitled by law to bring an action against the wrongdoer in its own name. In the light of the *Vorarlberger* decision it is possible that it might be held that an English court would not have jurisdiction under the *Odenbreit* principle to determine the part of a claim which represented the subrogated claim of an English insurer in an action brought by for example, the English domiciled victim of a road traffic accident in Portugal against the Portuguese-domiciled insurer of the driver involved. That part of the claim could be said to be exclusively for the benefit of the insurer, which is not the 'weaker party' and therefore would be held not to be entitled to rely on the *Odenbreit* exception. However, this scenario would clearly be a case under a civil law system where the claim would be brought by the insurer. That being so, and as the English courts would have no jurisdiction to determine the travel insurer's claim against the Portuguese motor insurer, it seems anomalous that it should make any difference that the claimant is only nominally the victim.

(e)   Article 12

An insurer is much more restricted as to the courts in which he can bring proceedings. Article 12 provides that, without prejudice to Art 11(3) (as to which see **4.4.4.7**(f)), an insurer (which the House of Lords in *Jordan Grand Prix Ltd v Baltic Insurance Group*[83] decided means any insurer, whether domiciled in a Regulation or Convention state or elsewhere) can sue a defendant (irrespective of whether he is the policyholder, insured or a beneficiary) only in the courts of the Regulation or Convention state in which that defendant is domiciled, although this does not affect the right of the insurer to bring a counterclaim in the court in which the original claim is pending in accordance with Arts 8 to 14. As noted above in relation to Art 6(3),[84] this counterclaim can only be against a claimant in the original proceedings.

(f)   Article 11(3)

This Article provides an additional basis of jurisdiction over a policyholder or an insured in situations where an injured party brings a

---

[83]   [1999] 2 AC 127.
[84]   See **4.4.4.6**.

direct action against an insurer, but its exact scope is a matter of controversy. The issue is whether, when it provides that the court where the direct action is proceeding, 'shall have jurisdiction over them',[85] it means that they can be joined as additional defendants to the claim.

It is clear from the opening words of Art 12(1),[86] which deals with proceedings which an insurer can bring, that Art 11(3) must contemplate an insurer who is being sued by an injured party joining the policyholder or insured as a third party to the direct action against him and that therefore 'shall have jurisdiction over them' means that an insurer can join one or both of them as a third party. If the jurisdiction over an insurer which is allowed by Art 11(1) is limited to the insurer being joined as a third party and does not extend to the insurer being made an additional defendant to an action by the injured party against the insured (as is submitted above), it could be said to follow that a similar limitation applies here. Both provisions appear to refer to existing proceedings and in that context the use of the phraseology 'may be joined', indicates something other than commencement of proceedings against two defendants (one being the insurer and the other being the policyholder or insured), namely introducing a third party. This interpretation of Art 11(3) receives support from the relevant part of the *Jenard* report (p 32), where when talking about the equivalent provision in the Brussels Convention he mentions only the third party situation.

However, although at first instance in *Maher v Groupama*,[87] Blair J expressed a preliminary view at para 25 that this interpretation might be right, on the appeal[88] Moore-Bick LJ inclined to the view that Art 11(3) allowed the insured to be joined as an additional defendant.[89] For the moment it would appear that the wider interpretation has the upper hand, in terms of obiter dicta at least.

(g) Jurisdiction agreements – Arts 13 and 14

The provisions of Arts 8 to 14 may only be departed from by an agreement and then only by an agreement which is of a type specified in Arts 13 and 14. For present purposes in practice this means that the parties can confer jurisdiction on an English court by an agreement:

(i)   which is entered into after the dispute has arisen;[90] or
(ii)   which allows the *policyholder, insured or beneficiary* to sue in a court other than one indicated by Arts 8 to 14;[91] or

---

[85] Ie the policyholder or the insured.
[86] 'Without prejudice to Article 11(3)'.
[87] [2009] 1 WLR 1752.
[88] [2010] 1 WLR 1564 (paras 14 to 21).
[89] Neither considered it was necessary to decide the point in the case because it was immaterial in their view given their decision on other issues.
[90] Article 13(1).
[91] Article 13(2).

(iii) which was entered into by the parties when they were both domiciled or habitually resident in England and Wales and the agreement is not contrary to English law;[92] or

(iv) which was concluded with a policyholder not domiciled in a Regulation or Convention state, unless the insurance was compulsory or relates to immovable property in a Regulation or Convention state.[93]

4.4.4.8 *Consumer contracts – Arts 15 to 17*

Articles 15 to 17 provide special jurisdiction rules for matters relating to certain categories of contracts concluded by consumers. They have many similarities with the special rules for matters relating to insurance, which is understandable as both sets of special rules have been inspired by the policy that weaker parties should be protected by jurisdiction rules which are more favourable to them than the general rules.[94] In relation to contracts to which they apply, subject to Arts 4 and 5(5) and to a submission to the jurisdiction under Art 24, jurisdiction is determined exclusively by the rules in Arts 15 to 17.

The special rules will apply if the contract was concluded by a person, the consumer, for a purpose which can be regarded as outside his trade or profession *and* the contract is one of the following:

(a) a contract for the sale of goods on instalment credit terms;

(b) a contract for a loan repayable by instalments, or any other form of credit, made to finance the sale of goods; or

(c) any other contract where the other party to the contract either (i) pursues commercial or professional activities in the Regulation or Convention state in which the consumer is domiciled or (ii) directs, by any means, such activities to that state, or several Regulation or Convention states including that state, and in either case (i) or (ii) the contract falls within the scope of such activities,[95]

but they will not apply if the contract is a contract of transport, unless it one which provides for a combination of travel and accommodation for an inclusive price.[96]

If the non-consumer party to the contract is not domiciled in a Regulation or Convention state but has a branch, agency or other establishment[97] in such a state, that party is deemed to be domiciled in

---

[92] Article 13(3).
[93] Article 13(4).
[94] See recital 13 to the Regulation.
[95] Article 15(1).
[96] Article 15(3).
[97] See **4.4.4.3** for what constitutes a branch, agency or other establishment.

that state in relation to disputes arising out of the operations of that branch agency or other establishment.[98]

In situations where these special rules apply an English-domiciled consumer can sue the other party either in an English court or the courts of the Regulation or Convention state where that party is domiciled,[99] however, the non-consumer party can sue the English-domiciled consumer only in an English court,[100] but this does not affect the right to bring a counterclaim in the court where the original claim is pending in accordance with Arts 15 to 17.[101]

In addition, the parties can confer jurisdiction on an English court by an agreement but only if it is one:

(i)   which is entered into after the dispute has arisen;[102] or
(ii)   which allows the *consumer* to sue in a court other than one indicated by Arts 15 to 17;[103] or
(iii)   which was entered into by the parties when they were both domiciled or habitually resident in England and Wales and the agreement is not contrary to English law.[104]

(a)   Consumer

It is important to note that, in accordance with the principle that exceptions to the general rule under Art 2 are to be construed narrowly, it has been held by the CJEU that this special regime does not apply to contracts which have a dual purpose, such as a purchase of goods for both private use and for use in connection with the buyer's trade or profession, unless the non-private aspect of the contract is negligible; *Gruber v Bay Wa AG*.[105] Even where the non-private aspect is negligible (and it would seem if even if there were no non-private aspect at all), the consumer regime will not apply if the commercial or professional party to the contract is reasonably unaware of the private nature of the purpose of the 'consumer' because of the conduct of the 'consumer', such as ordering goods which could be used for a business without saying anything to indicate that they are intended for private use, using business notepaper when communicating, requesting delivery to his business address or asking about recovery of VAT; see paras 51 to 53 of *Gruber*.

---

[98]   Article 15(2).
[99]   Article 16(1).
[100]   Article 16(2) combined with Civil Jurisdiction and Judgments Act 1982, Sch 4, r 8(2).
[101]   Article 16(3).
[102]   Article 17(1).
[103]   Article 17(2).
[104]   Article 17(3) combined with Civil Jurisdiction and Judgments Act 1982, Sch 4, r 9(c).
[105]   (C-464/01) [2006] QB 204. See also *Benincasa v Dentalkit Srl* (C-269/95) [1997] ECR I-3767 (goods purchased with intention to run a business which in fact did not trade).

(b)   Package travel

The exclusion of contracts of transport from the scope of these special rules should be noted, but because this exclusion expressly does not apply to contracts which, for an inclusive price, provide for a combination of travel and accommodation, this regime will apply to claims arising out of most package tours which fulfil the other requirements of this section of the Regulation and Convention. On a very strict interpretation of the proviso which brings contracts for a combination of travel and accommodation within the scope of the special regime, one could conclude that a contract which, for an inclusive price, combined not only travel and accommodation but also other tourist services fell outside it, but this is almost certainly not the case. In *Pammer v Reederei Karl Schlüter GmbH*,[106] the CJEU held that Art 15(3) was to be interpreted consistently with the definition of 'package' in the Package Travel Directive[107] and 'package travel' in Rome I,[108] and as the inclusion of other tourist services would not cause such a contract to fall outside the definition of 'package' or 'package travel', it is extremely unlikely that it would be treated differently to a package which included only travel and accommodation. The position is perhaps rather less clear in relation to other package deals which fall within the relevant definition for the Package Travel Directive and Rome I, such as one for travel and other tourist services (say ski lessons) but no accommodation. It is difficult to see how the language of Art 16(3) can be legitimately interpreted so as to bring these within the scope of the special regime.

(c)   Pursuing or directing commercial activities

In the context of claims arising out of accidents abroad, the question which will most frequently arise under this section of the Regulation and Convention is whether the contract falls within Art 16(3) so as to engage the special rules as to jurisdiction. There will normally be no difficulty in determining if the non-consumer party pursues commercial or professional activities in the Regulation or Convention state in which the claimant is domiciled or whether the contract in question falls within the scope of such activities, and if the answer to both questions is 'yes' then the special rules are engaged. It is the second limb (directing such activities, by any means, to the state of the consumer's domicile or to several states including that state), which may give rise to more difficulties when determining whether it applies. This formulation was intended to recognise the development of e-commerce and to be capable of bringing contracts resulting from internet marketing into the special consumer regime, but although the answer may be clear in the case of direct e-mails to potential customers in another Regulation or Convention state, in the case of a website (interactive or not) it is a question of fact in each case

---

[106]   (Cases C-585/08 and C-144/09) [2012] Bus LR 972.
[107]   Directive 90/314.
[108]   Regulation (EC) No 593/2008.

whether what the supplier has done by means of that website amounts to directing such activities to the state of the consumer's domicile. Some guidance can be obtained from the CJEU's decision in *Pammer*.[109] The fact that the trader's website is accessible in the consumer's state of domicile or that an e-mail address and other contact details are given is insufficient; these do not on their own show that the trader has manifested an intention to establish commercial relations with consumers from other Regulation states including that of the consumer's domicile, which is what is necessary to engage this limb of Art 15(3). Nor can that intention be established by use of a language or currency which is generally used in the Regulation state where the trader is established. However, the necessary intention can be inferred from the inclusion on the website of other matters which indicate that the trader is addressing potential customers outside his own state. The court identified a number of such matters, not by way of an exhaustive list, amongst which were the international nature of the activity, mentioning itineraries from other Regulation states to the place where the trader is established, use of a language or currency not generally used in the trader's state, mentioning telephone numbers with an international prefix, having a domain name with a suffix which is neither neutral (such as '.com' or '.eu') nor the one of the state in which the trader is established (eg '.de' for Germany) and mentioning an international clientele from different Regulation states. The necessary intention could also be shown by the trader spending money on an internet referencing service which could direct potential customers to its website.

The decision in *Pammer* does not address directly whether there is a requirement for the consumer to show that the contract was concluded through or as a result of the trader's activities which were directed to the consumer's state. However, it is suggested that the phrase 'falls within the scope of such activities' has the effect of restricting jurisdiction to those cases where there is a factual or causal link between such activities and the actual contract in issue. Accordingly, in a case where a contract is concluded face-to-face in the German office of a lawyer, it will not avail the English client to point to a subsequent discovery that the lawyer had a website which addressed UK nationals in need of German legal services.

4.4.4.9 *Individual contracts of employment – Arts 18 to 21*

Articles 18 to 21 provide special jurisdiction rules for matters relating to individual contracts of employment.[110] In relation to such matters, subject to Arts 4 and 5(5) and to a submission to the jurisdiction under Art 24, jurisdiction is determined exclusively by the rules in Arts 18 to 21. If the individual contract of employment is with an employer not domiciled in a Regulation or Convention state but who has a branch, agency or other

---

[109] Cases C-585/08 and C-144/09.
[110] These provisions are also founded on the protection of a weaker party to an employment contract, allowing the employee more favourable choice of jurisdiction than the general rules in relation to contracts (recital 13).

establishment[111] in such a state, the employer is deemed to be domiciled in that state in relation to disputes arising out of the operations of that branch agency or other establishment.[112]

Where these special rules apply an employee of an employer domiciled in a Regulation or Convention state (or deemed to be so domiciled under Art 18(2)) who has suffered an accident abroad for which he wishes to hold his employer liable can sue the employer in an English court only if:

(a) the employer is domiciled in England and Wales;[113] or
(b) England and Wales is the place where he habitually carries out his work or is the last place where he did so;[114] or
(c) in the case where the employee did not habitually carry out his work in any one country, England and Wales is the place where the business which engaged him is or was situated;[115] or
(d) there is an agreement on jurisdiction which allows him to bring proceedings in an English court.[116]

In the event that the application of paragraphs (a), (b/c) or (d) above points to the courts of more than one state having jurisdiction, the claimant is entitled to choose where to bring his claim. Whilst it may be thought that given the overall scheme of the Regulation this could scarcely be in doubt, it was bravely and unsuccessfully argued by an employer to the contrary in an equal pay claim in *Simpson v Intralinks Ltd.*[117]

On the other hand, as is clear from the drafting of (c), it can only apply in circumstances where it is not possible to determine where the employee habitually carries out his work. In determining the place 'from which' the employee habitually carries out his work, the court must first examine whether the employee principally carries out his work within one single country.[118] That will generally be where the employee actually carries out his working activities although in the absence of a centre of activities, it can be the place where he carries out the majority of his activities.[119] Factors which are relevant to identify the principal place of work include where he carries out his tasks, the place from which he receives his instructions, where his tools are situated and where he organises his work.

---

[111] See **4.4.4.3** for what constitutes a branch, agency or other establishment.
[112] Article 18(2). See also *Mahamdia v People's Democratic Republic of Algeria* (C-154/11) [2012] IL Pr 41, where it was held that an embassy was capable of being an 'establishment'.
[113] Article 19(1).
[114] Article 19(2)(a).
[115] Article 19(2)(b).
[116] Article 21(2).
[117] EAT, Langstaff P, [2012] ICR 1343.
[118] *Koelzsch v Luxembourg* (C-29/10) [2012] 2 WLR 262; [2011] IL Pr 25, a case concerning an international lorry driver under the parallel provisions of the Rome Convention, which fall to be interpreted consistently with the Regulation, see eg recital 7 to Rome I.
[119] *Koelzsch* at [45].

Where no habitual place of work can be established, then jurisdiction can be founded in the courts of the place where the business through which the employee was engaged is situated. The relevant point in time is when the contract of employment commenced, regardless of subsequent working activities.[120] A 'place of business' need not have distinct legal personality, but must have a degree of permanence and be an integral part of the structure of the entity which engages the employee.[121]

By contrast, the default position for an employer wishing to sue his employee is that the employee can be sued only in the Regulation or Convention state in which he is domiciled,[122] but that is without prejudice to the employer's right to bring a counterclaim in pending proceedings which the employee has commenced.[123]

It is possible for the employer and employee, by agreement, to confer jurisdiction on particular courts or to restrict the courts which can have jurisdiction, but this can only be by an agreement which is entered into after the dispute has arisen.[124] In *Mahamdia v Algeria*, the CJEU held that a jurisdiction agreement contained within the contract of employment was ineffective insofar as it purported to preclude the employee from bringing a claim before the courts which would ordinarily have jurisdiction pursuant to Arts 18 to 21. Accordingly, Art 21(2) takes priority over the general provisions in Art 23 regarding jurisdiction agreements.

4.4.4.10   *Exclusive jurisdiction – Art 22*

Article 22 contains rules which in relation to specified categories of actions, subject to one exception (which is material to claims arising out of accidents abroad), confer exclusive jurisdiction on the courts of one Regulation or Convention state, regardless of domicile. These rules apply whether or not the defendant is domiciled in a Regulation or Convention state,[125] and they cannot be overridden by a jurisdiction agreement[126] or a submission to the jurisdiction under Art 24.

(a)   Property rental and timeshare

The only one of these rules which has any relevance to claims arising out of accidents abroad is that under Art 22(1), which concerns proceedings which have as their object rights in rem in, or tenancies of, immovable property situated in a Regulation or Convention state, and it provides

---

[120] *Voogsgeerd v Navimer* (C-384/10) [2012] IL Pr 16.
[121] *Voogsgeerd v Navimer* at [53]–[58].
[122] Article 20(1).
[123] Article 20(2).
[124] Article 21(1).
[125] See the opening words of Arts 22 and 4(1).
[126] Article 23(5).

that, subject to the above-mentioned exception (which is dealt with below), such proceedings can be brought only in the courts of the Regulation or Convention state in which the immovable property concerned is situated.

This rule is relevant because in *Rösler v Rottwinkel*,[127] a case decided under the Brussels Convention, the CJEU held that disputes concerning the obligations of a landlord or tenant under a tenancy which was a holiday letting came within the concept of 'proceedings which have as their object ... tenancies of immovable property'. The concept also, it would seem, includes timeshare agreements. Timeshares are undoubtedly tenancies for the purposes of English law[128] and there is nothing in the judgment of the CJEU in *Klein v Rhodos Management Ltd*[129] to indicate that a timeshare would not be a tenancy within the meaning of this rule.[130]

However, not all agreements which involve the provision of holiday letting accommodation attract the application of the rule. It will apply if there are additional services which are merely ancillary to the rights of occupation, but the CJEU decision in *Hacker v Euro-Relais GmbH*[131] makes it clear that if there are additional services bundled up with accommodation in a package deal offered by someone other than the owner of the property the case will be outside the scope of this rule. It is a question of fact and degree as to how much more an owner would need to provide in order for it to be said that the rule does not apply, but it is suggested that if the additional services included substantial transport, that would be sufficient for the contract to be taken out of the scope of the rule.[132]

In the cases where it has been decided that a holiday let falls within this rule the claims have been brought by landlords for, for example, unpaid charges[133] or in respect of damage to the property,[134] however, there is no reason to conclude that a claim founded on an obligation owed by the landlord to the tenant would not also fall within it. Accordingly, in relation to a claim arising out of an accident abroad in the course of a holiday let which is founded on an allegation of breach on the part of the landlord of an express or implied term in the tenancy agreement relating

---

[127] (C-241/3) [1986] 1 QB 33.

[128] See the Court of Appeal decision in *Jarrett v Barclays Bank plc* [1999] QB 1.

[129] (C-73/04) [2005] ECR I-8667.

[130] The action concerned an agreement, part of which related to the right to acquire occupancy rights in a timeshare property. It was held that the exclusive jurisdiction rule did not apply to the proceedings, but this was because the agreement was predominantly concerned with membership of a club rather than with the timeshare occupancy rights and therefore fell outside the scope of the rule.

[131] (C-280/90) [1992] ECR I-1111.

[132] For further discussion on where services are ancillary to accommodation rather than components of a package in their own right see Chapter 2, Package Travel I at **2.3.3**.

[133] *Rösler v Rottwinkel* (C-241/3) [1986] 1 QB 33.

[134] *Dansommer A/S v Götz* (C-8/98) [2001] 1 WLR 1069.

to the state of the premises, the courts of the Regulation or Convention state in which the property is situated will have exclusive jurisdiction, unless either (i) the rule does not apply because one is concerned with a package deal or there are other substantial services provided by the owner or (ii) the exception discussed below applies.

(b)   Short-term lets exception

There is, however, an exception to the exclusive jurisdiction rule which was introduced as a result of the decision in *Rösler v Rottwinkel*. A subparagraph of Art 22 provides that if the tenancy is for temporary private use for a maximum period of 6 consecutive months and provided that the tenant is a natural person (ie an individual) and the landlord and tenant are domiciled in the same Regulation or Convention state, the courts of the Regulation or Convention state in which the defendant is domiciled will also have jurisdiction.

This exception is relatively narrow with its requirement that both the landlord and tenant have the same domicile. It meets the situation in *Rösler v Rottwinkel* (where they were both domiciled in Germany), but does not give the consumer the advantage which one might expect him, as the weaker party, to be given in the case of, for example, a French-domiciled landlord letting out a villa in Tuscany to an English-domiciled holidaymaker. The unsatisfactory nature of the narrowness of the exception in this regard is underlined if, as would appear to be the case, the requirement that the landlord and tenant are domiciled in the same Regulation or Convention state has to be satisfied at the time that proceedings are commenced. It is noticeable that, unlike the provisions at Arts 13(3) and 17(3), the requirement of a common domicile is not expressly stated to have to be satisfied at the time that any relevant agreement is concluded, and that suggests that the normal rule that the date of institution of proceedings is relevant to the question of domicile applies. Although, if this is the correct interpretation of the requirement of common domicile, it would help the English-domiciled holidaymaker in the above example in the event that the landlord's domicile changed to England by the time that the proceedings were commenced, it would mean that an English court would not have jurisdiction in the case of a letting of a holiday home in Spain between two persons both domiciled in England at the time of the letting if the landlord subsequently lost his English domicile by moving abroad before the action was started.

4.4.4.11   Jurisdiction agreements – Art 23

By virtue of Art 23, subject to complying with requirements as to form and subject to certain restrictions, the parties to litigation can in some situations, by agreement, override the rules as to jurisdiction which would otherwise apply and (i) confer jurisdiction on a particular court, or the courts generally, in a Regulation or Convention state, as the case may be, and/or (ii) deprive the court or courts in a Regulation or Convention state of jurisdiction which would otherwise have jurisdiction. The provisions of Art 23 are in practice most unlikely to change the position with regard to the jurisdiction of an English court in respect of a claim by the victim of an accident occurring abroad. In a purely tort-based claim it is barely conceivable that a potential claimant who would normally wish to sue in England will enter into a jurisdiction agreement after the event which deprives him of the possibility of suing there, and in a claim founded on contract he will most probably have the protection of one or other of the special regimes for insurance, consumer contracts or employment contracts which limit the ways in which the favourable jurisdiction rules under those regimes can be departed from to his disadvantage (agreements contrary to such provisions being of no effect for the purposes of Art 23).[135]

However, jurisdiction agreements will not infrequently have an effect in cases where a defendant to a claim wishes to pursue a claim against another party based on the claim made against it, such as where a tour operator wishes to claim an indemnity or contribution from the local supplier who was actually responsible for the accident.[136]

The requirements as to form for a jurisdiction agreement to have effect under Art 23 are that it is either:

(a)   in writing or evidenced in writing;[137]
(b)   in a form which accords with practices which the parties have established between themselves; or
(c)   in international trade or commerce, in a form which accords with the usage of which the parties are or ought to have been aware and which in such trade or commerce is widely known to, and regularly observed by, parties to contracts of the type involved in the particular trade or commerce concerned.

The effect which a valid jurisdiction agreement can have varies according to whether at least one of the parties to it is domiciled in a Regulation or Convention state, as the case may be, or whether none is so domiciled.[138] In the former case, if the parties have agreed that a court or courts in the Regulation or Convention state are to have jurisdiction to settle any disputes which have arisen or may arise in connection with a particular

---

[135]   Article 23(5).
[136]   See also Chapter 3, Package Travel II at **3.4**.
[137]   Article 23(2) provides that any communication by electronic means which provides a durable record of the agreement shall be equivalent to 'writing'.
[138]   This distinction will disappear for Regulation cases when Regulation (EU) No 1215/2012 applies as from 10 January 2015 in relation to legal proceedings instituted on or after that date, when jurisdiction agreements between parties neither of whom are domiciled in a Regulation state will then have the same effect as is currently the case for ones between parties one or more of whom are so domiciled.

legal relationship, that court or those courts will have jurisdiction, and unless otherwise agreed, such jurisdiction will be exclusive. In the latter case such an agreement has the effect of conferring jurisdiction on the chosen court or courts and also excluding the jurisdiction of the courts in other Regulation or Convention states over the disputes, unless the chosen court or courts have declined to exercise jurisdiction.

It should be noted that where a valid choice of jurisdiction exists between the parties in favour of the courts of a state other than England and Wales, the English courts have no power to determine a claim based on the Civil Liability (Contribution) Act 1978 between those parties.[139]

In addition to the restrictions already mentioned as to the effect which jurisdiction agreements can have in the context of insurance matters, consumer contracts and contracts of employment, they will also have no legal force if the courts whose jurisdiction they purport to exclude have exclusive jurisdiction under Art 22.[140]

However, even if the effect of a valid jurisdiction agreement is, by virtue of Art 23, to exclude the jurisdiction of the courts of a Regulation or Convention state, such a court can acquire jurisdiction under Art 24 if the defendant enters an appearance which is not for the purpose of challenging that court's jurisdiction.

4.4.4.12 *Submission to the jurisdiction – Art 24*

Except in a case where a Regulation or Convention state has exclusive jurisdiction by virtue of Art 22, a defendant will confer jurisdiction on any court in Regulation or Convention state before which he enters an appearance, but this will not apply where the appearance was entered in order to challenge that court's jurisdiction over him. In *Elefanten Schuh GmbH v Jacqmain*,[141] the CJEU ruled that under the equivalent provision in the Brussels Convention[142] the entry of an appearance which combines a challenge to the jurisdiction with presenting a defence on the merits will not confer jurisdiction, and this will still be the case under the Regulation and the Convention. However, the presenting of a defence on the merits from which it is not apparent that there is an intention to challenge the jurisdiction of the court will confer jurisdiction, and once that has occurred it is too late to challenge jurisdiction at a later stage.

---

[139] *Hough v P & O Containers Ltd* [1999] QB 834; see also **4.4.4.5** regarding Art 6(2).

[140] Article 23(5).

[141] (C-150/80) [1981] ECR 1671.

[142] In the English and some other versions of the Convention (but not the French version) the exception to the rule that the entry of an appearance would confer jurisdiction was differently worded to the equivalent under the Regulation and the Convention in that it said that the rule should not apply where the appearance was 'entered *solely* to contest the jurisdiction' (emphasis added).

This provision does not, however, provide a claimant with a carte blanche to trick gullible or inattentive defendants into conferring jurisdiction on an English court when it would not otherwise have jurisdiction by issuing and serving a claim form in a case where he knows that the court does not have jurisdiction and hoping that the defendant will, through ignorance or inadvertence, enter an appearance. This is because CPR, r 6.34 combined with CPR PD 6B, para 2.1 requires a claimant who intends to serve a claim form outside England and Wales without requiring the court's permission by virtue of the Regulation or Convention to file and serve with the claim form a completed Form N510 setting out the grounds on which he is entitled to do so verified by a statement of truth.

4.4.4.13   *Lis pendens and related actions – Arts 27 and 28*[143]

One of the main objectives of the Regulation and the Convention is to reduce the risk of irreconcilable judgments in courts of different states.[144] Under these Articles a court in a Regulation or Convention state seised of a matter is, in certain circumstances, either required to decline jurisdiction over the matter or given a discretion to do so because of the existence of other proceedings in another Regulation or Convention state. The general rule is that the court 'first seised' of an action has priority.

The concept of the court first seised is common to both Articles, and Art 30 now identifies the point in time when a court is deemed to be seised of a matter for the purposes of determining which of the courts in question was seised first. The question still turns to some extent on the procedural rules of the forum. If, as in England, proceedings are commenced by issuing (and lodging) a document such as a claim form at court and then serving a copy on the defendant, the court is deemed to be seised of the matter at the point in time when the document is lodged, provided that the claimant does not then subsequently fail to take the steps required to effect service on the defendant. If, however, as in many other Regulation or Convention states, the document is first served and then lodged with the court, the court is deemed to be seised when the document is received by the authority responsible for service, provided that the claimant has not subsequently failed to take the steps required for having the document lodged at court.

(a)   Mandatory stay and declining of jurisdiction

By virtue of Art 27 if there are two or more sets of proceedings in more than one Regulation or Convention state which involve the same cause of action and are between the same parties, any court other than the one first seised must stay its proceedings of it own motion until the jurisdiction of

---

[143] As noted above, as from 10 January 2015, when Regulation (EU) No 1215/2012 will apply in respect of legal proceedings instituted on or after that date, there will be changes to the existing scheme concerning these matters in Regulation cases.

[144] Recital 15 of the Regulation.

the court first seised is established, and then, when the jurisdiction of the court first seised is established it must decline jurisdiction in favour of that court. There is no discretion for the court.

In the light of the CJEU decision in *Gubisch Machinenfabrik KG v Palumbo*[145] it is clear that a claim for damages by the victim of an accident and a claim by the person alleged to be liable for a declaration of non-liability involve the same cause of action for the purposes of Art 27. This means that a person who is susceptible to the jurisdiction of an English court in respect of an accident abroad and who wishes to avoid what he perceives to be the more claimant-friendly regime in England with regard to damages and costs can, by bringing a claim[146] in another Regulation or Convention state which has jurisdiction over the victim before the victim commences proceedings in England, prevent the English court from exercising jurisdiction. This potential for preventing a claimant from pursuing a claim before an English court is a factor which should be borne in mind by all practitioners in this area and should deter them from delaying the commencement of proceedings unnecessarily.

It is possible for the different sets of proceedings to be between the same parties for the purposes of this rule even though all the names may not be identical. Two distinct legal entities, such as an insurer and its insured, may be the 'same party' if their interests are identical and indissociable.[147] Accordingly, a claim by a victim brought in England against a road traffic insurer under the *Odenbreit* principle and a claim seeking a declaration of non-liability brought in another Regulation or Convention state by the driver against that victim are likely to be seen as being between the same parties.

In some civil jurisdictions where following an accident the wrongdoer is prosecuted by the local state authorities in respect of criminal offences relating to the accident (e g careless driving), it is common for an injured victim to be named as, or invited to be, a party to the criminal action in order that, in the event of a conviction, an order for compensation in respect of the victim's losses may be made.[148] It is suggested that in such circumstances, civil proceedings in the English courts for damages against the wrongdoer or his insurer, if commenced after the initiation of the local proceedings (or the victim accepting an invitation to present a claim for compensation, if later), could fall to be stayed and dismissed in accordance with Art 27, notwithstanding the criminal nature of the local proceedings, where the same issues fall for determination between the same parties. This is because the clear dividing line between criminal and civil courts which exists in English law may not exist in the country where

---

[145] (144/86) [1987] ECR 4861.
[146] This could be a claim for a declaration of non-liability or one seeking the quantification of the damages which exist in some countries.
[147] *Drouot Assurances SA v Consolidated Metallurgical Industries* (C-351/96) [1999] QB 497.
[148] For example, in Spain.

the accident occurred and the judge, when ordering compensation, may be exercising a civil jurisdiction and awarding compensation in accordance with the same principles which would be applicable to an independent claim brought before a civil tribunal.[149] In any case where, in accordance with the local law and procedure, a claim by a victim for compensation is being entertained by a local court in the context of proceedings which are essentially or predominantly criminal in nature, it may therefore be necessary to ascertain, with the assistance of local lawyers, whether the claim is the equivalent of an ordinary civil claim for compensatory damages. If it is the equivalent of such a claim, so that there is a risk that Art 27 may lead to English proceedings being dismissed, the position is not necessarily irrecoverable, as it is often possible for the claimant to detach herself from such criminal proceedings before a determination has been reached.

(b)   Discretionary stay and declining of jurisdiction

Article 28 deals with certain situations involving two or more sets of proceedings in different Regulation or Convention states which do not involve the same cause of action between the same parties. It is concerned with 'related actions' pending before the courts of different Regulation or Convention states, and for these purposes actions are, by Art 28(3), 'deemed to be related where they are so closely connected that it is expedient to hear and determine them together to avoid the risk of irreconcilable judgments resulting from separate proceedings'.[150] In these circumstances any court other than the one first seised may, but is not obliged to, stay its proceedings.

Article 28(2) further provides that if the related actions are pending at first instance, any court other than the one first seised may decline jurisdiction, but it can do this only if an application in that regard is made by one of the parties and if the court first seised has jurisdiction over the actions and its law permits the consolidation of the actions.

4.5   DIFFERENCES WHEN A DEFENDANT IS DOMICILED IN SCOTLAND OR NORTHERN IRELAND

The Regulation and the Convention are not concerned with the distribution of jurisdiction between the courts of separate constituent parts of a non-unitary state such as the UK. The UK has, however, enacted a set of jurisdiction rules to address the question of which courts within the UK will have jurisdiction over a matter which falls within the

---

[149] In contrast to the limited powers which English criminal courts have to award compensation to victims of crime when sentencing Defendants.

[150] For discussion of the question of when actions are sufficiently 'closely connected' see **4.4.4.4** in relation the same wording in Art 6(1).

scope of the Regulation or the Convention and in respect of which the relevant instrument confers jurisdiction on the courts of the UK generally (as opposed to conferring jurisdiction on the courts of a particular 'place' as in eg Art 5(1)).[151] These are to be found in Sch 4 to the Civil Jurisdiction and Judgments Act 1982 ('the Schedule'), and subject to the material differences set out below, they provide for a scheme identical, mutatis mutandis, to that under the Regulation and the Convention.

Accordingly, there is a general rule (para 1) that a person is to be sued in the part of the UK in which he is domiciled, and a person domiciled in a part of the UK may be sued in the courts of another part only by virtue of rules 3 to 13 in the Schedule (para 2). Save that (i) there is no section dealing with insurance matters and (ii) there are no provisions relating to lis pendens and related actions, there are equivalents to all of the exceptions and qualifications under the Regulation and the Convention dealt with above, although there are the following material differences to those exceptions and qualifications. First, it should be noted that in para 3(a), which is the equivalent of the contract exception under Art 5(1), there is no equivalent of Art 5(1)(b), which qualifies the meaning of the phrase 'the place of performance of the obligation in question'. Secondly, the provisions concerned with jurisdiction agreements (para 12) are different. In particular there are no formal requirements for such an agreement to be valid, and it will only confer jurisdiction on the courts of a part of the UK as opposed to conferring exclusive jurisdiction on those courts.

4.5.1 Insurance matters

It follows from the absence of any special regime for matters relating to insurance that in proceedings between an insurer and a policyholder, insured or beneficiary involving a defendant domiciled in Scotland or Northern Ireland where the Regulation or Convention does not have the effect of conferring jurisdiction specifically on the courts of England and Wales and only has the effect of conferring jurisdiction on the courts of the UK generally, whether an English court will have jurisdiction will be determined by the general scheme under the Schedule, ie paras 3 to 13.

4.5.2 Lis pendens and related actions

The absence of any provisions equivalent to Arts 27 and 28 indicates that in cases where the Regulation or the Convention confers jurisdiction on

---

[151] In these cases the 'place' will be wholly within one of the constituent parts of the UK, and accordingly only courts within that part can have jurisdiction. There may be arguments as to whether every county court within England and Wales is a court for every 'place' within England and Wales (because the jurisdiction of a county court is geographically limited for some purposes, although not in relation to claims in tort and contract generally), but no such county court could possibly be the court for the 'place' in which a party is domiciled if that party is domiciled in Scotland alone.

the courts of the UK generally and the courts of more than one part of the UK can exercise jurisdiction, the principles of forum non conveniens can be invoked and a court in one of the parts can stay its proceedings in favour of the courts of another part in accordance with those principles. It would follow from this that a court on which jurisdiction is conferred by a valid jurisdiction agreement under para 12 could in an appropriate case decline jurisdiction and a court which also has jurisdiction could in such a case override the agreement and exercise jurisdiction.

4.6   CLAIMS OUTSIDE THE SCOPE OF THE REGULATION OR CONVENTION AND CLAIMS IN WHICH THE DEFENDANT IS NOT DOMICILED IN A REGULATION OR CONVENTION STATE

In relation to any claim which falls outside the scope of the Regulation or the Convention the jurisdiction of an English court is determined by the rules discussed below, ie English law unaffected by either instrument, irrespective of the domicile of the defendant. Even in relation to claims within the scope of the Regulation or Convention, except in cases to which Art 22 (exclusive jurisdiction) or Art 23 (jurisdiction agreements) of the Regulation or Convention apply, jurisdiction over a defendant who is not domiciled in a Regulation or Convention state will also be determined by those rules.[152] There are three bases for jurisdiction:

(1)   due service on the defendant while present in England and Wales;
(2)   service on the defendant outside England and Wales with permission pursuant to CPR, r 6.36; and
(3)   submission to the jurisdiction by the defendant.

4.6.1   Presence in England and Wales

Service of process on an individual physically present in England and Wales will confer jurisdiction on an English court, even if his presence is only temporary. So far as foreign domiciled partnerships and corporations are concerned, if they carry on business within England and Wales they are present for the purposes of establishing jurisdiction under this rule.

---

[152]   It should, however, be noted that the lis pendens and related actions provisions of the Regulation and the Convention (Arts 27 to 30) apply irrespective of the domicile of a defendant, so that, in a claim within the scope of either instrument, a court may be required to stay its proceedings and/or decline jurisdiction (or have a discretion so to do) in accordance with those provisions even where jurisdiction is established under the principles discussed below.

4.6.2 CPR, r 6.36

An English court will exercise jurisdiction over a defendant who has been duly served with process outside England and Wales if the claimant has been granted permission by the court to effect such service. Permission can be granted only if the claimant can pass through one of the gateways set out in CPR PD 6B, para 3.1 and in addition show that there is a serious issue to be tried and that an English court is the proper place (forum conveniens) in which to bring the claim. The gateways which are most likely to be material for establishing jurisdiction in claims arising out of accidents abroad are discussed below. In order to pass through one of these gateways the claimant has to establish a good arguable case that the basis for jurisdiction relied upon exists. Showing a 'good arguable case' does not require proving the matters in question on the balance of probabilities, but it does require something more than just showing that there is a serious issue to be tried. It must appear to the court that the claimant has the 'much better argument on the material available'.[153]

4.6.2.1 *Claims in tort – para 3.1(9)*

Permission to serve outside England and Wales may be granted where a claim is made in tort and either (a) the damage was sustained within England and Wales or (b) the damage sustained was the result of an act committed within England and Wales.

First instance decisions have interpreted the requirement for damage to have been sustained within England and Wales quite differently from the way in which decisions of the CJEU have confined the place where the resulting damage was sustained for the purposes of Art 5(3) to the place where the initial physical damage occurred.[154] In *Cooley v Ramsey*,[155] which involved a claim for personal injuries arising out of a road traffic accident in Australia, it was held by Tugendhat J to be sufficient if, following the claimant's repatriation to England, he had sustained further pecuniary losses in England. In so holding he followed an earlier case, *Booth v Phillips*,[156] in which a loss of dependency suffered in England and Wales as a result of a death in Egypt was held to be sufficient to establish damage sustained in England and Wales. In the context of a claim for loss of dependency under the Fatal Accidents Act 1976 there is a reasonably convincing argument for saying that that the damage is sustained in the place where the dependants are located. It is, however, less convincing to say in a claim for damages for personal injury where the injuries were sustained abroad that consequential economic losses suffered in England and Wales by a claimant who returns there later (or even just moves there) constitute damage sustained within England and Wales for the purposes

---

[153] Per Waller LJ in *Canada Trust v Stolzenberg (No 2)* [1988] 1 WLR 547.
[154] See **4.4.4.2**.
[155] [2008] EWHC 129.
[156] [2004] 1WLR 3292.

of para 3.1(9). This is particularly so when one bears in mind that the current wording derives from a change introduced to RSC Ord 11 which was apparently intended to reflect the CJEU's interpretation of 'the place where the harmful event occurred' in Art 5(3). The objection that the wide interpretation employed in *Cooley v Ramsey* creates an unjustifiably wide gateway is said to be met by the point that it will still be necessary to show that an English court is the forum conveniens. However, unless it is overruled by the Court of Appeal, English courts are almost certainly going to follow *Cooley v Ramsey*, and it is likely that the forum conveniens test will be met in most cases involving claimants with an established connection with England and Wales, especially where there is no dispute as to liability and the majority of the lay and expert evidence will be from witnesses in England.

4.6.2.2   *Contractual claims – para 3.1(6)–(8)*

Where a claim is made in respect of a contract, permission to serve the proceedings outside England and Wales may be granted if:

(a)   the contract:

  (i)   was made within England and Wales;
  (ii)   was made by or through an agent trading or residing in England and Wales;
  (iii) is governed by English law; or
  (iv)   contains a term conferring jurisdiction to determine any claim in respect of the contract on an English court; or

(b)   the claim is in respect of a breach of contract committed within England and Wales; or
(c)   the claim is for a declaration that no contract exists where, if a contract were found to exist, it would meet the conditions set out in (i) above.

Self-evidently it is the gateways under (i) and (ii) which will be of potential relevance in relation to claims arising out of accidents abroad.

In (a)(ii) the use of the word 'through' in addition to the word 'by' means that it is not necessary for the contract to have been concluded by the agent trading or residing in England and Wales. It is sufficient to provide a basis for jurisdiction if the involvement of the agent was merely as a negotiator with the contract having been concluded direct with the overseas principal. However, this provision has been interpreted so as to exclude cases where the claimant is a foreign principal who has made a contract by or through his agent trading or residing in England and Wales[157] and it therefore only applies to claimants seeking to bring a claim against a foreign principal.

With regard to (a)(iii), whether the contract is governed by English law will be determined by the relevant applicable principles discussed in the chapter on applicable law.[158]

Although the requirement that the claimant show that an English court is the forum conveniens applies equally to all of the gateways relating to contractual claims, that requirement is in most cases likely to be easily satisfied when reliance is placed on the gateway described at (a)(iv), and there would need to be very strong reasons for ignoring the parties' agreement as to jurisdiction in such a case.

4.6.2.3 Suing an additional defendant – para 3.1(3)

If a claim is being made against a defendant on whom a claim form has been or will be served ('the anchor defendant'), permission to serve another defendant with process outside England and Wales may be granted if certain conditions are met.

First, the service or intended service on the anchor defendant must be 'otherwise than in reliance on this paragraph'. In this context 'this paragraph' must mean the whole of para 3.1 of the Practice Direction, and therefore the service or intended service on the anchor defendant has to be as of right rather than pursuant to any discretionary ground for the grant of permission under that paragraph. Subject to that, the service or intended service on the anchor defendant can be either within or outside of England and Wales. This means that the scope for bringing additional defendants into the proceedings through this gateway is much larger than under the equivalent provision in the Regulation and the Convention (Art 6(1)) which requires, in the context of English proceedings, that the anchor defendant is domiciled in England and Wales, although this wide scope will in many cases be narrowed by the additional forum conveniens requirement.

Secondly, there must be a real issue between the claimant and the anchor defendant which it is reasonable for the court to try. If there is such a real issue it is not fatal that the claim against the anchor defendant is being invoked purely for the purpose of providing a platform for bringing a claim against the additional defendant, but it will be a factor in the exercise of the court's discretion, the weight of which will vary according to all the circumstances of the case. However, if the case against the anchor defendant is bound to fail permission cannot be granted. This

---

[157] *Union International Insurance Company Ltd v Jubilee Insurance Company Ltd* [1991] 1 WLR 415.

[158] See Chapter 5, Applicable law at **5.3**.

requirement is reinforced by CPR, r 6.37(2) which requires an application on this ground to state the grounds on which the claimant believes that there is a real issue between him and the anchor defendant which it is reasonable for the court to try.

Thirdly, the additional defendant must be shown to be a necessary or proper party. The threshold for showing someone to be a proper party is much lower than the one for showing that they are a necessary party, and in practice it will be the lower threshold with which one will usually be concerned. A person will be considered by the courts to be a proper party if by joining them it will be possible to resolve all matters in dispute in the proceedings or there is an issue involving the proposed new party and an existing party connected with the matters already in dispute in the proceedings and it is desirable, in order to resolve that issue, that the new party be joined.

4.6.2.4   *Joining a third party – para 3.1(4)*

Permission to serve the proceedings outside England and Wales may be granted where the claim is an additional claim under CPR Part 20 and the person to be served is a necessary or proper party to the claim or additional claim. This gateway enables a defendant to join a person who is not already a party to the proceedings for the purposes of either bringing an independent claim against that party or making him an additional defendant to a counterclaim he is bringing against the claimant (provided of course that the proposed new party is a necessary or proper party in the above sense to the claim or additional claim).

4.6.3   Submission to the jurisdiction

If a defendant submits to the jurisdiction of an English court, then even if the court would or could not otherwise exercise jurisdiction over him it has jurisdiction conferred on it.[159] Once there has been an effective submission to the jurisdiction by a defendant he cannot thereafter resile from it.

If a defendant is served with proceedings making a claim against him, even if such service is not justified by the court's procedural rules or is for any reason defective or invalid, and then takes a step which is consistent only with the court having power to decide the claim on its merits, he will be taken to have submitted to the jurisdiction of the court and to have waived any defect or invalidity in service. Conduct which is equivocal in this regard or is undertaken subject to an express reservation of his right to challenge the court's jurisdiction will not have this effect, but if it is

---

[159] This is subject to the qualification that jurisdiction cannot be conferred on a court by submission in a case which is within the scope of the Regulation or the Convention and where the courts of another Regulation or Convention state have exclusive jurisdiction under Art 22.

intended to challenge jurisdiction the best advice is to do nothing other than what is required under CPR Part 11 to mount such a challenge (see **4.7**). The test of whether there has been a submission to the jurisdiction is an objective one and the issue is determined by answering the question of whether a reasonable bystander would view the defendant's conduct as being consistent only with an acceptance that the merits of the case are to be determined by the English court.[160]

Steps which will be treated as a submission to the jurisdiction include filing a defence on the merits, making an application for security for costs, applying to strike out the claim or part of it or asking for further time to file a defence. However, filing an acknowledgement of service in which the box indicating an intention to challenge jurisdiction is not ticked or even one in which only the box indicating an intention to defend the claim is ticked will not be fatal as long as the procedure for making a challenge under CPR Part 11 is then scrupulously followed.

It is also possible to submit to the jurisdiction before being served with proceedings. Informing a claimant that an English solicitor has instructions to accept service unaccompanied by a reservation of the right to raise a challenge to the jurisdiction will amount to a submission to the jurisdiction. There will also be a submission to the jurisdiction in relation to a counterclaim by a defendant if proceedings are brought against that defendant in an English court, and this applies even to a counterclaim which could not have been brought in England as a free-standing claim.

4.7 CHALLENGING JURISDICTION – CPR PART 11

Any defendant who has been served with proceedings and believes that he has grounds for contending that the court in question does not have jurisdiction over him in relation to the subject matter of those proceedings must act quickly if he wishes to obtain a ruling from that court that it does not have jurisdiction. This applies equally to cases where the claimant is relying on the substantive provisions of the Regulation or the Convention and to cases where the claimant has relied on the English procedural rules. If he does nothing and thereby enables the claimant to obtain a default judgment, he runs the risk of the claimant being able to seek enforcement of that judgment, not only in an English court but also elsewhere. The enforceability of a default judgment varies according to the basis of jurisdiction relied on and the country in which the attempt to enforce is made, but in a case where jurisdiction was derived from the substantive provisions of the Regulation or Convention and enforcement is sought in a Regulation or Convention state there is a strong likelihood that enforcement will be possible even though it is a default judgment.

---

[160] *Sage v Double A Hydraulics Ltd* [1992] *The Times* 2 April 1992.

The procedure for challenging the court's jurisdiction is found in CPR Part 11. The need to follow this procedure is not limited to disputes as to the court's jurisdiction in the narrow sense of challenging the existence of the court's power to hear and adjudicate upon the claim which is made against the defendant.[161] It is also to be used where the defendant's wish to challenge the court's power to deal with the matter is founded on an allegation of defective or invalid service as well as in situations where the defendant is asking the court to stay its proceedings or to decline to exercise jurisdiction.[162]

In order to challenge the court's jurisdiction or to argue that the court should not exercise its jurisdiction a defendant must first file an acknowledgement of service in accordance with CPR Part 10,[163] but by doing so he does not lose any right he may have to dispute the court's jurisdiction.[164] He must then, within 14 days of filing the acknowledgement of service, make the application challenging the court's jurisdiction (or asking it not to exercise its jurisdiction), which must be supported by evidence,[165] and if he does so he does not need to serve a defence until after the application has been heard.[166] If, having filed an acknowledgement of service, a defendant does not make the application within 14 days of filing it he will be treated as having accepted that the court has jurisdiction to hear the claim,[167] but this time limit can be extended under CPR, r 3.1(2)(a), even, in an appropriate case after the period has expired.[168] If the defendant's application is successful that will be an end to the matter, and the court is likely to make consequential orders under CPR, r 11(6) setting aside the claim form etc as appropriate according to the facts of the case. If on the defendant's application the court does not make a declaration that it does not have jurisdiction to try the claim or that it will not exercise its jurisdiction, the acknowledgement of service will cease to have effect,[169] so that if the defendant takes no further steps he will not be treated as having accepted that the court has jurisdiction to try the claim, ie he will not be taken to have entered an appearance for the purposes of Art 24 nor will he be treated as having submitted to the jurisdiction solely by virtue of filing the acknowledgement of service. The defendant does, however, then have the option of filing a further acknowledgement of service (within 14 days of the

---

[161] *Hoddinott v Persimmon Homes (Wessex) Ltd* [2007] EWCA Civ 1203; [2008] 1 WLR 806.
[162] The stay or declining of jurisdiction may be sought under Arts 27 and 28 or on the basis of forum non conveniens, depending on the nature of the case.
[163] CPR, r 11(1) and (2).
[164] CPR, r 11(3).
[165] CPR, r 11(4).
[166] CPR, r 11(9).
[167] CPR, r 11(5).
[168] It can also be extended by the written agreement of the parties under CPR, r 2.11, but it would be wise for a defendant who obtains an extension in this way to include an express statement that he is not waiving any of his rights with regard to challenging the court's jurisdiction etc.
[169] CPR, r 11(7)(a).

decision on his application or such other period as the court may direct) and if he does so he will then be treated as having accepted that the court has jurisdiction to try the claim.[170]

On such an application the burden of establishing the facts on which it is claimed the court has jurisdiction will normally be on the claimant and in the event of a factual dispute the standard to which the facts need to be proved is that of a good arguable case (see above under the heading of CPR, r 6.36).[171] If the claimant is relying on one of the gateways under CPR, r 6.36 the burden of showing that an English court is the forum conveniens will continue to be on him. However, if the court has jurisdiction as of right and the defendant is asking the court not to exercise it on the grounds of forum non conveniens in a situation where such an argument is possible,[172] the burden of showing why the court should stay its proceedings lies on the defendant.[173]

4.7.1 Forum conveniens

The question of whether an English court or a court elsewhere is the forum conveniens arises in the context of a discretionary decision as to whether to grant permission to serve proceedings outside England and Wales or whether to stay existing English proceedings. As in all discretionary decisions there is the scope for a large number of factors to be relevant, all needing to be taken into account when balancing the merits for granting permission or granting a stay, as the case may be. The number of factors and the weight to be attached to each of them will vary enormously between cases, so although there are some general principles, each case will depend on its own facts.[174]

4.8 SERVICE

In order for an English court to exercise the jurisdiction over a defendant which the rules discussed above allow it to do it is necessary to effect valid service of the claim form on that defendant. It is beyond the intended scope of this chapter to provide a detailed treatment of the law relating to service, and, accordingly, what follows is principally confined to identifying the sources of the relevant rules as to the methods by which

---

[170] CPR, r 11(8).

[171] *Canada Trust Co v Stolzenberg (No 2)* CA [1998] 1 WLR 547.

[172] It is of course not possible in a situation where the jurisdiction of the English court is founded on one of the substantive provisions of the Regulation or the Convention (see *Owusu v Jackson* (C-281/02) [2005] ECR I-1383; [2005] QB 801), save possibly where the suggested other forum is in Scotland or Northern Ireland. In this situation the English court can be asked to stay the proceeding or to decline jurisdiction only on the basis of Art 28.

[173] *Spiliada Maritime Corp v Cansulex Ltd* [1987] AC 460.

[174] Helpful guidance as to the applicable principles and the materiality of a variety of factors can be found in the notes to the White Book at paras 6.37.15.4 to 6.37.20. Civil Procedure (Sweet & Maxwell, 2013).

service may be effected in the situations which may arise. There will of course be cases where it is possible to effect service within England and Wales, for example, on an English-domiciled defendant or on an English solicitor who has given notice in writing that he is instructed to accept service on behalf of a non-English-domiciled defendant, in which case service can be by any of the methods permitted by CPR, r 6.3, but where this is not possible it is necessary to have regard to the rules for service elsewhere, which are found at section IV of CPR Part 6.

4.8.1   Section IV of CPR Part 6

This section applies to all situations where it is necessary to serve a claim form outside of England and Wales, whether it is possible to serve only with the court's permission or as of right. This means that it also applies in situations where a defendant must be served elsewhere than England and Wales by virtue of CPR, rr 6.7(2), 6.7(3) or 6.8(1)[175] (including a defendant on whom service might otherwise be effected within England and Wales). The permissible methods of service vary according to the place where service is to be effected, each place falling into one of the categories set out below.

(1)   *Scotland and Northern Ireland*
A claim form must be served by one of the methods applicable to service within England and Wales (ie section II of CPR Part 6).[176] The local rules in Scotland and Northern Ireland relating to service are irrelevant.

(2)   *EU states*
A claim form may be served by a method:

   (a)   provided for by Council Regulation (EC) 1393/2007 ('the Service Regulation');

   (b)   provided for by CPR, r 6.42 (service through foreign governments, judicial authorities and British Consular Authorities);

   (c)   provided for by a Civil Procedure Convention[177] or Treaty;[178]

   (d)   permitted by the law of the country in which it is to be served.[179]

---

[175] Note that the decision in *Murphy v Staples UK Ltd* (one of the conjoined appeals reported in *Cranfield v Bridgegrove Ltd* [2003] 1 WLR 2441) indicates that the mandatory requirement under these rules to serve at a specified address in an EEA state (but outside England and Wales) in certain circumstances does not prevent valid service being effected on a corporate defendant by a method permitted under the provisions of the Companies Act 2006 or on an LLP by the equivalent methods applicable to LLPs.

[176] CPR, r 6.40(2).

[177] As defined in CPR, r 6.31(c).

[178] The text of any such Treaty can be found at www.fco.gov.uk/en/publications-and-documents/treaties/lists-treaties/bilateral-civil-procedure.

[179] CPR, r 6.40(3).

Notwithstanding Art 1(3) cf the Service Regulation, by virtue of a parallel agreement between Denmark and the EU, it does apply to Denmark. It should be noted that by Art 20 of the Service Regulation it prevails over a Civil Procedure Convention or Treaty (although this does not affect agreements or arrangements which expedite further or simplify the transmission of documents and are compatible with it). It is to be noted that the mandatory words used in Art 1 of the Service Regulation may have the effect, in relation to cases within its scope, of excluding as a valid method of service any method which is not authorised by its provisions, even if that method otherwise appears to be permitted by the provisions of the CPR. For this reason it is advisable, wherever possible, to use a method which is clearly provided for by the Service Regulation.

(3) *Lugano Convention states (ie Norway, Switzerland and Iceland)*
A claim form may be served by a method:

(a) provided for by CPR, r 6.42 (service through foreign governments, judicial authorities and British Consular Authorities);
(b) provided for by a Civil Procedure Convention or Treaty;[180]
(c) permitted by the law of the country in which it is to be served.[181]

All three states are now parties to the 1965 Hague Convention on the Service Abroad of Judicial and Extrajudicial Documents in Civil and Commercial Matters ('the Hague Convention'). This means, in the light of the decision of the CJEU in *Scania Finance France SA v Rockinger Spezialfabrik für Anhängerkupplungen GmbH & Co*,[182] that in relation to claims within the scope of the Lugano Convention the methods by which service may be effected in any of them are exhaustively provided for in the Hague Convention and Art I(2) of Protocol 1 to the Lugano Convention.

(4) *States other than (1) and (2) above which are party to a Civil Procedure Convention or Treaty with the UK*
A claim form may be served by a method:

(a) provided for by CPR, r 6.42 (service through foreign governments, judicial authorities and British Consular Authorities);
(b) provided for by the Civil Procedure Convention or Treaty in question;[183]
(c) permitted by the law of the country in which it is to be served.[184]

---

[180] See nn 178 and 179.
[181] CPR, r 6.40(3).
[182] (C-522/03) [2005] ECR I-8639.
[183] See fns 178 and 179.
[184] CPR, r 6.40(3).

(5)   *States which are not party to a Civil Procedure Convention or Treaty with the UK*
       A claim form may be served by a method:

       (a)   provided for by CPR, r 6.42 (service through foreign governments, judicial authorities and British Consular Authorities);
       (b)   permitted by the law of the country in which it is to be served.[185]

Note that CPR, r 6.40(4) provides that nothing in the rule permitting the above methods of service[186] authorises or requires any person to do anything which is contrary to the law of the country in which the claim form is to be served.

---

[185] CPR, r 6.40(3).
[186] CPR, r 6.40(3).

CHAPTER 5

APPLICABLE LAW

Pierre Janusz

5.1 APPLICABLE LAW

It does not follow from the fact, under the rules discussed in the preceding chapter, that an English court has jurisdiction to determine a claim arising out of an accident abroad that the court will decide the matter by applying the same rules of substantive law that it would use if the claim was a purely domestic one, ie a claim arising out of events in England and Wales and there being nothing with regard to the parties themselves or their relationship which imported a foreign element into the case. The likelihood in most cases arising out of accidents abroad is that, to a greater or lesser extent, the substantive rules of some foreign system of law will be material. In these cases the way in which one determines whether foreign law is relevant, and if so the law of which country, is by identifying what is the applicable law of the claim.

The need to identify the applicable law of the claim arises in both contractual and tort-based claims, but as will be seen below, the rules for identifying the applicable law differ according to whether one is concerned with a claim founded on the law of tort or based on a contract between the parties.

The potential impact of different rules of law under a foreign system of law is, however, generally restricted to questions of substantive law. In an English court matters of procedure[1] (which include matters of evidence) will be governed exclusively by English law, subject only to the effect of specific statutory provisions, such as the Foreign Limitation Periods Act 1984 (which in certain situations gives effect to foreign rules as to limitation, even ones which are characterised as procedural by both their own system of law and English law).

The desire for certainty which underlies the enactment of the Rome I and II Regulations may not have fully achieved its object. In non-contractual claims, the dividing line between substance and procedure has definitely moved. The position where it now lies, is not entirely clear.

---

[1] It should be noted that as a result of the Rome Convention, Rome I and Rome II (see below) the scope of procedure has been significantly narrowed from what it was previously considered to be by English law. These pieces of legislation transfer the assessment of damages from the area of procedural law to that of substantive law.

5.1.1 How does the court know what the rules of the 'applicable law' are?

The traditional analysis is that matters of foreign law constitute questions of fact, and the consequence of this is that if a provision of foreign law is to be relied upon by one or other party, that party must plead and prove the rule in question exactly as if it was a material fact relevant to the cause of action. In practice this generally means that, even in a case where it is clear (or even pleaded) that the applicable law is other than English law, if no specific rule differing from what would be the case under English law is pleaded, or, if it is pleaded, it is insufficiently supported by admissible evidence, the court will proceed by applying English law to the situation.

This result is often said to be the effect of a rebuttable presumption under English law that the law of a foreign state is the same as English law, and this is probably a correct statement of the law, but there are limits to the application of such a presumption. For example, the court may take judicial notice of a rule of foreign law under s 4(2) of the Civil Evidence Act 1972 or on the basis that it is notorious,[2] so that the need both to plead and prove it as a fact is removed, and it is accepted as a matter of common sense that the presumption of similarity should not be applied to a very specific rule dealing with special local situations (a 'special institution' of English law).[3]

It is worth noting that other European countries take a different approach to prove foreign law. In Germany, the courts would use their own research to identify the foreign law and in France it is common for the court to have a single expert witness to determine the law. There is also a question mark as to whether the traditional common law rule whereby the foreign law is assumed to be the same as English law can survive the arrival of the principles of effectiveness and loyal co-operation[4] in this area, where the Rome I and II Regulations expressly require the application of a foreign law to the claim.

5.1.2 Which choice of law regime?

The regime relevant for identifying the applicable law of the claim varies according to whether the claim is founded on an allegation that a tort has been committed or on an allegation of breach of contract,[5] and then within both categories there is further variation dependent on the factor

---

[2] *Dicey and Morris* gives the example of roulette not being unlawful in Monte Carlo.

[3] *Shaker v Al-Bedrawi* [2002] EWCA Civ 1452; [2003] Ch 350 in which it was held that it would not be presumed that an accounting rule under the Companies Act 1985 applying to public companies and deriving from an EU Directive would exist in Pennsylvanian law.

[4] Article 4(3) of the Treaty of the European Union.

[5] The so-called 'characterisation' issue which is discussed in detail in relation to direct actions against insurers in Chapter 6, Direct Actions Against Insurers at **6.3.2.1**.

of time, as legislation has introduced successive changes to the position at common law. It will be necessary to discuss the earlier regimes because the changes which have been made are not retroactive in effect and therefore cases governed by those regimes can still present themselves.

5.2 TORT

5.2.1 History of applicable law

This chapter is entitled applicable law because that is the concept and terminology used in the successive pieces of legislation[6] which have in general[7] replaced the common law rules governing actions brought before the English courts concerning tort-based claims arising out of events which have taken place outside England and Wales. However, this was not a concept at common law. The focus at common law was on the essential elements of the claim. As eventually developed the rule was that it was necessary to show not only that had the events taken place in England and Wales an action would have lain but also that there was an actionable wrong by the law of the place where the events took place, so-called double actionability.

It was, however, established in *Boys v Chaplin*[8] that in order to do justice in specific cases there was an exception to the general rule which meant that it was possible for discrete issues to be determined by reference to only one of the relevant systems of law. In *Boys v Chaplin* itself this meant that the claimant, a British soldier, who was injured in a road traffic accident which occurred in Malta as a result of the negligence of another British soldier, could recover general damages for pain and suffering (in accordance with English law principles) even though under Maltese law such damages were not recoverable and therefore would have been precluded under the general rule.

The double actionability rule was the subject of considerable criticism and a Law Commission Report[9] recommended its abolition and replacement with the concept of the applicable law of the tort. This Report was acted upon and the result was Part III of the Private International Law (Miscellaneous Provisions) Act 1995 ('the 1995 Act'), which applies to claims arising out of acts or omissions occurring on or after 1 May 1996 (other than defamation claims), but leaves the common law rules in effect for claims arising out of acts or omissions occurring before that date. The 1995 Act provides a general rule for identifying the applicable law of the

---

[6] First the Private International Law (Miscellaneous Provisions) Act 1995 and subsequently Council Regulation (EC) No 864/2007 ('Rome II').

[7] The common law rules continue to apply to defamation as it was expressly excluded from both pieces of legislation.

[8] [1971] AC 356.

[9] No 193 Private International Law Choice of Law in Tort and Delict.

tort but allows that rule to be displaced under certain circumstances in favour of the law of a different country.

Further reform has come from the direction of Europe in the form of Regulation (EC) No 847/2007 of the European Parliament and of the Council ('Rome II'), which, so far as concerns tort-based claims within the scope of this work, replaced the regime under the 1995 Act in relation to claims arising out of events giving rise to damage which occur on or after 11 January 2009.[10] Rome II continues to employ the concept of applicable law, but where it applies; the rules for identifying the applicable law differ from those under the 1995 Act. There are also significant material changes in the scope of the applicable law. Each of these three regimes will be discussed below, but because of the ever diminishing applicability of the earlier regimes they will be dealt with in reverse chronological order, followed by a separate section addressing the different rules with regard to limitation under each of them.

5.2.2 Claims arising out of events occurring on or after 11 January 2009: Rome II

5.2.2.1 *Material scope*

In common with Council Regulation (EC) No 44/2001 ('Brussels I') (which deals with inter alia issues of jurisdiction amongst the courts of the member states of the EU) Rome II is confined in its application to 'civil and commercial matters', and Art 1(1), which defines its scope in this regard, also contains the same express exclusions of revenue, customs and administrative matters as appear in Brussels I. Article 1(1) in addition also specifies that it does not apply to the liability of the state for acts and omissions in the exercise of state authority (acta iure imperii), thereby expressly stating what had been held in cases such as *LTU GmbH v Eurocontrol*[11] as to what did not fall within the expression 'civil and commercial matters' for the purposes of Brussels I.[12][13] The only other provision dealing with the material scope of Rome II which is relevant for the purposes of this work is Art 1(3), by which it is stated not to apply to evidence and procedure and which is dealt with below in the context of Art 15 (matters to be governed by the applicable law). The non-participation of Denmark in the adoption of Rome II (see recital 40

---

[10]   Articles 31 and 32 of Rome II as interpreted by the CJEU in *Homawoo v GMF Assurances SA* (Case C-412/10) [2012] IL Pr 2.

[11]   (C-29/76) [1976] ECR 1541.

[12]   It is to be noted that this addition to the definition of material scope for the purposes of Rome II has also been included in the new Regulation dealing with jurisdiction (Council Regulation (EU) 1215/2012) which will apply as from 10 January 2015 in relation to legal proceedings instituted on or after that date.

[13]   For a discussion of what relevance this aspect of the definition of the material scope of Rome II may have in claims arising out of accidents abroad reference should be made to the relevant part of the chapter dealing with jurisdiction.

and Art 1(4)), has no impact on its effect in England and Wales, save that it must be remembered that references to 'member state' in Rome II do not include Denmark.

5.2.2.2 Temporal scope

As stated above, the Rome II regime will apply to claims arising out of events which occur on or after 11 January 2009. In ordinary accident cases (such as road traffic accidents, slips, trips and falls) there will be no difficulty in knowing whether Rome II applies as the event (the collision, slip etc, the date of which will be known) will coincide exactly with the occurrence of and appreciation of damage (or if the incident is initially perceived to have involved no injury but symptoms attributable to it subsequently occur, there will still be the knowledge of the date of the incident). However, difficulties could arise in cases where there is a lapse of time between what must be the 'event' and the sustaining or appreciation of damage, such as in illness cases. The potential for such difficulties will of course diminish the further one is away in time from 11 January 2009, not least of all because of the need to avoid the expiry of limitation periods, but given the relatively long limitation periods and/or the possibility of them being interrupted or suspended under some systems of law which may be applicable, they may nevertheless crop up for some time to come.

5.2.2.3 Choice of law rules

The provisions for determining the law applicable to a claim founded on tort consist of a general rule (Art 4) and a number of special rules (Arts 5 to 9) which deal with specific species of tort claims and override the general rule where they are of application. Of these special rules only Art 5 (product liability) and Art 7 (environmental damage) are potentially of any relevance to personal injury claims and they are dealt with briefly below. Article 14 makes it possible in certain circumstances for parties to choose an applicable law different to that which is indicated by these rules.

Exclusion of renvoi

It should be noted that, by Art 24 (which has the effect of excluding the principle of the renvoi) the applicable law identified by all of these rules is the internal law of the country in question, excluding its rules of private international law. Under the principle of the renvoi, if the rules of private international law of the country whose law is the applicable law provide that the law of another country should apply, then it is that other country's law which will be used by the forum. Taking the example of a claim by a passenger habitually resident in England arising out of a single vehicle road traffic accident in France involving a German registered vehicle, as will be seen below, the general rule under Rome II says that the applicable law is that of France. A French court dealing with the case would not, however, apply French law to the case because, by Art 28, Rome II is overridden by relevant international conventions to which one or more member states were parties when the Regulation was adopted, namely the 1971 Hague Convention on the Law applicable to Traffic Accidents. Article 4(a) of that Convention would direct a French court to apply German law. However, because of the exclusion of the renvoi, an English court would ignore the Hague Convention rule directing one to German law and would apply only French internal law.

5.2.2.4   The general rule: Art 4(1)

Under Art 4(1), subject to any other provision in Rome II, the applicable law for a tort-based claim is the law of the country in which the damage occurs, irrespective of the country in which the event giving rise to the damage occurs and irrespective of the country or countries in which the indirect consequences of that event occur.[14] For these purposes one of a number of distinct territorial units of a state, each of which has its own rules of law in respect of tort/delict, is considered to be a separate country,[15] so that, for example, each of the United States of America and each of England and Wales, Scotland and Northern Ireland are all separate countries when identifying the applicable law.[16]

The very clearly expressed choice of the lex loci damni as the basic rule to be applied provides certainty in the vast majority of cases but there may be room for doubt as to which law one is being directed to in some cases where what constitutes the damage (or relevant damage) for the purposes of Rome II may be uncertain. In a case where a claimant sustains physical injury in a road traffic accident in France the position is quite clear: the physical damage was sustained in France, and decisions of the CJEU in relation to Art 5(3) of Brussels I (or its predecessor the Brussels Convention) have established that subsequent financial loss or further pain and suffering experienced in another territory do not constitute damage for the purpose of that Article, and recital 17 to Rome II makes it clear that the same would be decided in relation to Art 4(1) of Rome II.[17]

However, the position may not be so clear in a case where a holidaymaker consumes infected food on the last day of his holiday and due to the incubation period for the bacterium in question he does not suffer any symptoms until a few days after his return to England. An analysis based

---

[14]   By virtue of Art 3 of Rome II, the law of the country which is to be applied need not be that of a member state.

[15]   Article 25(1).

[16]   Under Art 25(2), the United Kingdom (as a member state comprising such separate territorial units) had the option of not applying the Regulation to conflicts between its constituent parts, but by reg 6 of the Law Applicable to Non-Contractual Obligations (England and Wales and Northern Ireland) Regulations 2008 (SI 2008/2986) it is applied to such conflicts.

[17]   See Chapter 4, Jurisdiction at **4.2.4.3**, matters relating to tort.

on the pleural plaques cases[18] would indicate that there would have been no damage for the purposes of completing the cause of action in tort until he was back in England. Does this mean, however, that under Art 4(1) the applicable law will be English law? Instinctively one may feel that this would be an odd result. It may be the case, however, that such a conclusion only arises because it is the consequence of applying a literal interpretation based on an Anglo-centric and parochial definition of the word 'damage' drawn from the English law of negligence and that it would not arise if one properly interpreted 'damage' in the context of it being an autonomous concept for the purposes of Rome II (which is what the CJEU is likely to say it is). So interpreted, it might be held to mean that damage is sustained in such a case as soon as the foreign organism is in the holidaymaker's body, irrespective of whether there is only a delayed, rather than an immediate, onset of symptoms. Alternatively, if properly interpreted, Art 4(1) would mean that English law was the applicable law; the 'odd result' could be avoided by invoking the 'escape clause' of Art 4(3) (see below).

Another situation in which there may be some uncertainty as to what law Art 4(1) points to is a claim which arises out of a fatal accident abroad. The problem arises in its clearest form if at the time of the death all the victim's dependants are in England. Leaving aside the claims which the victim might have for his personal losses and whether, and if so by whom, they can be pursued after his death, the claims which his dependants might have can only be for bereavement and loss of dependency (or for some broad equivalents to these under a foreign law), but these losses are suffered in England. Does that mean that English law is applicable to the dependants' claim? The literal reading which points to that conclusion is if anything reinforced by the words in Art 4(1) that it is the law of the country where the damage occurred which is applicable 'irrespective of the country in which the event giving rise to the damage occurred'. There are, however, pointers in the opposite direction. The desideratum of Rome II being construed consistently with Brussels I (recital 7 of Rome II) would indicate that the reasoning used by the CJEU in its decisions in relation to Art 5(3) of Brussels I would apply, so that it would be the initial physical damage to the victim which Art 4(1) is referring to, and there are additional pointers in Rome II itself. If a claim by the dependants is categorised as a personal injury claim, recital 17 indicates that it is the law where the injury was sustained which is applicable, and the provision at Art 15(g) that the applicable law will govern 'persons entitled to compensation for damage sustained personally' appears to be addressing the question of claims brought by persons other than the actual victim of personal injury. In the light of these opposite indications, it is preponderantly likely that the law applicable to fatal accident claims will be held to be the law applicable to the tort which caused the relevant death.

---

[18] *Rothwell v Chemical & Insulating Co Ltd* [2008] 1 AC 281.

5.2.2.5   *Common habitual residence: Art 4(2)*

The basic rule under Art 4(1) is subject to the exception provided for by
Art 4(2) that if the person claimed to be liable and the person sustaining
damage both have their habitual residence in the same country at the time
when the damage occurs, it is the law of that country which will be
applicable. If the condition of common habitual residence is fulfilled then
the exception applies without any element of discretion, subject only to
being overridden by one of the rules dealing with special situations
(Arts 5 to 9) or by Art 4(3).

The term 'habitual residence' is only partially defined in Rome II.
Article 23(1) defines it for companies, and other corporate or
unincorporated bodies, as the place of their central administration, with
the qualification that if the event giving rise to the damage occurs, or the
damage arises, in the course of the operation of a branch, agency or other
establishment,[19] the place where the branch agency or other establishment
is located shall be treated as its habitual residence. Article 23(2) defines
habitual residence for a natural person acting in the course of his or her
business activity as his or her principal place of business.

This leaves the habitual residence of individuals not acting in the course
of any business activity of theirs undefined. It is fairly certain that what
constitutes habitual residence for such individuals will be treated as an
autonomous concept in order to avoid different approaches being taken
by different member states. There were presumably good reasons for not
using the concept of 'domicile' as used in Brussels I, but it is likely that in
most cases the 'habitual residence' of such an individual will be the same
as his or her 'domicile' as that term is generally understood in civil law
systems. It will not be the same, therefore, as the English law concept of
'domicile of birth', but more fluid.

In a fatal accident or other secondary victim case[20] questions similar to
those under Art 4(1) can arise with regard to identifying the nature of the
damage which is referred to (and therefore the person whose habitual
residence is in issue, namely the primary or secondary victim).

There could also be room for uncertainty with regard to the person whose
habitual residence is material when looking at the person claimed to be
liable. In a case where an employer is alleged to be vicariously liable for
the negligence of his employee and they have different habitual residences,
it is the employer's or the employee's habitual residence which is material?
If, as is generally likely to be the case, it is only the employer who is being
sued, it is suggested that as he is the person whose legal responsibility is in
issue in the case it is upon him that the focus should be and it is his

---

[19]   For the meaning of 'branch, agency or other establishment' see **4.2.4.3**(3) in Chapter 4
       on jurisdiction.
[20]   Such as psychiatric loss claims.

habitual residence which is material, and there is probably no reason for a different approach even if the employee is also sued, given the separate treatment for multiple claimants and/or defendants discussed below. A similar question arises when a direct claim against an insurer is being made and the insurer has a different habitual residence to that of the insured. Such a claim does not of course involve a question of vicarious liability for the acts of another person, and it is considered that as the focus is on the insured's liability to the victim it is the habitual residence of the insured which is to be taken into account.

In cases where there are multiple claimants and/or defendants it would seem that the question of whether Art 4(2) displaces the basic rule under Art 4(1) has to be decided separately as between each pair of claimants and defendants. Accordingly, in relation to a road traffic accident in Greece between one car in which the driver and passenger were habitually resident in England and another car in which the driver was habitually resident in Greece, but the passenger in England, where both drivers and both passengers are injured and both drivers are alleged to be liable, the situation is as follows. All claims against the Greek driver and the claim of the Greek driver against the English driver would have Greek law as the applicable law, but the applicable law of the claims by both passengers against the English driver would be English law. It is apparent that in a more extreme example with more vehicles involved and greater multiplicity of common habitual residences the number of material applicable laws could become such as to make the situation become undesirably complex if not absurd. In such a case it is conceivable that recourse could be had to the 'escape clause' of Art 4(3).

5.2.2.6   *Escape clause: Art 4(3)*

The description of 'escape clause' for this provision comes from recital 18. It provides that where it is clear from all the circumstances of the case that the tort or delict is manifestly more closely connected with a country other than that indicated in Art 4(1) or (2), the law of that country shall apply.

A very literal reading of Art 4(3) would mean that in a case where the exception under Art 4(2) prima facie applied it would not be possible for the law indicated under the basic rule of Art 4(1) to apply in place of the law indicated under Art 4(2), but only the law of some third country. It is submitted, however, that such a literal reading is not justified, given that the intended purpose of Art 4(3) must be to do justice in particular cases. That purpose would be defeated by limiting the flexibility of the rule by giving it a restrictive reading.

Article 4(3) gives one specific example of a factor which might give rise to its application, namely 'a pre-existing relationship between the parties, such as a contract, which is closely connected with the tort/delict in question', but this is far from being an exhaustive statement of the factors which might be relevant. The court will need to have regard to all the relevant factors in the case, such as the parties, the events and their circumstances and the direct and indirect consequences thereof, but it is clear from the words 'manifestly more closely connected' that the threshold is quite high and it is only an exceptional case which will bring Art 4(3) into operation.

It should be noted that Art 4(3) is an all or nothing provision in the sense that it either has the effect of making another system of law applicable to all the issues in the case or it leaves the choice of law dictated by Art 4(1) and (2) unaffected. It is not worded so that a different applicable law can be 'chosen' to apply to one or more separate issues in the case according to the connection of those issues with a particular country. Accordingly the *dépeçage* possible under the 1995 Act (see below) is unavailable under Rome II.

5.2.2.7   *Product Liability: Art 5*

The scheme of the rules used in determining the applicable law in product liability cases is described as a 'cascade system' (recital 20), with five rules in a hierarchy in which, if the condition for applying the primary rule is not met, one moves on to the next rule, and if the condition for applying that rule is not met one moves to the next rule and so on. As will be seen below, the hierarchy of these rules is not the same as the order in which they appear in Art 5. There is in addition an 'escape clause' similar to that in Art 4 which, if it applies, overrides the choice of law dictated by the first five rules.[21]

The primary rule is that under Art 4(2), which is imported by the opening words of Art 5(1), so that if the person claimed to be liable and the person sustaining damage both have their habitual residence in the same country at the time when damage occurs, the applicable law will be the law of the country of their common habitual residence. See above for observations and comments on Art 4(2).

If Art 4(2) does not apply, then by a proviso at the end of Art 5(1), the applicable law will be that of the country in which the person claimed to be liable is habitually resident if it was not reasonably foreseeable to him that the product, or a product of the same type, would be marketed[22] in (i) the country where the person sustaining the damage had his or her habitual residence at the time when the damage occurred, (ii) the country

---

[21]   Although, as seen below, there is one view that it cannot override the first rule, and also there is a question as to whether it can lead to the application of a law which would be indicated by one of the four subsequent rules in the hierarchy.

[22]   There is no definition of what amounts to 'marketing', but as the question of whether a defendant reasonably foresees the marketing of a product arises, it is clear that it does not have to be by, or with the consent of, the defendant.

where in which the product was acquired or (iii) the country in which the damage occurred in any case where the marketing of the product in one of those countries would cause the law of that country to be the applicable law by virtue of Art 5(1)(a), (b) or (c) as the case may be.

Then, if the proviso does not apply and the product was marketed in the country in which the person sustaining the damage has his or her habitual residence, by Art 5(1)(a) the law of that country will apply.

Then, if Art5(1)(a) does not apply and the product was marketed in the country in which it was acquired, by Art 5(1)(b) the law of that country will apply.

Finally, if Art 5(1)(b) does not apply and the product was marketed in the country where the damage occurred, by Art 5(1)(c) the law of that country will apply.

The 'escape clause' (Art 5(2)) is materially identical to Art 4(3). A similar question arises as that under Art 4(3) as to whether the law to be applied by use of the escape clause cannot be one of the laws which would be applicable under Art 5(1)(a), (b) or (c) if the case fulfilled the conditions to engage them. It is again suggested that this narrow interpretation would defeat the intended purpose of the escape clause. A further question arises as to whether the escape clause can be used to displace the law which would be applicable if the parties had a common habitual residence as it can be read as only enabling the law 'indicated in' Art 5(1) to be disapplied and that law could be said not to be indicated 'in' Art 5(1) because it comes to be applied by reason of Art 5 being subordinate to Art 4(2). Again, it is submitted that the desirable flexibility intended to be imported by the escape clause would be defeated by such a narrow construction.

5.2.2.8 *Environmental Damage: Art 7*

In cases of claims for compensation for damage to property or sustained by persons resulting from environmental damage[23] the person seeking compensation has a choice as to which is to be the applicable law. The default position is that the rule under Art 4(1) applies, but the person seeking compensation can instead choose the law of the country in which the event giving rise to the damage occurred. Rome II is silent as to how a claimant makes or manifests his election, but it is likely that how or when the election has to be made will be treated as a question for the procedural law of the forum.

---

[23] Environmental damage is not defined in the body of the Regulation, but recital 24 gives guidance as to what the term is intended to cover: '"Environmental damage" should be understood as meaning adverse change in a natural resource, such as water, land or air, impairment of a function performed by that resource for the benefit of another natural resource or the public, or impairment of the variability among living organisms.'

It should be noted that the rule under Art 7 cannot be overridden by use of the 'escape clause' under Art 4(3).

5.2.2.9   Freedom of choice: Art 14

All the choice of law rules discussed above can be overridden by the agreement of the parties pursuant to Art 14. The freedom to submit tort or delict claims to a law of the parties' choice is however restricted in a number of ways, and these restrictions mean that effective agreements by which another applicable law replaces that chosen by virtue of the above rules are very unlikely to arise in the vast majority of accident and illness cases. First, the agreement must have been entered into after the event giving rise to the damage occurred,[24] unless all parties are pursuing a commercial activity and the agreement was freely negotiated[25] before the event giving rise to the damage occurred.[26] Secondly, the choice must be expressed or demonstrated with reasonable certainty by the circumstances of the case and must not prejudice the rights of third parties.[27] Thirdly, the parties' choice of applicable law cannot prejudice the application of provisions of law of another country which cannot be derogated from by agreement if that other country is one where all the elements relevant to the situation at the time when the event giving rise to the damage occurs are located.[28] Fourthly, the parties' choice of applicable law which is not that of a member state[29] cannot prejudice the application of provisions of EU law, where appropriate as implemented in the member state of the forum, which cannot be derogated from by agreement if all the elements relevant to the situation at the time when the event giving rise to the damage occurs are located in one or more member states.[30] Finally, Art 14 is subject to Art 16 (see below).

5.2.2.10   Scope of the applicable law: Art 15

It is provided by Art 1(3) that, without prejudice to Arts 21 and 22 (entitled 'Formal validity' and 'Burden of proof' respectively), Rome II does not apply to evidence and procedure. Of these two Articles, which Rome II thereby expressly acknowledges amount to possible encroachment into the area of procedure (which as a matter of general principle is to be governed exclusively by the lex fori and therefore unaffected by any rules of the law rendered applicable to the tort or delict by the choice of law rules), it is only Art 22 which is likely to be of any relevance in claims arising out of accidents abroad. Article 22(1) provides that the applicable

---

[24]   Article 14(1)(a).
[25]   This requirement will generally prevent valid agreements based on a party's standard terms and conditions.
[26]   Article 14(1)(b).
[27]   The last sentence of Art 14(1).
[28]   Article 14(2).
[29]   It should be remembered here that Denmark is not a member state for these purposes.
[30]   Article 14(3).

law shall apply to the extent that, in matters of non-contractual obligations (ie tort or delict for our purposes), it contains rules which raise presumptions of law or determine the burden of proof. So if, for example, the applicable law contained a rule that in the case of a collision between a pedestrian and a motor vehicle there was a presumption of liability on the part of the driver of the vehicle and the burden was on him to establish facts which could exonerate him, that rule would have to be applied by the forum.

It is apparent, however, from Art 15, which sets out in some detail the matters which are to be governed by the applicable law, that the encroachment of Rome II into the area of procedure as it is understood by English law goes beyond that which is provided for by Arts 21 and 22. In addition to identifying the matters which English law would see as naturally falling on the substantive side of the dividing line between substance and procedure (and therefore to be governed by the applicable law rather than the lex fori) it specifies two matters which are to be governed by the applicable law which the common law would characterise as being partially or wholly matters of procedure: the assessment of damage (Art 15(c)) and limitation (Art 15(h)). The inclusion of these matters as ones to be governed by the applicable law makes it clear that the concept of 'procedure' in Art 1(3) is not exactly the same as that word has been traditionally understood in English law.

The provisions of Art 15 which are likely to be relevant to personal injury claims are discussed below.

(i)   Art 15(a): 'the basis and extent of liability, including the determination of persons who may held liable for acts performed by them'

This means that the applicable law will govern whether liability is strict or fault-based and what is meant by fault (including for example if it comprises omissions as well as positive acts). It would also seem to govern the maximum extent of liability (although that would also appear to be addressed in Art 15(b), which deals with defences). Additionally, questions such as whether minors can be held liable for their acts would fall within the scope of the applicable law.

(ii)   Art 15(b): 'the grounds for exemption from liability, any limitation of liability and any division of liability'

The applicable law will accordingly also govern, in addition to general defences, matters such as the availability and extent of contributory negligence as a defence, the equivalent of volenti non fit injuria etc. Statutory caps on damages under the applicable law will be given effect to the extent that they are not covered by Art 15(a). This provision would also seem to cover the question of whether two or more tortfeasors who have contributed to the damage suffered by a claimant can be held liable for the full extent of the damage sustained (as in English law) or whether their separate liability to the claimant is restricted to the proportion of the claimant's loss which represents their own share of responsibility or blame for the incident or damage. It is not entirely clear whether it also addresses the question of contribution claims by one tortfeasor against another, as such claims, or certainly some types of such claims, fall under a separate provision (Art 20).

(iii)   Art 15(c): 'the existence, the nature and the assessment of damage or the remedy claimed'

By virtue of this provision questions of remoteness of damage, mitigation and the available heads of damage will all be governed by the applicable law. This does not represent a change from the perspective of English law, but the inclusion of the assessment of damage and the reference to the remedy claimed does constitute a departure from the previous position in English law, which has treated remedies as a matter of procedure and has included within the concept of remedies the quantification or assessment of damages, as shown by the decision of the House of Lords in *Harding v Wealands*.[31] For a fuller discussion of the implications of this change, and the effect of recital 33 on the assessment of damages, please see the chapter on damages.

(iv)   Art 15(d): 'within the limits of powers conferred on the court by its procedural law' the court is required to apply the lex causae to, 'the measures which the court may take to prevent or terminate injury or damage or ensure the provision of compensation'

These words are potentially wide enough to cover the power to award interest. It has been held previously that s 35A of the Senior Courts Act 1981 creates a 'procedural' remedy,[32] but whether the same conclusion would be reached under Rome II is doubtful. Also, the words of Art 15(d) suggest that the applicable law governs the right of the English court to award damages in a foreign currency. As a matter of English law, the court has power to award damages in a foreign currency.[33]

(v)   Art 15(e): 'the question whether a right to claim damages or a remedy may be transferred, including by inheritance'

In English law the question of whether in the context of personal injury the whole or part of a claim can be assigned arises relatively rarely. However, in civil law systems, it is not uncommon for assignment of some or all of a claimant's losses to take place, whether by operation of automatic statutory assignment or specific agreement. Partly this reflects the fact that under many civil law systems the concept of subrogated loss

---

[31]   [2007] 2 AC 1.

[32]   *Maher v Groupama EST* [2009] EWCA Civ 1191 [2010] 1 WLR 1564.

[33]   *Miliangos v George Frank (Textiles) Ltd* [1976] AC 443.

claims are not recognised, but title passes to the third party which has reimbursed the victim's loss. So, in German law, for example, where an injured party receives sick pay from his employer's compulsory insurance body, the right to claim recovery of that part of the loss passes automatically to the insurer and the injured person is no longer entitled to sue for those losses. Article 15(e) ensures that these issues are governed by the same law as that which relates to the tort.

By virtue of Art 15(e) the applicable law will also govern whether a cause of action survives the death of the claimant such that his heirs may bring a claim for the losses he sustained. It does not, however, address the question of the availability (in principle and if so to whom) of a claim for bereavement or loss of dependency (or their equivalents) in a fatal accident case, which, if it is specifically addressed in the provisions dealing with the scope of the applicable law, is covered by Art 15(f).

(vi)   Art 15(f): 'persons entitled to compensation for damage sustained personally'

This provision establishes that the applicable law will determine who, other than the primary victim of a tort, may make a claim for losses they may have suffered in consequence of the damage to the primary victim. As discussed under Art 4(1) above, it would seem that this covers claims which are equivalent to ones under the Fatal Accidents Act 1976, but its application is wider than that in that it also covers claims by secondary victims generally, not only claims which arise out of fatal accidents.

(vii)   Art 15(g): 'liability for the acts of another person'

This provision makes it clear that whether someone can be held vicariously liable for the torts of another, not only in the context of employer and employee, but also in that of principal and agent or of parent and child, will be a matter for the applicable law. It is suggested that this wording does not, on the other hand, encompass the question of whether a wrongdoer's insurer can be sued directly by the victim, because such actions depend on the obligation of the insurer to indemnify the wrongdoer, not as a result of liability for his acts.

(viii)   Art 15(h): 'the manner in which an obligation may be extinguished and rules of prescription and limitation, including rules relating to the commencement, interruption and suspension of a period of prescription'

The greatest significance of this provision is that the rules of the applicable law with regard to limitation will govern such issues. Although this is a change to the position at common law, it is not radically different to the position immediately before Rome II began to apply, which was brought about by the combination of the Foreign Limitation Periods Act 1984 and the 1995 Act (see below). It expressly mentions rules concerning commencement, suspension and interruption of limitation, but omits reference to substantive law regarding what acts are necessary in order to stop time running. It is suggested that the questions of whether (and more importantly for practical purposes) when time has been stopped will be governed by the lex fori as a matter of procedure. Accordingly, where the English court has jurisdiction, issue of a valid claim form will stop time running, even where the relevant limitation rules are of a foreign applicable law.

The provision also means that the applicable law will govern the issue of how liability may be extinguished, for example by the death of the tortfeasor.

5.2.2.11   Overriding mandatory provisions and public policy: Arts 16 and 26

Article 16 states that nothing in Rome II shall restrict the application of provisions of the law of the forum in a situation where they are mandatory irrespective of the law otherwise applicable. In doing so it gives effect to a recognised concept in private international law that respect must be given to certain provisions in the system of law of a country which that country regards as crucial for safeguarding its public interests to the extent that they should apply to any situation regardless of the law which would otherwise be applicable.[34] Recital 32 makes it clear that the circumstances in which such overriding mandatory provisions should be applied will be exceptional. The CJEU has held that the term applies to 'national provisions ... crucial for the protection of the political, social or economic order'.[35]

To the extent that the UK is party to international conventions which include their own rules of jurisdiction which apply regardless of the applicable law (for example the Montreal and Athens Conventions), these are likely to constitute overriding mandatory provisions for the purposes of this rule.

There is a general rule in English private international law that an English court will not give effect to a rule of foreign law the application of which would be contrary to English public policy, and is a rule which has its counterpart in foreign systems of law. The focus when considering whether a rule is objectionable is its application in practice, not the rule in the abstract. Article 26 recognises this rule, but restricts its application to situations where the application of the foreign rule would be 'manifestly incompatible' with the public policy of the forum. Again, recital 32 clarifies that invoking the public policy exception is limited to exceptional

---

[34]   The definition is taken from Art 9(1) of Rome I.
[35]   *Arblade* Case C-369 and 376/96 [1999] ECR I-8453.

circumstances.[36] It is for the English court to determine what is English public policy, however, the CJEU will no doubt wish to place constraints on the ability of national courts to have recourse to the concepts, to prevent the general rules of choice of law being undermined.

5.2.2.12   *Direct claims against insurers: Art 18*

In the vast majority of claims arising out of accidents abroad the claimant does not expect to receive his compensation from the tortfeasor himself, but rather, directly or indirectly, from the tortfeasor's liability insurer. In many systems of law, such as French law, the availability of a direct cause of action in favour of a victim against a liability insurer has been well established for many decades, but there has been a debate within English private international law as to whether the availability of such direct claims depends on the rules of the applicable law of the tort or the applicable law of the contract of insurance. Article 18 cuts through this debate and says that a direct claim against an insurer can be brought if either the law applicable to the tort or the applicable law of the contract of insurance allows it.

5.2.2.13   *Contribution claims between tortfeasors: Art 20*

This Article, whilst using the slightly unusual terms in the context of tort liability of creditor and debtor,[37] provides that where a claimant has the same claim against more than one tortfeasor and one of the tortfeasors has satisfied the claim against him in whole or in part, the issue of that tortfeasor's right to demand compensation from another tortfeasor will be governed by the law applicable to his tortious liability to the claimant. This provision clearly covers the situation of a contribution claim where there has been at least a partial satisfaction of the claim, but it is thought that a legitimate purposive interpretation would mean that the same law would be applicable to decide questions of contribution before any payment was made, and if not, the same result could be achieved by an appropriate interpretation of the scope of the provision as to division of liability under Art 15(b) (at least in situations where the same law applied to the liability of both tortfeasors). Similarly, it is considered that the words 'liable for the same claim' should not be interpreted so narrowly as to cover only the case of claims which have exactly the same factual and legal basis and the applicable law of which is the same, but that the provision should cover situations, for example, where the injuries of a victim of a road traffic accident have been made worse by negligent medical treatment (even in a different country). Given the apparent intention under Rome II of dealing with at least some forms of contribution claim it is difficult to see how the approach of the English

---

[36] See Chapter 9, Remedies at **9.3.2.5** in relation to awards of multiple damages being contrary to public policy.

[37] Using these terms as defined in the preceding Article which deals with subrogation, where for present purposes they can be taken as equivalent to claimant and tortfeasor.

courts in the pre-Rome II setting to applicable law questions in relation to contribution claims as discussed at **5.2.3.6**(iii) can continue to be correct.

5.2.3   The 1995 Act – Claims arising out of acts or omissions occurring on or after 1 May 1996 and not falling under Rome II

5.2.3.1   Material and temporal scope of the 1995 Act

Part III of the 1995 Act came into force on 1 May 1996, and its rules for determining the applicable law in non-defamation tort-based claims apply to all such claims arising out of acts or omissions occurring on or after that date save to the extent that they fall within the material and temporal scope of Rome II. As set out above, Rome II applies to civil and commercial matters which arise out of events occurring on or after 11 January 2009, so unless a claim falls outside the definition of 'civil and commercial matters' the 1995 Act will not apply to it if the 'event' occurred on or after 11 January 2009 even if the act or omission which gave rise to the event occurred after the Act's entry into force and before 11 January 2009. In the case of claims falling within the material scope of Rome II it will in the vast majority of cases be obvious whether they also fall within its temporal scope, but in a small number of cases, such as ones involving the contraction of illness, identifying the date of the 'event' could be problematic as it will not coincide with the date of the onset of symptoms and it will have preceded the latter by an unknown (and possibly unknowable) number of days.

5.2.3.2   Choice of law rules

The 1995 Act operates by abolishing, save in respect of defamation, the common law double actionability rule and the qualification to it established by *Boys v Chaplin*[38] and developed in *Red Sea Insurance Co v Bouygues SA*[39] (s 10) and replacing it with a general rule for determining the applicable law of the tort (s 11), which can be displaced in particular circumstances (s 12). By s 9(6) the rules for determining the applicable law apply equally to events occurring in England and Wales as they do to events occurring elsewhere, so contrary to the position at common law it would be possible for the applicable law in relation to a claim arising out of a road traffic accident in England to be the law of another country.

---

[38]   [1971] AC 356.
[39]   [1995] 1 AC 190.

5.2.3.3   *The general rule: s 11*

By s 11(1) the general rule is that the applicable law is the law of the country[40] in which the events constituting the tort occur. As with Rome II, the law of a particular country in this context is its internal law, excluding its rules of private international law, the principle of renvoi[41] being excluded by s 9(5). The general rule is easy to apply where all the elements of a tort (relevant act or omission, event caused thereby and the damage resulting from the event) take place in a single country, but because of the possibility of one or more elements occurring in different countries additional rules are set out in s 11(2) to deal with such situations. Where the elements of the events constituting the tort occur in different countries the applicable law under the general rule is to be taken as being:

(a)   the law of the country where an individual was when he sustained injury in the case of a cause of action in respect of personal injury[42] suffered by an individual or death resulting from personal injury (s 11(2)(a));

(b)   the law of the country where the property in question was when it was damaged in the case of a cause of action in respect of damage to property (s 11(2)(b));

(c)   in any other case, the law of the country in which the most significant element or elements occurred (s 11(2)(c)).

The combination of the definition of personal injury and s 11(2)(a) would indicate that the applicable law for a claim by a secondary victim who has suffered nervous shock or some other form of psychiatric damage in consequence of the death of or personal injury to another person which occurred in a different country would not be the law of that other country but the law of the country where the secondary victim was when he or she sustained the psychiatric damage. This result would be different to the result under Rome II (see comments above in relation to Art 15(f) of Rome II).

5.2.3.4   *Displacement of the general rule: s 12*

Under s.12 the law which would be the applicable law under the general rule can be displaced in favour of the law of another country. This can happen in relation to either all the issues which arise in a case or just one or more of them, so the possibility exists of there being a different

---

[40]   The term 'country' is not defined, but it must be taken that separate jurisdictional units of a unitary state such as the United Kingdom or the Unites States of America are all different countries.

[41]   See **5.2.2.3** as to the effect of the principle of renvoi. In the example given there the result would be the same under the 1995 Act.

[42]   By s 11(3) 'personal injury' is defined as including disease or any impairment of physical or mental condition.

applicable law for each of a number of separate issues in a case, so called *dépeçage*, a result which is not possible under the Rome II regime.

The displacement of the law applicable under the general rule will only occur, however, if it appears, as a result of a comparison of the significance of the factors which connect a tort with the country whose law would be applicable under the general rule and the significance of any factors which connect the tort with another country, that it is substantially more appropriate for the issues (or particular issue or issues, as the case may be) to be determined by the law of that other country. The factors which may be taken into account include in particular those related to the parties, to any of the events constituting the tort and to any of the circumstances or consequences of the event.[43] The use of the words 'substantially more appropriate' indicates that there is a significant threshold and that the general rule should not be dislodged easily.

Accordingly, an argument that English law (the applicable law under the general rule) should be displaced in favour of Dutch law in relation to the issue of assessment of damages was rejected by the Court of Appeal in *Roerig v Valiant Trawlers Ltd*,[44] where a claim under the Fatal Accidents Act 1976 was brought on behalf of the Dutch widow and dependants of a Dutch seaman employed by a Dutch company who had been fatally injured on an English registered vessel which had been on a fishing expedition to and from a Dutch port.

However, the general rule was displaced in the earlier decision of *Edmunds v Simmonds*,[45] a claim arising out of a road traffic accident in Spain where the claimant and defendant were both English residents on a short holiday together. The defendant was driving a Spanish registered hire car which was insured by a Spanish insurer with the claimant as a passenger when it came into collision with a Spanish registered lorry, also insured by a Spanish insurer, driven by a Spanish national. The preliminary issues before Garland J included not only that of what the applicable law was but also liability. He decided the issue of liability first, finding that the defendant was 100% responsible for the accident, thereby exonerating the Spanish lorry driver of all blame, and went on to hold that the applicable law for the purposes of quantum was English law because it was substantially more appropriate for that to be the applicable law; the factors such as the nationality or residence of the parties and England being the place where the claimant's damages arose were 'overwhelming' as compared with the factors such as the defendant's insurer being Spanish. Whether his approach of deciding liability first, so that his decision on applicable law was taken in the context of the case being more 'domestic' than it would have been with the issue of the Spanish driver's liability still being live, was correct is open to doubt, and

---

[43] The last paragraph of s 12.
[44] [2002] 1 WLR 2304.
[45] [2001] 1 WLR 1003.

others might find the choice between Spanish law and English law being rather more evenly balanced (particularly if one looked at the claim as a whole rather than just the issue of quantum).[46] However, it is noteworthy that the decision drew no adverse comment in *Roerig*, where Waller LJ said:[47]

> 'One can entirely understand that, if fortuitously two English persons are in a foreign country on holiday and one tortiously injures the other, the significant factors in favour of England being the place by reference to which the damages should be assessed may make it *substantially* more appropriate that damages should be assessed by English law.' (original emphasis)

Notwithstanding Waller LJ's dictum quoted above, the different outcomes in *Roerig* and *Edmunds v Simmonds* with regard to displacement of the general rule are not entirely easy to reconcile. A cynic might say that whether the general rule is displaced or not appears to be very significantly affected by the factor of which law will give the claimant a higher award of damages. However, in practice the decision in *Edmunds v Simmonds* has had a wide influence in both courts and the approach of parties to litigation in similar situations.

5.2.3.5 *Overriding Mandatory provisions and public policy*

By s 14 (3)(a)(ii) nothing in Part III of the 1995 Act authorises the application of a foreign law as the applicable law insofar as to do so would conflict with principles of public policy. The commonest example of a rule of the forum which amounts to a reflection of public policy is the Human Rights Act 1998. it is suggested that for a rule to be part of *public* policy, it needs to be of a more fundamental nature than simply having been government policy at the time it was enacted by Parliament. By s 14(4) the mandatory rules of the law of the forum are also applied in preference to the applicable law. It is difficult to give guidance on the type of rule which is likely to be considered, 'mandatory' and to override the rules of jurisdiction in the 1995 Act, but as this is a matter of construction, it is more likely that such a rule would be found in a statute. One analysis of the decision in *Arab Monetary Fund v Hashim* (discussed under **5.2.3.6**(iii)) is that s 1(6) of the Civil Liability (Contribution) Act 1978 overrides the 1995 Act rules regarding choice of law.

5.2.3.6 *Scope of the applicable law*

(i)   Substance and procedure

By virtue of s 14(3)(b) nothing in the 1995 Act affects any rules of evidence, pleading or practice or authorises questions of procedure in any

---

[46] But, of course, under the 1995 Act *dépeçage* is possible, so one can focus on one or more specific issues.

[47] At 2310D–E.

proceedings to be determined otherwise than in accordance with the law of the forum. This preserves the common law rule that matters of procedure are to be determined exclusively according to the lex fori, but the Act has the effect of making the applicable law govern all substantive matters.

Therefore the applicable law will determine, amongst other things, whether a tort has been committed and whether it is fault based or one of strict liability, what type of damage is necessary to found a cause of action and what heads of damage are recoverable, questions of causation and remoteness, who has title to sue, whether a cause of action survives death (of either the victim or the tortfeasor), whether and in what circumstances a person can be vicariously liable for the tort of another, as well as general defences including contributory negligence (and whether it is a complete or only partial defence). As explained below it will also govern questions of limitation and prescription (but that is by virtue of the effect of the provisions the Foreign Limitation Periods Act 1984 combined with the 1995 Act).

(ii)   The assessment of damages

However, the preservation of the rule that the lex fori governs matters of procedure means that questions of what remedy is to be granted, including the quantification or assessment of damages, are to be determined by the lex fori and not the lex causae. It was held by the House of Lords in *Harding v Wealands*[48] that the word 'procedure' in s 14 of the 1995 Act was to be interpreted according to its meaning in English law at the time the Act was passed and did not have a more restricted meaning in the Act (as had been held by the Court of Appeal). The claimant in the case had suffered very serious injuries in a road traffic accident in New South Wales when a passenger in a car driven by the defendant. The claimant was domiciled in England, but was on holiday with the defendant, who was an Australian national. The car involved belonged to the defendant and was insured by a New South Wales insurance company. New South Wales legislation provided for restrictions on awards of damages in road traffic accident claims, including thresholds for certain types of claim (such as care) and also caps on damages under specific heads of loss. The decision with regard to the scope of procedure had the consequence that English law alone governed the assessment of damages and that no regard was to be had to the restrictions on awards contained in the provisions of the New South Wales statute, which were procedural and therefore of no application in an English court.

(iii)   Contribution claims

Unlike under Rome II there is no express provision dealing with the question of claims for contribution by one tortfeasor ('T1') against

---

[48]   [2007] 2 AC 1.

another tortfeasor ('T2'). As a matter of principle it might be thought that, even in an English court, the availability of a claim for contribution and the circumstances in which it could arise would depend on the availability and basis of such a claim under the law which applied to the substantive issues in the claims by the victim against the two tortfeasors, so that if under the law applicable to the claims which the claimant could make against T1 and T2 there was no possibility of T1 obtaining a contribution from T2, such a claim could not succeed in an English court.

English courts have, however, not given this answer to the question. In *Arab Monetary Fund v Hashim (No 9)*[49] (a decision made before the abolition of the common law double actionability rule by the 1995 Act) Chadwick J held that in an English court the availability of a claim for contribution between tortfeasors depended only on whether the provisions of the Civil Liability (Contribution) Act 1978 established the availability of such a claim and it was unnecessary to decide as a precondition to applying the 1978 Act that the claim fell to be determined by reference to the 1978 Act and not some other system of law by applying rules of private international law. There have been decisions since the regime under the 1995 Act came into force which follow the same approach, including the decision of the Court of Appeal in *Petroleo Brasiliero v Mellitus Shipping Inc (the Baltic Flame)*,[50] where the unavailability in Saudi Arabian law of a contribution claim against a Saudi Arabian third party was held to be immaterial to the viability of a claim under the 1978 Act which was 'unequivocal in its application to all proceedings brought in England'.

5.2.4 Claims arising out of acts or omissions occurring before 1 May 1996: the common law

Although it is relatively unlikely that there will still be existing or new litigation involving foreign accident claims arising out of acts or omissions occurring before 1 May 1996 it is not inconceivable that such claims may present themselves. Long limitation periods, the deferment of time running for limitation purposes until a claimant reaches his or her majority and the possibility of interruption or extension of limitation periods all mean that one cannot completely exclude the possibility of claims from this period cropping up. As explained under the heading 'History of applicable law' above, the common law required double actionability as a general rule. The exception to this established by *Boys v Chaplin*[51] (see above) was developed in subsequent cases and it was eventually established, shortly before the 1995 Act was passed, in the case of *Red Sea Insurance Co v Bouygues*[52] (a decision of the Privy Council on

---

[49]   *The Times*, 11 October 1994.
[50]   [2001] 2 Lloyds Rep 203.
[51]   [1971] AC 356.
[52]   [1995] 1 AC 190.

an appeal from Hong Kong) that in an appropriate case all substantive issues in a case could be determined by reference to the lex loci delicti alone.

5.2.5   Limitation

5.2.5.1   The common law

At common law, in a situation where the double actionability rule came into play (because the cause of action arose out of events which took place outside England and Wales), the distinction between substantive and procedural law was taken to its logical conclusion with regard to the effect which limitation periods had. When applying the principle of double actionability, an English court would pay heed to any rule of English law which was characterised as a procedural rule, but would not take any account of a rule of the foreign law which English law characterised as being procedural. On the other hand, if it appeared that a rule of foreign law was substantive in nature, the English court would give effect to it.

In the context of tort-based personal injury claims the statutory provisions of English law relating to limitation are ones which English law views as procedural, because they simply bar the remedy of court proceedings to enforce the claim rather than extinguish the right, or cause of action, itself. Therefore, as part of the lex fori, they were applied irrespective of the foreign aspects of the action. If there was a limitation provision of the lex loci delicti which appeared also to be procedural, the expiry of the period of limitation under that law would not prevent an action being brought in an English court, but if by its terms it appeared to extinguish the right rather than merely bar the remedy, and was therefore a rule of substantive law, then the expiry of the period meant that no action could succeed in an English court even if the English limitation period had yet to expire.[53] The common law rules are most unlikely[54] to affect any existing or new proceedings as, acting on the basis of the recommendations in a Law Commission report,[55] Parliament intervened in the form of the Foreign Limitation Periods Act 1984, which in turn has been superseded by the provisions of Rome II in relation to more recent cases (see below as to the temporal scope of these pieces of legislation).

---

[53]   If the limitation period under the English (procedural) rule expired before the right became extinguished under the lex causae, then the English rule would prevail.

[54]   'Most unlikely' because the common law rules cannot affect any proceedings brought on or after 1 October 1985 (see below), save in the exceptional case where, under s 2(1) of the Foreign Limitation Periods Act 1984, s 1 of that Act is held not to apply because its application would conflict with public policy (again, see below).

[55]   *Classification of limitation in Private International Law,* Law Com No 114 (TSO, 1982).

5.2.5.2 The Foreign Limitation Periods Act 1984 ('the 1984 Act')

(i) Temporal scope

The 1984 Act applies only to proceedings commenced on or after 1 October 1985 (the date on which it came into force),[56] and it does not apply to any matter if the limitation period which would have applied to it apart from the 1984 Act expired before 1 October 1985.[57] Its substantive provisions (ss 1, 2 and 4) are disapplied in situations where Rome II applies,[58] which in essence means civil and commercial matters arising out of events occurring on or after 11 January 2009 (see above). It can therefore apply to both claims governed by the common law and ones governed by the 1995 Act.

(ii) Effect of the 1984 Act

Section 1 has the effect, in the case of proceedings before an English court where the law of any country other than England and Wales falls to be taken into account in the determination of any matter, of changing the rules to be applied with regard to limitation. Its exact effect varies according to whether one is concerned with a claim to which the 1995 Act applies or a claim subject to the double actionability rule. In the former case, where there is a single lex causae, it states that the law relating to limitation[59] of that other country shall apply in those proceedings to the exclusion of English law in that area. This means that in such a case the foreign law is to be used to determine questions of limitation, irrespective of whether its provisions are characterised as substantive or procedural, and even if the provisions of English law which would otherwise be applicable are substantive, they will not affect the matter.[60] In the latter case, where there are two leges causae (one of which is English law), the foreign law relating to limitation also applies to the proceedings, but the exclusion of English law relating to limitation does not apply. This has the effect that the proceedings will be time barred if they would be time barred under either English law or the foreign law.[61]

---

[56] Section 7(3)(a).

[57] Section 7(3)(b).

[58] Section 8 (inserted by SI 2008/2986).

[59] What is meant by law relating to limitation is defined in s 4.

[60] This is certainly the effect in the paradigm case under the 1995 Act where there will be only one lex causae. If, however, the general rule is displaced under s 12 in relation to at least one issue in the case in favour of English law, on a literal reading of s 2(2) the case would appear to fall under that subsection (as both English law and the law of some other country would fall to be taken into account in the determination of the matter) with the result that English law relating to limitation would apply in the same way as it would in relation to a paradigm common law case.

[61] Again, this description of the effect of the 1984 Act is certainly correct in relation to a paradigm common law double actionability case, because there will be two leges causae, one of which will be English law. However, if under the exception to the general double actionability rule as exemplified by the *Red Sea Insurance* case [1995] 1 AC 190 only the foreign law is to be applied, so that there is only one lex causae (and that is not English

(iii)   Other material provisions

The following matters should be noted. First, by s 1(5) the renvoi is excluded.

Secondly, by s 1(3), even in a case where the law of limitation of another country applies, English law provisions will apply for the purposes of determining whether and at what time proceedings have been commenced and accordingly s 35 of the Limitation Act 1980 will apply in relation to time-limits applicable under the foreign law in the same way that it applies to time-limits under that Act.

Thirdly, by s 1(4) an English court is required, so far as is practicable, to exercise any discretion which is conferred by any foreign law in the same way that the courts of the foreign country would exercise it in comparable cases.

Fourthly, by s 2(1), if the application of s 1 would to any extent conflict with public policy, that section shall not apply to the extent that such conflict arises. What is meant by a conflict with public policy is partially defined in s 2(2), which provides that there will be a conflict to the extent that the application of s 1 would cause undue hardship to any person who is or might be a party to proceedings. As noted above, the effect of s 1 being disapplied under this provision is that the common law rules with regard to the effect of limitation provisions will apply.

Fifthly, s 2(3) imposes a restriction on the applicability of certain provisions of a foreign law which allow for the extension or interruption of a limitation period. Provisions which extend or interrupt a limitation period on the basis of the absence of any party to the proceedings from a specified country or jurisdiction are to be disregarded.

(iv)   Pleading and proving foreign limitation law.

It should be remembered that it will be necessary to plead the effect of any foreign law as to limitation relied on, and unless all material allegations about the foreign law in question are unconditionally admitted it will also be necessary to adduce expert evidence from a lawyer qualified in the relevant jurisdiction.

---

law), then it would seem that the effect of the 1984 Act would be that only the law relating to limitation of the lex causae would be applicable.

5.2.5.3 *Rome II*

(i) Temporal scope

The provisions of Rome II relating to questions of limitation will apply to proceedings involving civil and commercial matters which arise out of events occurring on or after 11 January 2009.

(ii) Material provisions

By Art 15(h) the law applicable to the tort governs the 'rules of prescription and limitation, including rules relating to the commencement, interruption and suspension of a period of prescription or limitation'. This has the effect of importing wholesale the rules relating to limitation under the applicable law and excluding the limitation law of the forum.

Although the effect of this provision is broadly similar to the position which, by virtue of the combination of the 1984 Act and the 1995 Act, existed immediately before Rome II began to apply, two differences should be noted. First, there is no restriction on the application in certain respects of the rules relating to the extension and interruption of periods of limitation as provided for by s 2(3) of the 1984 Act. Secondly, although Art 15(h) is subject to the public policy exception under Art 26, that exception is probably narrower than the public policy exception under s 2(1) of the 1984 Act, which was engaged if 'undue hardship' was caused to a party. It is doubtful whether all instances of undue hardship which would engage the public policy exception under the 1984 Act would be sufficient to justify refusing to apply a foreign law on the basis of public policy under Rome II given the requirement under Art 26 that the foreign rule must be 'manifestly incompatible' with the public policy of the forum.

(iii) Pleading and proving foreign limitation law

The same considerations as arise in relation to cases governed by the 1984 Act also arise in ones governed by Rome II.[62]

5.3 CONTRACT

5.3.1 History of applicable law

As in the above section dealing with tort-based claims, the term 'applicable law' is used because that is the concept and terminology which is used in the successive pieces of legislation which have replaced the common law rules in this area of private international law. At common

---

[62] See **5.2.5.2**.

law, in a case where the claim was founded on contract and there were features of the case which were not entirely domestic in nature, the concept of the 'proper law of the contract' was used for determining what system of law should govern the questions which might arise in the claim. In general, subject to any considerations of public policy, an express choice of law would determine what the proper law of the contract was. In the absence of an effective express choice the court would look for indicia from the terms and nature of the contract and from the general circumstances of the case as to what the intention of the parties had been as to which system of law should govern their contract.

If there was no express choice and the parties' intention could not be inferred from the circumstances, the proper law of the contract would be the law with which the transaction had its closest and most real connection.

The rules of the common law were in general superseded by the provisions of the Rome Convention[63] in relation to contracts concluded after 1 April 1991, and this in turn has been superseded by the provisions of Regulation (EC) 593/2008 of the European Parliament and of the Council ('Rome I') in relation to contracts concluded on or after 17 December 2009.[64] As with the section above in relation to tort-based claims, because of the ever diminishing applicability of the earlier regimes they will be dealt with in reverse chronological order, followed by a separate section dealing with limitation.

5.3.2 Contracts concluded after 17 December 2009: Rome I

5.3.2.1 *Material scope*

In harmony with Brussels I and Rome II, Art 1(1) provides that Rome I applies to civil and commercial matters and expressly excludes revenue, customs and administrative matters from its scope. Art 1(2) contains a number of additional excluded matters, the only ones of real potential significance to personal injury claims being the exclusion of arbitration agreements and agreements on the choice of courts (Art 1(2)(c)).[65] By Art 1(3) it does not apply to evidence and procedure (but, as with Rome II, procedure has a narrower meaning here than it does at common law in the light of subsequent provisions regarding the scope of the applicable law).

---

[63] Given the force of law by the Contracts (Applicable Law) Act 1990.

[64] Notwithstanding recital 45 to Rome I, which records that the United Kingdom was not participating in the adoption of the Regulation and was not bound by or subject to its application, Rome I does apply to the whole of the United Kingdom as the Government notified the European Commission that it intended to opt into the Regulation, and the Commission decided by Decision 2009/26/EC that Rome I would apply to the United Kingdom.

[65] As these are also excluded from the scope of the Rome Convention, the choice of law in relation to them will be governed by common law principles.

The non-participation of Denmark in the adoption of Rome I (see recital 46), has no impact on its effect in England and Wales, save that, except in Articles 3(4) and 7, the term 'member state' does not include Denmark.[66]

As with Rome II, the law to be applied need not be that of a member state (Art 2) and one of a number of distinct territorial units of a state which has its own rules in respect of contractual obligations is considered to be a separate country for the purposes of identifying the applicable law (Art 22(1)). By virtue of Art 22(2) the United Kingdom was not required to apply Rome I to conflicts between the laws of its constituent parts, but it has chosen to do so, save with regard to insurance contracts falling within Art 7.[67]

5.3.2.2 Temporal scope

By Art 28, Rome I applies to all contracts within its material scope which were concluded after 17 December 2009.

5.3.2.3 Choice of law rules

As with Rome II the renvoi is excluded (Art 20), so the law of the country which is applicable under the rules contained in Rome I does not include the rules of private international law of that country.

Party autonomy and freedom of choice are the starting points for determining the applicable law. but there are a significant number of limitations to those principles. There are two Articles (3 and 4) which provide general rules, but these are subject to Arts 5 to 8, in which special rules are set out dealing with specific classes of contract (contracts of carriage, consumer contracts, insurance contracts and individual employment contracts respectively).

The rules relating to insurance contracts (both under Rome I and the previous regimes) are dealt with in the chapter on direct actions against insurers. This is due to the materiality which the availability of a direct right of action against an insurer under the applicable law of a contract of insurance can have for the existence of jurisdiction over an insurer domiciled in another member state (or a Lugano Convention state) under the *Odenbreit*[68] principle.

5.3.2.4 The general rules: Arts 3 and 4

Article 3 deals with the situation where there has been a choice of applicable law, either expressly or 'clearly demonstrated by the terms of

---

[66] Article 1(4).
[67] See SI 2009/3064, reg 5; SI 2009/3075, reg 3; SSI 2009/410 (Scotland); SI 2001/2365.
[68] (C-463/06) [2007] ECR 1–11321.

the contract or the circumstances of the case', and Art 4 deals with situations where there is no such choice.

Under Art 3(1), the applicable law will be that chosen by the parties, and they are free to choose different laws to apply to different parts of the contract. By Art3(2), the parties may agree to subject the contract to a law different to the one which previously governed it, but such a change made after the conclusion of the contract shall not affect its formal validity or prejudice the rights of third parties.

The freedom of choice granted by Art 3(1) and (2) is however restricted by Art 3(3) and (4). If all the other elements relevant to the situation at the time that the choice is made are located in a country other than the one whose law has been chosen, under Art 3(3) that choice of law shall not prejudice the application of provisions of the law of that other country which cannot be derogated from by agreement. Article 3(4) addresses a similar situation in relation to EU law, and it is engaged if all the other elements relevant to the situation at the time that the choice is made are located *in one or more* member states, in which case a choice of law other than that of a member state shall not prejudice the application of provisions of Community law (where appropriate as implemented in the member state of the forum) which cannot be derogated from by agreement.

The classes of contract for which Art 4 provides rules in the absence of choice which are of potential relevance for personal injury claims are as follows.

5.3.2.5 *Special types of contract*

(a)   Sale of goods.

Under Art 4(1)(a) a contract for the sale of goods (other than a sale of goods by auction, which is dealt with by Art 4(1)(h)) is governed by the law of the country in which the seller has his habitual residence. The term 'habitual residence' is partially defined in Art 19 in terms which are equivalent to the partial definition given in Art 23 of Rome II, with the additional provision that the relevant point in time for determining habitual residence is the time of the conclusion of the contract. There is therefore no definition of habitual residence for a natural person not acting in the course of any business activity.

(b)   Provision of services.

By Art 4(1)(b) a contract for the provision of services shall be governed by the law of the country where the service provider has his habitual residence.

(c)   Tenancies of immovable property.

Under Art 4(1)(c) and (d) a contract relating to a right in rem in immovable property or to a tenancy of immovable property shall be governed by the law of the country where the property is situated, unless the contract relates to a tenancy of immovable property concluded for temporary private use for a period of no more than 6 consecutive months, in which case it shall be governed by the law of the country where the landlord has his habitual residence, provided that the tenant is a natural person and has his habitual residence in the same country.[69]

(d)   Sale of goods by auction.

By Art 4(1)(h) a contract for the sale of goods by auction shall be governed by the law of the country where the auction takes place, if such a place can be determined.

(e)   Cases not covered by Art 4(1) or covered by more than one of Art 4(1)(a) to (h).

By Art 4(2) such contracts in such cases are governed by the law of the country in which the party required to effect the characteristic performance of the contract has his habitual residence.

5.3.2.6   *The 'escape clause': Art 4(3)*

If it is clear from all the circumstances of the case that the contract is manifestly more closely connected with a country other than that indicated by Art 4(1) or (2), the law of that other country will apply. This is the equivalent of the escape clause in Rome II (also Art 4(3)), and is also only to be brought into operation by exceptional cases.

5.3.2.7   *Where the law cannot be determined by Art 4(1) or (2): Art 4(4)*

This is a mop up clause designed to deal with contracts which do not fall exclusively into one of the specific categories under Art 4(1) and in respect of which an applicable law cannot be determined by the rule under Art 4(2). In relation to such a contract the applicable law will be the law of the country with which it is most closely connected.

---

[69]   These provisions correspond with the provisions under Art 22(1) relating to exclusive jurisdiction under Brussels I, and reference should be made to the relevant part of the chapter on jurisdiction for fuller commentary.

5.3.2.8   *Contracts of carriage: Art 5*

Article 5 does not apply to contracts relating to package travel, which are dealt with under Art 6 (consumer contracts). Subject to that, and to what follows below with regard to international conventions, it is considered that a contract which provides, in addition to carriage simpliciter, other services which are no more than ancillary to the carriage will also be governed by Art 5.[70] It is only if the additional services exceed what can properly be called ancillary that it would be said that the contract has moved from being simply a contract of carriage and therefore one which falls outside the category of 'a contract of carriage'.

It should also be noted that because, by Art 25(1), Rome I shall not prejudice the application of international conventions to which one or more member states were party when the Regulation was adopted which lay down conflict of laws rules relating to contractual obligations, Art 5 will not apply to contracts which come within the scope of such conventions, for example the Montreal Convention.[71] An alternative basis for Art 5 not being applicable in relation to contracts falling within the scope of such international conventions is Art 9, on the grounds that they constitute overriding mandatory provisions.

Contracts for the carriage of goods and contracts for the carriage of passengers are dealt with differently by Art 5. In relation to the former, Art 5(1) provides that the parties are free to agree an applicable law in accordance with Art 3, but if they have not so agreed, then the applicable law will be that of the country in which the carrier has his habitual residence, as long as the place of receipt or the place of delivery or the place of the habitual residence of the consignor is located in the same country. If those requirements are not met, then the applicable law will be that of the country where the agreed place of delivery is located. With regard to the latter, Art 5(2) restricts the parties' freedom to agree an applicable law in accordance with Art 3 to the law of the country of (i) the passenger's habitual residence, (ii) the carrier's habitual residence, (iii) the carrier's place of central administration, (iv) the place of departure or (v) the place of destination. If they have not so agreed, the applicable law will be that of the country where the passenger has his habitual residence, provided that the either the place of departure or the place of destination is situated in that country. If those requirements are not met, then the applicable law will be that of the country where the carrier has his habitual residence.

---

[70]   See Chapter 2 on package travel contracts at **2.3.3** for a discussion as to what will be considered significant enough to exceed being 'merely ancillary' to some other service.

[71]   See Chapters 7 and 8 for a discussion of the jurisdiction rules in relation to both Athens and Montreal Conventions.

In relation to all contracts of carriage within Art 5 there is also an escape clause (Art 5(3)), which provides that, in the absence of a choice of law,[72] if it is clear from all the circumstances of the case that the contract is manifestly more closely connected with a country other than that indicated in Art 5(1) or (2), the law of that other country shall apply. Again, this escape clause will only be engaged in exceptional cases.

5.3.2.9 *Consumer contracts: Art 6*

Article 6 governs the choice of applicable law in respect of certain types of contracts between a consumer (a natural person who has concluded a contract for a purpose which can be regarded as being outside his trade or profession) and a professional (a person acting in the exercise of his trade or profession). In the case of such a contract, unless it is excluded expressly by Art 6(4) or is an insurance contract within Art 7, and subject to an agreement as to applicable law which is allowed by Art 6(2), the applicable law will be that of the country of habitual residence of the consumer, provided that the professional (i)(a) pursues his commercial or professional activities in the country where the consumer has his habitual residence or (b) by any means directs such activities to that country or to several countries including that country and (ii) in either case the contract falls within the scope of such activities.[73]

Contracts expressly excluded by Art 6(4) which are material to personal injury claims are:

(i)   contracts for the supply of services where the services are to be supplied to the consumer exclusively in a country other than that where he has his habitual residence;[74]
(ii)   contracts of carriage other than those relating to package travel within the meaning of Council Directive 90/314/EEC of 13 June 1990[75] (thus relevant package travel contracts are within the scope of Art 6 and not Art 5); and
(iii)   contracts relating to a right in rem in immovable property or a tenancy of immovable property other than a contract relating to the right to use immovable property on a timeshare basis within the meaning of Directive 94/47/EC.[76]

The conditions for the application under Art 6(1) of the law of the country of the consumer's habitual residence in the absence of any valid choice of law and the restriction under Art 6(2) on the parties' freedom with regard to a choice of applicable law (see below) are the same mutatis

---

[72]   Which must be in accordance with Art 3, and in the case of the carriage of passengers also subject to the restrictions imposed by the second paragraph of Art 5(2).
[73]   Article 6(1).
[74]   Article 6(4)(a).
[75]   Article 6(4)(b).
[76]   Article 6(4)(c).

mutandis as some of the conditions for the application of the special consumer contracts regime under Brussels I (Arts 15 to 17). Reference should be made to the relevant part of the chapter on jurisdiction for a detailed commentary as to how these conditions are to be interpreted, in particular with regard to contracts which have a dual purpose and with regard to the professional directing his commercial or professional activities to the country of the consumer's habitual residence.

By Art 6(2) a departure from the default position under Art 6(1) is possible by an agreement in accordance with Art 3, but such an agreement will not be effective to deprive the consumer of the protection afforded to him by provisions which, in the absence of choice, would have been applicable by virtue of Art 6(1) and cannot be derogated from by agreement.

In relation to a contract between a consumer and a professional[77] which would fall within Art 6(1) if either of the provisos in Art 6(1) were fulfilled,[78] but in relation to which neither proviso is in fact fulfilled, it is provided by Art 6(3) that the applicable law will be determined pursuant to Arts 3 and 4.

5.3.2.10   *Individual contracts of employment: Art 8*

Article 8 is concerned with identifying the applicable law in the case of contracts of employment for individuals; it does not apply to collective agreements between employers and employees. Article 8(2) to (4) sets out rules for determining the applicable law of a contract of employment in the absence of a choice made by the parties, but under Art 8(1), although the parties are free to choose the applicable law of an individual contract of employment in accordance with Art 3, such a choice will not have the result of depriving the employee of the protection of provisions which cannot be derogated from under the law which would have applied, in the absence of choice, under Art 8(2) to (4).

By Art 8(2) the applicable law will be the law of the country in which or, failing that, from which the employee habitually carries out his work in performance of the contract. The words 'or, failing that, from which' have been incorporated in order to reflect the effect of decisions of the CJEU in relation to Art 18 of Brussels I. The second sentence of Art 8(2) makes it clear that temporary employment in another country will not change the position with regard to the country in which the employee's work is habitually carried out for the purposes of Art 8(2).

By Art 8(3), if the applicable law cannot be determined pursuant to Art 8(2), the contract will be governed by the law of the country where the

---

[77]   These terms are to have the meaning given to them under Art 6(1).
[78]   This will not include a contract excluded by Art 6(4) or an insurance contract within Art 7.

place of business through which the employee was engaged is situated. This provision will apply only in a very narrow range of situations given the wide scope of Art 8(2). Even if an employee works in a number of different countries (such as an airline pilot), he will normally have a base or somewhere which can be considered to be the centre of his activities, so there will be a country 'from which' he habitually carried out his work.

Article 8(4) provides a rule of displacement for the rules under Art 8(2) and (3) if it appears from the circumstances as a whole that a contract is more closely connected with a country other than that indicated by either of those Articles. In such a case, the law of that other country will be applicable.

5.3.2.11   Scope of the applicable law: Art 12

Art 12(1) sets out the matters which, in particular, are to be governed by the applicable law. They are:

(a)   the interpretation of the contract;[79]
(b)   the performance of the contract;[80]
(c)   within the limits of the powers conferred on the court by its procedural law, the consequences of a total or partial breach of obligations, including the assessment of damages insofar as it is governed by rules of law;[81]
(d)   the various ways of extinguishing obligations, and prescription and limitation of actions;[82]
(e)   the consequences of nullity of the contract.

In addition, Art 12(2) provides that in relation to the manner of performance and the steps to be taken in the event of defective performance, regard shall be had to the law of the country in which performance takes place.

The non-exhaustive list of matters which are to be governed by the applicable law reflects the general principle that the applicable law governs substantive matters, but that matters of procedure and evidence are for the lex fori. This general principle is, however, subject to some exceptions. First, there is the provision under Art 18(1) regarding rules which raise presumptions of law or determine the burden of proof, which is identical in effect to Art 22(1) of Rome II (see above). Secondly, the use of the applicable law in relation to questions of limitation involves moving the line between substance and procedure from where English law traditionally drew it, as limitation provisions which bar a remedy rather than extinguishing a right are seen as purely procedural in the eyes of

---

[79]   Article 12(a).
[80]   Article 12(b).
[81]   Article 12(c).
[82]   Article 12(d).

English law. However, Art 12(1)(d), like its predecessor under the Rome Convention,[83] does not change the position from what it would otherwise be under English law, because of the Foreign Limitation Periods Act 1984, the effect of which in contractual claims was to make the lex causae rather than the lex fori govern matters of limitation.

Thirdly, it would appear that a change has been made to the English law position that the assessment or quantification of damages is a question of remedy and therefore procedural. The language used in Rome I (ie that the applicable law shall govern 'the assessment of damages in so far as it is governed by rules of law') is the same as was used in the Rome Convention, but is not as clear as it might be. The qualification 'in so far as it is governed by rules of law' does not appear in the equivalent provision in Rome II (Art 15(c)), where the intention, and therefore the effect, is accordingly rather clearer. However, it is clear that the lex causae is to have relevance to the assessment of damages and one possible interpretation of the qualification is that it merely emphasises that questions of fact remain exclusively within the sphere of the lex fori.

5.3.2.12   Overriding mandatory provisions and public policy: Arts 9 and 21

The term 'overriding mandatory provisions' is defined in Art 9(1) as:

> '... provisions, the respect of which is regarded as crucial by a country for safeguarding its public interests, such as its political, social or economic organisation, to such an extent that they are applicable to any situation falling within their scope, irrespective of the law otherwise applicable to the contract under this Regulation.'

By Art 9(2), nothing in Rome I shall restrict the application of the overriding mandatory provisions of the law of the forum, but as is made clear by recital 37, exceptional circumstances will be required to justify the use of provisions of the law of the forum on the basis that they are overriding mandatory provisions.

The wording of the public policy exception under Art 21 is exactly the same as the equivalent under Rome II (Art 26), and it is therefore also restricted to situations where the application of a foreign rule of law would be 'manifestly incompatible' with the public policy of the forum. Again, recital 37 makes it clear that exceptional circumstances are required for this exception to be invoked.

5.3.2.13   Contribution claims: Art 16

Rome I contains a provision similar to that in Rome II (Art 20) with regard to the law applicable to claims by one debtor against another

---

[83]   Article 10(1)(d) of the Rome Convention.

debtor of the same creditor. It is stated that the law governing the obligation of the debtor who has wholly or partly satisfied the creditor is to govern that debtor's right to claim recourse from any other debtor.

5.3.3 Contracts concluded on or before 17 December 2009: the Rome Convention and the common law

For the reasons given above under the section dealing with Rome I, the following treatment does not deal with insurance contracts, which are dealt with in the chapter on direct actions against insurers.

5.3.3.1 The Rome Convention

Material scope

In the context of claims arising out of accidents abroad the material scope of the Rome Convention is no different to that of Rome I, save that by Art 1(3) and (4) it does not apply to contracts of insurance which cover risks situated in the territories of the member states of the European Economic Community (other than contracts of re-insurance).[84] Therefore, subject to that exclusion, it applies to contracts generally, with the material exceptions for present purposes of arbitration agreements and agreements on the choice of court (Art 1(2)(d)). Without prejudice to Art 14 (presumptions of law and burden of proof) it does not apply to evidence and procedure (Art 1(2)(h)).

The law specified as being applicable need not be the law of one of the contracting states (Art 2), and as with Rome I, one of a number of distinct territorial units of a state which has its own rules in respect of contractual obligations is considered to be a separate country (Art 19(1)). The Rome Convention rules apply as to conflicts between England and Wales, Scotland and Northern Ireland (s 2(3) of the 1990 Act).

Temporal scope

In relation to contracts within its material scope, the Rome Convention determines the applicable law of any contract which was concluded after 1 April 1991 and on or before 17 December 2009.

Choice of law rules

The principle of renvoi is excluded (Art 15).

The overall scheme of the choice of law rules is very similar to that under Rome I, which is a development from and refinement of the Rome

---

[84] See the chapter on direct actions against insurers for the effect of this exception and the parallel scheme which was introduced after the Rome Convention was enacted into English law.

Convention. Accordingly, the following account will focus on drawing attention to the differences as compared to Rome I rather than repeating what has been set out above in relation to the Rome I scheme.

As with Rome I, there are general rules (Arts 3 and 4), which are either displaced or modified if the contract falls within one of the special regimes for specified types of consumer contracts or employment contracts.

The general rules: Arts 3 and 4

The rules under Art 3, with the starting point of freedom of choice, are identical to those under Rome I, save that the restriction under Art 3(4) of Rome I with regard to non-derogable provisions of Community law is absent. The rules under Art 4, which are to be used in the absence of a choice by the parties, are, however, quite different from those under Art 4 of Rome I.

By Art 4(1), in the absence of choice by the parties in accordance with Art 3, a contract will be governed by the law of the country with which it is most closely connected. The second sentence of Art 4(1) contemplates that exceptionally a severable part of a contract may be governed by the law of another country if that severable part has a close connection with that other country. Article 4(1) is then supplemented by a series of sub-Articles which provide presumptions in certain situations as to the country with which the contract is most closely connected.

By Art 4(2), there is a presumption, which is subject to the subsequent paragraphs of Art 4, that a contract is most closely connected with the country where the party who is to effect the performance which is characteristic of the contract has his habitual residence,[85] or in the case of a corporate or incorporate body, has its central administration. However, if the contract is entered into in the course of that party's trade or profession, that country shall be the country in which the party's principal place of business is situated or, where under the terms of the contract the performance is to be effected through a place of business other than the principal place of business, the country in which that other place of business is situated.

In the case of personal injury claims the likelihood is that the contracts concerned will be ones for the provision of services or goods, and in such cases the performance which is characteristic of the contract will be the provision of the goods or services and not the payment for them. Accordingly, in cases which do not fall within the special regime for

---

[85]   The term 'habitual residence' is not defined in the Rome Convention, but as in other places where it is undefined in respect of individuals not acting in the course of his business activity, it is likely that it means much the same as 'domicile' as that term is understood in most civil law systems.

consumer contracts (see below), the applicable law in such cases will be determined by the habitual residence etc of the provider of the goods or services.

Article 4(3) overrides the presumption in Art 4(2) in the case of a contract whose subject matter is a right in, or a right to use, immovable property, in which case it is to be presumed that the contract is most closely connected with the country where the immovable property is situated.

Article 4(4) provides that the presumption under Art 4(2) shall not apply to a contract for the carriage of goods. Such contracts will not be relevant in personal injury cases.

Article 4(5) provides that if the performance which is characteristic of the contract cannot be determined, then Art 4(2) shall not apply, so in the absence of the presumption specified therein Art 4(1) will apply on its own and the applicable law will be the law of the country with which the contract is most closely connected. Article 4(5) also provides that if in any case to which one of the presumptions under Art 4(2) to (4) applies it appears from the circumstances as a whole that the contract is more closely connected with a country other than the one to which the presumption points, then the presumption shall be disregarded.

Certain consumer contracts: Art 5

By Art 5(1) the special regime for certain consumer contracts applies to contracts the object of which is the supply of goods or services to a person ('the consumer') for a purpose which can be regarded as being outside his trade of profession, or a contract for the provision of credit for that object, but by Art 5(4) the regime does not apply to a contract of carriage (other than a contract which, for an inclusive price, provides for a combination of travel and accommodation)[86] or a contract for the supply of services where the services are to be supplied to the consumer exclusively in a country other than the one in which he has his habitual residence. The decisions of the CJEU in relation to dual purpose contracts in the context of Arts 15 to 17 of Brussels I discussed in the chapter on jurisdiction will be relevant here if the contract is not, or may appear not to be, for exclusively non-business purposes.

In relation to a contract with a consumer which is within the special regime the parties are free to agree a choice of law in accordance with Art 3, but in the case of any of the following situations it is provided by Art 6(2) that such choice shall not have the result of depriving the consumer of the protection afforded to him by the mandatory rules[87] of the country in which he has his habitual residence:

---

[86] This exception to the exclusion under Art 5(4) is provided by Art 5(5).
[87] Here, as elsewhere in the Rome Convention, 'mandatory rules' are the rules of the law of a country which cannot be derogated from by contract: see Art 3(3). They are not the

(i)   where in the country of the consumer's habitual residence the conclusion of the contract was preceded by a specific invitation addressed to him or by advertising, and he had taken all the steps necessary on his part for the conclusion of the contract in that country;

(ii)   where the consumer's order was received by the other party or his agent in the country of the consumer's habitual residence; or

(iii) where the contract is for the sale of goods and the consumer travelled from the country of his habitual residence to another country and gave his order there, provided that the consumer's journey was arranged by the seller for the purpose of inducing the consumer to buy.

If in relation to a contract within the special regime for consumers one of the three above situations applies and there has been no choice of law by the parties, by Art 6(3) the contract will be governed by the law of the country in which the consumer has his habitual residence.

Individual employment contracts: Art 6

The effect of Art 6 is in substance the same as the provisions for individual contracts of employment at Art 8 of Rome II, although the structure of the rules is different. The only difference of significance in the differently structured and worded Art 6 in the Rome Convention is that the refinement in Rome I of the added words 'or, failing that, from which' (introduced in order to reflect the approach of the CJEU in relation to the equivalent provisions in Brussels I regarding jurisdiction in individual employment situations) is absent. The absence of these words should not, however, cause the Article as a whole to be interpreted differently from Rome I.

Scope of the applicable law

Art 10 contains identical provision to the ones under Art 12 of Rome I, and accordingly reference should be made to the above discussion in relation to that Article. It should, however, be noted that Art 10(e), unlike its equivalent in Art 12(e) of Rome I, does not apply in the United Kingdom (see s 2(2) of the 1990 Act).

Mandatory rules and 'ordre public' (public policy): Arts 7(2) and 16

The effect of these provisions is identical to the equivalent Articles in Rome I (Arts 9 and 21 – see above).

---

same as 'overriding mandatory provisions' within Art 9 of Rome II, which have their equivalent in the Rome Convention at Art 7(2). Note that Art 7(1) does not apply in the United Kingdom (s 2(2) of the 1990 Act).

Contribution claims: Art 13(2)

Art 13(2), when read together with Art 13(1), makes a similar provision to that under Art 16 of Rome I (see above) with regard to contribution claims between persons who are subject to the same contractual claim, save that in the case of Art 13(2) the rule speaks of the person who is seeking contribution having satisfied the creditor (the natural meaning of which is full satisfaction), but in Art 16 of Rome I the rule is engaged also in the case of partial satisfaction of the creditor.

5.3.3.2 The common law

Temporal and material scope

The rules of the common law with regard to the identification of the proper law of the contract will not apply to contracts concluded after 1 April 1991 (save for those which are excluded from the material scope of the Rome Convention and Rome I). Although this could mean that some insurance contracts concluded after that date are governed by the common law rules, it will be very rare now that such contracts will be relevant in personal injury cases because they will already be relatively old.

In practical terms it is only claims arising out of employment contracts which could still require reference to the position at common law, as the relationship of employer and employee could have commenced years, if not decades, before the events giving rise to a claim occur. The basic rules of the common law are summarised sufficiently for present day practical purposes under the heading of 'History of applicable law' above. If further detail is required it is recommended that recourse is had to earlier editions of standard works on conflicts of laws, such as the 13th and earlier editions of *Dicey & Morris*.

Scope of the proper law of the contract

At common law the proper law of the contract governed the substantive issues in the case, but questions of procedure were governed entirely by the lex fori, and in this respect the traditional line drawn by English law between substance and procedure was fully respected, subject only to the effect of the Foreign Limitation Periods Act 1984 after it came into force on 1 October 1984 (see below under 'Limitation').

5.3.4 Limitation

At common law the situation with regard to limitation in relation to contract-based claims was the same as it was in relation to tort-based claims. An English court would always apply English statutory provisions relating to limitation on the grounds that they were characterised as procedural, but if there were provisions relating to limitation under the proper law of the contract which an English court characterised as substantive because they extinguished the right of action rather than just barring the remedy, then effect would be given to them if the limitation period set by them expired before any limitation period under English law. The 1984 Act, discussed above under the section relating to tort, applied equally to contract-based claims, but in such cases that Act was superseded first by the Rome Convention and then subsequently by Rome I. As with tort-based claims, the common law principles cannot affect any proceedings commenced after 1 October 1985 (the date when the 1984 Act came into force), save where, in a case in which the 1984 Act applies (because, for example, the contract in question was concluded on or before 1 April 1991 so that the Rome Convention does not apply to it), s 1 of that Act is held not to apply because its application would conflict with public policy.

5.3.4.1   The 1984 Act

The 1984 Act is discussed in detail in the above section dealing with tort-based claims. By s 8 of the Act it is expressly disapplied in relation to cases where Rome I applies,[88] and it can be of no effect in relation to contracts within the scope of the Rome Convention as the latter's provisions with regard to limitation override it (although the effect is in substance the same). Because in the case of contractual claims there is only one lex causae, its effect in cases where the proper law of the contract was not English law was to make the limitation law of the lex causae apply to proceedings in England and Wales (and to exclude the application of the English law of limitation).

5.3.4.2   The Rome Convention and Rome I

As noted above in the respective passages dealing with the scope of the applicable law under each of these instruments, they both provide expressly that the applicable law of the contract is to govern matters of limitation.

---

[88]   Amended by SI 2009/3064.

CHAPTER 6

DIRECT ACTIONS AGAINST INSURERS

Howard Stevens QC and Alexander Halban

6.1 INTRODUCTION

When an individual suffers illness or accident, he is usually able to sue the person responsible for the wrongful acts or omissions which caused his loss. The advent of widespread third party liability insurance, particularly in the field of motor accidents, has created a new feature in the landscape of English law, namely the right to bring action directly against the wrongdoer's insurer.

This chapter addresses the rights of action which exist directly against an insurer before the courts of England and Wales. Where an accident occurs abroad and an insurer is domiciled outside England and Wales but inside the EU, generous special rules of jurisdiction in favour of the injured party permit the English courts to determine many claims. In these circumstances, notwithstanding the fact that the English courts are a permissible forum, it is, nevertheless, more likely that foreign law will apply to some or all the issues in the claim. There are limited circumstances under which English law provides for a claim to be pursued directly against the insurer. This chapter focuses on cross-border cases, when it is necessary to use the rules of private international law to determine which law applies to a case or to issues in a case, and whether the injured party can rely on a direct right of action existing within that law against the insurer of the person liable. It also deals with some of the practical implications of litigating a claim before the English courts, but utilising a foreign law.

6.1.1 History: direct action against insurers

Until relatively recently, English law provided for limited direct action against insurers only in cases where the wrongdoer was insolvent.[1] In all other cases, the claim could only be brought against the wrongdoer. In practice, the insurer would conduct the litigation in the name of the insured wrongdoer and would satisfy any judgment in favour of the injured party directly. This practice did not preclude an insurer from refusing to provide an indemnity to his policyholder in accordance with the policy terms (and the limitations of the general law).

---

[1]   Third Parties (Rights Against Insurers) Act 1930.

The position in England and Wales can be contrasted to that of some civil law jurisdictions in Europe, where direct rights of action against insurers have existed for decades. In France and Spain, individuals are able to bring a claim directly against an insurer where they are providing public liability insurance. In addition, direct actions also exist in some international conventions, such as the Hague Convention on the Law Applicable to Traffic Accidents 1971[2] and the 2002 Protocol to the Athens Convention.[3]

The introduction of the Fourth Motor Insurance Directive in 2000 resulted in some harmonisation of direct action against insurers within Europe. All member states were required to provide victims of motor accidents with a direct right of action against the insurer of the person responsible.[4] In addition, the landmark decision of the CJEU in *FBTO Schadeverzekeringen NV v Odenbreit*,[5] confirmed that the victim of an accident had a choice whether to bring proceedings before the courts of his own domicile or those of the insurer of the wrongdoer. The effect of this has been to open the door to significant numbers of potential claimants who are resident in the UK, but whose accident occurred elsewhere in the EU. Furthermore, such jurisdiction is not limited to motor accidents.

6.1.2   The benefits of a direct action

Direct actions against the insurer of the wrongdoer have a number of specific litigation advantages for the claimant. According to the Fourth Motor Insurance Directive, these benefits are said to ensure that victims of motor accidents are treated equally, irrespective of the state where the accident occurred.[6] In addition, the preamble to the Fifth Motor Insurance Directive[7] emphasises the promotion of the efficient and fair settlement of claims:[8]

> 'The right to invoke the insurance contract and to claim against the insurance undertaking directly is of great importance for the protection of victims of motor vehicle accidents. In order to facilitate an efficient and speedy settlement of claims and to avoid as far as possible costly legal proceedings, a right of direct action against the insurance undertaking covering the person responsible against civil liability should be provided for victims of any motor vehicle accident.'

---

[2]   Article 9. Note that the UK is not a signatory to this Convention, although many other European States are.
[3]   See Chapter 7 on Athens Convention claims for further detail.
[4]   Directive 2000/26/EC of 16 May 2000.
[5]   (Case C-463/06) [2007] ECR I-11321.
[6]   Directive 2000/26/EC, recitals 8–10.
[7]   Directive 2005/14/EC of 11 May 2005.
[8]   Recital 21.

A direct action can make the service of proceedings simpler. An insurer can be served with documents at its place of business, or in the case of a foreign domiciled insurer, may nominate solicitors or handling agents within England and Wales to accept service of proceedings. Even in a domestic context this is a genuine advantage where the wrongdoer may have changed address or be seeking to evade service. In an international context, it brings an additional advantage of by-passing the need for service out of the jurisdiction, with the attendant delay and costs of intermediaries, translations and other fees as well as the not insignificant risk that service will not be validly effected in accordance with the permitted methods.

Where an injured party is able to bring his claim before the English court in respect of an accident abroad, there are clear practical advantages to litigating in his own country, such as using a familiar court procedure, enabling more effective choice of representation and being able to litigate in his own language. There are potential juridical advantages including English procedural rules in relation to costs, evidence and interest. There is also the subtle, but very real, advantage of having the factual issues, including quantum, decided in a forum will be in a much better position to assess his true loss and damage.

6.2 DIRECT RIGHTS OF ACTION UNDER ENGLISH LAW

It is necessary first of all to consider the circumstances in which English law provides a direct right of action in favour of a victim against the wrongdoer's insurer. As noted above, the victim has rights against the insurer in case of the insolvency of the wrongdoer under the Third Parties (Rights Against Insurers) Act 1930.[9] This statute achieves the transfer to the victim of the insured wrongdoer's right to be indemnified by his insurer, but examination of its precise mechanism lies largely outside the scope of this work. The focus of this section will be on the creation of a new direct right of action against insurers under English law. Currently, this only exists in road traffic accidents in the UK. The UK has only to a limited extent implemented the European requirement to confer on residents of the member states a new right to bring proceedings directly against the insurer in cases of motor accidents. As noted below, this has ramifications for those who are injured in another member state or outside the EU, but who are resident in the UK at the time proceedings are issued.

The obligation on the UK to provide a direct right of action in motor cases is derived from what is now Art 18 of the Codified Directive[10] which states:

---

[9] Third Parties (Rights Against Insurers) Act 1930. The 1930 Act is due to be replaced by the Third Parties (Rights Against Insurers) Act 2010, but this has not yet been brought into force. Both Acts also apply to Scotland, with some modifications.

[10] Directive 2009/103/EC of 16 September 2009.

'Member States shall ensure that any party injured as a result of an accident caused by a vehicle covered by [compulsory third party] insurance ... enjoys a direct right of action against the insurance undertaking covering the person responsible against civil liability.'

It has been noted by several commentators that this obligation is not limited by the residence of the injured party, or the location of the accident.[11] Further, recital 30 to the Codified Directive speaks of 'victims of any motor vehicle accident', which is materially wider than the corresponding phrase in the predecessor legislation, Art 3 of the Fourth Motor Insurance Directive, which refers to the Art 1 definition of accident as being limited to those 'caused by the use of vehicles insured and normally based in a Member State'. It remains a matter of debate whether this alteration of the wording was intended by the legislator to bring about substantive changes in meaning and effect.

Returning to the UK's implementing legislation, the European Communities (Rights Against Insurers) Regulations 2002[12] ('the 2002 Regulations') provide that where an 'entitled party' has a cause of action against an 'insured person' in tort which arises out of an 'accident' he also has a right of action directly against the insurer. An 'entitled party' is the victim of a road accident (or his dependants or estate in a wrongful death claim). The 'insured person' is, in practice, the driver whose negligence caused or contributed to the accident.[13]

Although no case has directly considered the point, it is suggested that, as a matter of English law at least, little turns on the reference to a duty arising 'in tort'. Even where cause of action against the wrongdoer arises out of a breach of contract the existence of a concurrent duty of care in tort will suffice to meet the threshold test of 'giving rise to an action in tort'. In the context of limitation periods where the issue of concurrent liability has been considered it has been held that the claimant can choose to advance the claim on the basis which is most advantageous to him.[14]

The definition of 'accident' is more difficult and has given rise to debate about whether the Regulations implement the Directive effectively. 'Accident' is confined to an:[15]

'Accident on a road or other public place in the United Kingdom caused by, or arising out of, the use of any insured vehicle.'

Neither the Fourth Motor Insurance Directive nor the Codified Directive contains restrictions which would limit the provision of a direct right of

---

[11] Dickinson *The Rome II Regulation: the Law Applicable to Non-Contractual Obligations* (Oxford University Press, 2008) paras 14.102–14.104.
[12] SI 2002/3061.
[13] Regulation 2(1).
[14] *Coupland v Arabian Gulf Oil Co* [1983] 1 WLR 1136 at 1153 per Goff LJ.
[15] Regulation 2(1).

action against the relevant insurer to accidents occurring solely in the state concerned. To this extent at least, the 2002 Regulations appear to be narrower in scope than the two Directives. This means that under the 2002 Regulations, the British victim of an accident which occurs in a member state other than the UK has no cause of action against the insurer of the vehicle *as a matter of English law*. Where English law is the proper law of the direct action,[16] the victim may have no direct right of action at all.[17] However, not all claimants will necessarily have no right of action whatsoever, but, as will be seen, they may be constrained to relying on a cause of action arising under the relevant applicable foreign law only.

This chapter is therefore concerned with:

(i)   the circumstances in which the English court has jurisdiction to determine a direct claim by a victim against an insurer in respect of injury or illness sustained outside England and Wales;
(ii) the applicable law issues which arise in such claims; and
(iii) the practicalities for the practitioner in bringing such actions.

6.3   DIRECT RIGHTS OF ACTION UNDER A FOREIGN LAW

6.3.1   Jurisdiction

6.3.1.1   *Insurer domiciled in an EU member state*

Jack Odenbreit was a German national, resident in Germany, who sustained injury and loss as a result of a road accident which took place in the Netherlands. He brought proceedings before the German courts against the Dutch insurer of the person responsible for the accident.[18] The German court made a reference to the CJEU on whether it had jurisdiction to hear the claim. The CJEU considered whether, under the Brussels I Regulation,[19] an injured party could bring an action directly against an insurer in the courts of the member state where he (the injured party) was domiciled. The case turned on the proper interpretation of Arts 9(1)(b) and 11(2) of the Brussels I Regulation, which provide:

'9(1)   An insurer domiciled in a Member State may be sued:
(a)   in the courts of the Member State where he is domiciled, or
(b)   in another Member State, in the case of actions brought by the policy holder, the insured or a beneficiary, in the courts for the place where the plaintiff is domiciled, ...

---

16   A topic covered in detail at **6.3.3**.
17   This point was made in *Jones v Assurances Generales de France (AGF)* [2010] IL Pr 4 at [16] and [34].
18   (Case 463/06) [2007] ECR I-11321.
19   Regulation EC 44/2001.

11(2)　Articles 8, 9 and 10 shall apply to actions brought by the injured party directly against the insurer, where such direct actions are permitted.'

The Court answered the question in the affirmative for two reasons. First, it pointed out that Art 9(1)(b) does not merely attribute jurisdiction to the courts for the place where the persons listed in the subparagraph are domiciled, but provides that the courts for the place where the plaintiff is domiciled have jurisdiction. To interpret the reference in Art 11(2) to Art 9(1)(b) as permitting the injured party to bring proceedings only before the courts for the place of domicile of the policyholder, the insured or the beneficiary, would run counter to the wording of Art 11(2). This led to a widening of the scope of that rule to categories of plaintiff other than the policyholder, the insured or the beneficiary of the insurance contract. The reasoning was also informed by recital 13 in the preamble to the Regulation which aimed to guarantee more favourable protection to the weaker party than was provided by the general rules of jurisdiction. Secondly, the Court noted that such an interpretation was supported by the Fourth Motor Insurance Directive, as amended by the Fifth Motor Insurance Directive, recital 16(a) of which referred expressly to Arts 9(1)(b) and 11(2) of the Brussels I Regulation when mentioning the right of injured parties to bring proceedings against the insurer in the courts for the place where they are domiciled. Moreover, the Court held that it mattered not how the direct action against the insurer might be classified as a matter of national law.[20] The nature of the action in national law was irrelevant since the rules of jurisdiction were contained in a section of the Brussels I Regulation which concerned, in general, matters relating to insurance as distinct from those relating to special jurisdiction in matters relating to contract, tort or delict.

A person injured in a road traffic accident in a member state in which he is not domiciled may therefore bring proceedings against the insurer of the person responsible in the member state in which he (the injured party) is domiciled. The only conditions which Art 11(2) lays down for the application of this rule of jurisdiction is that a direct action must be permitted under the national law and that the defendant insurer is domiciled in an EU member state. Whilst, as will be seen, the words 'where such direct actions are permitted' in Art 11(2) have been the subject of debate, they are unlikely to cause particular difficulty in a motor case following *Odenbreit*, bearing in mind the obligation on member states to ensure that an injured party enjoys a direct right of action against the relevant insurer.

The interpretation of Arts 9 and 11 of the Brussels I Regulation in *Odenbreit* applies equally to direct actions in the non-motor context. But in such cases there is no EU requirement (such as is laid down in the Fourth Motor Insurance Directive and the Codified Directive) that

---

[20]　The vexed question of characterisation of the direct right of action is considered at **6.3.2**.

member states ensure that injured parties enjoy direct rights of action against insurers. It is therefore necessary in every case to consider whether a direct right of action exists; a process which engages conflict rules and will often require evidence of foreign law, which is considered further below.

6.3.1.2 *'Where such direct actions are permitted by the national law'*

The meaning of the words 'where such direct actions are permitted by the national law' appears to be answered by Art 18 of Rome II. In cases which relate to events which took place on or after 11 January 2009 (when Rome II took effect), a claimant can rely on Art 18, which provides:

> 'The person having suffered damage may bring his or her claim directly against the insurer of the person liable to provide compensation if the law applicable to the non-contractual obligation or the law applicable to the insurance contract so provides.'

The article seeks to strike a balance between the interests of the insurer and those of the person suffering damage. It allows the insurer the relative comfort that it can only be sued under two possible systems of law: the law applicable to the insurance contract (which it will usually have chosen) and the law applicable to the non-contractual obligation (where the damage caused by its insured occurred). The victim of the accident therefore cannot rely on other systems of law, such as the law of the country in which he is resident, which may be different. However, as between these two systems of law, the victim has a free choice of the system most favourable to him. The law of the place where the accident occurred may even provide a direct action, where the law of the insurance contract does not. The rules for determining the law applicable to the non-contractual obligation and of the insurance contract are considered in **6.3.3**. Reference should also be had to Chapter 5, Applicable Law.

In cases that pre-date Rome II, however, it will be necessary to ask whether the 'direct action is permitted by the national law'. It is difficult to ascertain precisely to what the CJEU was referring in *Odenbreit* when it referred to the requirement for the direct right of action to be 'permitted' by the national law. The words 'by the national law' do not appear in Art 11(2), there is no consideration in the judgment itself of the rationale underlying the requirement and the CJEU has not been invited to consider the point since. Certainly, given that *Odenbreit* is a case solely concerned with jurisdiction, the reference to 'national law' may suggest that some confusion between the distinct concepts of jurisdiction and applicable law has crept in.

6.3.1.3   *Determined by the law of the insurer's domicile?*

The better view may be that these words are merely intended to prevent the insurer's exposure to direct claims in the courts of a victim's member state where in fact it would not have been subjected to a direct claim before the courts of its own domicile. On this basis, the correct meaning is simply that the 'national' law of the domicile of the insurer should permit him to be sued directly by the third party victim. That was the extent of the question which was being addressed in *Odenbreit* itself. The Dutch courts would have had power to determine a direct claim by Mr Odenbreit against the insurer by virtue of Art 2 of Brussels I. The only question was whether the German courts had jurisdiction to hear the same claim *in addition.*

So, for example, should a Frenchman suffer injury as a result of an accident at work in England, he cannot sue the English domiciled insurer of his employer in England directly. English law recognises no cause of action in favour of the injured employee against his employer's insurer. Accordingly, he cannot bring such a claim before the French courts, even if his contract of employment was governed by French law which would otherwise recognise a direct right of action against the employer's insurer. The logic behind this is that the English insurer should not be exposed to direct actions in a foreign jurisdiction in circumstances where he would not face such a claim at home. It should be remembered that, *Odenbreit* itself was a motor case, for which all member states were obliged to create a direct right of action. In non-motor cases the question whether 'a direct right of action is permitted' will vary according to the national laws of the countries involved.

6.3.1.4   *Determined by the applicable law?*

In contrast, in the English courts the issue has been analysed with reference to concepts of applicable law.[21] This has led to substantial debate about (i) how to characterise the direct right of action – that is, whether the issues are tortious or contractual in nature, and (ii) in the event that they are tortious, whether they are one for the applicable law or for the law of the forum.

The point was touched on at first instance in *Maher v Groupama Grand EST,*[22] a motor case, but was not in issue, either at first instance or on appeal.[23] Nevertheless, Blair J, applying the principles set out in *Dicey, Morris and Collins,*[24] held that the question whether a claim can be

---

[21]   See Chapter 5, Applicable Law.
[22]   [2009] EWHC (QB) 38, [2009] 1 WLR 1752.
[23]   [2009] EWCA Civ 1191, [2010] 1 WLR 1564 at [20].
[24]   *Dicey, Morris and Collins on the Conflict of Laws* (14th edn, 2006) vol 2 at para 35-043; see now (15th edn, 2012), vol 2 at para 35-012.

brought by an injured party directly against the wrongdoer's insurers was a contractual question, governed by the law applicable to the insurance contract.[25]

In two subsequent cases in the county court however, the point was in issue. In the first, *Jones v Assurances Generales de France (AGF) SA*,[26] again a motor case, the defendant contended that the question whether a direct action was permitted fell to be determined according to the law of the forum, that is English law, and that there was no direct right of action because the 2002 Regulations did not extend to accidents which occurred outside the UK.[27] This submission depended on the foreign insurer establishing both (i) that the relevant issues in the direct action fell to be categorised as tortious and then also (ii) that the existence of a right of action was a procedural matter, not a substantive one.[28] In the second, *Thwaites v Aviva Assurances*,[29] a non-motor case arising out of an accident at an adventure park in France (decided by a different judge in the same county court), the defendant contended for similar reasons that the direct action against the French insurer could only be brought in France, English law not permitting such an action. In both cases it was held that it was the law of the insurance contract (in both cases, French law) which determined whether an action could be brought, and as a result that the proceedings in the English court in each case were competent.

As mentioned above, these arguments are now only of relevance in cases to which Rome II does not apply. Article 18 of Rome II has overtaken this debate. But even in pre-Rome II claims, it is suggested that the argument unsuccessfully advanced in *Jones* and *Thwaites* (that the existence of a right of action is a matter of procedure which falls to be governed by the law of the forum) is incorrect. It is highly likely that in future cases the courts will follow either the main ratios of both cases – that the question was determined by French law as the law of the insurance contract – or the alternative ratios – that even had the question fallen to be determined as a question arising in tort French law would have applied.

In practice, therefore, where a claimant is able to establish that the relevant choice of law rules in tort point to a proper law which recognises a direct right of action on the facts of his case, and provided the insurer is domiciled in a member state, the English court will most likely have jurisdiction to hear the claim.

---

[25] See also *Knight v AXA Assurances* [2009] EWHC (QB) 1900 at [26].

[26] [2010] IL Pr 4.

[27] As explained at **6.2**.

[28] For the full discussion of this distinction created by s 14(3)(b) of the Private International Law Act 1995 and see Chapter 9, Remedies at **9.33** and Chapter 5, Applicable Law at **5.2.3.6**.

[29] [2010] I L Pr 47.

There may be some cases, however, where the proper law of the tort does not recognise the direct right of action. For example where a French skier with voluntary third party insurance cover is at fault for knocking over an English snowboarder in Germany, the law applicable to the tort (whether under Rome II or otherwise) is German law. German law does not recognise a direct right of action in this context, but French law does. In such a case, if the English claimant wishes to bring a claim against the insurer in his home courts, it may be necessary to ascertain whether the proper law of the contract of insurance is French law. In practice, this is unlikely to present a significant challenge. It will be a rare contract of insurance which does not expressly choose an applicable law, usually one convenient to the insurer.

However, if there is no such express choice, then regard must be had to the conflict rules applicable to contracts of insurance in order to determine whether the 'direct action is permitted' for the purposes of jurisdiction under *Odenbreit*. In respect of contracts of insurance entered into on or after 17 December 2009, these rules are contained within the general rules governing choice of law in all contracts, the Rome I Regulation,[30] and for contracts entered into before this date, the rules are contained in domestic regulations of similar effect. These rules are discussed in **6.3.3.2**.

6.3.1.5   Choice of jurisdiction is with the injured party

Once the laws applicable to the tort and to the insurance contract have been determined (see **6.3.3**), the claimant can rely on a direct right of action against the insurer which exists in either system of law. In many cases, this will not be problematic. As discussed above, in motor cases a direct right of action exists in all EU member states. For non-motor cases, the position differs between states. In France and many other civil-law jurisdictions, the direct action exists in all cases of liability insurance.[31] However, other jurisdictions limit direct actions to specific circumstances. In English law, they only exist where the policyholder is insolvent.[32] In German law, they are restricted to cases where liability insurance is compulsory, where the policyholder is bankrupt, or where the policyholder's whereabouts are unknown.[33]

---

[30]   Regulation (EC) No 593/2008 of 17 June 2008 on the law applicable to contractual obligations (Rome I).

[31]   French Insurance Code (*Code des Assurances*), art L 124-3, para 1. Similar provisions exist in Belgium, Luxembourg, the Netherlands and Spain.

[32]   Third Parties (Rights Against Insurers) Act 1930, s 1.

[33]   German Insurance Contract Act (*Versicherungsvertragsgesetz*), s 115, para 1.

6.3.1.6 *Insurer domiciled outside the EU*

Where the insurer is not domiciled in an EU member state, the question of jurisdiction is not governed by Brussels I. Rather, the common law rules on jurisdiction apply.[34]

Since the common law rules depend on establishing which is the relevant 'gateway' to jurisdiction,[35] this requires the courts to characterise the direct right of action for jurisdiction purposes as either tortious or contractual.

As above, in claims to which Rome II applies, Art 18, it is suggested, will still apply to answer this question. This is because the provisions of Rome II have universal application.[36] This, it is submitted, will have the effect of permitting the claimant to choose which gateway is most favourable to him or her for jurisdiction purposes.

In pre-Rome II cases, where liability for an accident is not in dispute, it is likely that, following *Maher*, the correct characterisation is tortious. In cases where liability is in dispute, it may well be a question to be considered as a matter of the foreign applicable law as to whether, the issues arise in tort or contract under that foreign law. It is suggested that in most cases the potential 'gateway' to jurisdiction for the purposes of obtaining permission to serve the claim form outside of England and Wales will arise under ground (9)(a) of CPR PD 6B, 'claims in tort'. Provided that the English court is the convenient forum, there would appear to be no reason in practice why an insurer against whom a non-contractual direct right of action lies should not potentially be exposed to determination of the claim before the English court. That would be the location where a personal injury victim has suffered substantial consequential or indirect loss in economic terms, even where the illness or injury itself was sustained outside England and Wales, mirroring the case-law in relation to claims against his insured: see *Booth v Phillips* and *Cooley v Ramsey*.[37]

It is inherently less likely that the 'contract' gateway in ground (6) of CPR PD 6B will avail an English victim of an accident or illness abroad because it is unlikely that the insurance contract will have the relevant links to England and Wales (for instance, being governed by English law or being made in England or through an agent trading or residing in England). But, in theory, if the issue in the direct action is characterised as contractual, it would be this gateway which is relevant to the claim.

---

[34]   In respect of which see Chapter 4, Jurisdiction at **4.2.6**.

[35]   See Chapter 4, Jurisdiction at **4.2.6.2**.

[36]   See Art 3.

[37]   [2004] 1 WLR 3292 and [2008] EWHC 129 (QB) respectively.

6.3.2   Applicable Law

6.3.2.1   *Characterisation of the direct action and why it matters*

In order to select which set of rules determine the law applicable to an issue or a claim in litigation, it is first necessary to 'characterise' that issue as belonging to one or other species of claim. This is an exercise which is done in accordance with English law.

A direct action by the victim of an accident against the insurer of the wrongdoer is a hybrid of contractual and tortious issues. From the perspective of the insurer, the claim appears contractual, because it amounts to reliance by the third party victim on the benefit of the contractual indemnity under the insurance policy. The insurer may wish to rely on the terms of the policy, such as notification requirements or exclusions or limitations in order to defeat or reduce the claim for an indemnity and use those terms in defence of a direct action by the third party victim. On the other hand, from the victim's point of view, the same action is closely linked to an underlying wrong, which is very often (although not always) tortious in nature. His objective is to obtain damages for the tortious wrong which caused his loss and damage, and he is not concerned with who pays those damages.

The significance of this is that contractual defences and limitations may not apply to the tortious claim. Equally, as discussed above, if the claim is entirely contractual in nature, then this affects the rules governing the choice of law.

Many questions therefore arise, including:

(i)   which law determines whether a direct right of action exists and whether the victim can bring this action?

(ii)   which law governs whether contractual terms of the policy of insurance are relevant in respect of the insurer's liability to the victim?

(iii)   which law governs the scope and nature of the remedy available to the victim?

6.3.2.2   *Discussion in case-law*

It was long the opinion of the German courts that direct actions are to be characterised as arising out of tortious liability and only exist if the law applicable to the tort so provides.[38] In contrast, the European Commission's proposal for Rome II provides some support for the

---

[38]   See decision of the *Bundesgerichtshof* (German Federal Supreme Court), VIZR 1/92, BGHZ 119, 137, 139 and see Gruber 'Article 18 Direct Action against the Insurer of the Person Liable' in Calliess (ed) *Rome Regulations: Commentary on the European Rules of the Conflict of Laws* (The Hague, 2011) p 587.

argument that the direct action is contractual. The explanatory memorandum accompanying the proposal states: '[T]he scope of the insurer's obligations is determined by the law governing the insurance contract'.[39]

The predominant view in English law is that the direct action is a contractual right. This is supported by the wording of the 2002 Regulations,[40] which, as discussed above, create the direct right of action in motor cases in the UK. Regulation 3(2) provides that the insurer shall be directly liable to the claimant 'to the extent that he is liable to the insured person'. The insurer's liability to the insured arises out of the insurance contract and the Regulations transfer the right to bring an action in respect of this liability from the insured to the claimant. Thus, it is the same contractual liability which is being enforced and the same limits to that liability which apply.

A number of English cases have discussed the characterisation of the direct action. In *Through Transport Mutual Assurance (Eurasia) Ltd v New India Assurance Co Ltd*,[41] New India had insured a party who shipped a cargo of textiles which were lost in transit through Finland. The carrier of the goods, which had become insolvent, was insured by Through Transport. New India paid out to the owner of the goods and obtained an assignment of the owner's rights against the carrier. It then sued Through Transport directly in Finland, relying on s 67 of the Finnish Insurance Contracts Act 1994, which allowed a direct action against an insurer. Through Transport sought an anti-suit injunction in England, relying on a provision in its agreement with its members (which was governed by English law) that all disputes were to be submitted to arbitration in London. At first instance, Moore-Bick J issued the injunction, but this decision was set aside by the Court of Appeal. In the course of its judgment, the Court of Appeal discussed the issue of characterisation of the direct action.

The question of how the claim was to be characterised depended on whether it was a claim under the Finnish statute and therefore governed by Finnish law, or whether it was a claim to enforce a contractual obligation and therefore governed by English law as the law of the contract. Both the trial judge and the Court of Appeal analysed the Finnish statute and held that, although Finnish law applied, the statute simply gave the injured party a right to enforce the contract as the insured could, according to the terms of the contract. Therefore, since New India's claim was to enforce the insurance contract, Through Transport could rely on defences in the contract, such as a 'pay when paid' clause. The anti-avoidance provisions in the Finnish statute (which declared void

---

[39]   Com (2003) 427 final, p 26.
[40]   SI 2002/3061.
[41]   *The 'Hari Bhum'* [2004] EWCA Civ 1598, [2005] 1 Lloyd's Rep 67.

any clause in the insurance contract which conflicted with the statute[42]) were applied to the extent that the direct action could be brought against the insurer. But nonetheless, the claim was still to enforce the contract and was therefore subject to defences and restrictions in the contract.

Similarly, in *Maher* the Court of Appeal provisionally reached the view that the availability of the direct action and the insurer's liability were issues in contract, governed by the law of the contract.[43] In doing so, the Court of Appeal agreed with Blair J in the same case at first instance,[44] and with Sharp J in *Knight*.[45] However, in both cases the Court took a narrower view of the issue of 'characterisation' and held that the actual issue in both cases was the quantification of the claimant's damages, which was an issue which arose in tort, not contract, and which – in accordance with the pre-Rome II distinction at common law between substantive and procedural issues – then fell to be determined by English law.

It is clear from the analysis in *Maher* that there is not a single characterisation for all the issues in a typical direct action against a motor insurer. Indeed, , Moore-Bick LJ appears to embrace a hybrid approach, whereby questions of liability of the driver (a necessary precondition to liability under the policy of insurance) are tortious, but questions of say a contractual limit of indemnity would arise in contract.[46] It may be that the correct characterisation in any given case will depend on expert evidence of the relevant foreign law as to the nature of the direct right of action.[47] However, there was no evidence in *Maher* before the Court as to the precise nature of the French law direct right of action and whether it exists independently of the contract of indemnity or solely subject to its terms.

There are other English cases in which the issues were not characterised as contractual where the evidence indicated that the direct right of action was independent of the contract of insurance. In *Markel International Co Ltd v Craft*,[48] Mr Craft was killed in a fire aboard a ship, while returning to port in Tunis from working on a drilling rig. His widow and children issued proceedings in the Tunisian courts against the ship's owners and insurer, Markel. Markel sought an anti-suit injunction to restrain the Craft family from continuing with the Tunisian proceedings, relying on a clause similar to that in *Through Transport*. The Craft family

---

42 These provisions were similar to the Third Parties (Rights Against Insurers Act) 1930, s 3.

43 *Maher* [2009] EWCA Civ 1191 at [11]–[12].

44 *Maher* [2009] EWHC 38 (QB), at [20]–[23].

45 *Knight v AXA Assurances* [2009] EWHC (QB) 1900 at [25].

46 As demonstrated by Moore-Bick LJ's examples in his judgment: *Maher* [2009] EWCA Civ 1191 at [11].

47 This is the preferred solution of Plender and Wildespin *The European Private Law of Obligations* (Sweet & Maxwell, 2009) paras 28-012–28-015, discussed below.

48 [2006] EWHC 3150 (Comm).

relied on the direct right of action in art 26 of the Tunisian Insurance Code.[49] Morison J analysed this statutory provision and relied on evidence from Tunisian lawyers to the effect that the Tunisian direct right of action exists independently of both the injured person's rights against the tortfeasor and the insured tortfeasor's rights against the insurer. This direct right of action was different to the right in *Through Transport*, which was simply a right to enforce the contract.[50] Accordingly, in *Markel*, the Court held that the direct action was not subject to defences or limitations in the insurance contract, such as the English arbitration clause.

6.3.2.3 Discussion in academic commentary

The authors of *Dicey, Morris and Collins* are also of the view that there may not be one single law applicable to a direct right of action against an insurer. They point out that, whichever applicable law the injured party relies on, it may still be necessary to take account of the other law referred to in Art 18 of Rome II. Thus, a direct action under the law applicable to the non-contractual obligation may be limited to the amount which the insurer would be liable to the insured under the contract; the law applicable to the contract may or may not be effective to limit the insurer's liability. Similarly, if the injured party relies on the law of the contract, it may be necessary to take account of conditions in the law applicable to the non-contractual obligation. The law of the contract may, for instance, require the injured party first to prove the insured's liability to him, before proving that the insurer is liable to the injured party.[51]

Gruber, on the other hand, argues that Art 18 is concerned mainly with whether a direct action exists at all, while its scope is determined by the law applicable to the insurance contract, particularly in the case of the events which are covered by the insurance and the insured sum.[52] Defences which the insurer could raise are governed by the law applicable to the insurance contract, not to the law determined by Art 18 of Rome II (if different). However, even in this case, there are certain defences which the insurer could have raised against the insured, which it is prevented from raising against the injured party, as a matter of policy of the law applicable to the insurance contract.[53]

Plender and Wildespin argue that the characterisation of the direct action depends on its status in whichever applicable law is relied on by the injured party to bring the action. They note that in *Through Transport*, the Court characterised the direct action as contractual only after analysing

---

[49] This provision of the Tunisian insurance code was worded similarly to art L 124-3 of the French Insurance Code.

[50] [2006] EWHC 3150 (Comm) at 24, 26, 27.

[51] *Dicey, Morris and Collins* (15th edn, 2012) vol 2 at para 34-072.

[52] Gruber (n 39), p 591.

[53] Gruber, pp 591-592.

the Finnish statute which created it. Therefore, the question of who counts as a 'person having suffered damage' in Art 18 can only be resolved by reference to whichever applicable law is relied on for the direct action. Further, Rome II does not limit the scope of recoverable damage, nor does it broaden it; this is a matter only for the applicable law.[54]

6.3.2.4 *Suggested view*

These issues have not yet been determined either by a national court or the CJEU and so we can only proceed from first principles and by analogy with pre-Rome II cases.

The starting point is that Rome II is a regulation on the conflict of laws, designed to standardise rules as to which law applies in cross-border cases. It is not a source of rights or obligations in itself. Those rights and obligations remain determined by the applicable law which creates the claim in the first place.[55] In *Through Transport,* the Court of Appeal did not decide that *all* direct rights of actions are contractual. Rather, it was analysing the characterisation of the particular right of action created by the Finnish statute. This is supported by the subsequent decision in *Markel.* There, Morison J determined that the Tunisian direct right of action relied on was a separate statutory right and not a right to enforce the contract. The judge applied the reasoning in *Through Transport* to decide that the characterisation depends on an analysis of the provisions in the applicable law which create the action.[56]

It is therefore suggested that the question of who is entitled to be a claimant and bring a direct action is also determined by the applicable law relied on for the action. The concept of 'a person having suffered damage' in Art 18 does not have an autonomous definition under Rome II separate from that given under the applicable law, nor does Rome II restrict that definition to certain types of damage. This is reflected in Art 15 of Rome II: the applicable law governs 'the question of whether a right to claim damages or a remedy may be transferred, including by inheritance' and 'persons entitled to compensation for damage suffered personally'.[57]

Therefore, the injured party is bound by any rules in the applicable law which restrict the type of damage recoverable or which prescribe the particular relationship between the injured party and the wrongdoer necessary to bring a claim. No hardship is caused to an injured party who

---

[54] Plender and Wildespin, paras 28-014–28-015. Dickinson advances a fairly similar argument at para 14.95A of the updating supplement (2010) to his work on Rome II.

[55] It is true that under Rome II a non-contractual obligation has an autonomous definition, not dependent on its categorisation under national law: recital 11. However, that autonomous definition is designed to avoid differences between national laws as to what falls within the scope of the Regulation. This definition cannot be relied on to suggest that Rome II creates new rights or non-contractual obligations.

[56] *Markel* (n 48), paras 26, 27, 31.

[57] Rome II, Art 15(e) and (f).

has to rely on an applicable law with such restrictions; if he wishes to rely on a direct right of action in that law, he also has to accept its limitations.

The events which fall within the scope of the coverage provided by the insurer are defined by the insurance contract itself, and by the law applicable to it. The same applies to any limits or defences which apply to the insurance contract, including a maximum insured sum. These limits and defences define the scope of the insurer's liability to the insured. Similarly, in most cases, they will also apply to determine the insurer's liability to the injured party in a direct action.

However, there can be situations in which such limits and defences would not apply. In some cases it may be that the law applicable to the insurance contract provides that an insurer cannot raise certain defences against an injured party which it could raise against the insured.[58] It is also possible, but unlikely, that a term of the insurance contract could be void for breach of a provision in the law which governs it. More commonly, defences or limits in the insurance contract may be effectively disapplied when they conflict with provisions of the law applicable to the tort, where the injured party relies on this law for the direct action. For instance, in *Markel*, the Tunisian direct action was held to be a separate claim under the insurance code, independent from the contract, and therefore defences in the insurance contract (such as the arbitration clause) could not be raised against the injured party.

This potentially puts the insurer in a worse position than it would have been in had it been sued under the law of the insurance contract. But this is not a great hardship, because the insurer can foresee that the victim of an accident caused by its insured may be able to rely on a different law to that governing the insurance contract and will make provision accordingly. Clearly, for travel insurers, the insured will necessarily be abroad and it is inevitable that persons injured by the insured will be able to rely on the law of the foreign state where the damage occurs (which governs the non-contractual obligation), as well as the law governing the contract. The same is quite likely for motor insurers; it is foreseeable that the insured will drive abroad and that victims of accidents which they cause can rely on the law of that foreign state.

6.3.3 Determining the applicable law

6.3.3.1 *Law of the tort*

Article 18 of Rome II does not itself provide rules on how the applicable laws to which it refers are to be determined. However, it is clear that the law applicable to the non-contractual obligation is determined by the

---

[58] For instance, in German law, the insurer can avoid liability to the insured where an accident was caused by the insured's deliberate act, but the insurer cannot raise this defence against the injured party pursuing a direct action: Gruber, pp 591–592.

other rules in Rome II. In the case of a tort, the general rule is contained in Art 4(1): the applicable law is the law of the country in which the damage occurs, irrespective of the country in which the events giving rise to the damage occurred and irrespective of the country in which the indirect consequences of the damage occurred. This is subject to an exception in Art 4(2), when the person seeking compensation and the person said to be liable are both resident in the same state, in which case the law of that state will apply. Further, Art 4(3) provides that where the case is 'manifestly more closely connected' with another country rather than those above, then the law of that country will apply. This will usually be a high threshold to satisfy.[59]

6.3.3.2 *Law of the insurance contract*

For contracts entered into on or after 17 December 2009, the applicable law is determined by the rules in the Rome I Regulation. Article 7 of Rome I lays down special rules for choice of law in relation to insurance contracts. In general terms, subject to some limitations, the parties to an insurance contract can choose the law which applies to the contract in accordance with the general rules set out in Art 3.[60]

Article 7 then provides default rules in the absence of choice of applicable law. In the case of 'large risks' wherever that risk is situated in the world, the default rule is that the law of the country of the habitual residence of the insurer shall apply.[61] For other insurance contracts covering risks situated inside the member states, the default provision is the law of the country where the risk is situated.[62]

There are provisions which place restrictions on which choice of law the parties to an insurance contract are entitled to make[63] and, where an insurance contract arises by virtue of a legal obligation to be insured, the member states are given the power under national law to require that the applicable law be that of the country whose law requires the insurance to be held.[64]

For contracts entered into before 17 December 2009, the relevant rules are set out in the Financial Services and Markets Act (Law Applicable to Contracts of Insurance) Regulations 2001,[65] which, with some modification, implemented the Second and Third Directives on Non-Life Insurance.[66] The number of cases to which these Regulations will apply

---

[59]   For further discussion, see Chapter 5, Applicable Law at **5.2.3.6**.
[60]   In respect of which see Chapter 5, Applicable Law at **5.3.2.4**.
[61]   The definition of 'large risk' in Art 7(2) depends on factors relating to the size of the insured's operation in terms of turnover and number of employees.
[62]   Article 7(3).
[63]   Article 7(3).
[64]   Article 7(4)(b).
[65]   SI 2001/3542.
[66]   Directive 88/357/EEC of 22 June 1988 and Directive 92/49/EEC of 18 June 1992.

will become fewer and fewer following their amendment (in response to Rome I) and accordingly a detailed treatment of the complex provisions regarding choice of law falls outside the ambit of this work.

6.4   BRINGING AN ACTION DIRECTLY AGAINST THE INSURER

Where a claimant has been injured in an accident abroad it is important, given the potential complexity of the claim, that early steps are taken to gather the necessary evidence for the claim. This is particularly so in cases of serious injury. In some respects, that evidence will mirror that which would be appropriate were the claim entirely domestic. On the other hand, the international element means that not all the material issues are the same.

6.4.1   Identifying the issues in the claim

The applicable law generally determines what are the facts in issue. Sometimes the applicable law will contain a provision which states that no evidence may be given on a certain matter. Other times an applicable law will state that no evidence need be given in respect of a matter.[67] It is essential therefore to have a clear outline of the material issues in a foreign law claim as this guides the entire evidence gathering process.

The substantive law will determine the burden of proof on a particular issue. In the event that the substantive applicable law has a presumption in respect of a matter, the English court will apply that presumption.[68]

However, once the relevant issues have been identified, where the proceedings are before the English court, it will be the English rules of procedure which determine the manner in which those issues can be proved. This is clear from Rome I and Rome II (both at Art 1(3)) which expressly reserve issues of evidence and procedure for the law of the forum.[69] Accordingly, the question of whether hearsay evidence is admissible to prove a particular matter would fall to be determined by the law of the forum, as would questions of privilege attaching to communications.

6.4.2   Liability issues

It is not uncommon in claims where there is a significant dispute concerning the legal issues, including those discussed above, for the basic

---

[67]   *See Dicey, Morris and Collins* (15th edn, 2012) at para 7-022.
[68]   Rome I, Art 18 and Rome II, Art 22. See also *Bacon v Nacional Suiza Seguros y Reaseguros* [2010] EWHC 2017 (QB), [2010] IL Pr 46 in which the presumption of Spanish law in favour of the victim of a road accident was applied.
[69]   See Chapter 9, Remedies.

element of liability to be overlooked. It remains essential to obtain the best possible evidence of the actual circumstances of the accident. Of course, it is the custom and practice of the place of the accident which will govern the relevant standards by which conduct falls to be judged, regardless of the law applicable to the claim. Recital 34 of the preamble to Rome II gives the English court guidance to this effect:

> 'In order to strike a reasonable balance between the parties, account must be taken, in so far as appropriate, of the rules of safety and conduct in operation in the country in which the harmful act was committed, even where the non-contractual obligation is governed by the law of another country. The term "rules of safety and conduct" should be interpreted as referring to all regulations having any relation to safety and conduct, including, for example, road safety rules in the case of an accident.'

In larger claims it will almost always be justified to send an investigator to gather evidence locally. The sooner that this can be done following the accident, the better. In many countries the quality of police investigation of even serious accidents leaves a lot to be desired and it is rare that police reports contain scale drawings, good quality photographs of the vehicles or locus (in road accident cases). There is unlikely to be any evidence to assist with allegations of contributory negligence for issues concerning seatbelts.

An independent investigation of the accident circumstances can be crucial. The reputation of English holidaymakers in some parts of the Mediterranean is such that there is a tendency for local investigators to assume that all accidents are entirely attributable to inebriation, recklessness and a lack of familiarity with the local customs and practices. Foreign insurers are used to being able to rely on a favourable police report in order to defeat claims in some jurisdictions and are resistant to any further investigations taking place.

6.4.3   Policy and indemnity issues

It seems likely that in light of the decision in *Maher* that issues relating to the extent of an indemnity under the policy or any possible defences advanced by an insurer on the basis that they have no obligation to indemnify their insured due to a breach of contract or exclusion, would be governed by the law applicable to the contract of insurance. This may or may not be the same as the law applicable to the tort. For example, where a road accident occurs in Bulgaria involving a Polish vehicle, insured by a Polish insurer, with British passengers, the extent of cover under the policy of insurance and the correct interpretation of its terms will fall to be determined under Polish law, even though Bulgarian law will determine the driver's liability for the accident. The claimants would have a choice between Polish law (as the law of the contract) and Bulgarian law (as the law of the tort) on which to base their direct actions.

Such policy questions depend first and foremost on the proper interpretation of the insurance contract. This must be done in accordance with the proper law of the contract and therefore foreign law expert evidence as to the principles of construction is required. However, it remains the task of the English court to determine what the words in question mean and their effect by reference to the facts of the particular case.

Another factor to bear in mind is that the proper law may have rules which affect the validity of the policy wording, especially where it purports to limit or exclude the insurer's liability to indemnify his insured. If there is an issue that the law applicable to the tort (if the claimant relies on it for the existence of the direct action) affects a term of the policy or the insurer's ability to rely on those terms, then expert evidence of that law will also be required.

When dealing with limits of recoverability under insurance policies, it is important from a practical perspective to have accurate information as to whether the limit is inclusive of costs as well as damages and whether it is per incident or per victim.

6.4.4   Heads of loss

It is necessary to identify with some care what relevant heads of loss will be recoverable pursuant to the applicable law. It is essential to have the right expert who has practical experience of acting in such claims to advise on the types of loss which the local law will recognise at an early stage.

Common areas of dispute include whether claims for care and assistance provided on a gratuitous basis are recoverable. Such claims are often alien to the law of countries other than England and Wales and therefore expert witnesses are apt to indicate that this head of loss is not recoverable. Deeper exploration of the nature of the objection of the local law to a particular head of claim can reveal that the difference may be one of evidence and procedure rather than substance. For example, if the local courts apply a rule that only actual financial loss evidenced by documentary evidence is recoverable, then that may be the sole basis that a claim for gratuitous care and assistance would never succeed. That is not the same as saying that the head of loss is not recognised. Given that questions of evidence are reserved to the law of the forum, the English court could permit such a claim whilst applying the foreign law. Indeed, in many countries care and assistance is in principle recoverable, insofar as it has been professionally provided and there is evidence that the fees have been incurred.

Care should also be taken not to overlook heads of loss which are recoverable pursuant to the applicable law which would not be recoverable under English law. For example, French law recognises loss to parties other than the direct victim (so-called *victimes par ricochet*) in a much broader category of circumstances than English law. Similarly, under Italian law it is possible to advance claims for 'bereavement' on behalf of a large number of relatives of the deceased in a wrongful death case. It is therefore important not to assume an anglo-centric approach to the quantification of loss, but to invite the local law expert or agent to advise specifically on the types of loss which they would expect to seek if they were pursuing the claim in the court of the country whose law applies.

6.4.5   Medical expert evidence

It is clear that the question of assessment of damage in a personal injury or wrongful death claim is an issue which arises 'in tort' for the purposes of applicable law characterisation. In cases under Rome II, this gives rise to the question of which aspects of 'assessment of damages' in Art 15(2)(c) amount to rules of evidence or procedure which fall to be governed by English law as the law of the forum. A particular difficulty arises where the applicable law scheme for assessment of damage involves the local courts using the assistance of local experts.[70] In such cases, it will be essential to have evidence from an expert in the local law and procedure who is able to discuss in detail how the rules operate in order to determine whether they are in fact rules which govern the basis of assessment, or whether they are procedural rules which set out how the assessment is to be carried out.

There is no reason why a claim governed by a foreign law requires the medical expert witnesses to come from the country whose law applies. A medical expert's competence to give opinion evidence arises from his medical expertise, not his nationality. However, care may be necessary to ensure that the medical expert addresses the material facts in his report which puts the claimant in a position to prove his claim at trial. Whilst therefore for reasons of linguistic and geographical convenience it is easier to instruct English medical experts, care will be needed to ensure that they are instructed to address the correct factual issues. It may be foolhardy for a claimant simply to present his claim as if it were an entirely domestic one.

6.5   CLAIMS AGAINST THE MOTOR INSURERS' BUREAU

Where a road traffic accident is caused by an uninsured driver, there is clearly no insurer whom the victim can sue. The victim can sue the tortfeasor personally, but most drivers will not have sufficient assets to satisfy a judgment in a large personal injury case. In the UK the victim

---

[70]   See, for example, the detailed account by Tugendhat J in *Wall v Mutuelle de Poitiers* [2013] EWHC 53 (QB) at [29] and [30], which is discussed further in Chapter 9, Remedies.

can recover compensation from the Motor Insurers' Bureau (MIB) in such a case, but must join the tortfeasor in the proceedings. The MIB now includes all insurers licensed to provide motor insurance. Under the green card system, operated between insurers throughout the European Economic Area (EEA),[71] representatives of an insurer in one state handle claims on behalf of an insurer based in another state. The MIB is also the body which operates the green card system in the UK.

The green card system was extended by the Fourth Motor Insurance Directive, which required states to establish a compensation body against which the victim of an accident could claim if an insurer's representative failed to respond to a claim promptly, or the vehicle was not covered by insurance, or it could not be traced. Again, the MIB is the compensation body for such claims in the UK. When acting as the compensation body, the MIB operates pursuant to the Motor Vehicles (Compulsory Insurance) (Information Centre and Compensation Body) Regulations 2003 ('the 2003 Regulations').[72] Under these Regulations, the injured party receives compensation from the compensation body in his state, which then in turn recovers compensation from the body in the state where the tortfeasor's vehicle is insured, which in turn claims an indemnity from the driver's insurer (where it is possible to do so).

6.5.1   Where the foreign insurer is identified

Regulations 11 and 12 of the 2003 Regulations create the entitlement to compensation from the MIB where the insurer of the tortfeasor is identified. They apply where:

(i)   the injured party is resident in the UK;
(ii) he claims to be entitled to compensation for an accident in another EEA state;
(ii) the injury was caused by the use of a vehicle normally based in another EEA state and insured through an insurer in another EEA state.

Where reg 11 applies, the injured party may claim compensation from the MIB where he has not commenced legal proceedings against the insurer of the vehicle which caused the accident and either:

(i)   the injured party has claimed compensation from the insurer or its representative in the UK, but the insurer or representative has not provided a reasoned reply to the claim within 3 months; or
(ii) the insurer failed to appoint a representative in the UK and the injured party has not claimed compensation directly from the insurer.

---

[71]   The EEA comprises the member states of the EU plus Iceland, Liechtenstein and Norway.
[72]   SI 2003/37.

Regulation 12 lays down the procedure for the MIB to respond to the claim. It must reply within 2 months. The MIB will indemnify the injured party for loss or damage, provided the injured party establishes:

(i)   that the insured is liable to the injured party for the accident; and
(ii)   the amount of loss or damage which is properly recoverable in that part of the UK where the injured party is resident at the date of the accident.

The MIB ceases to act in the claim if the insurer appoints a representative in the UK or the injured party starts proceedings against the insurer.

6.5.2   Where the foreign insurer is not identified

Regulation 13 of the 2003 Regulations covers the injured party's entitlement to compensation where the vehicle or the insurer is not identified. The regulation applies where:

(a)   an accident caused by a vehicle based in an EEA state occurs in an EEA state other than the UK and the injured party is resident in the UK;
(b)   the injured party has made a request for information about the vehicle under reg 9(2); and
(c)   it has proved impossible to identify the vehicle responsible or, within 2 months, to identify the insurer for the vehicle.

In this case, the injured party can claim compensation from the MIB. The MIB is required to compensate the injured party:[73]

> 'in accordance with the provisions of article 1 of the Second Motor Insurance Directive as if it were the body authorised under paragraph 4 of that article and the accident had occurred in Great Britain.'

The MIB is also the body authorised under that article of that Directive for the purposes of accidents caused by uninsured drivers in the UK.

Regulation 13 was discussed by the Court of Appeal in *Jacobs v Motor Insurers' Bureau*.[74] The claimant, who was resident in the UK, was involved in a road traffic accident in Spain caused by an uninsured German national, who was then resident in Spain and whose vehicle was normally based in Spain. The claimant brought a claim for compensation against the MIB as the UK compensation body and, in court proceedings sought a declaration that the MIB was liable to pay compensation in accordance with English law under reg 13. The MIB claimed that Spanish law applied to the assessment of compensation, either because Spanish law was the applicable law under Rome II, or because the compensation

---

[73]   Regulation 13(2)(b).
[74]   [2010] EWCA Civ 1208, [2011] 1 WLR 2609.

which the MIB had to pay was limited to the amount for which the tortfeasor would have been liable, and he could only have been sued in Spain, not in England.

The Court of Appeal held that reg 13(2)(b) implied that the injured party had to show that the tortfeasor would have been liable to him for the accident. The judge at first instance had held that the regulation included a choice of law, so that the assessment of damages was governed by the applicable law under Rome II. In the Court of Appeal, it was agreed that the regulation did not contain a choice of law. It was held that the regulation meant that compensation was to be assessed as if the accident had occurred in Great Britain, applying the law of that part of Great Britain in which the injured party was resident. The Court also stated that Rome II had no application to the assessment of compensation under reg 13, since the regulation was concerned with the existence and extent of compensation payable by the MIB, not with the extent of the tortfeasor's liability. The MIB appealed to the Supreme Court, but the case was settled before the appeal could be heard. Therefore the decision of the Court of Appeal stands and compensation payable under reg 13 is unaffected by the entry into force of Rome II.

A slightly different issue was raised in *Bloy and Ireson v Motor Insurers' Bureau*.[75] Here, the MIB sought to rely upon a maximum cap on damages available to a victim of a road accident in an action against the Lithuanian equivalent of the MIB, were that action to be brought under the relevant Lithuanian law. It argued that the issue of a limit on recoverable damages was not decided in *Jacobs*, and that it was therefore distinguishable. HHJ Platts rejected this suggestion, holding instead that a cap on damages was exactly the kind of assessment of loss issue which had been agreed to be solely a concern for English law under the 2003 Regulations. In so doing, he referred to the fact that Lithuanian law would have permitted the claimant to pursue losses over and above the indemnity limit of the Lithuanian guarantee fund directly against the driver responsible. He further reaffirmed the implicit reasoning of the Court of Appeal in *Jacobs* that concepts of applicable law had no place in the discussion.

However, the law of the country where the accident takes place does have some relevance to claims under the 2003 Regulations. That law will continue to govern the issues in relation to the underlying liability of the uninsured or unidentified driver to the victim. Therefore, it may be necessary to obtain expert evidence of foreign law if there is an issue as to the relevant principles of law. For example, if the accident occurred in a country whose law provides for strict liability on the part of a driver whose vehicle is involved in an accident, it will be necessary for foreign

---

[75]   QBD (Manchester), unreported, 11 January 2013, Lawtel 6 February 2013. There is an outstanding appeal to the Court of Appeal against this decision; permission to appeal was granted on paper and the hearing is listed for the second half of 2013.

law evidence to be adduced in the event that there is a dispute as to what connection a vehicle must have to an accident in order to be 'involved' and subject to liability for damages. Similarly, questions of any contributory fault on the part of the injured party will be dealt with in the same fashion.

Rome II was intended to achieve harmonisation throughout the EU in the assessment of damages, making this a matter for the applicable law. English law had often led to awards of damages which were considerably higher than those in other countries.[76] However, in those specific cases where the 2003 Regulations apply, injured parties may be better off claiming compensation from the MIB, perhaps enjoying strict liability under a foreign applicable law and yet with damages assessed according to the English law, rather than pursuing a direct action against the insurer, with damages assessed under the foreign applicable law. Whether or not, as was suggested to the Court of Appeal in *Jacobs*, this is an unintended consequence of the 2003 Regulations, it would appear now to be primarily a matter for Parliament or the Secretary of State to correct.

---

[76] See further discussion in Chapter 9, Remedies.

CHAPTER 7

ACCIDENTS AT SEA

Sarah Crowther

with Helen Pugh and Patricia Londono

7.1 INTRODUCTION

International cruising by ship is no longer the domain of the super-rich or celebrities. The cruise ship industry has broadened its appeal and shed its stereotyped image of retirement holidays and strict rules about dressing for dinner. It is anticipated that 1.76 million British passengers will take a cruise in 2013.[1] This chapter concerns the legal liabilities of both cruise and other commercial carriers such as ferry companies to their passengers in the event of personal injury or death. It also looks at the principles which apply in the event that employees or others who are not passengers sustained illness or injury whilst at sea.

Other legal rights which are available to passengers being carried at sea are outside the scope of this work. In particular, the rights of disabled persons and persons with reduced mobility when travelling by sea[2] and the obligations of carriers in the event of interrupted travel, although issues which sometimes arise when addressing personal injury or accident at sea, require more detailed consideration than can be permitted here.

7.2 PASSENGER CLAIMS – THE ATHENS CONVENTION 1974

7.2.1 The Athens Convention

The Convention relating to the Carriage of Passengers and their Luggage by Sea, 1974 was concluded at Athens on 13 December 1974. The Convention is deposited with the International Maritime Organisation (IMO),[3] whose purpose is to develop and maintain responsibility for the safety of shipping. The original Convention was written in both English and French.[4] It entered into force on 28 April 1987. There is a Protocol

---

[1] According to the Passenger Shipping Association (www.the-psa.co.uk).
[2] Regulation EU 1177/2010. For guidance on these provisions including their interface with other legislation see www.gov.uk/government/publications.
[3] The IMO is an agency of the United Nations and has its headquarters in London.
[4] Article 28. Both versions have equal authenticity.

which effectively amends the original Athens Convention which was adopted on 1 November 2002 but as at the date of writing only nine states had signed the 2002 Protocol and therefore it has not yet entered into force.[5] The EU is a signatory to the 2002 Protocol.[6]

The main innovation of the 2002 Protocol is the compulsory requirement for all carriers performing carriage by sea of more than 12 passengers to have indemnity insurance in respect of liability for death and personal injury to passengers in accordance with Athens Convention limits. It also provides for a direct right of action in favour of the victim against the carrier's insurer.[7] Finally, the provisions of Art 3 which set out the scheme for carrier's liability to his passenger for personal injury and death have been reshaped and clarified.

7.2.1.1   Athens Convention in English law

The original Athens Convention was originally implemented into English law by the Merchant Shipping Act 1995.[8] However, from 31 December 2012 Regulation (EC) No 392/2009 of the European Parliament and of the Council on the liability of carriers of passengers by sea in the event of accidents[9] ('the 2009 Regulation') applies.[10] It has created a modified regime relating to liability and insurance for the carriage of passengers by sea. The 2009 Regulation effectively adopts the Athens Convention as amended in accordance with the 2002 Protocol.[11] The 2009 Regulation obviously has direct effect in English law, but it is supplemented by the Merchant Shipping (Carriage of Passengers by Sea) Regulations 2012.[12] References in this chapter to the 'Convention' or the 'consolidated Convention' mean the Convention as amended in accordance with the 2002 Protocol. References to the 'original Athens Convention' mean the text as it stood following the Athens Conference on 13 December 1974.

The effect of these changes is that the original Athens Convention will no longer apply to carriage to which the 2009 Regulation applies. It is not made explicit in the text of the 2009 Regulation whether it applies to contracts for carriage concluded before 31 December 2012 but where the incident giving rise to the loss and damage occurs after that date. It is suggested that the better view is that the consolidated Convention will

---

[5]   Article 20. It will enter into force 12 months following the date on which 10 States have signed the Convention.
[6]   www.imo.org since 15 December 2011.
[7]   See Chapter 6 Direct Actions Against Insurers for a detailed consideration.
[8]   Sections 183 and 184 and Part I of Sch 6.
[9]   OJ L131, 28 May 2009, p 24.
[10]   Article 12.
[11]   Annex I to the 2009 Regulation. It must also be read in conjunction with the IMO Reservation and Guidelines for the Implementation of the Athens Convention adopted by the Legal Committee of the IMO on 19 October 2006 (Annex II of the 2009 Regulation). See also Appendix 5 in this book.
[12]   SI 2012/3152.

apply to claims for personal injury and death where the incident took place after 31 December 2012. The contract of carriage defines the context in which liability attaches, but it is the timing of the carriage not the contract which is pertinent to liability pursuant to the Convention. This view is supported by the text of the 2002 Protocol to the Athens Convention which states that it applies to claims arising out of 'occurrences' which take place after its entry into force.[13]

In these circumstances the law in this chapter is stated as it stands in accordance with the Convention. For claims where the incident occurred before 31 December 2012 it will be necessary to have regard to the original Athens Convention. Cross-referencing is however assisted by the fact that consistency of numbering has been maintained between the original Athens Convention and the consolidated version following the 2002 Protocol. Where points of difference arise, they are identified as appropriate.

7.2.1.2 *Jurisdiction of the English courts and recognition of foreign judgments*

There is a special jurisdiction regime for Convention claims. It is not governed by either Brussels I or the common law.[14] The Art 17 Convention provisions do not form part of the 2009 Regulation but nonetheless apply since the accession of the EU to the 2002 Protocol.[15]

The claimant is given a choice of forum, subject to some limitations.[16] He must choose the courts of a country which is a state party to the Convention. That state must also be one which is either:

(i) the country of permanent residence or principal place of business of the defendant; or
(ii) the country of departure or destination according to the contract of carriage; or

provided that the defendant has a place of business in the chosen country and is subject to the jurisdiction in that country additionally

(iii) the place of the claimant's domicile or permanent residence; or
(iv) the country where the contract of carriage was made.

It is open to the parties to agree to submit to any jurisdiction or arbitration after the occurrence of an incident causing damage.[17] The question of whether submission to the jurisdiction of the English court

---

13 Article 15(2).
14 As discussed in Chapter 4, Jurisdiction.
15 Preamble recital 11 of the 2009 Regulation.
16 Article 17(1).
17 Article 17(3).

has taken place is decided in accordance with the usual procedural principles of English law.[18] However, the English court has no discretion to decline jurisdiction on forum non conveniens grounds.[19] The provisions of the Brussels I Regulation[20] with respect to lis alibi pendens have no application.[21]

In most cruise cases departing from or arriving in the UK, the claimant will have jurisdiction under (ii). In a fly–cruise holiday where the cruise element departs from, say Fort Lauderdale, it will be necessary to consider the defendant's country or permanent residence or principal place of business in order to establish jurisdiction under limb (i) or if necessary (iii) or (iv). In practice, the choice is broadened considerably by the fact that the claimant can also elect to pursue either the carrier with whom he has contracted for carriage or the carrier who performed the relevant part of the carriage.[22]

The concepts of 'permanent residence' and 'principal place of business' are autonomous and will not necessarily bear the same meaning as they do in any domestic or European legislation. The jurisdiction rules in the Convention are a self-contained code. In the context of Carriage by Air it has been held that the phrase, 'where the carrier is *ordinarily* resident' must be narrowly construed. It is not enough that the carrier holds a branch office in England and Wales. Nor does it suffice that the carrier would be amenable to service within England and Wales under the domestic procedural rules.[23]

In the context of interpretation of a bill of lading which contained a jurisdictional clause in favour of the courts 'where the carrier has its principal place of business', it has been held that this phrase means:[24]

> '... the centre from which instructions are given, and from which control is exercised on behalf of the company over the employees of and the business of the company, and where control is exercised, and the centre from which the company is managed without any further control.'

This means that the focus is the decision-making on the part of the company, even where the day-to-day management of the ship itself is carried out elsewhere. The phrase 'principal place of business' appears in Brussels I in relation to the 'domicile' of a company[25] and *The Rewia* has been followed when considering the same words in that context. It is

---

[18] *Rothmans v Saudi Airlines* [1981] 1 QB 368, 377.
[19] *Milor Srl v British Airways plc* [1996] QB 702.
[20] EC 44/2001, Arts 27–28. See **4.4.5.13**.
[21] *Deaville v Aeroflot* [1997] 2 Lloyd's Rep 67.
[22] Article 4(1) and **7.2.2.2**.
[23] *Rothmans v Saudi Airlines* [1981] 1 QB 368, 374–375 and 386.
[24] *The Rewia* [1993] I L Pr 507, 521, following *The Polzeath* [1916] P 241.
[25] EC 44/2001, Art 60.

likely, although not certain, that a similar approach will be adopted by the English court to these words as they appear in the Convention.

One of the changes to Art 17 brought about by the 2002 Protocol is that in claims which are pursued directly against the carrier's insurer,[26] jurisdiction of the English court will exist where the claimant could have brought a claim against either the carrier or performing carrier. The Protocol also clarifies that where a state party contains multiple possible forums, the domestic law of that state will determine the correct venue.[27]

Article 17bis requires the English court to recognise the judgment of any competent court pursuant to Art 17 unless it was obtained by fraud or without reasonable notice or a fair opportunity to the defendant to present a case.[28] It is not permissible for an English court to reopen the merits of a case. Once recognised, a judgment of a foreign court is enforceable in the UK.[29]

In accordance with Art 17bis(3) the EU has given a declaration regarding the recognition of judgments on matters covered by the consolidated Convention in the courts of a member state which is bound by the Brussels I Regulation, as well as Denmark and any Lugano Convention country. In such cases the relevant rules on recognition of judgments under the Brussels I Regulation, Denmark Agreement or Lugano Convention apply. In the event of conflict, those rules most favourable to the claimant will prevail.

7.2.1.3   *Direct right against carrier's insurer*

Any claim for compensation may be brought directly against the insurer[30] of the carrier who actually performs the whole or part of the carriage.[31] All performing carriers[32] are compelled to hold insurance cover in relation of liability under the Convention for the death of and personal injury to passengers of not less than 250,000 units of account[33] per passenger on each distinct occasion.[34] There are no apparent preconditions to the

---

[26]   Pursuant to Art 4bis see **7.2.1.3**.

[27]   Article 17(1). In the UK this is governed by the Civil Jurisdiction and Judgments Act 1982, Sch 4.

[28]   Article 17bis(1).

[29]   Article 17bis(2) and (3).

[30]   Or other person providing financial security.

[31]   Article 4bis(10).

[32]   Save where the ship is licensed to carry 12 or fewer passengers.

[33]   For discussion of units of account see **7.2.4.1** on caps on damages.

[34]   Article 4bis(1). The details of the 'Blue Card' certificate of insurance are in Appendix B to Annex I of the 2009 Regulation and are implemented in detail by the Merchant Shipping (Carriage of Passengers by Sea) Regulations 2012.

existence of the direct right of action, such as insolvency of the carrier. The claimant can elect to pursue the insurer alone.[35]

The insurer is only liable to a claimant to the extent of the liability limits under the policy, even if the insured carrier's liability would have been greater. The Convention is silent as to whether the insurer is liable in respect of interest or costs over and above the compulsory indemnity limits.

On the other hand, the insurer's entitlement to rely on other policy defences is restricted to asserting the 'wilful misconduct' of the carrier. It is not clear in cases of deliberate injury such as assault whether the 'wilful misconduct' of an employee or agent of the carrier will suffice to give the insurer a defence against a claimant victim. The insurer cannot rely on other policy defences or terms as against the claimant. It is assumed therefore that in the event of insolvency of the carrier, 'pay and be paid' clauses and notification requirements would be of no avail to the insurer.

The claimant cannot be in a better position against the insurer than he would have been against the carrier and consequently the insurer can invoke such defences as the carrier himself would have been able to maintain pursuant to the Convention against the claimant. Accordingly, the claimant's claim on the merits will be judged as if it were in fact the carrier who was the defendant to the claim.[36]

7.2.1.4   *Exclusivity of the Convention regime*

Article 14 states that no action for damages for the death of or personal injury to a passenger shall be brought against a carrier or performing carrier, 'otherwise than in accordance with this Convention'.

Accordingly, where a claim for damages arises out of an incident occurring in the course of carriage, no claim for negligence or breach of contract will lie against the carrier. Such causes of action cannot be used as means of circumventing Convention limits on damages or time bars.[37] Another point to note is that the exclusivity zone applies only to claims against the carrier or performing carrier. Where an incident giving rise to damage occurs in the course of carriage but as a result of the acts or omissions of a third party who is neither servant nor agent of the performing carrier, it is not a claim to which the Convention applies.

In principle at least, some services provided to passengers whilst on board a ship at sea may be said to be unrelated to the contract of carriage even though they take place at the same time as the carriage and on board the

---

[35]   Although the insurer has the right to join the carrier and/or performing carrier to proceedings.

[36]   Article 4bis(10).

[37]   See the discussion in Chapter 8 Travel by Air.

ship. For example many cruise ships have on-board medical facilities which are privately paid for services provided by independent medical staff. It is arguable that a claim for loss and damage arising out of clinical negligence of the medical team would not occur 'in the course of carriage', in which case the claim lies not against the performing carrier but the medical staff directly.

Even if the phrase 'in the course of the carriage' can be legitimately be interpreted so as to exclude services which are provided on board and during the carriage, such questions are ones of fact and degree and will ultimately turn on close analysis of the contract of carriage, brochures for cruise holidays and any documentation concerning the provision of the service in question. However, it is suggested that the court will look critically at any attempt by cruise operators to side-step Convention liability by reference to small print which is unlikely to have been at the forefront of the passenger's mind at the time of the provision of the service or arrangements which seek to suggest that crew are 'self-employed'. It is more likely that the court will adopt the viewpoint of whether the reasonable passenger would have thought that the services in question were being provided, 'in the course of the carriage'.

7.2.1.5 *Notice of Convention rights*

The carrier and the performing carrier are obliged to provide passengers with appropriate and comprehensible information regarding their rights under the Convention.[38] Non-compliance is a criminal offence.[39] Similar provisions exist in relation to the original Athens Convention. Failure to comply does not invalidate the carrier's right to rely on the Convention's provisions.[40]

7.2.2 Definitions and scope of the Convention

7.2.2.1 *Contract of carriage*

Liability under the Convention depends on there being a 'contract of carriage', which is defined as being, 'a contract made by or on behalf of a carrier for the carriage by sea of a passenger'.[41]

In claims before the English courts, questions regarding the formation and validity, terms and interpretation of a contract fall to be determined in accordance with English law. The identification of those entitled to sue and be sued is also left to domestic law, so that where an issue regarding the correct parties to a contract arises, such as where a passenger alleges that he was unaware that he was dealing with an agent rather than the

---

[38]   The 2009 Regulation, Art 7.
[39]   Merchant Shipping (Carriage of Passengers by Sea) Regulations 2012, reg 12.
[40]   *Mayor v P&O Ferries ('The Lion')* [1990] 2 Lloyd's Rep 144.
[41]   Article 1(2).

carrier, English law principles apply.[42] Similarly, in a wrongful death claim, questions of which parties are entitled to bring proceedings is a matter for English law.[43] However, the Convention itself is a code which applies to govern the rights and liabilities of carriers and passengers; it is not a scheme which depends on the incorporation of particular provisions of the Convention into a contract. It imposes its provisions as a matter of law on the parties.[44]

In cases under the original Athens Convention contracts of carriage which are other than 'for reward' are excluded.[45]

The scope of 'carriage' is defined as including the periods when the passenger is, 'in the course of embarkation or disembarkation'.[46] This phrase is not comparable with the sister provision in the Carriage by Air Conventions. There is a specific exclusion for any period when the passenger is in a 'marine terminal or station or on a quay or in or on any other port installation', thus fairly comprehensively excluding land-based activities, even if they are necessary steps to embarkation of the vessel.[47]

On the other hand, once the passenger takes to the water, he is in the 'course of carriage', even if such travel is by auxiliary transport rather than the ship, so long as it is the carrier which provides the transport or if the cost is included in the contract of carriage.[48] In a case where a passenger fell overboard from a ferry in the Irish sea, notwithstanding the fact that he was overboard when he met his death, it was common ground that the incident occurred 'during the course of the carriage' within the meaning of the Convention and that its liability regime, in particular Art 3 applied.[49]

7.2.2.2   Carrier and performing carrier

The carrier is the party who promises to provide the passenger with carriage pursuant to the contract. This is the case notwithstanding the fact that the party who enters the contract might not itself perform any of the carriage.[50] For example, in *Lee and Another v Airtours Holidays Ltd,* where an agent took a booking for a cruise holiday on behalf of a tour operator (which was not the operator of the ship), the latter was a 'carrier' because 'the agreement with the claimants included obligations pertaining

---

[42]   *Western Digital Corpn and others v British Airways plc* [2001] QB 733.
[43]   See Fatal Accidents Act 1976.
[44]   *RG Mayor v P&O Ferries ('The Lion')* [1990] 2 Lloyd's Rep 144, per Hobhouse J.
[45]   Merchant Shipping Act 1995, Sch 6, para 9.
[46]   Article 1(8)(a).
[47]   In contrast to the Montreal Convention.
[48]   Article 1(8)(a).
[49]   *Davis v Stena Line Ltd* [2005] 2 Lloyd's Rep 13.
[50]   Article 1(1)(a) and (b).

to carriage by sea and to that extent, it represented a contract for the carriage by sea of the claimants by the defendants'.[51]

By contrast, the 'performing carrier' is the party to whom performance of some or all of the carriage has been entrusted.[52] The performing carrier must also be either the 'owner, charterer or operator' of the ship who actually performs the carriage.[53]

Where a carrier delegates performance of some or all of the carriage to a performing carrier, the carrier remains liable to the passenger for the entire carriage and his liability is joint and several with the performing carrier.[54] It is no defence on the part of the (contracting) carrier that the fault arose as a result of acts or omissions of the employees or agents of the performing carrier. The carrier is vicariously liable in these circumstances.[55]

The passenger can therefore choose whether to pursue the party with whom he has a contract or the actual operator of the ship. The Convention provisions apply equally to both actions. The only point of difference is where a contracting carrier has agreed obligations to the passenger over and above those in the Convention in which case any performing carrier is not bound by those terms unless he has expressly agreed in writing.[56]

Where both a carrier and performing carrier are parties to an action in the English court for damages by a passenger, any claims for a contribution, indemnity or other remedies as between them are not governed by the Convention.[57]

7.2.2.3 *Ship*

'Ship' under the Convention is defined as 'only a seagoing vessel, excluding an air-cushion vehicle'.[58] In the context of the Merchant Shipping Act 1995, it has been held that a jet-ski is not a 'seagoing vessel' because they do not go to sea on voyages and would not be seaworthy in heavy weather. It is not, however, clear whether a ship which remains within coastal waters is or is not a seagoing vessel.[59]

---

[51]   [2004] 1 Lloyd's Law Reports 683 at [32].
[52]   Article 4(1).
[53]   Article 1(1)(b).
[54]   Article 4(2) and (4).
[55]   Article 4(2).
[56]   Article 4(3).
[57]   Article 4(5). For discussion as to the law applicable to contribution claims see **5.2.2.13** and **5.2.3.6**(iii).
[58]   Article 1(3).
[59]   *R v Goodwin* [2006] 1 WLR 546, 558D.

In *Michael v Musgrave* it was held that the question of whether a vessel was 'seagoing' depended upon its actual business at the time of the incident. The issue is not whether the ship *can* go to sea but whether in fact it does go to sea.[60] Therefore, on the facts, it was held that a rigid inflatable boat without a cabin which was used for the purposes of taking day-trippers along the Menai Strait to see places of scenic and wildlife interest was 'going to sea' at the time when the claimant passenger lost his footing. A significant evidential factor in the decision was the fact that the local maritime authorities had identified the stretch of water where the incident took place as being 'sea' for the purposes of the Merchant Shipping legislation.

Similarly it has been held that neither a 17 foot long marine assault craft nor the inflatable banana raft being towed behind it were, whether taken together or individually, seagoing vessels capable of falling within the Convention definition of ship. The marine assault craft was not seagoing because that would suggest, 'something more than progressing a short distance up and down a bay, namely a vessel capable of a voyage of some length'.[61]

Several of the English authorities make reference to a requirement that a vessel be capable of being used in 'navigation'.[62] In cases under the original Convention this creates a second limb to the test of whether a craft is a 'ship'. Navigation is the nautical art or science of conducting a ship from one place to another.[63] In practice, this establishes a pragmatic dividing line between the use of vessels which is partially if not even predominantly to get from A to B and situations which might be described as 'messing about in boats'.[64] It is unclear whether in cases under the consolidated Convention this part of the test can survive as it would now appear to be an unnecessary domestic gloss on the Convention definition which might not be consistent with European authority.

7.2.2.4 *Passenger*

The Convention defines a passenger as:

> '... any person carried in a ship (a) under a contract of carriage, or (b) who, with the consent of the carrier, is accompanying a vehicle or live animals which are covered by a contract for the carriage of goods not governed by this Convention.'

---

[60] *The Sea Eagle* [2011] EWHC 1438 (Admlty); [2012] 2 Lloyd's Rep 37 at [31]–[32].

[61] *McEwan v Bingham (t/a Studland Watersports)* [2000] CLY 4691.

[62] A test apparently derived from what is now s 313(1) of the Merchant Shipping Act 1995 and imported by the Merchant Shipping Act 1983, Sch 7, Part II, para 12 see e g *The Sea Eagle* [2012] 2 Lloyd's Rep 37 at [20] and [28].

[63] *Steedman v Scofield* [1992] 2 Lloyd's Rep 163, 166.

[64] *R v Goodwin* [2006] 1 WLR 546, 558D at [27] per Lord Phillips MR.

This definition will include not only those who are party to the contract of carriage, but others, such as children or protected parties, on whose behalf a contract has been made. Limb (b) in practice is directed towards ferry passengers accompanying vehicles or goods.

Those on board who are not 'under' a contract of carriage or without consent, such as stowaways, are not covered. Persons who are on board as crew are not carried under a contract of carriage, but under a contract either of employment or for services and are not passengers.[65] This is probably the case whether or not they are actually acting in the course of their employment at the time of an incident or not.

On the other hand, there is no distinction between business and leisure passengers. A passenger is still a passenger even where the purpose of his journey is to fulfil his work obligations for a third party.

Where individuals are on board as volunteer crew, there is some authority for the proposition that they will also be 'passengers'.[66] However, this decision arises in the context of a domestic statutory definition of 'passenger' which was construed in light of the historical English law approach to the term.[67] As the Convention text does not share any of the wording or the history, it is suggested that a different result is likely to be achieved in a Convention case.

7.2.2.5   *International carriage*

'International carriage' for the purposes of the Convention means any carriage in which, according to the contract of carriage, the place of departure and the place of destination are situated in two different states, or in a single state if, according to the contract of carriage or the scheduled itinerary, there is an intermediate port of call in another state.[68] Therefore, a cross-channel ferry from Calais to Dover provides international carriage. A round-trip cruise from Miami which is scheduled to call at a port outside the US is also international carriage, even if (a) the scheduled call never in fact takes place or (b) the passenger disembarks before the scheduled call or (c) the port of call is situated in a non-contracting state.[69]

---

[65]   *Haley v Western Airlines Inc (Mexico City Aircrash of 31 October 1979)* 708 F 2d 400 (9th Cir, 1983, US Court of Appeals) in relation to air crew.
[66]   *Secretary of State for Trade v Booth* [1983] 1 WLR 243.
[67]   Merchant Shipping (Safety Convention) Act 1949, s 26(1)(a).
[68]   Article 1(9).
[69]   See e g *Rotterdamsche Bank NV v British Airways Corp* [1953] 1 WLR 493.

7.2.2.6   *Domestic carriage*

For present purposes claims in respect of incidents arising in the course of carriage of passengers by sea in the UK are governed by the original Athens Convention.[70]

The 2009 Regulation will in due course additionally extend the Convention provisions to the carriage of passengers by sea within a single member state on certain classes of ship[71] if any of the following applies:

(a)   the ship is flying a flag of or is registered in a member state;
(b)   the contract of carriage has been made in a member state; or
(c)   the place of departure or destination, according to the contract of carriage, is in a member state.[72]

The classification of passenger ships is designated according to the sea area in which they operate.[73] The scheme of the 2009 Regulation is gradually to cover all domestic passenger ships, starting with those which operate closest to international waters.[74] The UK has taken advantage of the transitional provisions and therefore the 2009 Regulation will not apply to carriage on Class A ships before 31 December 2016 and on Class B ships before 31 December 2018.[75]

7.2.3   Liability for personal injury

Article 3 of the Convention provides the basis of liability of the carrier to his passenger for personal injury and death. It is the most substantially revised provision in the consolidated Convention text following the 2002 Protocol. This has clarified the scheme of liability as it stood under the original Convention in many significant respects.

Some aspects of the scheme of the original Convention have been maintained. Accordingly the liability of the carrier falls effectively into two categories, depending on whether personal injury or death is caused by either (what is now defined in the consolidated Convention as) a:

(a)   shipping incident; or
(b)   any other kind of incident.[76]

---

[70]   Merchant Shipping Act 1995, s 184; Carriage of Passengers and their Luggage by Sea (Domestic Carriage) Order 1987/670.
[71]   Article 1(2).
[72]   Article 2.
[73]   Directive 98/18/EC, Art 4, see also guidance at www.gov.uk/vessel-classification-and-certification.
[74]   The 2009 Regulation, Art 1. The Commission is obliged to lay proposals to extend the application to Class C and D ships by no later than 30 June 2013.
[75]   The 2009 Regulation, Art 11 and Merchant Shipping (Carriage of Passengers by Sea) Regulations 2012, reg 4.
[76]   Article 3(1) and (2).

7.2.3.1 *Shipping incident*

A 'shipping incident' means, 'shipwreck, capsizing, collision or stranding of the ship, explosion or fire in the ship, or defect in the ship'.[77]

Liability in such cases is in two stages. First, if personal injury or death is caused by any of the 'events' identified on this exhaustive list, then the carrier is strictly liable up to a limit of 250,000 units of account.[78] The carrier can only avoid liability by proving that the incident either (i) was wholly caused by the deliberate act of a third party or (ii) resulted from one of a list of exceptional circumstances, namely, act of war, hostilities, civil war, insurrection or a natural phenomenon of an exceptional, inevitable and irresistible character.[79]

This represents a significant change of emphasis from the text of the original Convention. In the original Art 3, there was a rebuttable presumption of fault in a case which arose from or in connexion with, 'shipwreck, collision, stranding, explosion or fire, or defect in the ship'. Fault on the part of the carrier was presumed, but it was open to the carrier to prove he was not at fault.

Under the consolidated Convention, the defence of the carrier is in some senses narrower. The defendant carrier must show that one of the listed events caused the incident in order to be exonerated from liability, not merely that he was not at fault. Further, in cases where a third party is said to be culpable, the defendant carrier will now generally be liable to his passenger save where a third party intentionally caused the incident *and* was wholly to blame for it. Therefore, for example in a collision case, it is no longer sufficient for the carrier to demonstrate that the carrier's navigation was not at fault. He must also show that the third party intended to cause a collision.

Conversely, the new list of exceptional circumstances potentially widens the scope of the defence. It certainly has the effect of unifying the scope of the defence, which under the original Convention would have been a matter for the law of the courts where the claim was heard. The concepts of 'act of war, hostilities, civil war and insurrection' are likely to be sufficiently wide to encompass criminal activity motivated by political or terrorist purposes.[80] The phrase, 'natural phenomenon of an exceptional, inevitable and irresistible character' reflects events which are often generically described as 'acts of God' but would, it is suggested, include extreme weather conditions or earthquake. These terms will acquire an autonomous meaning in the case-law.

---

[77] Article 3(5)(a).
[78] Units of account are discussed at **7.2.4.1.**
[79] Article 3(1)(a) and (b).
[80] IMO Guidelines, para 2.2.

Secondly, for loss and damage over the 250,000 units of account limit in a shipping incident case, the carrier is presumed to be liable to the passenger. The presumption is rebuttable and therefore if the carrier proves that the shipping incident arose otherwise than through his fault or neglect, he is not liable to the passenger for this second layer of loss and damage.

7.2.3.2   Defect in the ship

The Convention defines 'defect in the ship' for the first time as:[81]

> '... any malfunction, failure or non-compliance with applicable safety regulations in respect of any part of the ship or its equipment when used for the escape, evacuation, embarkation and disembarkation of passengers, or when used for the propulsion, steering, safe navigation, mooring, anchoring, arriving at or leaving berth or anchorage, or damage control after flooding; or when used for the launching of life saving appliances.'

The definition was a significant feature of the negotiations at the conference which agreed the text of the 2002 Protocol. It is clearly wide enough to encompass incidents which are caused by a failure to operate the ship and its equipment in accordance with the applicable safety regulations as well as mere physical defects in the vessel or its equipment.

It can be seen from the travaux preparatoires[82] that there was significant concern to limit the concept of 'defect' to exclude accidents which occur in the ordinary operation of the ship and its equipment. Accordingly, a claimant must show malfunction of failure of the ship or its equipment or non-compliance with a safety regulation to come within the definition.

On this basis, slipping accidents due to spilled drinks on board will not fall within the definition of 'defect in the ship'.[83] However, where a cruise operator fails to follow the guidance for containment of norovirus[84] and the ship remains contaminated as a result, it is arguable that such a failure brings the operator within the definition of, 'defect in the ship'. Whether in practice this amounts to a significant litigation advantage to the passenger is doubtful because, in such an example, it would only be a short step to prove fault-based liability.

7.2.3.3   Other 'incidents'

All other 'incidents' which are not 'shipping incidents' and which give rise to personal injury or death are governed by Art 3(2). In such cases the carrier is liable if the incident was due to his fault or neglect. The

---

[81]   Article 3(5)(c).
[82]   Available at www.imo.org (account log in required to access documents).
[83]   See e g *Dawkins v Carnival plc* [2012] 1 Lloyd's Rep 1.
[84]   www.hpa.org.uk.

Convention does not provide any assistance with the meaning of 'incident'. It would seemingly have a wider meaning than the word 'accident' used in the Montreal Convention.[85] There are some personal injury contexts in which it is somewhat artificial to speak of an 'incident'. For example, in a case where a claimant alleges that the on-board medical staff failed to treat her appropriately which led to an exacerbation of a pre-existing condition, in practical terms it might be difficult to identify a specific 'incident' from which the injury loss and damage results. The better view is that an instance of fault or neglect will probably constitute an 'incident' even if the injury is not immediate.

The claimant must prove that there was fault or neglect.[86] The question of what is the relevant standard by which conduct should be judged is governed by the law of the country where the claim is heard. In the context of international carriage, it is generally difficult for defendant carrier's to argue the 'local standards' defence which is the stalwart of tour operator claims.[87] The fault or neglect need not be that of the carrier itself; it is enough that the carrier's agents or employees acting within the course of their employment are responsible.[88]

7.2.3.4   *Fault or neglect*

Whilst the claimant bears the burden of proving the carrier's 'fault or neglect', it is apparent that in cases where the allegation is that the carrier failed to take adequate steps to avoid or manage a known hazard or risk, it is incumbent on the carrier to adduce adequate evidence that its systems were implemented effectively.

In *Dawkins v Carnival (t/a P&O Cruises)*,[89] the claimant was a passenger on the cruise liner *Oriana* when she slipped and fell whilst walking through the Conservatory Restaurant. It was found that the cause of the slip was a spillage of water. There was no evidence as to how and when precisely the spillage occurred. The restaurant was in constant use throughout the day and the area where the accident occurred was near a clearing station which should have been permanently manned. The carrier defended the claim on the basis that the claimant had failed to prove that it ought to have identified and cleared the spill by the time of her fall. It was held that where there was a hazard present this raised a prima facie case of negligence and on the facts in the absence of evidence from the carrier from members of staff claiming to be implementing the cleaning system at the relevant time, the only logical inference was that the spill

---

[85]   See Chapter 8 Travel by Air.
[86]   Article 3(2).
[87]   See Chapter 3 Package Travel II.
[88]   Article 3(5)(b).
[89]   [2012] 1 Lloyd's Rep 1.

had been present on the floor for longer than the very brief period which would have excused the carrier liability.[90]

Norovirus outbreaks are sadly a relatively common feature of cruise ships. Whilst norovirus is prevalent in the population at large and therefore it is unlikely that a carrier would be found to be at fault merely because its passenger contracted the illness, in cases of either repeated, sustained or substantial outbreaks it will be incumbent on the carrier to demonstrate that it implemented effectively and thoroughly the guidance for the management of such outbreaks.[91]

7.2.4   Limitation of the carrier's liability

7.2.4.1   Caps on damages

The carrier's liability to the passenger for loss and damage caused by personal injury or death under the Convention is capped at 400,000 units of account.[92] The same limit applies to any action against the servant or agent of the carrier or performing carrier in respect of loss or damage covered by the Convention.[93] The limit applies 'on each distinct occasion' and is 'per passenger'. It is open to the carrier and the passenger to agree expressly and in writing to higher limits.[94] Examples of such agreement are, unsurprisingly, vanishingly rare.

The insurer's Convention liability to the passenger in respect of a direct right of action is 250,000 units of account.[95]

A unit of account is a 'special drawing right' (SDR) which is a unit of currency defined by the International Monetary Fund (IMF). Damages in a Convention claim remain payable in the currency of the country in whose courts the claim is being heard, with any exchange from SDRs being carried out as at the date of the judgment or settlement agreement and in accordance with IMF methods of valuation at that time.[96] At the date of writing the pound sterling is roughly in parity with the SDR.

In a case where several dependants are entitled to damages in respect of the wrongful death of a single passenger, the limit is applied in respect of the total loss and damage arising out of the death and not in respect of each claim or claimant. Similarly where the law of the country whose courts are determining a claim permits recovery of loss and damage on the part of a secondary victim (eg for psychiatric harm) following death

---

[90]   See also *Ward v Tesco Stores Ltd* [1976] 1 WLR 810.
[91]   www.hpa.org.uk.
[92]   Article 7(1).
[93]   Articles 4(1) and 11.
[94]   Article 10(1).
[95]   Article 4(10).
[96]   Article 9(1).

or personal injury to a passenger, the claims of the primary and secondary victim are aggregated before the cap is applied.[97]

In periodical payment cases, the periodical payments must be capitalised and the relevant cap on damages is applied to the capitalised value.[98] The cap on carrier's liability applies only to claims for damages. It does not affect claims for interest or costs.[99] However, the Convention is silent as to whether the cap on insurer's liability is inclusive or exclusive of interest or costs.

Where a claimant is entitled to recover against more than one defendant, such as the carrier, as well as a performing carrier or the performing carrier's servants or agents, the total amount recovered by the claimant cannot exceed the highest limit on damages and each individual defendant is only liable to the extent of limit specifically applicable to him.[100]

In claims which proceed pursuant to the original Athens Convention, where the defendant is a carrier whose principal place of business is in the UK, the limit on liability is 300,000 units of account.[101]

7.2.4.2 *Loss of the cap on damages – reckless or intentional conduct*

The carrier is not entitled to the benefit of the limit on liability either in Art 7 or any higher limit agreed pursuant to Art 10(1):[102]

> '... if it is proved that the damage resulted from an act or omission of the carrier done with the intent to cause such damage or recklessly and with knowledge that such damage would probably result.'

There are some useful parallels which can be drawn between the Convention case-law and that decided in respect of Air Passenger claims pursuant to the Montreal Convention regime.[103] It is well established that, in common with limitation under other Maritime Conventions, the burden of proof rests on the claimant who is trying to 'break' the limits of liability.[104]

There are two separate limbs to the test. The conduct in question has to be both 'reckless', as well as 'with knowledge that damage would probably

---

[97] Article 12(1).

[98] Article 7(1).

[99] Article 10(2).

[100] Article 12(3).

[101] Carriage of Passengers and their Luggage by Sea (United Kingdom Carriers) Order 1998, SI 1998/2917.

[102] Article 13(1).

[103] See for example *Goldman v Thai Airways International Ltd* [1983] 1 WLR 1186.

[104] *Margolle v Delta Maritime Co Ltd ('The Saint Jacques II' and 'Gudermes')* [2003] 1 Lloyd's Rep 203; [2003] EWHC 2452 (Admlty).

result'. 'Recklessness' has been explained as being, 'conduct ... [which] engenders the risk of undesirable consequences ... [and] which indicates a decision to run the risk or a mental attitude of indifference to its existence'. Furthermore the test is subjective and there has to be actual conscious knowledge on the part of the carrier.[105]

Therefore in a case where a pilot of an international air liner had failed to switch on the fasten seat belt signs when entering an area of turbulence, even if this had been reckless, the claimant had failed to show that the pilot had knowledge of the likelihood of severe turbulence likely to cause injury.[106]

However, the terminology in the Carriage by Air Conventions is wider and there is an additional element to the test in Athens Convention claims. It has been held that the act or omission which is done either recklessly or with intention to cause damage in maritime cases must be that of the carrier or his alter ego and not merely one of his servant or agent.[107] In doing so, Hobhouse J placed reliance on what he described as a 'consistent policy' in interpreting similar provisions in other Maritime Conventions[108] as well as the precise drafting of the original Athens Convention itself. In this regard the Convention regime differs from the Carriage by Air Conventions.

In practical terms, where a claim for death or personal injury arises from a collision between vessels, it is virtually axiomatic that the carrier will be able to limit his liability[109] and in practice the same applies for all passenger claims against his own carrier.

There are a few examples of the limits been successfully 'broken'. Where cargo which was liable to be damaged if exposed to water was subjected to 'deplorably bad handling' and the carrier failed to call evidence to explain, inferences were drawn that the damage was as a result of reckless acts and omissions with the knowledge that damage would probably result.[110]

7.2.4.3   Contributory fault

In a Convention case the carrier can exonerate himself either wholly or partly from liability in respect of personal injury to or death of a passenger where the carrier proves that the personal injury or death was caused or contributed to by the passenger's own fault or neglect.

---

[105] *Nugent and Killick v Michael Goss Aviation Ltd* [2000] 2 Lloyd's Rep 222, 227 and 229.
[106] *Goldman v Thai Airways Ltd* [1983] 1 WLR 1186; *Gurtner v Beaton* [1993] 2 Lloyd's Rep 369.
[107] *Mayor v P&O Ferries ('The Lion')* [1990] 2 Lloyd's Rep 144, 149; *Margolle v Delta Maritime Co Ltd ('The Saint Jacques II' and 'Gudermes')* [2003] 1 Lloyd's Rep 203, 208.
[108] For example the Convention on Limitation of Liability for Maritime Claims 1976.
[109] *Margolle v Delta Maritime Co Ltd ('The Saint Jacques II' and 'Gudermes')* [2003] 1 Lloyd's Rep 203, 209; *The Leerort* [2001] 2 Lloyd's Rep 291.
[110] *SS Pharmaceutical v Quantas Airways Ltd* [1991] 1 Lloyd's Rep 288.

It is the law of the court in which the claim is proceeding which determines the extent of the availability of the defence.[111] There is no reason in principle why the Law Reform (Contributory Negligence) Act 1945 should not apply in personal injury and wrongful death claims before the English Courts. However, it is well established that as a matter of English law, contributory fault is only a partial defence.[112]

In cases which proceed under the original Athens Convention, the application of the 1945 Act is expressly confirmed in statute.[113]

7.2.4.4 *Contractual defences*

It is not permissible for a carrier to seek to contract out of the Convention regime, whether by seeking to fix lower limits for damages, reducing the jurisdiction options available to a claimant, shifting the burden of proof or purporting to relieve any person from liability altogether.[114]

7.2.4.5 *Time bars*

The time-limit for bringing proceedings for personal injury or wrongful death pursuant to the Convention is 2 years.[115] Such a time-limit applies where the carrier is also a tour operator and where the booking conditions incorporate Convention limits.[116]

Time starts to run in a personal injury action from the date of disembarkation of the passenger.[117] In a wrongful death claim where the death occurs during the carriage, time starts at the date when the passenger should have disembarked. Where the death of the passenger occurs following disembarkation, the date of death is used for the calculation of time, however, there is a maximum time period of 3 years from the date of disembarkation.[118]

A new provision in the consolidated Convention arises in cases before courts whose domestic law permits interruption or suspension of limitation, so that there is a long-stop time bar of 5 years from the later of actual or intended disembarkation. However, if the claimant knows or ought reasonably to know of the injury, loss or damage caused by the incident, the maximum period for bringing proceedings is 3 years from the date of such knowledge (which under the original Convention was the

---

[111] Article 6.
[112] *Pitts v Hunt* [1991] 2 QB 24.
[113] Merchant Shipping Act 1995 Sch 6, Part II, para 3.
[114] Article 18.
[115] Article 16(1).
[116] *Norfolk v MyTravel Group plc* [2004] 1 Lloyd's Rep 106.
[117] Article 16(2)(a).
[118] Article 16(2)(b).

longest possible limitation period in any event). As English law does not recognise the concepts of either suspension or interruption of limitation in the strict sense of these terms as used in civil law systems, these provisions will have marginal if any relevance in claims before the English courts.

Section 33 of the Limitation Act 1980 does not apply to Convention claims and therefore it is not permissible to extend time once the primary limitation period has expired.[119] Nor is there any equivalent of the extension to limitation in cases of 'disability' in favour of children or protected parties,[120] although conceivably on a purposive interpretation it might be argued that this amounted to a 'suspension' of limitation for the purposes of the Convention.

It has been held that where a claimant to a Convention claim applies after expiry of the limitation period in Art 16 to amend his claim so as to add or substitute a party, the English court has power to entertain such an application pursuant to CPR, r 19.5,[121] notwithstanding the restrictive wording of CPR, r 19.5(1)(c).

The period of limitation set down by Art 16 may be extended once a cause of action has arisen by two methods. First, the carrier may declare an extension of limitation. Secondly, the parties may agree an extension. Either way, the extension must be in writing.[122]

7.2.5   Damages in Convention cases

7.2.5.1   Advance payment

Carriers who perform the whole or the part of the carriage must make an 'advance payment' in the case of death or personal injury in shipping incident cases only. The payment should be, 'sufficient to cover immediate economic needs on a basis proportionate to the damage suffered within 15 days of the identification of the person entitled to damages'.[123] In the case of death, the minimum amount of the payment is €21,000.

Such 'advance payments' do not constitute an admission of liability. They can be offset against any subsequent sums paid by way of damages. There are limited circumstances in which the advance payment is refundable by the receiving party, namely:[124]

(a)   where the receiving party is not the person entitled to damages;

---

[119]   *Higham v Stena Sea Link* [1996] 1 WLR 1107.
[120]   Limitation Act 1980, s 28.
[121]   *Adams v Thomson Holidays Limited* [2009] EWHC 2559 (QB), unreported.
[122]   Article 16(4).
[123]   The 2009 Regulation, Art 6.
[124]   The 2009 Regulation, Art 6(2).

(b) where contributory fault is established (presumably to an extent which means that the carrier has paid more than his liability to the claimant); or

(c) where the carrier is exonerated from liability in one of the exceptions in Article 3(1).[125]

7.2.5.2 Punitive/exemplary damages

Punitive and exemplary damages are specifically excluded from the definition of loss under the Convention.[126] This provision did not feature in the original Athens Convention.

7.2.5.3 Heads of loss

Save for the exclusion of exemplary and punitive damages referred to above, there is no definition of damage within the Convention. It is left to the adjudicating court to determine which loss is 'cognisable' for the purposes of a Convention claim.[127]

It is conceivable that the contract of carriage is governed by a law other than English law. Any express provisions regarding loss and damage would fall to be interpreted in accordance with the proper law of the contract.[128] It is suggested, however, that the cognisable loss and damage would still fall to be determined in accordance with English law. The claim is not one for damages for breach of contract and no issue of applicable law arises.

Claims for loss of enjoyment are in principle permissible as part of the general damages arising out of a personal injury claim. Although the claim is not for breach of contract, the better view is that diminution in the value of the contract services can still be recovered, on the basis that the phrase 'loss and damage' in the Convention is wide enough to encompass this loss.

Similarly the Convention is silent as to the method by which damages should fall to be assessed, but for the same reasons there is no reason why any difference of approach from a purely domestic case is needed.

In wrongful death claims, the usual heads of loss recoverable in a Fatal Accidents Act 1976 or Law Reform (Miscellaneous Provisions) Act 1934 claim can be claimed.

---

[125] See **7.2.3.1**.

[126] Article 3(5)(d).

[127] *Morris v KLM Royal Dutch Airlines* [2002] QB 100 at [70]–[77]. See Chapter 9 Remedies for consideration of recoverable loss under English law.

[128] Bearing in mind the limitations on such clauses imposed by Art 18 discussed at **7.2.4.4**.

7.3   OTHER PERSONAL INJURY AND WRONGFUL DEATH CLAIMS AT SEA

7.3.1   Employer's Liability

7.3.1.1   *Jurisdiction and applicable law*

There are no special rules to consider regarding the question of whether the English court has power to hear and determine a claim brought by an employee as against his employer simply because the accident occurred at sea.[129] It is necessary to bear in mind that an employee's claim might well arise in tort as in contract. There are specific rules concerning jurisdiction over employment contract disputes generally in Brussels I.[130]

Insofar as the applicable law is concerned, specific rules also apply in Rome I and the Rome Convention to employment contract claims.[131] Where the claim is raised in tort, the general rules will apply.[132] This poses no problem so long as the ship is in the territorial waters of a country at the time that an accident occurs. However, the position in respect of accidents on the high seas is less clear. Such accidents do not take place in a 'country' whose law can then be applied. However, it is suggested that in such cases the law of the country whose flag the ship carries should be adopted as a starting point for the purposes of Rome II, Art 4(1).[133] This may represent a departure in many cases from the pre-Rome II law, when English law adopted the general 'maritime law' in such cases.

It should also be borne in mind that when considering personal injury and wrongful death claims, any relevant provisions of health and safety law may well be considered by mandatory and to override any 'choice' of law in any event.[134]

7.3.1.2   *Relevant health and safety legislation*

Parliament has given the Secretary of State power to make regulations regarding the safety of persons whilst on UK ships.[135] A UK ship is one which is registered in the UK or which is not registered elsewhere and its owners have links to the UK.[136] The power has been utilised copiously and many of the Regulations made under this power apply to non-UK

---

[129] For consideration of the general rules on jurisdiction see Chapter 4.
[130] See **4.4.5.9**.
[131] See **5.3.2.10**.
[132] See **5.2**.
[133] *Dicey, Morris and Collins on the Conflict of Laws* (15th edn, 2012), vol 2 at para 35–033.
[134] Rome II, Art 16, see **5.2.2.11**.
[135] Merchant Shipping Act 1995, s 85.
[136] Merchant Shipping Act 1995, s 85(2).

ships. Many of these Regulations make specific provision regarding their territorial scope. It is beyond the scope of this work to list or consider them all.[137]

It is worth noting that s 85 of the Merchant Shipping Act does not, unlike its sister legislation the Health and Safety at Work Act 1974 carry a presumption that breach of its provisions gives rise to civil liability. In practice, however, it is suggested that it is highly unlikely that a court would wish to draw any distinction between the position under the 1974 Act and the provisions in relation to working seamen.[138]

7.3.1.3 *Convention on Limitation of Liability for Maritime Claims 1976*

If a member of a ship's crew has a contract of employment which is governed by English, Scots or Northern Irish law, then the shipowner is not permitted to limit his liability in claims for personal injury or wrongful death.[139] Where, in accordance with the relevant choice of law rules, the contract of employment is governed by a proper law which permits the shipowner to limit liability, it is not clear whether s 185(4) of the Merchant Shipping Act would be regarded as either an overriding mandatory rule of English law or applied by reason of public policy.[140]

7.3.2 Collision cases

It should be explained that the possible relevance of the general rules on collision cases is as an option of last resort. It will only arise where the claimant is a passenger who wishes to pursue a party other than his carrier or the carrier's insurer. In such a case a passenger on ship A might want to sue the operator or master of ship B, usually in the case of a collision. Where the incident arises under the consolidated Convention, it would be a rare case where the carrier could avoid liability below the 250,000 units of account limit.[141] However, in a large claim where the loss exceeds this amount, it might be necessary to pursue the ship which was at fault for the collision.

Liability in such cases arises in the tort of negligence. The possible factual circumstances in which such claims arise are too numerous to discuss in this text and reference should be had to specialist works regarding

---

[137] A useful starting point is www.dft.gov.uk/mca/mcga07-home/workingatsea/mcga-healthandsafety/mcga-dqs-shs-health_and_safety.htm (as at 1 April 2013).

[138] For example see the somewhat unconvincing reasoning deployed to find civil liability in *Ziemniak v ETPM Deep Sea Ltd* [2003] EWCA Civ 636; [2003] 2 Lloyd's Rep 214.

[139] As a result of Merchant Shipping Act, s 185(4) in combination with Art 3(e) of the Convention itself.

[140] See Chapter 5.

[141] The narrowness of the exceptions is described at **7.2.3.1**.

collision cases. The applicable law and jurisdiction in such claims are governed by the general principles in relation to tort claims.[142]

The liability of shipowners where a person suffers death or injury as a result of the fault of more than one ship is joint and several.[143] The court has power to apportion liability in such cases as between defendant shipowners.[144] However, it is not permissible for a claimant to circumvent the limits on damages by proceeding against several defendants.[145]

The Convention on Limitation of Liability for Maritime Claims 1976 permits a shipowner to limit his liability to claimants in such cases. The 1976 Convention has a similar structure to the Athens Conventions and the right to limit damages is lost under mirror terms to that in Art 13 of the Athens Convention.[146] Limits are calculated by reference to the tonnage of the ship.[147]

The limitation period for an action to which English law applies is 2 years from the date of loss or damage[148] or the date of death.

7.4   PROCEDURAL ISSUES IN ADMIRALTY CLAIMS

An important, but often overlooked, feature of all claims which involve personal injury on a ship is that the only court which is competent to issue such a claim is the Admiralty Division of the High Court.[149] It is not permissible to issue such a claim out of the county court or any other division of the High Court. In light of the rigid limitation scheme in Athens Convention and Convention on Limitation of Liability for Maritime Claims 1976 cases, this is a detail which should not be disregarded. The author is aware of claims which have been started in the county court, but then transferred to the Admiralty Court, but the power of the county court to transfer a claim which it has no power to issue is uncertain. In practice, low value personal injury claims are routinely transferred out of the Admiralty Court to the claimant's local county court following issue.

---

[142] See Chapters 4 Jurisdiction and 5 Applicable Law.
[143] Merchant Shipping Act 1995, s 188.
[144] Merchant Shipping Act 1995, s 189. The limitation period for such a claim is 1 year from the date of payment, s 190(4).
[145] Merchant Shipping Act 1995, s 189(3).
[146] See **7.2.4.2**.
[147] www.imo.org/About/Conventions/listofconventions/pages/convention-on-limitation-of-liability-for-maritime-claims-(llmc).aspx.
[148] *Sweet v Owners of Blyth Lifeboat, The Times*, 22 February 2002.
[149] Senior Courts Act 1981, s 20(2)(f).

CHAPTER 8

TRAVEL BY AIR

Sarah Crowther

8.1 INTRODUCTION

In line with the title of this work, the focus of this chapter is on claims for death or personal injury which arise out of air travel.

As with travel by sea[1] there are myriad legal rights which affect passengers and crew whilst in the course of carriage by air. Specific legislation deals with such topics as the rights of those whose mobility is reduced, allegations of disability discrimination and also the rights of recourse in the event that a flight is delayed or baggage is lost or damaged.[2] The legal and policy issues which are raised are complex and deserve more detailed treatment than can be provided here.

8.2 CARRIAGE OF PASSENGERS BY AIR

8.2.1 History

The first commercial passenger flight took place in 1919. It was very soon apparent that international air transport poses many challenges for national legal systems and that an international solution was necessary. The fledging commercial passenger air carriage industry was subject to the vagaries of numerous competing national law regimes of jurisdiction and applicable law, sometimes throughout the course of a single carriage.[3] For example, in England and Wales, such carriage was governed by the common law rules in relation to carriers and bailment. There could hardly have been a clearer case for harmonisation and increased certainty.

The origin of the modern law governing the liability of the carrier to his passenger is the Convention for the Unification of Certain Rules Relating to International Carriage by Air. Signed at Warsaw on 12 October 1929, better known as the Warsaw Convention 1929.[4]

---

[1] Discussed in Chapter 7.
[2] Topics which are dealt with in the main work on aviation law, *Shawcross & Beaumont: Air Law* (Looseleaf, LexisNexis Butterworths).
[3] As envisaged by Greene LJ in *Grein v Imperial Airways* [1937] 1 KB 50, 75.
[4] Referred to throughout this Chapter as 'the Warsaw Convention'.

The Warsaw Convention was the result of a proposal by the French Government in 1923 and followed several years of deliberations by CITEJA,[5] a body which has since become known as the International Civil Aviation Organisation (ICAO) and is part of the United Nations based in Montreal. The Warsaw Convention came into effect on 13 February 1933. Between 1948 and 1951 a further legal committee was set up by ICAO with a view to writing a replacement draft convention, however it was not until 1955 following the ICAO conference at The Hague that a protocol for the amendment of the Warsaw Convention was adopted. Over time there were further revisions to the Warsaw system of conventions,[6] culminating in the Montreal Convention 1999.[7]

It has been said both that:[8]

> '... it is clear that what was sought to be achieved was a uniform international code which could be applied to all [international carriage by air] contracts. One of the objects of the Convention was to encourage the development of the airline industry, which it was felt might be unduly inhibited by the increasing legal complexity of conducting a business of that kind across international frontiers. The aim was to reduce the opportunity for litigation and to provide a more definite and equitable basis on which airline operators could negotiate rates with their insurers.'

And at the same time that:

> '... it should not be forgotten that one of the advantages of excluding the rules of the common law is that the United Kingdom rules are designed to impose liability on the carrier without proof of fault in respect of the death of or injury to passengers and to nullify contractual provisions the effect of which would be to relive the carrier of liability or to restrict his liability in amount.'

8.2.2   Scheme of the Warsaw Conventions

The history is of practical relevance for practitioners today. It must be noted that not all states parties to the Warsaw Convention have ratified all subsequent revisions. Equally, some states, which were not party to the Warsaw Convention, have since joined into later Conventions or Protocols. A further complicating factor is that the Conventions require a minimum number of states parties to ratify before the Convention comes into effect. As revisions generally have the effect of superseding previous treaties, in the case of international carriage by air, in order to determine

---

[5]   Comité International Technique d'Experts Juridiques Aérien.

[6]   Including the Guadalajara Convention, the Guatemala City Protocol and the Montreal Protocol.

[7]   Done at Montreal on 28 May 1999.

[8]   *Herd v Clyde Helicopters* [1997] AC 534, 553A per Lord Hope.

which Warsaw system Convention applies to a claim, it is necessary to identify the most recent effective Convention which has been ratified by both states parties.[9]

8.2.3 Montreal Convention 1999

The Montreal Convention entered into force on 4 November 2003 and has been in force in England and Wales since June 2004. It has 103 states parties.[10] In the overwhelming majority of cases the relevant Convention will be Montreal and this chapter deals with the Montreal provisions.[11] The most notable non-party to the Montreal Convention is the Russian Federation.

Both the UK[12] and the EU are parties to the Montreal Convention.[13] Where the EU concludes an international agreement, they are binding on its institutions and prevail over secondary legislation of the Union.[14] Accordingly the CJEU is competent to determine Montreal Convention disputes.

8.2.4 What does the Montreal Convention do?

It is worth noting that, in common with the Athens Convention regimes, the Warsaw Conventions amount to a partial harmonisation of international law in the field of civil liability for injury and death. The Warsaw Conventions are not a comprehensive code.

The important contributions of the Warsaw Conventions are to introduce a uniform scheme governing legal liability in the event of bodily injury or death. There is a two-tier system of civil liability of the air carrier to his passenger, of which the first tier is no-fault. The second tier is now unlimited. In addition, carriers are obliged to make advance payments to meet immediate needs. The rules of jurisdiction are harmonised and the need for choice of law is removed. The ability to contract out is limited in favour of the passenger.

However, the domestic law of the courts where the claim is proceeding will determine questions such as who can claim, what are the heads of cognisable loss, what damage is too remote, to what extent can a

---

9   Carriage By Air Act 1961, s 1(4).
10   As at the date of writing. See the full list online at www.icao.int/secretariat/legal/List%20 of%20Parties/Mtl99_EN.pdf.
11   For a detailed treatment of the Warsaw Convention or the preceding protocols and Conventions see *Shawcross & Beaumont, Air Law.*
12   In English law the Carriage by Air Acts (Implementation of the Montreal Convention 1999) Order 2002, SI 263/2002.
13   Council Decision 2001/539/EC of 5 April 20001 on the conclusion by the European Community of the Montreal Convention and Regulation EC 889/2002.
14   Treaty on the Functioning of the European Union, Art 216(2) and *Wallentin-Herman v Alitalia – Linee Acree Italiano* [2008] ECR I-11061.

passenger be considered to have contributed to his own loss and damage and how should loss and damage be assessed. In this way, the Convention scheme avoids a traditional conflicts of laws approach, and sidesteps potentially complex questions of applicable law and jurisdiction.

8.2.5   Interpreting the Warsaw Conventions

As provisions of multilateral international agreements, the general domestic rules of statutory interpretation do not apply.[15] As with all international treaties, the Montreal Convention 1999 must be interpreted in good faith in accordance with the ordinary meaning to be given to the terms of the treaty in its context and in the light of its object and purpose.

The general principles of construction are as follows. First, the words are to be given their natural meaning.[16] It is worth, however, bearing in mind that the primary language of the Warsaw (although not Montreal) Convention is French and comparison can provide insight into the intention of the parties.[17] Secondly, the Conventions fall to be interpreted as a coherent whole, with an emphasis on seeking to achieve the purpose of the parties.[18] When considering what purpose was intended, the travaux préparatoires of the relevant ICAO working group or conference debates are, if publicly accessible and where they indisputably point to a definite legislative intention, accordingly admissible as evidence.[19] Thirdly, interpretation must take place without reference to the domestic legal meaning of words or, indeed rules of interpretation. Fourthly, the courts are permitted to derive assistance from the decisions of the courts of other states parties, but the weight to be attached will depend on both the standing of the courts in question generally and the quality of the specific analysis to which reference is made.[20] It cannot be assumed that the view which appears to have been formed on an issue in the courts of one state party would be the same as that which would be taken in other countries which are party to the Conventions.[21]

Overall, the judicial approach has been to promote certainty of interpretation, even where this comes at the price of 'harshness' in the individual case. The potential injustice such an approach can cause has been judicially recognised, but the courts have insisted that the Warsaw code was intended to be 'uniform and exclusive of any resort to rules of domestic law'.[22]

---

[15]   *Fothergill v Monarch Airlines* [1980] 2 All ER 696 at 706 per Lord Diplock.

[16]   *The Deep Vein Thrombosis and Air Travel Group Litigation* [2006] 1 AC 495 at [11] and [12] per Lord Scott of Foscote.

[17]   Only the English language version of the Montreal Convention has the force of law in England and Wales.

[18]   *The Hollandia* [1983] 1 AC 565.

[19]   Vienna Convention, Art 32; *Morris v KLM* [2002] UKHL 7, [2002] 2 AC 628.

[20]   *Abnett v British Airways* [1997] AC 430 per Lord Hope.

[21]   *Herd v Clyde Helicopters* [1997] AC 534, 554F per Lord Hope.

[22]   *Sidhu v British Airways* [1997] 2 AC 430 at 453D per Lord Hope.

8.2.6 Some features of the Montreal Convention scheme

8.2.6.1 *Exclusivity*

Article 24 of the Montreal Convention provides that in cases 'covered by Article 17' that 'any action for damages, however founded, can only be brought subject to the conditions and limits set out' in the Montreal Convention.

The words 'however founded' serve to impose the Montreal Convention limits and conditions regardless of the type of action on which relief is sought, whether contract, tort or statute. If injury occurs in circumstances 'covered' by Article 17, then whatever basis the passenger chooses in law to seek damages or recompense, her claim is subject to the conditions and limitations of the Montreal Convention.

The remedy provided by Art 17 of the Montreal Convention is exclusive. No other common law or civil law remedy (eg contractual or negligence) is available to a passenger who sustains bodily injury or dies in the course of international carriage by air, but has no claim against the carrier under Art 17 (eg because the event giving rise to the damage is not an 'accident').[23]

In *Sidhu v British Airways plc*,[24] the claimants were passengers on board a commercial airline flight which had a scheduled stopping point in Kuwait. In an extreme case of unfortunate timing, this scheduled stop occurred very shortly before the invasion of Iraqi forces in August 1990 and the passengers were held hostage. In a second episode of unfortunate timing, the claim form was not issued until nearly 3 years after the events in question and well outside the time-limit for Convention actions.[25] Their Art 17 action inevitably failed and the claimant passengers were left completely without remedy. It was held that Art 24 precludes a passenger from asserting any personal injury claim under local law, including those which do not satisfy Art 17 liability conditions, for example because the injury did not result from an 'accident' or because the injury was not a 'bodily' one.[26]

It is suggested, therefore, that where negligence occurs before embarkation but that the accident causing injury takes place within the Art 17 timeframe, then Art 17 still 'covers' the injury and unless it comes within the terms of Art 17, the passenger is unable to recover. So, for example, where a passenger is a patient on a medical repatriation flight and a decision to embark the passenger is negligently taken by the

---

[23] See **8.2.8.4(1)**.
[24] [1997] 2 AC 430.
[25] See **8.2.8.3(6)**.
[26] This reasoning is followed by that of the Second Circuit of US Court of Appeal in *El Al Israel Airlines Ltd v Tsui Yuan Tseng* (1999) 525 US 155.

carrier's medical staff, when pressure sores develop during the flight, unless this is an 'accident' for the purposes of Art 17, the passenger has no remedy against the carrier.

Exclusivity is reinforced by the fact that it is not possible in an agreement concluded prior to an accident causing personal injury or death to contract out of the Convention provisions.[27]

8.2.6.2   *Jurisdiction*

The Montreal Convention provides its own rules governing which courts have power to hear and determine civil liability claims between passengers and air carriers for injury and death.[28] The right to choose is given to the claimant.[29] However, the choice is limited to one of the following where they are the courts of a state party to the Montreal Convention:

(a)   the country of domicile of the carrier;[30]
(b)   the country of the carrier's principal place of business;
(c)   the country where the carrier has a place of business through which the contract of carriage was made;
(d)   the country which is the place of destination; or
(e)   the country in which the passenger at the time of his accident has his principal and permanent residence and from to or which the carrier operates services and conducts business from leased or owned premises, whether itself or by another carrier with which it has a 'commercial agreement'.[31]

The scheme of Art 33 is to create a 'cascade' of possible jurisdictions, increasingly favourable to the passenger because they are more likely to result in a choice of the court of his home country.

There is no definition of 'domicile' in the Montreal Convention. In light of the possible jurisdiction in (b) principal place of carrier's business, it is likely that 'domicile' will focus on the administrative centre of the carrier's business interests.

The term 'principal place of business' has been considered in the context of carriage by sea and it is likely that the courts would strive to achieve consistency of approach.[32] In those cases it has been held that the test is to identify the centre from where instructions are given and from which

---

[27]   Article 49.
[28]   Article 33. There are similarities with the scheme in respect of carriage by sea; see **7.2.1.2**.
[29]   The carrier has no right to challenge the choice of the English court by a passenger either on grounds of forum non conveniens or lis alibi pendens (see *Milor Srl v British Airways plc* [1996] QB 702 and *Deaville v Aeroflot* [1997] 2 Lloyd's Rep 67).
[30]   Discussion of the term carrier is at **8.2.7.6**.
[31]   Article 33(2).
[32]   See discussion at **7.2.1.2** *The Rewia* [1993] I L Pr 507, 521.

control is exercised, even where the day-to-day management of the aircraft in question is carried out elsewhere.

Bases (c) and (d) are likely to cause more factual than legal difficulty in practice, although it is suggested that in line with the general approach to Montreal Convention claims, the starting point for any consideration of the facts of a given case is the written contract.[33] Therefore the place of destination remains as in the contract even if in the event travel was terminated before that point. For the purposes of (c) having a 'place' of business suggests more than temporary or transient presence in a country at the time of contract.

The final possible jurisdiction (e) is the route most likely to point towards the courts of the passenger's own 'home' country. However, in order for these courts to have the power to hear a Montreal Convention claim, all three limbs of the test must be met. First, the passenger's 'principal and permanent residence' is defined as 'the one fixed and permanent abode of the passenger at the time of the accident'.[34] By referring back to the time of the accident, this rule of jurisdiction is at odds with most jurisdictional rules which fall to be determined at the time of the proceedings, not the events which give rise to the claim.[35] Additionally, the nationality of the passenger is not 'the determining factor in this regard'. This explanation implies, however, that nationality remains a relevant factor. Secondly, the carrier must operate services to or from the country of the passenger's principal and permanent residence. Thirdly, the carrier must lease or own premises in that country. The scope of this clause is broadened considerably by the inclusion of not only services and premises directly operated or owned by the carrier, but also those of partner airlines, because '"commercial agreement" means an agreement, other than an agency agreement, made between carriers and relating to the provision of their joint services for carriage of passengers by air'.[36]

Finally, all procedural questions in relation to jurisdiction, such as service of proceedings and challenge to the jurisdiction are governed by English law when the claim proceeds in the English court.[37] It has been held that 'procedure' in this context is sufficiently wide to encompass the English law concept of submission to the jurisdiction, even in circumstances where under a strict interpretation of Art 33, the English court would not have power to hear the claim.[38]

---

[33] Article 11(1) which provides that the air waybill is prima facie evidence of the conclusion of the contract and the conditions of carriage.

[34] Article 33(3)(b).

[35] See discussion at **4.2.2**.

[36] Article 33(3)(a), such as code sharing agreements.

[37] Article 33(4).

[38] *Rothmans v Saudi Airlines* [1981] 1 QB 368, 377. There is nothing in the Montreal Convention to preclude jurisdiction agreements where they are entered after the events giving rise to loss and damage, see Art 49.

8.2.7 Scope and definitions

8.2.7.1 Aircraft

It might be thought surprising that the Montreal Convention does not attempt to define what is an 'aircraft'. A hot air balloon is capable of carrying passengers from one place to another and is capable of being used as a means of international transport. Accordingly as the natural and ordinary meaning of the word, 'aircraft' is wide enough, it has been held to qualify as an 'aircraft' for Convention purposes.[39] A paraglider being used for recreational activity and tuition is not an aircraft.[40]

8.2.7.2 Contract of carriage

In common with the other major concepts already discussed, 'carriage' is not separately defined in the Montreal Convention. The discussions leading to the Warsaw Convention focused on the traditional model of international carriage in an aircraft from point A to point B. However, the Conventions are not inconsistent with a wider definition to encompass more unusual forms of 'carriage' by air.[41] It is established that 'carriage' includes carriage on a so-called 'voyage charter' flight where the owner charters his fully equipped plane and crew for a predetermined voyage,[42] although the position in respect of other types of charter ('bare charter' or 'time charter') is less clear and would raise consequential issues as to whether the 'carrier' is properly said to be the owner of the aircraft or its operator.

It has been held that a contract of carriage need not identify the point of destination prior to embarkation[43] in order to amount to 'carriage'. However, the agreement must have some element of carrying the person from A to B, so, for example, where an accident occurred during a test flight, the purpose of which was to test the aircraft, the Convention did not apply.[44]

The contractual relationship requires only that the carrier consents to undertake the international carriage of the passenger from one designated spot to another. There is no requirement to establish the formation of a contract in the strict common law formulation; less still is there need for evidence of negotiation over specific terms. There is therefore no objection to the application of the Montreal Convention to contracts which have been concluded by a third person acting as agent of either

---

[39] *Laroche v Spirit of Adventure* [2009] QB 778, 789 at [45]–[48].
[40] *Disley v Levine* [2002] 1 WLR 785, 795G.
[41] *Herd v Clyde Helicopters* [1997] AC 534, 552G per Lord Hope.
[42] *Block v Air France*, 386 F2d 323 (5th Cir, 1977, US Court of Appeals) at 23.
[43] *Laroche v Spirit of Adventure (UK) Ltd* [2009] QB 778 at [56], in the case of a hot-air balloon.
[44] *Aéro-Club de l'Aisne v Klopotowska*, 24 RFDA 195 (Cour de Cassation).

passenger or carrier himself even though there is no express provision in the Montreal Convention to this effect.[45] Nor does the passenger need to have provided 'consideration' for the contract.[46]

Therefore, it has been held that where passengers in an aircraft were military personnel of the US, who had no direct contractual relationship with the airline, that in fact the Warsaw Convention did apply and that the airline was carrier.[47]

Finally, there is an exception to the Convention regimes for 'carriage performed in extraordinary circumstances'. As the wording suggests, this is a very narrow exception.[48]

8.2.7.3   *International carriage*

The Montreal Convention applies to all international carriage of persons performed by aircraft.

'International carriage' means any carriage in which the place of departure *and* the place of destination, whether or not there be a break in the carriage, are situated either within the territories of two states parties or within the territory of a single state party if there is an agreed stopping place within another state, even if that third state is not a state party.[49]

It is the agreement[50] between the parties which determines whether the carriage is international or not.[51] There is only one contractual place of departure and destination, even though there could be breaks in the journey. The phrase 'stopping place' encompasses not only situations where the aircraft touches down but also where the passenger is entitled to break his journey.[52] Accordingly, where a passenger was killed in a crash during a flight between London and Antwerp, because the contract was for return travel, it was 'international carriage', even though the tickets for each leg were issued as wholly separate documents showing individual fares.[53]

---

[45]   *Block* at 29.
[46]   *Block* at 33.
[47]   *Mertens v Flying Tiger Line Inc*, 341 F2d 851 (2nd Cir, 1965).
[48]   Article 51.
[49]   Article 1(2).
[50]   In fact a direct translation of the original French is 'conditions' or 'stipulations' of the parties: *Block v Air France* at 32.
[51]   *Grein v Imperial Airways* [1937] 1 KB 50, 77 per Greene LJ.
[52]   *Grein v Imperial Airways* [1937] 1 KB 50, 79 and 80.
[53]   *Grein v Imperial Airways* [1937] 1 KB 50, 82. See also *Holmes v Bangladesh Biman* Corpn [1989] 1 AC 1112, 1131B–D.

Carriage between two points within the territory of a single state party without an agreed stopping place within the territory of another state is not international carriage.[54]

8.2.7.4   *Application to domestic or 'non-international' carriage*

The Montreal Convention has been applied to non-international carriage[55] by English law. For present purposes 'non-international carriage' simply means such carriage as is not covered by the Montreal Convention, either because it lacks the relevant international character and is domestic or internal to a single country, or because despite being across national borders, it does not connect countries which are states parties to Montreal.

Whilst the ordinary meaning of the words 'all carriage' in the 2004 Order are potentially wide enough to encompass contracts of carriage made and to be performed wholly within the territory of a foreign state, in fact they fall to be interpreted in accordance with the presumed intention of Parliament not to seek to legislate in the affairs of foreign nationals who did nothing to bring themselves within the jurisdiction. Accordingly, where a passenger was killed during an internal flight in Bangladesh, the widow's damages were limited in accordance with the domestic Bangladeshi law principles and not the Conventions.[56]

The 2004 Order applies the Montreal Convention to all carriage by air which touches the UK. Accordingly, in a case of non-Convention carriage involving a place of departure or destination or an agreed stopping place in a foreign state and a place of departure or destination or an agreed stopping place in the UK or other British territory, the Montreal Convention will apply.[57]

The 2004 Order also applies the Montreal Convention to domestic UK carriage by air.

Some significant alterations apply where the claim is brought by virtue of the 2004 Order rather than directly under the Montreal Convention itself. In particular, the 2004 Order only applies to carriage by air 'for reward' and therefore in non-international carriage cases it is generally necessary

---

[54]   Article 1(2).
[55]   Carriage by Air Acts (Application of Provisions) Order 2004, SI 2004/1899 ('the 2004 Order'), Art 4 and Sch 1, pursuant to the power in Carriage by Air Act, s 10(1).
[56]   *Holmes v Bangladesh Biman Corpn* [1989] 1 AC 1112.
[57]   *Holmes v Bangladesh Biman Corpn* [1989] 1 AC 1112, 1131F and 1132G per Lord Bridge.

to ensure that the carriage was not gratuitous.[58] Generally, this is not an issue, but can arise, such as in *Disley's* case where it was held that the £177 fee related to tuition, not carriage.[59]

The other significant point to note is that where reliance is placed on the 2004 Order, it will be necessary to utilise the general English law rules as to jurisdiction of the English courts, because the specialist provisions of the Montreal Convention regarding jurisdiction do not apply.[60]

In accordance with Art 3(1) of EC Regulation 2027/97 all carriage by a Community air carrier[61] is subject to the provision of the Montreal Convention.

8.2.7.5 *Passenger*

Although in Art 1(1) the Montreal Convention is stated to apply to the carriage of all 'persons' the obligations of the carrier in respect of liability refer to the narrower category of 'passengers'.[62]

There is no specific definition of 'passenger' in the Montreal Convention. However, the texts of the Conventions do provide some assistance as to how the term should be interpreted. As the Montreal Convention applies to 'gratuitous carriage' the status of passenger cannot turn on whether a fare is paid.[63] Nor does it matter whether a ticket has been issued.[64] It is implicit from the requirement of the carrier's contractual consent to undertake carriage that stowaways are not passengers.[65]

Where a person is on board a flight because they are working towards the operation of the flight, it is well established that where such individuals are not 'passengers' as defined by the Montreal Convention.[66] Further, it has been held that a police officer who was working (not in the employment of the carrier) on board a police helicopter in course of his aerial surveillance and detection police duties was a passenger.[67]

In practice, issues have arisen where persons are on board an aircraft in the situation known in the industry as 'deadheading', namely where they

---

[58] Unless the defendant is an 'air transport undertaking' under the Air Navigation Order 2005, SI 2005/1970.

[59] *Disley v Levine* [2002] 1 WLR 785, 800 at [64] per Buxton LJ. For the same reason, the defendant was not an air transport undertaking.

[60] See Chapter 4, Jurisdiction.

[61] Those carriers obliged to hold an operating licence in accordance with Regulation EEC No 2407/92.

[62] Article 17.

[63] Article 1(1); *Sulewski v Federal Express Corpn* 933 F2d 180 (2nd Cir, 1990, US Court of Appeals).

[64] Article 3(2).

[65] *Block* at 334.

[66] *Mexico City Aircrash*, 708 F2d at 417.

[67] *Herd v Clyde Helicopters* [1997] AC 534.

are in the employment of the carrier, but are not on the particular flight in question for the purposes of their employment, even if the individual is being paid for his time on board or is travelling in order to fulfil contractual employment obligations. The test as to whether such a person is a 'passenger' appears to be purposive. Accordingly, in the *Mexico City Aircrash* litigation, the question whether the deadheading flight attendant was on board, 'primarily for the purpose of travelling or ... to perform her employment obligations' was left to the jury.

By contrast, in *Sulewski v Fed Ex*,[68] the deceased was a ground staff mechanic employed by the carrier, but who contributed nothing to the operation of the flight on which he died. As he was contractually obliged as part of his employment to be on the fatal flight and was not free to choose other transport, his primary purpose of being on board was to fulfil his somewhat specialist employment responsibilities, which was inconsistent with the status of 'passenger'. This was notwithstanding the fact that he did not have any in-flight duties.[69]

A purposive approach to the definition of 'passenger' has also been embraced by the English courts.[70] A 'passenger' is a person who is not contributing to the carriage of himself or other persons on board.[71] Furthermore, it is somebody who is on board with the predominant purpose of being conveyed from one place to another.[72] In *Laroche v Spirit of Adventure*,[73] 'obvious examples' of non-passengers were stated to be trainee pilots, pilots, stewards and other members of the crew. Other examples of non-passengers in the decided cases include, where a person agreed verbally to take part in an aerial survey[74] and those carried by an emergency state-organised ski slope helicopter rescue service.[75]

A person can be a 'passenger' even if his predominant purpose in being on board is for the recreation of the flight itself and where the actual destination is wholly unpredictable (such as in *Laroche*). However, a trainee under instruction on a tandem paraglider training flight is not a passenger.[76]

---

[68]   933 F2d 180.
[69]   *Sulewski* at 41.
[70]   *Disley v Levine* [2002] 1 WLR 785 at [70] per Buxton LJ.
[71]   *Herd v Clyde Helicopters* [1997] AC 534, 542, 548.
[72]   *Disley v Levine* [2002] 1 WLR 785.
[73]   [2009] QB 778 at [61].
[74]   *Ortet v Georges* (1975) 30 RFDA 490 (Cour d'Appel de Paris).
[75]   *Barnes v Service Aérien Français* (1993) RFDA 343 (Cour d'Appel de Paris).
[76]   As the above principles were applied to the facts in *Disley's* case. See also *Société Mutuelle d'Assurance Aériennes v Gauvain* (1967) 21 RFDA 436, a decision of the French courts concerning a trainee pilot under instruction who was not a passenger.

8.2.7.6 *Carrier*

This issue is relevant to personal injury actions in an aviation context for two reasons. First, it may be necessary to exercise some care as to who is the correct party to name as defendant to an Art 17 claim.[77] In a charter flight situation, it may not necessarily be immediately apparent who is the 'carrier' as between the owner or charterer of the aircraft. Secondly, there may be other defendants who are not carriers against whom claims are not governed by the Convention regimes.

Where carriage is to be performed by 'several successive carriers' the carriage is deemed to be undivided where the parties (both of them, not just the passenger) consider it to be a single operation.[78] This is the case notwithstanding the fact that the carriage may be formed of several separate contracts. Where successive carriage exists, it is possible for the first carrier to adopt liability for the entire carriage.[79] If this does not occur, each carrier is liable for that portion of the carriage which he performs[80] and the passenger can only sue that particular carrier in respect of a personal injury loss.

This situation should not be confused with subcontracting by the carrier. In a case where the carrier subcontracts performance of his obligations under the contract of carriage with his passenger, he is known, under Montreal Convention terminology as the 'contracting carrier'.[81] The carrier which performs the carriage is referred to as the 'actual carrier'.[82] In these situations the passenger can choose whether to proceed against either or both the contracting or actual carrier, thus avoiding the risk of disputes as to responsibility for performance of contractual obligations.[83] To facilitate this choice, an actual carrier is exposed to all the jurisdictions in which the contracting carrier would have been able to be sued in addition to the courts for the place of his own domicile and principal place of business.[84] Furthermore, the contracting carrier is made vicariously liable for the employees and agents of the actual carrier. On the other hand, the actual carrier's vicarious liability for the employees and agents of the contracting carrier is limited.[85]

Where a claim is brought against only one of the actual or contracting carrier, the other can be joined as a third party to proceedings in

---

[77] See *Hall v Heart Balloons* [2010] 1 Lloyd's Rep 373.
[78] Article 1(3).
[79] Article 36(2).
[80] Article 36(1).
[81] Article 39.
[82] Articles 39 and 40.
[83] Article 45.
[84] Article 46.
[85] Article 41(2).

accordance with English law procedure on joinder[86] and any contribution or indemnity claims between them are unaffected by the Convention.[87]

Finally, should a claimant bring proceedings against the servant or agent of a carrier, employees or agents can invoke Convention limits and defences.[88] The exception is where the claimant shows that the damage resulted from an act or omission done with intent to cause damage or recklessly with knowledge that damage would probably result.[89]

In practice, there may not be any significant benefit to a claimant seeking damages as a result of injury or death to a passenger in suing multiple parties. As with claims against the servants or agents of carriers, this is not a route to circumventing the limits of liability and the passenger is not entitled to recover more than the limits in total.[90]

8.2.8   Obligations of the carrier

8.2.8.1   *Document of carriage*

It is the carrier's obligation to deliver to the passenger a document of carriage,[91] which indicates the international nature of the carriage. That is to say it must specify the places of departure and destination and, in the event that departure and destination are within the territory of the same state party, the location of at least one stopping point outside that state party.[92] The 'document' can be electronic or other form so long as a written statement is also offered.[93] Importantly, this document is required to provide the passenger with written notice of the carrier's right to limit his liability in respect of death and personal injury.[94] In a departure from previous Warsaw Convention wordings, the failure to comply with these obligations does not deprive the carrier of his right to limit his liability to the passenger in the event of death or injury.[95] This means that neither delivery of a defective ticket nor failure to deliver a ticket at all will not deprive the carrier of his right to limit damages.[96]

---

[86] Article 45.
[87] Article 48.
[88] Article 30.
[89] For discussion of the application of this exception in case-law see **7.2.4.2**.
[90] Article 44.
[91] Which can be either individual or collective; Art 3(1).
[92] Article 3(1)(a) and (b).
[93] Article 3(2).
[94] Article 3(4). In the case of Community air carriers in the EU, EC Regulation 2027/97 as amended imposes additional more specific information requirements.
[95] Article 3(5).
[96] See *Preston v Hunting Air Transport Ltd* [1956] 1 QB 454 for the previous law.

8.2.8.2 Insurance

A carrier is obliged to 'maintain adequate insurance covering their liability under this Convention'.[97] This is a strange requirement, given that there is effectively no upper cap on damages under the Montreal Convention, so it is difficult for carriers to know in advance what level of damages they might be required to meet.

8.2.8.3 Liability of the carrier for death and bodily injury

Article 17 of the Montreal Convention sets out the basis on which a carrier is liable for bodily injury sustained by a passenger during the flight (or during embarkation or disembarkation):

> 'The carrier is liable for damage sustained in case of death or bodily injury of a passenger upon condition only that the accident which caused the death or injury took place on board the aircraft or in the course of any of the operations of embarking or disembarking.'

It should be observed that this wording is modified from the original Warsaw Convention text.[98]

(1) Accident

It is worth noting at the outset of the discussion of the meaning of 'accident' that the term is only used in the Montreal Convention in respect of injury and death claims for Art 17. It is clearly intended to be a narrower term than the phrase 'event' which is used in the context of baggage claims.[99]

The leading decision is *Air France v Saks*,[100] in which the claimant brought proceedings after air pressure changes in the cabin during the landing descent, caused her to become deaf in one ear. The pressurisation system had operated normally. O'Connor J stated that an accident under Warsaw:

> '... arises only if a passenger's injury is caused by an unexpected or unusual event or happening that is external to the passenger. This definition should be flexibly applied after assessment of all the circumstances surrounding a passenger's injuries.'

Therefore, where the injury results from the passenger's own internal reaction to the usual, normal and expected operation of the aircraft, it has not been caused by an accident.

---

[97] Article 50 and EC Regulation 889/2002 amending EC Regulation 2027/97 on air carrier liability in respect of the carriage of passengers and their baggage by air, Art 3(2).

[98] Although it is suggested that no material difference in meaning arises.

[99] Article 17(2).

[100] 470 US 392.

Article 17 distinguishes between the bodily injury to the passenger on the one hand and the 'accident' by which the bodily injury was caused on the other, so that the injury could not itself be the accident. Accordingly, where the allegation was that normal cabin conditions during air travel contributed to the onset of deep vein thrombosis (DVT), there was no 'accident'.[101]

Similarly, many cases where the alleged injury is in essence a progression of a medical condition, such as wear and tear on a back injury, or a heart attack[102] or stroke, or a self-induced temporary condition,[103] it will in practice be difficult to establish that an 'accident' has occurred.

However, in a case where the widow of a passenger who died on board a flight made an Art 17 claim for damages against the carrier on grounds that the deceased was a congenital asthmatic who had repeatedly been refused his requests to be seated further away from the smoking section of the passenger cabin, it has been held that the failure of the flight attendant in contravention of industry standard policy to accede to the requests was an 'accident'.[104] The reliance on the cabin crew's refusal to heed the passenger's requests as a basis for determining that it was an 'external and unusual event' is questionable.

It has been held by the Court of Appeal that where there is no event entirely unconnected with the passenger, but the injury is not due to an autonomous collapse in the passenger's health, this is still insufficient to amount to an 'accident'. So, where a passenger slipped on standard fitting which was a narrow plastic strip running under the seats and covering the seat fix tracking as she was in the process of finding her seat as she boarded an aircraft, the injury was constituted by contact or interaction between the passenger and the aircraft in its normal state and no 'accident' had taken place.[105] In a US case where the accident occurred due to slipping on a wet step on some stairs at a terminal at Heathrow, it was considered that the presence of water on the stairs was external to the passenger and therefore an accident had taken place.[106] There is domestic county court level decision to the opposite effect.[107]

Where the injury or death results following unlawful deliberate activity, it is conversely, rather more straightforward to characterise such events as being 'external' to the passenger and 'unusual'. On 6 September 1970, in

---

[101] *Re Deep Vein Thrombosis and Air Travel Group Litigation* [2005] UKHL 72; [2006] 1 AC 495. The issue has been decided the same way in Australia: *Povey v Qantas Airways Ltd* [2005] HCA 33.

[102] This is essentially what happened in *Chaudhari v British Airways, The Times*, 7 May 1997.

[103] Such as alcohol intoxication as in *Padilla v Olympic Airways* 765 F Supp 835 (1991).

[104] *Olympic Airways v Husain* 124 S Ct 1221.

[105] *Barclay v British Airways plc* [2010] QB 187.

[106] *Gezzi v British Airways plc* 991 F 2d 603 (9th Cir, 1993, US Court of Appeals).

[107] *Cannon v MyTravel Airways Ltd* (Lawtel, 8 July 2005, Manchester County Court).

Zurich, TWA had a direct flight to New York which was hijacked shortly after take-off by terrorists. Despite the obvious tension between these facts and the natural and ordinary meaning of the language, it was clear that this situation represented an 'accident' for Convention purposes.[108] The English authority in respect of deliberate acts has followed the same approach.[109]

There is a line of US authority which suggests that in order to qualify as an accident, the incident must bear some relation to the carrier's operation of the aircraft or the services on board associated with the carriage. Thus, where one passenger punched another, there was no accident in respect of which the carrier was liable.[110] This was distinguished by the Court of Appeal in *Morris v KLM Royal Dutch Airlines*[111] on the basis that Art 17 did not require the accident to arise as a result of a feature which was unique to air travel. It was held that the circumstances in which the 15-year-old victim would settle down to sleep in close proximity to an unknown man represented a 'special risk' of air travel.

(2) Bodily injury

One of the more controversial aspects of the interpretation of the Montreal Convention is the limitation of the phrase 'bodily injury' to a narrow meaning excluding purely mental injuries. Where a passenger's plane barely avoided crash landing during a flight between Miami and Bahamas, causing entirely predictable psychological distress, it was held that the passenger had no entitlement to claim damages, because the loss fell outside that which was compensable pursuant to Art 17.[112] On a similar basis, the claimant in *Morris* was held not to be entitled to recover in respect of her claim which concerned purely mental injury as a result of the sexual assault.

The reasoning in *Floyd* is based on a supposed assessment of what would have been in the 'draftsman's mind'[113] when using the language 'bodily injury' in 1929.[114] In all likelihood, the question of recovery for pure psychiatric injury, unrecognised by most systems of civil justice at that stage, simply did not occur to anybody. This led the US Supreme Court to conclude that it was excluded from Art 17. Whether this approach of preserving the Convention wording in aspic is permissible is open to

---

[108] *Husserl v Swiss Air Transport Co Ltd* 388 FSupp 1238 (1975).

[109] See *Morris v KLM Royal Dutch Airlines* [2002] 2 AC 628, where the passenger was indecently assaulted by her neighbouring passenger.

[110] *Stone v Continental Airlines Inc,* 905 FSupp 823 (1995).

[111] [2002] 2 AC 628.

[112] *Eastern Airlines Inc v Floyd* 499 US 530 (1991).

[113] To the extent that any such Convention written in committee has a 'draftsman'.

[114] The year in which the Warsaw Convention was concluded.

doubt.[115] However, the authority has been extensively followed, including by the House of Lords in the leading English case: *King v Bristow Helicopters*.[116]

Attempts have been made to sidestep the obvious harshness of the narrow view of 'bodily injury'. In the US, it has been held that where a diagnosis of PTSD was described as resulting from physical and chemical changes to the passenger's brain, that this was sufficient to evidence a 'bodily injury' and to distinguish *Floyd*.[117]

In a case where a passenger suffers some physical injury and some psychological injury, but where there is no evidence that the psychological injury springs from or is caused by the physical injuries, damages will be limited to the physical injuries.[118] Conversely, where it can be shown that the psychological damage flows from the physical injury, it will be recoverable.

Despite the fact that the wording of Art 17 was amended slightly in the Montreal Convention version of the text, there is no reason to suppose that there was any intention to affect this case-law or to include psychological as well as physical injuries in the scope of Art 17.

(3)   Embarking and disembarking

In *Day v Trans World Airlines Inc Kersen*,[119] a hijacking case, a passenger had checked-in for his flight and had passed through passport and currency control and, after waiting in the transit lounge, was standing in a queue for a hand-baggage search at the departure gate, when the attack took place. A tripartite test of 'embarkation' was established (i) activity (what was the passenger doing at the time of the injury); (ii) control (at whose direction); and (iii) location. It was held that at the point of the attack, the passengers were not free agents roaming at will through the terminal.[120] The activity which they were undertaking was a condition to boarding the aircraft and boarding was imminent and they were close to the exit (and physically being on the aircraft).

In a case where a schoolgirl was arrested on board an aircraft which made an emergency landing following a hoax bomb threat, because the subsequent detention and intensive questioning which gave rise to her consequent psychiatric illness was carried out in the terminal building by

---

[115]   See eg the counterargument that the Convention is a living and developing document capable of accommodating changes in the world over time: *Herd v Clyde* Helicopters [1997] AC 534, 553D per Lord Hope.

[116]   [2002] 2 AC 628.

[117]   *Weaver v Delta Airlines Inc*, 56 FSupp2d 1190 (1999).

[118]   *Ehrlich v American Airlines Inc*, 360 F3d 366 (2004).

[119]   528 F2d 31 (2nd Cir, 1975, US Court of Appeals).

[120]   Paragraph 11.

the police authorities and was unconnected with disembarkation, the incident was not covered by Art 17.[121]

If the passenger is in the course of undertaking a necessary process towards embarkation when the accident occurs, then Art 17 is engaged. However, embarkation is not a continuous process and does not include common activities at air terminals, such as waiting, shopping, eating or drinking.[122]

In practice, therefore, the ambit of 'disembarkation' tends to be significantly more restrictively interpreted than 'embarkation'. Some commentators have suggested that there is a single test of location in respect of disembarkation, although on the decided cases this may represent no more than the reality that once inside the terminal building, a passenger is no longer effectively under the control of the carrier and is a free agent. In *Macdonald v Air Canada*,[123] the passenger was waiting in the baggage hall near the carousel at Boston International Airport when she fell. It was held that the operation of disembarking was terminated by the time the passenger has descended from the aircraft and reaches a safe point inside the terminal, even though he remains a passenger.[124] An example of an accident in the course of disembarkation is provided by *Ricotta v Iberia Lineas Aerea De Espana*[125] where the passenger fell off the transit bus between the aircraft and the terminal building.

(4)   Limits on liability

There are two tiers to liability for death or personal injury pursuant to the Montreal Convention. In respect of the first 113,100[126] SDRs,[127] it is not permissible for the carrier to limit his liability in anyway.[128]

For loss and damage over that limit, the carrier can avoid liability if it shows that either (a) the damage was not due to his negligence, or wrongful act or omission or that of his servants or agents or (b) the damage was solely due to the negligence or other wrongful act or omission of a third party.[129]

Fault still therefore has a role to play in Montreal Convention claims, especially where the loss and damage is significant. A carrier may

---

[121] *Schroeder v Lufthansa German Airlines* 875 F2d 613 (7th Cir, 1989, US Court of Appeals).
[122] *Phillips v Air New Zealand* [2002] EWHC 800 (Comm).
[123] 439 F2d 1402 (1st Cir, 1971, US Court of Appeals).
[124] See also *Adatia v Air Canada* [1992] PIQR P238, CA.
[125] 482 F Supp 497 (1979).
[126] Carriage by Air (Revision of Limits of Liability under the Montreal Convention) Order 2009, SI 2009/3018, in force from 30 December 2009.
[127] See **7.2.4.1** for discussion of special drawing rights.
[128] Article 21(1).
[129] Article 21(2).

stipulate that a contract of carriage be subject to higher limits of liability than provided for by the Montreal Convention.[130]

The Montreal Convention includes a mechanism by which the limits of liability are reviewed every 5 years with a view to maintaining the level of limits relative to inflation.[131] Revisions can then be implemented into English law by statutory instrument.[132]

It is worth noting that questions of court costs or other expenses of litigation incurred by the claimant, including interest[133] can be awarded in addition to the damages limits in accordance with the law of the court hearing the action.[134] The carrier is given the opportunity to limit his exposure to additional litigation expenses, costs and interest by making a written offer in respect of damages[135] to the claimant. The offer must be made by the later of either (i) 6 months after the accident or (ii) issue of the claim form. If the claimant's damages at trial (excluding costs and disbursements but including interest) do not exceed the sum offered by the carrier, the claimant is not entitled to claim costs, interest or disbursements.[136]

This rather rudimentary settlement mechanism does not state what happens in the event that a claimant wishes to accept an offer made by the carrier under this procedure. In particular it is not clear whether a claimant in such circumstances would be entitled to recover any costs or expenses incurred prior to the date of the offer.[137] If not, then this settlement procedure represents a more generous regime than the domestic rules of the English court under the CPR for pre-action offers. The better view is that the Montreal Convention, Art 22(6) settlement mechanism operates as an express limit on the power of the English court to award interest, pre-action costs or expenses.[138] It overrides domestic procedural rules and imposes its own structure and accordingly provides the sole settlement regime prior to issue of proceedings.

However, to the extent that CPR Part 36, or the more general costs rules in CPR Part 44 are not inconsistent with the Montreal Convention provisions, they will continue to apply. Accordingly, where offers are made post-issue, then CPR Parts 36 and 44 will govern the consequences for

---

[130] Article 25.

[131] Article 24.

[132] Made pursuant to Carriage by Air Act 1961, s 2(1A).

[133] Reversing *Swiss Bank v Brink's MAT* [1986] 1 QB 853.

[134] Article 22(6).

[135] Although the text is ambiguous as to whether the offer should be inclusive of costs and interest, it is submitted that the better view is that the offer should be in respect of the claimant's loss and damage including interest so that a 'like for like' comparison is possible at the conclusion of the litigation.

[136] Article 22(6).

[137] As would be the case for an offer to which CPR Part 36 applies: r 36.2(2)(c).

[138] In line with the reasoning in *Swiss Bank v Brink's MAT* [1986] 1 QB 853, above.

costs and interest, which from a defendant's perspective has the advantage that it could require an unsuccessful claimant not merely to forgo his own costs, but to meet the defendants'.

(5) *Exoneration and contributory fault*

If the damages was caused by or contributed to by the negligence of the injured person the court may exonerate the carrier wholly or partly from his liability.[139] The extent of the availability of the contributory fault defence depends on the law of the court where the action is to be heard. The burden of establishing contributory fault lies with the carrier. In English law this is governed by the Law Reform (Contributory Negligence) Act 1945[140] and as a result, the carrier is only entitled to a partial defence.

The Montreal Convention represents a significant departure from the previous Warsaw scheme Conventions in that it limits the defence which was previously open to the carrier, namely that the carrier would not be liable pursuant to Art 17 to his passenger if the carrier could prove that the accident which caused the damage was not the fault of the carrier, his servants or agents or was wholly the fault of some third party, to damages above 113,100 SDRs.

(6) *Time bars*

Any right to claim damages which is covered by the Montreal Convention is extinguished if action is not brought within 2 years.[141] Time runs from the date of actual or planned arrival at the destination or when the carriage ended, whichever is the sooner. The question of calculation of time is left to the law of the forum.[142]

Practitioners need to be wary of the fact that the provisions of the Limitation Act 1980 do not apply to Montreal Convention claims. There are no special rules for children or those under a disability. Nor is there the safety net of s 33 extension.

In stark contrast with the decided case-law in respect of amendment outside limitation to substitute a party in carriage by sea claims,[143] it has been held that the English court has no power to permit amendment of a personal injury claim brought by a passenger against a carrier so that the

---

[139] Article 21.
[140] Carriage By Air Act 1961, s 6.
[141] Article 35(1).
[142] Article 35(2).
[143] *Adams v Thomson Holidays Ltd* [2009] EWHC 2559 (QB), unreported.

correct carrier could be named as defendant where the Montreal Convention time-limit had expired.[144]

(7)   Damages in a Montreal Convention claim

The Montreal Convention makes only a very selective attempt to legislate for the type of loss and damage which the passenger may recover in a successful claim under Art 17 against the carrier. It has been said that the specification of what harm is legally cognisable is left to the domestic law of the forum where the claim is pursued.[145] The question of 'what are the respective rights' of the various parties who have right to bring an action are expressly left to the law of the court hearing the claim.[146]

As in the case of contracts of carriage by sea, it is theoretically possible that the contract itself would be governed by a law other than English law and may well contain provisions regarding loss and damage. However, in the absence of express stipulation, English law as the law of the forum would apply to questions regarding loss, including recoverable heads of loss, including loss of enjoyment, mitigation, remoteness as well as rules of quantification and assessment.[147]

In terms of loss of enjoyment claims, it is suggested that the usual principles of English contract law damages should apply. Accordingly, it is only in those cases where 'enjoyment' is part of the price of the contract and in the reasonable contemplation of the parties that this should be recoverable as a head of loss if events do not turn out as planned. In *Cowden v British Airways*[148] it was held that an action for delayed and damage to baggage arising out of a contract of carriage simpliciter did not give rise to any claim for loss of enjoyment. It is suggested that insofar as this county court decision indicates that loss of enjoyment damages are never recoverable in respect of a claim arising under Art 17 of the Convention, it is not authority for that proposition.

Punitive, exemplary or non-compensatory damages are all prohibited in an action under the Convention.[149]

A carrier is obliged in a case of personal injury or death to make advance payment of damages without admission of liability to the claimant entitled to damages by no later than 15 days after the accident.[150] Such

---

[144]   *Hall v Heart of England Balloons Ltd and Gabb* [2010] 1 Lloyd's Rep 373 (County Court, HHJ Worster).

[145]   *Zicherman v Korean Air Lines Co Ltd* 516 US 217 (1996) followed in *Morris v KLM Royal Dutch Airlines* [2002] QB 100.

[146]   As are questions of who can sue, which is often at issue in wrongful death claims, see Art 29.

[147]   See discussion at **7.2.5.3**.

[148]   [2009] 2 Lloyd's Rep 653.

[149]   Article 29.

[150]   Article 28.

payment is to be 'proportionate to the hardship suffered' and in case of death must be not less than 16,000 SDRs.[151] As with similar payments in carriage by sea cases, they are only returnable in accordance with the Convention defences and limits.

8.3 OTHER AIR TRAVEL CLAIMS

Where a claim is made outside the scope of the Warsaw Conventions, such as by a crew member, then general law principles will apply to determine such questions as whether a cause of action exists, who are the correct claimants and defendants and what heads of loss are recoverable.

However, there are some rules of jurisdiction and applicable law which are specific to international air travel which deserve brief mention. In respect of jurisdiction, if the claim arises out of a contract, then the general rules as to choice of law in a contractual situation will apply.[152] Where the contract is a consumer contract or one of individual employment, it will not generally be difficult to ascertain whether the English court has jurisdiction and the choice of law can be governed by the contract. However, in a tort case, where the jurisdiction depends on where the harmful events occur, there is potential difficulty in identifying a 'country' where the events occur. Similar issues arise when determining the applicable law, where Rome II requires identification of the place where the harmful event occurred.

The solution suggested by *Dicey, Morris & Collins*[153] is to apply imaginary territorial lines in the air and to apply a fiction that where an event takes place mid-air above a particular country, then it should be deemed to have taken place in that country. There are two obvious problems with this approach. First, there may not be a country over whose territory the aircraft is flying at the material time (if indeed the material time can be established with such precision on the facts of the claim). Secondly, it is wholly artificial to allocate jurisdiction or applicable law on this basis and arguably does not satisfy the underlying ambitions of European harmonisation of promoting certainty or basing choice of law in tort on lex loci delicti principle.

It is suggested that inevitably in a case where the harmful event occurred in the midst of international air travel and the claim is made in tort, then jurisdiction would have to follow the 'flag' of the aircraft and choice of law would be determined using the 'escape clause' of Rome II, Art 4(3). It is likely that such cases will be exceptionally rare.

---

[151] EC Regulation 2027/97 as amended, Art 5(2).
[152] See Chapter 4 Jurisdiction.
[153] *The Conflict of Laws* (Sweet & Maxwell, 15th edn, 2012) at para 35–033.

CHAPTER 9

REMEDIES

Daniel Clarke with Helen Pugh

9.1 OVERVIEW

This chapter is concerned with the remedies available in cases where the parties are involved in an accident abroad. There will be many cases involving accidents abroad where English law will apply to quantum issues. This may be by operation of the relevant regime for determining the applicable law, or by default, in a case where no point is taken on the foreign applicable law. In such cases, the English law and practice on quantum applies just as it would in any case involving an accident in England. This is dealt with at **9.2**.

This chapter is also concerned with the principles for assessing damages in claims in the English courts when a foreign law applies to the issue of assessment. This is dealt with at **9.3**.

9.2 DAMAGES UNDER ENGLISH LAW

The book is concerned with accidents abroad. Accordingly, the emphasis in this section is upon heads of loss which may be relevant in that context. For details on the usual heads of loss recoverable in all personal injury claims regard should be had to leading texts *Kemp & Kemp*[1] or *McGregor on Damages*.[2]

9.2.1 Contract

The aim of damages, contractual or tortious, is to provide the injured party with monetary compensation for the damage, loss or injury suffered. This is done by awarding 'that sum of money which will put the party who has been injured, or who has suffered, in the same position as he would have been in if he had not sustained the wrong for which he is now getting his compensation or reparation'.[3] In contract claims, the wrong is the breach of contract. The compensation aims to put the injured person in the position as if the contract had been properly performed. In other words, compensation is given for the loss of the

---

[1]   *Kemp and Kemp: Quantum of Damages* (Sweet & Maxwell).
[2]   *McGregor on Damages* (Sweet & Maxwell, 18th edn, 2012).
[3]   Per Lord Blackburn in *Livingstone v Rawyards Coal Co* (1880) 5 App Cas 25 at 39.

bargain.[4] All claims brought under the Package Travel Regulations 1992[5] are claims for breach of contract and are subject to the principles applicable to such claims.

As in tort claims, special damages and general damages for pain, suffering and loss in personal injury claims are recoverable in contract claims[6] and these will be assessed in the same way irrespective of whether the claim is brought in contract or in tort.

9.2.1.1   Loss of enjoyment

In personal injury claims sustained in breach of a holiday contract, there is an additional common law head of loss which aims to compensate an injured person for the non-pecuniary, intangible harm done to the enjoyment of their holiday. In the leading case of *Milner v Carnival plc*,[7] the Court of Appeal described this head of loss as damages for 'physical inconvenience, discomfort and mental distress'[8] although it is perhaps more commonly known as 'loss of enjoyment'. The Court of Appeal's definition makes it plain that the award is used to compensate for both the physical and mental harm to an injured party.

Loss of enjoyment is a type of general damage which is not susceptible of precise quantification. The following guidance can be distilled from the Court of Appeal judgment:

(a) Awards must take into account the physical inconvenience and discomfort, and also measure the level of distress by the extent of the failure to meet reasonable expectations.[9]

(b) This will be a very fact-specific exercise. However, the courts are likely to strive for consistency of approach between comparable cases and accordingly, regard should be had to awards in other ruined holiday cases but also to comparators in the field of psychiatric injuries, injury to feelings arising out of sex discrimination and awards for loss of a child.[10]

(c) Factors include whether the holiday was a special occasion or more ordinary annual holiday,[11] the nature of the breach and the extent of disappointment (so the sports fanatic denied his sporting facilities will be more disappointed than someone who didn't wish to use the sporting facilities anyway).

---

4   *McGregor on Damages* (Sweet & Maxwell, 18th edn, 2012) at 2-002.
5   SI 1992/3288.
6   *McGregor on Damages* at 3-017.
7   [2010] EWCA Civ 389; [2010] PIQR Q3.
8   *Milner* at [47].
9   *Milner* at [35].
10 *Milner* at [37]–[40].
11 *Milner* at [37].

Loss of enjoyment awards in holiday cases tend on the whole to show low awards. Awards varied depending on the factors above, thus:

- holidaymakers who planned to marry abroad and whose plans were ruined received £4,406–£4,360;
- disappointed honeymooners received £321–£1,890;
- other special occasion holidays attracted awards of £264–£1,161; and
- ordinary, run of the mill ruined holidays attracted £83–£1,876.

The Judicial College Guidelines suggest moderate injuries attract an award of £3,750–£12,250, minor injuries will attract an award of between £1,000 and £3,750, and so on. A table of comparators in holiday cases is at the end of this chapter. Whilst this table in intended to serve as a useful starting point, caution is required when relying on comparators awarded prior to the decision of the Court of Appeal in *Milner*.

For discussion about which party can claim 'loss of enjoyment' in a claim for improper performance of a package holiday contract under reg 15 of the Package Travel Regulations see Chapter 2, Package Travel at **2.5.2**.

9.2.1.2   *Diminution in value*

The aim of diminution in value awards is to compensate the consumer for the monetary difference between the holiday contracted for and the holiday actually received.[12] The Court of Appeal in *Milner* confirmed that diminution in value and loss of enjoyment are two separate heads of loss. The former is a type of pecuniary loss whereas the latter is a type of general damages to compensate for partly subjective harm.

Traditionally a strictly arithmetic approach has been taken to the calculation of loss. It has been suggested that the correct approach is to calculate the number of days affected by the diminution in value as a proportion of the total holiday period and then to award a pro rata refund of the total cost of the holiday. In cases where the complaint relates only to the accommodation, and the cost of the package covered the cost of both the accommodation and flights, the Association of British Travel Agents (ABTA) has suggested that half of the total cost of the holiday should be deemed to be the cost of the accommodation. The same arithmetical approach is then adopted on the basis of a pro rata refund of the accommodation-portion of the holiday.

It is now established that this approach is overly simplistic. It is necessary to consider the complaints 'in the round' and then to calculate the value by which the package holiday has been diminished.[13]

---

[12]   *Milner* at [43].
[13]   *Milner* at [46].

The table of comparators at the end of this chapter details the cost of some holidays and the awards in respect of diminution in value. Some of these awards may need to be revisited in light of the Court of Appeal guidance.

9.2.2   Tort

The aim of compensation in tort is to put the injured person back in the position he would have been in as if the tort had not occurred. In personal injury claims this will mainly comprise general damages for pain, suffering and loss and special pecuniary losses.

Parties routinely deal on the basis that separate damages awards for loss of enjoyment and diminution in value are recoverable in personal injury claims when the injury was sustained on holiday and where the cause of action is tortious rather than contractual. In fact this approach is incorrect. Where an injured person in say, a skiing accident, pursues a claim in tort against the party responsible for his injuries, the question of, 'diminution in value' of a contract for a holiday does not arise. Put another way, a skier owes no duty to his neighbours on the slopes in respect of performance of a contract for their holiday. He is not party to the holiday contract and cannot be liable for its breach.

On the other hand, in the scenario above, if the injured skier's enjoyment of his holiday is reduced by reason of his injuries, then the negligent party will have to pay general damages for that loss of enjoyment.

9.2.2.1   *Package travel non-injury remedies*

The following section deals with claims under the Package Travel Regulations which do not themselves involve personal injury, but are of a nature which are commonly made in claims arising out of package travel contracts. Very often alongside the main complaint of an accident or illness and consequential loss and damage come issues regarding the provision of the contracted services and their quality in general terms. As the Package Travel Regulations contain some specific remedies over and above those which arise at common law, it is appropriate to address briefly the effect of these provisions.

9.2.2.2   *Regulation 12*

Under reg 12(a) an organiser must notify a consumer as quickly as possible where it is constrained before departure to alter significantly an essential term of the contract so as to enable the consumer, amongst other things, to withdraw from the contract without penalty. If the consumer withdraws then they are entitled to the relief set out in reg 13.

In some cases reg 12 provides an entirely new right and remedy. Whether a departure is also a breach of contract at common law entitling the consumer to claim damages will depend on the terms of the particular contract.

In any event, the remedy for a breach of contract and the remedy prescribed by reg 12 are different. Even where a common law breach of contract claim lies, it may be in the consumer's interests to insist on its rights under reg 12 to avoid any penalty clause in the contract terms.

No express provision is made by the Regulations in the event that notification is not given by the tour operator as prescribed. In such a case either reg 13 remedies apply or apply by analogy; or the general principles of the assessment of damages for breach of contract may apply.

9.2.2.3 *Regulation 13*

Regulation 13 applies where the consumer withdraws pursuant to his rights under reg 12, or the organiser cancels the package other than by reason of the consumer's fault.

There is no definition of 'cancellation' in the Regulations and it is likely to depend upon the particular facts of the case. It has been held that 'cancelled' means 'either unable or unwilling to provide the cruise it had promised to provide'. Thus a cruise package was cancelled when the organiser sold the cruise ship to another operator who provided the cruise which was otherwise unchanged.[14]

We suggest that there will be some borderline cases where there is such a change to the contract that it could either be described as a significant alteration to an essential term of the existing package contract to which reg 12 applies, or described as a cancellation of the original package to which reg 13 applies.

Under reg 13(2) a consumer is entitled to the choice of an equivalent or superior package, an inferior package and compensation for the difference in value, or a refund. The obligation upon the other party to the contract to provide an alternative package is only triggered if it 'is able to offer' such a substitute.

There is no definition of 'equivalent', 'superior' or 'inferior' quality and this will be a question of fact. We would suggest that cost alone cannot be the sole determining factor. A consumer may well doubt that a 7-night stay at the 3-star Bulgarian Palace Hotel is an equivalent quality package to a 2-night stay at the 5-star Paris Ritz although both cost the same.

---

14 *All Leisure Holidays Ltd v Europaische Reiseversicherung AG* [2011] EWHC 2629 (Comm); [2012] Lloyd's Rep IR 193.

Similarly, there is no guidance on when the other party to the contract will be held to be 'able to offer' another package.

We would suggest that assistance in interpreting reg 13(2) lies in the words 'substitute package'. We would suggest that a package is only a 'substitute' if it has the same or substantially same length of stay, location and accommodation basis (all-inclusive, self-catering and so on). If a different package meets these criteria and is available, it is likely that an organiser or retailer will be obliged to offer it to the consumer irrespective of whether the substitute package is of lower, equivalent or superior quality.

There is no provision in reg 13 for the other party to the contract to refuse to supply a substitute package on the basis it is much more expensive. There is also no provision permitting a supplement to be levied in respect of a superior package, although we note that in contrast with reg 14(2) there is no express prohibition on charging a supplement.

In addition to a right to a substitute package or a refund, a consumer is also entitled to be compensated, if appropriate, and provided the cancellation is not by reason of insufficient take-up by holidaymakers or due to unusual and unforeseeable circumstance beyond the organiser or retailer's control which couldn't have been avoided if all due care had been exercised (reg 13(3)).

Compensation is likely to include any damages for loss of enjoyment and special losses such as additional travel expenses. A consumer is unlikely to have any loss arising from a diminution in value because reg 13(2) already provides for compensation in such cases.

Whether compensation is 'appropriate' will be a question of fact. In addition to being satisfied of the existence and cause of any loss, a court seemingly has a wide discretion to consider whether compensation should be awarded. Factors are likely to include the relative blame of the parties for the cancellation, steps taken by the organiser or retailer to accommodate the consumer, and perhaps whether the consumer obtained a much more superior quality package for no extra cost.

Regulation 13(2) and (3) are implied terms which give rise to damages if breached. It is likely that damages for breach would extend to any diminution in value or refund, loss of enjoyment or special losses which may have been suffered as a result of the breach.

9.2.2.4   *Regulation 14*

Regulation 14 follows the same pattern as reg 12. It both implies a term and prescribes a course of action which an organiser is required to take in certain circumstances, namely where 'after departure, a significant proportion of the services contracted for is not provided or the organiser becomes aware that he will be unable to procure a significant proportion of the services to be provided'.

Regulation 14(2) requires the organiser to make 'suitable alternative arrangements' at no extra cost for the continuation of the package and to compensate the consumer for any difference in the services to be supplied.

There is no definition of what a 'suitable alternative arrangement' but it is likely that a court will have regards to the alternatives in reg 13. It will undoubtedly be fact specific. The obligation to compensate the consumer for the diminution in value of the services only arises 'if appropriate'. As discussed in relation to reg 13(3), the court's discretion is broad. It is clearly unlikely to be appropriate to award any compensation if the consumer is supplied with a superior alternative service.

Loss of enjoyment is not expressly provided for under reg 14(2). It is unlikely that falls within the phrase 'the difference between the services to be supplied under the contract and those supplied'.

If an organiser finds it impossible to supply the suitable alternative arrangements required by reg 14(2), or the consumer declines the alternative for good reasons, the organiser is required to – 'where appropriate' (see above) – provide equivalent transport back to the place of departure or to another agreed place, and compensate the consumer. There is no reason why compensation pursuant to reg 14(3) could not include loss of enjoyment damages.

Regulation 14(2) and (3) are implied terms which give rise to damages if breached (and the right to terminate if the breach is so serious as to go to the root of the contract). The heads of loss will vary from one case to another but in principle will include any diminution in value, loss of enjoyment or special losses incurred, such as additional hotel or food costs. Where an organiser charges a supplement as a condition of providing a suitable alternative arrangement, it is likely that a consumer can claim this back in damages.

9.2.2.5 *Non-performance of the altered or substitute contract*

The language of reg 14 ('for the continuation of the package') and to some extent reg 12 ('to accept a rider to the contract'), suggests that there has been a variation or modification to the original package holiday contract but no more. In contrast, the language of reg 13 ('withdraws' and 'cancels') suggests that there is a new package holiday contract.

In most cases the difference will not matter but it may become important where there is non-performance of the replacement holiday itself.

The issue is most likely to arise where an organiser offers a consumer a 'complimentary' additional 'qualifying component' at the time of the change. A typical example may be a 'complimentary' excursion which is offered by an organiser who otherwise is only obliged to provide the hotel and flights.

If the original package is merely varied or modified then it is seems unlikely that the excursion will form part of the package because it was not prearranged. Regulation 15 would not apply to non-performance of the excursion. Unless a consumer could point to a collateral contract, there would be no breach of contract remedy for a failure to provide the excursion.

On the other hand, if there is a wholly new contract formed at the time of the alteration then it is much more likely that the excursion, the hotel and the flights will all form part of a new package. If the excursion is not provided or is performed inadequately then there is likely to be a contract claim brought pursuant to reg 15.

9.3   DAMAGES UNDER A FOREIGN LAW

As a matter of common law, it is well established that the usual rule in an English court is that a party wishing to rely on foreign law must plead and prove it. If foreign law is not pleaded or proved, the claim will not fail for this reason. Rather, the default rule is that the court will decide the case according to English law, following a presumption that English law and the foreign law are materially the same. The rule ultimately derives from English law's characterisation of foreign law as a matter of fact, not law.[15]

This approach prevails for now. However, there is some question as to whether the current pragmatic approach can survive the encroachment of European principles into the area of applicable law. In a case where the relevant choice of law rules require an English court to apply a law other than that of England and Wales to a claim or issue, there is an argument that the principle of effectiveness requires the English court to disapply its procedural rules in favour of substantive European law.[16]

The parties may be content to allow a case to proceed on the footing of the default rule. There may be no material or significant difference between English law and the applicable foreign law on a particular issue. Alternatively, there will be low value cases where the parties will not consider the differences between English law and foreign law proportionate to the expense of obtaining evidence as to the foreign law.

---

[15]   Per Lord Mansfield in *Mostyn v Fabrigas* (1774) 1 Cowp 161, 174.
[16]   See e g *Kongress Agentur Hagen GmbH v Zeehaghe BV* (C-365/88) [1990] ECR I-1845.

While this is not uncommonly the case where liability is concerned, it is rarely the case where remedies are concerned, certainly in cases of any significant value. When it comes to quantum, there are often fundamental differences between English law and that of other countries (and between different countries generally). For this reason, the applicability and content of foreign law as regards quantum is often a critical issue between the parties.

One example of an area where the differences between English law and that of another country is often significant is the assessment of general damages. In many countries general damages, or their equivalent, are assessed by means of a tariff or 'Baremo'.[17] This is usually more prescriptive, and less favourable to claimants, than the English law equivalent. Broadly speaking, the equivalent is the Judicial College Guidelines, but it is an imperfect analogy. Besides leaving less to the court's discretion, often foreign laws will have tariffs covering matters which would be treated separately to general damages in English law, such as claims for care and assistance. Practitioners must always beware assuming similarities between English and foreign systems in this field and early consultation with a locally qualified lawyer is always advisable.

Another example may be found in the approach taken to reducing a claimant's damages by reference to sums received by the claimant after the accident. *Cox v Ergo Versicherung*[18] was a claim by a widow, domiciled in England, for dependency as a result of her husband's death – a fatal road accident in Germany. German law imposed a duty on the claimant to mitigate and sought to compensate her in net terms only. By contrast, under the English regime, dependency is fixed at the moment of death. The majority of events occurring after the death are deemed irrelevant, in particular, a widow's re-marriage or prospects, as are any benefits which have accrued or will or may accrue as a result of the death. On the facts, the financial difference to the claimant was huge. Cue extensive litigation on which country's law applied to the issue.[19]

Significant points of departure from English law are by no means confined to EU or civil law countries. The Motor Accidents Compensation Act 1999 from New South Wales, which was the legislation in issue in the seminal case of *Harding v Wealands* (see below), provides at least seven other examples.[20] These include caps on various heads of loss, a concept largely unknown to the assessment of damages in personal

---

[17] A Spanish term meaning 'scale' or 'ready-reckoner'. For a brief summary of the way French law deals with the assessment of general damages see the Irish case of *Kelly v Groupama* [2012] IEHC 177.

[18] [2012] EWCA Civ 854.

[19] Fatal Accidents Act 1976, ss 3(3) and 4, respectively. See in particular the judgment of Smith LJ in *Williams v Welsh Ambulance Services NHS Trust* [2008] EWCA Civ 81 for a summary of the sweeping effect of these provisions on fatal accident damages.

[20] [2006] UKHL 32 at [17].

injury cases in England and Wales and significantly higher 'discount rates' which have the impact of reducing substantially lump sum damages in respect of future loss.

This section will consider: evidence required of foreign law (**9.3.1**); tortious claims under Rome II (**9.3.2**); assessment of damages for claims in tort covered by the pre-Rome II regime (**9.3.3**); assessment of damages under a foreign head of loss (**9.3.4**); claims with a foreign law element arising from a death (**9.3.5**); assessment of damages for claims in contract (**9.3.6**); and claims for interest (**9.3.7**).

9.3.1   Evidence of foreign law

There is no substitute for admissible and detailed evidence. Usually this must be in the form of a CPR-compliant expert report from a lawyer or jurist. The expert must be qualified in the relevant jurisdiction. An expert who is in practice is generally preferable because the English court may require evidence as to how the foreign law is actually applied. This does not necessarily rule out an academic lawyer, especially where the English court will have to grapple with a comparative law exercise requiring comprehension of the fundamentals of the relevant foreign law. But in most cases, particularly where losses are straightforward, a practising lawyer will be a better bet.

The expert must understand his or her role in the English proceedings. That role may differ substantially from what they are accustomed to in their own jurisdiction. For example, they are obliged to answer appropriate questions put to them under CPR Part 35. In some legal systems experts are appointed by the court and would not ordinarily expect to have to answer the parties' questions, which they may regard as impertinent. Further, they are not called upon to decide, or opine upon, the ultimate issue. This does not mean that they cannot provide worked calculations of quantum figures in appropriate cases. Often this will greatly assist the court. In any event it will be necessary for the instructing party to have a sense of what the claim would be worth before the courts from whose country the applicable law is derived, even if this is not strictly the same task which the English court will be invited to perform.

Timing is important. It is advisable to obtain and to seek permission to rely on such evidence early, for several reasons. First, if the parties ostensibly proceed on the footing that the default rule applies, there will come a point when obtaining the court's permission for expert evidence of foreign law will become impossible if it is left too late. At the least it will risk costs sanctions. The party may miss out on being able to prove and rely upon potentially helpful provisions of foreign law.

Secondly, knowledge is power. Take, for example, the case where an applicable foreign law prohibits the recovery of a certain head of loss, which makes up half the value of a claim as pleaded under English law. A party who is aware of the provision of foreign law early in the case will be greatly assisted in properly formulating, resisting or valuing the claim. They will be able to make a competitive offer to settle, with the costs consequences that flow from that.

Ideally such evidence (if not the permission to rely on it) should be obtained as early as possible and prior to issue of proceedings, so that it can be pleaded to, or form part of a schedule or counter-schedule. Apart from allowing a claim to be properly valued, it will direct the other factual and medical evidence towards the relevant issues.

Presentation is also important. If a party wishes to rely on foreign law, the written expert evidence of it must be suitably detailed. Unlike English law, the court cannot be presumed to know foreign law and cannot deduce or infer foreign law from incomplete evidence. It is severely limited in the assistance it can derive from counsel on such issues. In cases where there is no oral evidence from experts in foreign law, the written evidence will be all that the court has to go on. General or vague evidence will leave the court hard pressed to rely on it.

In some jurisdictions (eg France) it is common for courts to rely on the evidence of a medico-legal assessor, ie a qualified doctor who also calculates the appropriate level of damages under French law. There is nothing inherently wrong in such a dual, or overlapping expert (provided that they are appropriately qualified in both disciplines) giving evidence in English proceedings.[21] However, such experts must take care to keep separate their factual evidence on medical and legal matters so as to not to obscure the court's roles of finding the primary facts and applying the law to those facts.

The evidence must be tailored to the English court's needs. Compliance with the practice or standards of the courts of the foreign law will not necessarily suffice. A report which might have served the purposes of a foreign court may not necessarily serve the purposes of the English court.[22]

In cases where Rome II applies, it is clear that matters of expert evidence generally (including what expert evidence to order and what form the evidence should take) are matters of 'procedure' within the meaning of Art 1(3) of Rome II. They therefore fall to be determined in accordance with English law and practice, as the law of the forum. CPR Part 35, and the rules and practice that attaches to it, therefore apply to such issues.

---

[21] Indeed, this is the type of evidence relied on in *Kelly v Groupama* [2012] IEHC 177.
[22] See eg the sample report produced in *Wall v Mutuelle De Poitiers Assurances* [2013] EWHC (QB) at [41].

The court is not required to place itself in the position of the foreign court and adopt its practices, conventions or guidelines as to what expert evidence should be ordered.

This was confirmed in the recent High Court decision of *Wall v Mutuelle De Poitiers Assurances*.[23] The court was concerned in that case primarily with the provision of expert medical, or medico-legal, evidence. But the case has implications for expert evidence of all kinds. The claimant had suffered very severe injuries in a motorcycle crash with a French driver in France. Liability was admitted. The court was asked to determine as a preliminary issue whether the issue of the expert evidence the court should order fell to be determined by reference to English law (the law of the forum) or French law (the applicable law).

The claimant sought to adduce expert evidence in the usual way. He sought to rely upon the reports of 8–10 separate experts in various fields. These included spinal injuries, clinical psychology, care, rehabilitation costs, accommodation, assisted technology, neuro-physiotherapy, transport, and employment or accountancy. By contrast, the defendant submitted that the court should follow the French practice as regards experts.[24] This entailed giving permission for only one (perhaps one or two) experts to be called. Broadly speaking, in France there is less scope for separate instruction of experts in a range of disciplines. Usually one expert is appointed to report back to the court and to the parties. He may direct and collate the evidence of other, more specialised experts ('sapiteurs') when required. But the sapiteurs do not report to the court directly. The defendant provided a sample report to illustrate the French approach.

The defendant's approach was rejected by the court. Tugendhat J held that:[25]

> '… the court derived no assistance from the sample report … CPR r35 does not provide for the court to give permission to a single expert to convey to the court opinions of other experts whom s/he has consulted on matters which are not within the single expert's expertise … This court is not required to put itself in the position of a court in France and to decide the case as that court would have decided it. This court is not required to adopt new procedures.'

The same approach applies to pre-Rome II cases, where matters of expert evidence were equally considered to be matters of procedure and for English law and practice to determine.

---

[23]   [2013] EWHC 53 (QB). Thanks to Nicholas Richards for bringing this to the authors' attention.
[24]   The French practice is summarised at [27]–[30].
[25]   *Wall v Mutuelle De Poitiers Assurances* at [41]–[43].

9.3.2 Tortious claims under Rome II

Rome II[26] is now the key regulation for claims in tort. It represents the future. It will apply to all claims in tort where the accident occurred on or after 11 January 2009. It supersedes the pre-existing law.

9.3.2.1 *Scope of applicable law*

For claims under Rome II the starting point is Art 15, which defines the scope of the applicable law. It provides that the applicable law shall govern 'the existence, the nature and the assessment of damage or the remedy claimed' (Art 15(c)) and 'within the limits of powers conferred on the court by its procedural law, the measures a court may take to prevent to terminate injury or damage or to ensure the provision of compensation' (Art 15(d)).

It is apparent from the language of Art 15(c) that the applicable law therefore determines not just what the recoverable heads of loss are, but also how those heads of loss are, in principle, to be quantified. This represents a significant change. Application of foreign law by English courts is, of course, nothing new. But Art 15(c) is likely to compel its application in a larger number of cases than before and in ways to which English courts have not historically been accustomed.

For example, an English court, sitting in a case where Rome II provides that French law applies will now be required, first, to consider for what heads of general damages French law permits recovery and, secondly, to determine, by application of the French principles of quantification, what the correct figure for such damages should be.

Pre-Rome II law the court would have performed step 1, since this was regarded as 'substantive' and therefore a matter for the applicable law. But it would not have performed step 2. The quantification of damages was regarded as 'procedural' and therefore for English law as law of the forum. It would have applied the English law and practice on quantifying the loss.

By way of illustration, in the pre-Rome II case of *Hulse v Chambers*,[27] the claimants were injured in a road traffic accident in Greece. Liability was admitted. Greek law was the applicable law. It was agreed that Greek law would determine what the recoverable heads of loss were. At issue was whether general damages (or their Greek equivalents) should be quantified according to Greek principles or English. This would have made a significant difference. In particular, in the case of one claimant (a minor) general damages stood to be assessed at £125,000 if quantified according to English principles, but only in the range £56,000–£94,000 if

---

[26] Regulation (EC) 864/2007 on the law applicable to non-contractual obligations.
[27] [2001] 1 WLR 2386.

quantified according to Greek principles. The court held that 'assessment of the general damages justified as a head of claim by Greek law as the applicable law, is to be made by reference to English law, as the *lex fori*'.

This is to be contrasted with *Kelly v Groupama*,[28] a decision of the Irish High Court,[29] where Rome II applied. The plaintiff was struck by a van in France in 2009, suffering a fractured femur. Proceedings were issued against the defendant's insurer. French law applied not only to determine the recoverable heads of loss, but also how they were to be quantified. The court therefore proceeded to quantify the heads of loss by reference to the 'methodology of assessment of damages… prescribed by French law'. It was assisted in this task by the evidence of French legal experts for each party.

It should be noted, however, that, although the court in *Kelly v Groupama* notionally applied the correct approach under Rome II, it did so loosely. So loosely that it probably fell into error. The court noted that the French courts ultimately retained 'an unfettered discretion' in deciding the amount of damages to award in a particular case and that use of the official and widely used French comparators (the equivalent of the Judicial College Guidelines) was not compulsory in France but was more a matter of practice. The court then declared itself entitled in matters of practice to apply the *lex fori* and 'have regard to levels of compensation awarded in Irish courts in respect of similar losses'.[30]

This is to have too little regard to the French law and guidance. Most legal systems leave the final determination of the correct award in the court's hands. But it does not follow from this that in a Rome II case damages should be quantified according to, or taking into account, English (or here Irish) principles or comparators. It is, perhaps, understandable that a court would wish to seek refuge in the familiar and the tried and tested. However, such cases should properly be determined according to the principles of quantification of the foreign law. This is so even where application of the foreign principles of quantification leads to a result quite different from that which application of the domestic principles would provide. It is not correct to use the awards that would obtain in domestic law as a cross-check.

Because Rome II is relatively new, there remains a degree of uncertainty as to how far the scope of the applicable law extends. It is likely that the applicable law will apply to questions of mitigation of damage, contributory negligence, causation of loss, and foreseeability of loss.

---

[28]   [2012] IEHC 177.
[29]   The same principles would apply in the English courts.
[30]   *Kelly v Groupama* at [17].

These were all regarded as 'substantive' under the pre-Rome II regime and governed by the applicable law as opposed to English law. They are set to stay that way.[31]

There are limits to the extent to which the English courts are required to apply the foreign law. Most obviously, Rome II does not apply the applicable law to matters of evidence and procedure, which remain governed by English law.[32] The evidence of foreign law before the court is just that – evidence of the rules of the applicable law. The facts to which those rules or principles are to be applied are determined by the English court, applying the English rules of procedure and evidence.

For that reason, where an English court is provided with an uncontradicted expert's report which (as many do) provides a figure or calculation for damages or heads of damage, it is not bound to accept it. Nor is the court bound to accept one of two competing figures provided by experts instructed on each side.[33]

The precise boundaries of 'substance' and 'procedure' under Rome II are yet to be determined with certainty. However, the better view is that the Art 1(3) exclusion should be interpreted narrowly as covering only matters such as the constitution and powers of courts, case management, mode of proof of facts, costs and the mode of trial, that are an integral and indispensable feature of the forum's legal framework for resolving disputes, such that they cannot satisfactorily be replaced by corresponding rules of the applicable law. In *Wall v Mutuelle De Poitiers Assurances* (above) Tugendhat J gave obiter dicta approval to passages from *Dicey & Morris* and Andrew Dickinson's work, *The Rome II Regulation: The Law Applicable to Non-contractual Obligations,* in these terms.[34]

9.3.2.2 *Recital 33*

Plainly, a possible consequence of the application of a foreign law by a court (in whatever jurisdiction) is that a claimant may be awarded significantly less by way of damages than they would in the courts of their own country. Given that the strength of currencies and cost of living (not to mention cost of care) may vary considerably between jurisdictions, this may lead to under-compensation.

The drafters of Rome II clearly contemplated this possibility, at least in the context of the victims of road traffic accidents. It led them[35] to insert recital 33 to the preamble to the Regulation, which provides that:

---

[31] *Harding v Wealands* [2006] UKHL 32 at [24], [74].
[32] Article 1(3). Except for matters of formal validity and, importantly, burdens of proof which are matters for the applicable law (Arts 21 and 22).
[33] See e g the Irish High Court decision in *Kelly v Groupama* [2012] IEHC 177.
[34] See [2013] EWHC (QB) at [20]–[22], [43].
[35] In fact, this particular provision was inserted at the behest of the European Parliament.

'According to the current national rules on compensation awarded to victims of road traffic accidents, when quantifying damages for personal injury in cases where the accident takes place in a State other than that of the habitual residence of the victim, the court seised should take into account all the relevant actual circumstances of the specific victim, including in particular the actual losses and costs of after-care and medical attention.'

The status of recital 33 is uncertain. It appears intended to draw attention to, and to mitigate, the lot of potentially under-compensated claimants in road traffic cases. However, the recitals are, at most, statements of intent and aids to interpretation. They cannot alter or undermine the law which the Regulation determines is applicable to the case.

The better view is that, in concrete terms, its effect is negligible.[36] The English court is still obliged to apply the foreign law (as it would be applied in the foreign court), albeit subject to its own procedures and rule of evidence. This is so even if it leads to a potentially harsh result for the claimant. Recital 33 highlights the difficulty, but provides no solutions.

9.3.2.3   *Periodical payments*

In the majority of cases damages for personal injury in English law take the form of a lump sum payment. However, the award need not necessarily be in that form. English courts are empowered to make a periodical payment order for damages for future pecuniary loss in personal injury cases.[37] Indeed, the English courts are under a statutory obligation to consider making such an order and may impose one even if the parties do not consent.[38] In domestic litigation such orders are perhaps most common in the field of high value clinical negligence claims involving the NHS. They are certainly not restricted to this field. It is often the results of mathematical calculations which will determine whether a party will wish to seek such an order and in what form.

CPR, r 41.7 provides that courts shall have regard to all of the circumstances of the case when considering whether to make such an order and, in particular, the form of award which best meets the claimant's needs. CPR PD 41B sets out the factors to be considered. They include: the scale of the annual payments; the reason for the claimant's preference for a periodical payment; the nature of any financial advice received by the claimant on the form of award; and the defendant's preferred form of award and reason for that preference.

---

[36]   Although it may prove to be the springboard or inspiration for future, more concrete regulation of this issue. It is perhaps telling that it was not sought to be relied upon in *Kelly v Groupama* [2012] IEHC 177, a case where it would have applied.
[37]   Damages Act 1996, s 2(1) as amended by s 100 of the Courts Act 2003.
[38]   Damages Act 1996, s 2(1)(b).

The court may only make an order if satisfied that the continuity of the periodical payment is 'reasonably secure'.[39] The Damages Act 1996 deems certain payments to be 'reasonably secure', ie payments protected by a ministerial guarantee; payments protected by a scheme under s 213 of the Financial Services and Markets Act 2000; and payments where the source of the payments is a government or health service body.[40]

Several questions arise in cases where there is a foreign applicable law. First, if the foreign law makes provision for periodical payments, or their equivalent, which is more extensive than that provided for by English law, can the parties rely on the relevant provisions of foreign law? Secondly, can the English courts make a periodical payment order against a foreign defendant where the applicable foreign law makes no provision for such orders?

These matters have yet to be tested in the courts. The answers cannot be stated with certainty. It seems unlikely that the parties cannot rely on provisions of foreign law which makes provision for periodical payments, or their equivalent, which are more extensive than that provided for by English law. This is because Art 15(d) provides that the applicable law applies 'within the limits of powers conferred on the court by its procedural law' to the measures a court may take 'to ensure the provision of compensation'. Whether or not to order periodical payments is (certainly in English law) a matter of procedure. Rome II does not require the English courts to create new remedies or procedures to mirror those provided for by the applicable law.

Similarly, it would appear that the English courts can make a periodical payment order against a foreign defendant, even where the applicable foreign law makes no provision for such orders. Again this follows from the status of periodical payment orders as aspects of procedural, rather than substantive, law.

However, there is a tenable argument that the English courts are bound by the applicable foreign law as to the availability of periodical payment orders. The argument runs as follows. Matters such as the right to seek payment by way of periodical payments fall to be governed by Art 15(c), as opposed to Art 15(d), of Rome II. Article 15(c) provides that 'the nature of the remedy claimed' is governed by the applicable law. Article 15(c) is not qualified by reference to the limits of the powers conferred by the court's procedural law. The point awaits determination in the courts.

There is no reason in principle why a foreign defendant, such as an insurer, should not be ordered to make periodical payments by an English court. A recent example of a case where this occurred is *Billingsley v*

---

[39] Damages Act 1996, s 2(3).
[40] Damages Act 1996, s 2(4).

UPS Ltd,[41] where the defendant insurer was registered in the Republic of Ireland. In practical terms the biggest obstacle to such awards being made will be demonstrating that the continuity of payments from foreign defendants will be 'reasonably secure'. In *Billingsley* the defendant insurer was covered by the Financial Services Compensation Scheme and was a member of the MIB. Many foreign defendants will be less obviously secure.

9.3.2.4   *Provisional damages*

The English courts also have power to order provisional damages. In practical terms this permits the court to award the claimant damages assessed on the assumption that they will not develop a further disease or suffer a deterioration in their condition, and to award further damages if at a later date one or both of these eventualities occurs. The power is discretionary. It is derived from s 32A of the Senior Courts Act 1981. It arises where there is:

> '... a chance that at some definite or indefinite time in the future the injured person will ... develop some serious disease or suffer some serious deterioration in his physical or mental condition.'

If provisional damages are sought they must be specifically pleaded.[42] If a court awards provisional damages, its order must specify: the disease or type of deterioration; the period during which the application for further damages may be made; and the documents which are to be preserved and provided on a further application for damages. The claimant may apply to extend the specified period, but may only apply once for further damages in respect of each disease or deterioration.[43]

Such orders are most commonly sought in so-called 'disease' claims, such as claims for lung cancer or mesothelioma, but not exclusively so. They are, for example, potentially applicable in cases where the claimant has suffered a head injury and risks developing epilepsy or spinal cord injury cases where syringomyelia can have devastating consequences.

Similar questions will arise regarding provisional damages in cases where a foreign law applies as with periodical payment orders. They also await analysis by the courts. The analysis will be broadly similar. It will depend on a comparison between the foreign law provision and that under s 32A of the Senior Courts Act 1981. The best view is that if the foreign law makes provision for provisional damages, or their equivalent, which is more extensive than that provided for by English law, the court will not be able to rely on the relevant provisions of the foreign law. Whether or not

---

[41]   Unreported, Claim No HQ10X04473. It is clear that the MIB may be subject to a periodical payments order, *AC v (1) Farooq (2) MIB* [2012] EWHC 1484.
[42]   CPR, r 42.2(1), CPR, r 16.4(1)(d).
[43]   CPR, r 41.3(2).

to order provisional damages is a matter of procedure. Rome II does not require the English courts to create new remedies or procedures to mirror those provided for by the applicable law.

Further, in the converse case, the English courts are likely to be able to order provisional damages against a foreign defendant, even where the applicable foreign law makes no provision for such orders. Again this follows from their status as aspects of procedural law. However, as with periodical payment orders, there is a tenable argument that the English courts are bound by the applicable foreign law as to the availability of orders for provisional damages.

9.3.2.5   *Exemplary, aggravated and multiple damages*

Almost all personal injury claims are for compensatory damages. However, it is not the only type of award which may be sought. In certain cases English law allows for exemplary or aggravated damages. Foreign laws may also provide for similar remedies, and others, such as multiple damages.

A claim may be made for a remedy which is not known to English law. The question then arises, assuming that it is an appropriate case for the remedy on the facts, as to the extent to which an English court has power, or is obliged, to grant it. Such remedies are matters of substance, not procedure. The answer is, therefore, that the English court is obliged to grant the remedies provided for by the foreign law, save to the extent that they are contrary to public policy in English law.[44]

As to the public policy exception, the rule is that English court is not obliged to enforce foreign rules which are, in their application, 'manifestly incompatible with the public policy (*ordre public*) of the forum'.[45] The effect of the exception where it applies is to compel the English court to ignore and disapply the relevant provision of foreign law.

It is likely to be a rare case where this exception has practical application. It is possible for a rule to appear to be contrary to public policy in the abstract but not in its application to the facts of a particular case – in which case it will be upheld. It is only in its application to particular facts that the exception will bite. Further, the reference to 'manifestly incompatible', as opposed to merely 'incompatible', in the wording of the exception suggests that will only apply in clear or egregious cases.

Further still, the authorities suggest that the type of issues or concerns which are likely to render the applicable law incompatible with English

---

[44]   The English court is also obliged to disapply any penal laws of the foreign law or any laws that contradict English mandatory laws. Neither of these exceptions are likely to feature heavily in practice in this context.

[45]   Rome I, Art 21; Rome II, Art 26.

public policy are restricted to situations where the applicable law is an affront to basic principles of justice or fairness, or amounts to a fundamental breach of human rights.[46] It will be highly unusual for foreign laws (especially those from the EU) to fall foul of these stringent criteria, particularly in the field of personal injury.

Nevertheless, the exception may still have relevance. This is especially with regard to awards of exemplary or multiple damages. It is clear that this is an area which concerned the drafters of Rome II. The European Commission's final proposal for Rome II contained a draft Art 24 deeply hostile to such awards, providing that:

> '... the application of a provision of the law designated by this Regulation which as the effect of causing non-compensatory damages, such as exemplary or punitive damages, to be awarded shall be contrary to Community public policy.'

Perhaps unsurprisingly (especially in light of its wide and unprecedented reach) this was dropped from the final version. It was replaced by a rather watered down recital 32, which appears likely to have little practical effect:

> '... the application of a provision of the law designated by this Regulation which would have the effect of causing non-compensatory exemplary or punitive damages of an excessive nature to be awarded may, depending on the circumstances of the case and the legal order of the Member State of the court seised, be regarded as being contrary to the public policy (*ordre public*) of the forum.'

Where does this leave claims for remedies such as exemplary, aggravated, multiple or jury-assessed damages in personal injury cases? These issues require testing in the courts. The answer is likely to be that exemplary and aggravated damages are not manifestly contrary to public policy per se. Indeed English law provides for them in certain situations. It will take a rare case, or an astronomical award, for the award of such damages to be prohibited by public policy.

Multiple awards may, on the other hand, be difficult to enforce. Statute has intervened to prohibit the enforcement of an award of multiple damages by a foreign court (s 5 of the Protection of Trading Interest Act 1980).[47] There is therefore a credible argument that it would be contrary to public policy for such awards to be made by an English court applying the foreign law.

---

[46] See *Kuwait Airways v Iraqi Airways (Nos 4 & 5)* [2002] 2 AC 883. A similar analysis has been adopted in Continental systems.
[47] See *Lewis v Eliades* [2004] 1 WLR 692, heavyweight litigation that went the full 12 rounds.

9.3.3 Pre-Rome II tort claims

For claims in tort where the accident pre-dates 11 January 2009, Part III of the Private International Law (Miscellaneous Provisions) 1995 Act ('the 1995 Act') applies to determine the applicable law.

Section 14(3)(b) of the 1995 Act provides that questions of 'procedure' are governed by the law of the forum (ie England), by implication leaving matters of 'substance' to be governed by the applicable law. The 1995 Act did not define 'procedure', much less 'substance', nor did it specify the scope of the applicable law. This was left to the common law.

The leading case is the House of Lords decision in *Harding v Wealands*.[48] The claimant was injured and rendered tetraplegic in a road traffic accident in New South Wales. He brought his claim in England.[49] The defendant contended that the law of New South Wales applied to the assessment of damages and sought to rely on certain provisions of local law, namely the Motor Accidents Compensation Act 1999, which imposed restrictions on the amount of damages which could be recovered.[50] The question therefore arose as to whether these provisions formed part of the substantive law (in which case they applied) or procedural law (in which case English law applied and the provisions of local law did not).

The unanimous view of the House of Lords was that the provisions of the Motor Accidents Compensation Act 1999 constituted procedural matters. They were therefore not applicable to the dispute since this was the preserve of English law.

Where was the line to be drawn between procedure and substance? It was to be taken that Parliament of the 1995 Act, in passing s 14(3)(b), had intended to adopt the pre-existing common law understanding of 'procedural'. This was, as Lord Hoffmann put it, as follows:[51]

> 'In applying this distinction to actions in tort, the courts have distinguished between the kind of *damage* which constitutes an actionable injury and the assessment of compensation (i.e. *damages*) for the injury which has been held to be actionable. The identification of actionable damage is an integral part of the rules which determine liability. As I have previously had occasion to say, it makes no sense simply to say that someone is liable in tort. He must be liable *for* something and the rules which determine what he is liable for are inseparable from the rules which determine the conduct which gives rise to liability. Thus the rules which exclude damage from the scope of liability on the grounds that it does not fall within the ambit of the liability rule or does not have the prescribed causal connection with the wrongful act, or

---

[48] [2007] 2 AC 1.
[49] The claimant was the passenger in a car which the defendant, his girlfriend (an Australian), was driving.
[50] [2007] 2 AC 1 at [17] of the House of Lords judgment.
[51] [2007] 2 AC 1 at [24] of the House of Lords judgment.

which require that the damage should have been reasonably foreseeable, are all rules which determine whether there is liability for the damage in question. On the other hand, whether the claimant is awarded money damages (and if so, how much) or, for example, restitution in kind, is a question of remedy.'

Put shortly, what heads of loss are recoverable is a matter of substantive law, ie governed by the applicable law. But quantification of damages is a matter of procedure, to be governed by English law. Hence, the applicable law applies to determine what heads of general damages are recoverable;[52] mitigation of damage; contributory negligence; causation of loss; foreseeability of loss, since these were all regarded as 'substantive'.[53]

But the type of matters set out in the Motor Accidents Compensation Act 1999 was considered to be procedural matters for English law. These included: a cap on damages for non-economic loss, a rule of no award for the first 5 days' loss of earnings, a discount rate for future economic loss of 5% (compare the English rate of 2.5%), and a rule that credit was to be given for any payment made to the claimant by an insurer.

The decision was controversial in terms of its reasoning. Nor was the distinction between 'procedure' and 'substance' easy to apply in practice.[54] But there can be no doubt that it represents the law as it applies under the pre-Rome II regime. As set out above, there can be no doubt either that the Rome II brought about a significant change in the law and practice in this regard, leading to the application of foreign law to issues previously considered the preserve of English law.

9.3.4   Assessing damages under a foreign law head of loss

One consequence of a foreign law applying to a case is that the English court will be required to assess foreign heads of loss. Often these heads of loss will correspond to equivalent heads of loss in English law. But this is not necessarily the case.

In cases where Rome II applies, the foreign law will determine both the recoverable heads of loss and the principles for quantifying them. As set out above, the English court is therefore required to determine the case according to the methodology of, and as far as possible placing itself in the position of, the foreign court. This is so even where application of the foreign principles of quantification leads to a result markedly different to the one application of more familiar domestic principles would lead to.

---

[52]   The dictum to this effect in *Boys v Chaplin* [1971] AC 356, 394 was approved in *Harding v Wealands*.

[53]   *Harding v Wealands* [2006] UKHL 32 at [24], [74].

[54]   See e g *Roerig v Valiant Trawlers* [2002] EWCA Civ 21.

Undoubtedly, this will mean English courts undertaking tasks to which they have hitherto been unaccustomed. Hence, if French law requires assessment of general damages by reference to medico-legal evidence specifying a degree of disability expressed as a percentage, that is the exercise the English court should perform. It should not simply rely on the domestic formula of the judge's discretion, assisted by the Judicial College Guideline brackets and comparators. Further, it may lead English courts to have to assess and quantify heads of loss that have no equivalent in English law.

Courts may also be called upon to assess foreign heads of loss in pre-Rome II cases. However, in pre-Rome II cases the methods and principles of quantification are English, even if the heads of loss are not (see, for example, the assessment in *Hulse v Chambers*,[55] above).

This can lead to a situation where the English court is required to quantify a head of loss totally unknown to English law. An example is provided by the case of *Cox v Ergo Versicherung*,[56] a pre-Rome II wrongful death claim where it was held that German law applied to determine recoverable heads of loss. One of the heads of loss provided for by German law was loss of maintenance by the deceased (s 844 of the German Civil Code). This had no English law equivalent. How was such a head of loss to be quantified? The court gave a pragmatic answer – the starting point would be the methodology used by the foreign law when carrying out the assessment. As Maurice Kay LJ put it:[57]

> 'In theory, it would be perfectly open to the English court now to develop from scratch its own rules for the assessment of damages for loss of maintenance in a section 844 case. As a matter of expediency, however, it seems obvious to start by examining the way another jurisdiction carries out such an assessment where it has a section 844 head of loss. The only other jurisdiction to which we were referred was Germany itself ... I can see no good reason, therefore, why, purely as a matter of English law rather than comity, it would not be expedient to follow, at least as a starting point for assessment of damages, the way damages are assessed in Germany in cases under section 844. The English court is not bound by German methodology, and experience and precedent may result in deviation from German methodology.'

9.3.5 Claims arising from death

There are two types of claim which may arise on the death of a party who has suffered personal injury: wrongful death claims pursuant to the Fatal Accidents Act 1976 ('the 1976 Act'); and claims pursuant to the Law Reform (Miscellaneous Provisions) Act 1934 ('the 1934 Act').

---

[55]   [2001] 1WLR 2386.
[56]   [2012] EWCA Civ 854.
[57]   At [47].

9.3.5.1 *Wrongful death claims under the 1976 Act*

Broadly speaking the 1976 Act permits the dependants (as defined by the 1976 Act) of a deceased person to claim damages for their loss of dependency. It also permits a smaller class of persons to claim damages for bereavement (which are fixed at £11,800). By doing so, it creates a claim which does not exist at common law.

In order to make a claim under the 1976 Act the claimant must be able to show that the defendant would have been liable to the deceased for the injuries caused had the deceased not died.[58] The claimant must also fall within the definition of dependants, as defined by the 1976 Act, or the class of person entitled to claim bereavement damages. The 1976 Act makes specific provision as to quantification of claims for dependency. In particular, as noted above, for the purposes of assessment the claimant's dependency is fixed at the moment of death. In particular, a widow's re-marriage or prospects are deemed irrelevant, as are any benefits which have accrued or will or may accrue as a result of the death.[59]

In claims governed by English law (whether by default or otherwise) the 1976 Act applies just as it would in a domestic case. While the 1976 Act is silent as to its territorial scope, it can and does apply to accidents which occur abroad. Similarly, while the 1976 Act is also silent as to whom may be sued under it, it may be used to sue a foreigner or foreign legal person.

By contrast, in claims where a foreign law applies (whether pursuant to Rome II, or the pre-Rome II regime), the 1976 Act will have no role to play. The 1976 Act is not, as has been argued in the past, a procedural statute but a substantive one. As noted above, it provides for a claim, or cause of action which would not otherwise exist in English law. Therefore, in claims for wrongful death or dependency where a foreign law applies, the 1976 Act will not apply. Rather, the provisions of the applicable law will.

This is made explicit for cases where Rome II applies by Art 15(f) of Rome II. This provides that the applicable law will govern 'persons entitled to compensation for damage sustained personally'. The Explanatory Memorandum to Rome II[60] provides that this concept includes claims for 'pain and suffering caused by a bereavement, or financial, as in the loss sustained by the children or spouse of a deceased person'.

---

[58] Fatal Accidents Act 1976, s 1.
[59] Fatal Accidents Act 1976, ss 3(3) and 4.
[60] COM (2003)0427, p 24.

For pre-Rome II cases, the leading authority is the Court of Appeal decision in *Cox v Ergo Versicherung*.[61] The claimant was married to a British army major, stationed in Germany, who was killed riding his bicycle in 2004, leaving the claimant his sole dependant. The claimant issued proceedings in England directly against the German driver's insurer.

The claimant pleaded that the applicable law was German, but sought to rely on the 1976 Act, which, as set out above, offered her significant advantages when it came to the assessment of damages. In particular, the claimant had been, and would continue to be, in receipt of a war widow's pension from the MoD for life. Credit would have to be given for this pursuant to the German regime, but not the English.

The claimant relied on dicta by Waller LJ in *Roerig v Valiant Trawlers*[62] to the effect that claims for loss of dependency brought in England could only be brought under the 1976 Act. She also submitted that the assessment of damages was a procedural matter for English law, which included application of the 1976 Act, and that the application of the 1976 Act by the English court was mandatory on public policy grounds.

The court rejected each of these arguments. German law was the applicable law. Once identified, the applicable law determined whether there was liability and also for what heads of damage. It came as a package. There was no place for the 1976 Act. Further, in *Roerig* the applicable law was English. Anything said about the 1976 Act being the only procedure for recovering damages for dependency had to be read in that light.

English law did have a part to play in *Cox*, even if the 1976 Act did not. Because the claim was brought under the pre-Rome II regime, quantification of damages (as opposed to identification of heads of loss) was a matter for English law. The position under Rome II is that the applicable law will govern the availability of the cause of action, the heads of loss recoverable and quantification of loss.

9.3.5.2 Claims under the 1934 Act

Section 1 of the 1934 Act provides that on the death of any person all causes of action subsisting against or vesting in him shall survive against or, as the case may be, for the benefit of his estate. It abolished the rule that a personal injury claim dies with the claimant. Subject to certain limitations, it permits a claim by the estate of a deceased person to recover the damages to which the deceased person would have been entitled by

---

[61] [2012] EWCA Civ 854. The claimant has obtained permission to appeal to the Supreme Court in this case.
[62] [2002] 1 WLR 2304.

reason of the personal injuries. In claims governed by English law (whether by default or otherwise) the 1934 Act applies just as it would in a domestic case.

However, in cases governed by a foreign law, the 1934 Act will have no role to play. The applicable law will apply to this issue. It may not provide for such extensive rights as English law does. Like the 1976 Act, the 1934 Act is substantive, not procedural. It provides for a claim, or cause of action, which would not otherwise exist in English law.

This is made explicit for cases where Rome II applies by Art 15(e) of Rome II. This provides that the law applicable under Rome II determines the question whether a non-contractual obligation is personal to the person sustaining damage or may be passed to his heirs.

9.3.6   Contract claims

Some claims concerning accidents abroad are most appropriately (or most advantageously) brought, not in tort, but in contract. Classic examples are the (non-package) holiday let of a property abroad, where the claimant wishes to sue the owner of the property, or excursions on package holidays which do not form part of the package.[63]

Rome I applies to contracts concluded on or after 18 December 2009. The starting point under Rome I is Art 12, entitled 'Scope of the law applicable'. Article 12(c) provides that:

> 'The law applicable to a contract by virtue of this Regulation shall govern in particular ... within the limits of the powers conferred on the court by its procedural law, the consequences of a total or partial breach of obligations, including the assessment of damages in so far as it is governed by rules of law.'

As under Rome II, the applicable law therefore determines not just what the recoverable heads of loss are, but also how the recoverable heads of loss are, in principle, to be quantified. As with Rome II, Rome I does not apply the applicable law to matters of evidence and procedure, which remain governed by English law.[64] Further, Art 12 expressly limits the scope of the applicable law to governing matters 'within the limits of the powers conferred on the court by its procedural law'. One point of distinction is that Rome I has no equivalent of recital 33, although it is doubtful that this makes any difference in practice.

---

[63]   It should be noted that the claimant may not have an entirely free hand in this regard since some of the law in jurisdictions does not recognise concurrent liability and may, at the least, compel a claimant to elect between contract and tort rather than pursue them both.

[64]   Article 1(3), again subject to the matters of formal validity and burdens of proof, which are reserved to the applicable law.

Contracts entered into before 18 December 2009 are governed by the Rome Convention, given effect in English law by the Contracts (Applicable Law) Act 1990. As far as the issues discussed in this chapter are concerned there is no material difference between the two regimes.

9.3.7 Interest

In substantial or long-running claims, the ability to claim interest on damages will be important. In such cases significant sums may be at stake. In English law recovery of interest on damages is largely a matter of statute. Section 35A of the Senior Courts Act 1981 and s 69 of the County Courts Act 1984 give the courts a general power to award interest on damages. Interest is in the discretion of the court and must be awarded at a trial or assessment.[65] In claims where English law applies these provisions will apply in the usual way.

However, difficult questions arise when a foreign law applies. In particular, when a foreign law provides for a substantive right to recover interest (which may be more or less generous than what English law provides for), the question arises as to which country's law should determine the issue.

Pre-Rome II, the matter was considered in *Maher v Groupama.*[66] This was an *Odenbreit* claim against a French insurer. One of the issues was whether the award of pre-judgment[67] interest was to be determined in accordance with English or French law. The answer given was a nuanced one. The Court of Appeal held that s 35A of the Senior Courts Act 1981[68] created a remedy exercised at the court's discretion rather than a substantive right to interest. Therefore, although the existence of a legal right to claim interest was to be classified as a substantive matter, to be determined by applicable law (ie French law), whether such a substantive right existed or not an award of interest under s 35A of the 1981 Act was to be classified as a procedural matter, governed by English law. However, in exercising its discretion the court might well take into account any relevant provisions of the applicable law relating to the recovery of interest.

In practical terms this probably meant that a claimant was entitled to seek interest pursuant to the statute regardless of what the applicable law provided. However, since the powers under the English statute were discretionary the court was likely to take into account the scope of the power to award interest under the applicable law in exercising its discretion. Alternatively, if the foreign law gave the claimant a substantive right to interest the claimant was entitled to rely on it.

---

[65] A full exposition of the rules on interest is beyond the scope of this work.
[66] [2009] EWCA Civ 1191.
[67] It was agreed that post-judgment interest was governed by English law.
[68] The same analysis will apply to s 69 of the County Courts Act 1984.

The position under Rome II is less certain and awaits resolution by the courts. The better view is probably that the award of interest on damages is a matter for the applicable law by virtue of Art 15(d) of Rome II. The matter is therefore to be determined in accordance with the applicable law, save that the English court must act 'within the limits of powers conferred on the court by its procedural law', in this case the law on interest.

9.4 TABLE OF COMPARATORS

This table of comparators gives a brief description of the complaint and details the awards for diminution in value and/or loss of enjoyment which was made. It is hoped that it will be a useful guide in assessing future awards. Many of these awards were made before the Court of Appeal decision in *Milner v Carnival plc*[69] which we would suggest is now the starting point for loss of enjoyment and diminution in value cases. That case confirmed that diminution in value and loss of enjoyment were two separate heads of loss, gave guidance upon how to calculate each head of loss and also set out approximate award brackets for loss of enjoyment cases.

---

[69]   [2010] EWCA Civ 389.

Quantum: diminution in value and loss of enjoyment

Case	Length of Holiday	Cost	Complaint	Damages: Diminution in Value	Damages: Loss of Enjoyment	RPI
Personal Injury Cases						
Saga Holidays v Sewell (24/8/11)			C and wife on excursion whilst on holiday. Returned to cruise ship and had to cross a concrete pier, a concrete block and step on to a mesh plate. C attempted to cross and stumbled and fell.		£1576	£1640.75
Barnes v Thomas Cook Tour Operations Ltd (17/5/2011) [2011] CLY 2497	14 days		67-year-old male infected with legionella pneumophila whilst on holiday in Egypt.	£339	£500	£354.28 (Diminution) £522.53 (Enjoyment)
H (A Child) v First Choice Holidays and Flights Ltd (13/6/2007) [2007] LCY 3199			6-year-old boy tripped on set of unlit concrete steps whilst on holiday in Turkey. Was unable to go swimming, play football or expose injury to sand on the beach. Accident occurred on second day of holiday so much of it was ruined.	No separate award	£1000	£1185.72

Case	Length of Holiday	Cost	Complaint	Damages: Diminution in Value	Damages: Loss of Enjoyment	RPI
Borton v First Choice Holidays and Flights Ltd (12/5/2005) [2006] CLY 3253			C went on holiday to be married and then on honeymoon. On eve of wedding (half way through holiday) taken ill with infection of Cryptosporidium. Wedding, reception and honeymoon ruined.	No separate award.	£4000	£5120.83
Jones v First Choice Holidays and Flights Ltd (2/3/2005) [2006] CLY 3256	14 days	Over £2000 each for C and her husband (RPI £2580.58)	C contracted Salmonella poisoning on the third day of her honeymoon at the beginning of safari excursion.	No separate award.	£2,500	£3225.72
Hutchinson and others v First Choice Holidays and Flights (16/2/05)			C suffered food poisoning whilst on holiday in Mexico, after which she suffered from IBS.	£700	£500	£907.49 (Diminution) £648.21 (Enjoyment)
Battley v Thompson Holidays Ltd (12/3/2003) [2004] CLY 1878			C sustained head injuries when struck head on large and visible ornamental light fitting close to the end of his holiday.	No separate award.	£100 (50% contributory negligence)	£136.63
Non-Personal Injury Cases						

Case	Length of Holiday	Cost	Complaint	Damages: Diminution in Value	Damages: Loss of Enjoyment	RPI
Milner and Milner v Carnival plc (20/4/10) [2010] EWCA Civ 389	106 days	£59, 052 (RPI £65 148.03)	Voyage described as glamorous. Cabin damaged on the first night after entering stormy conditions, as a result of which they suffered two sleepless nights, then moved to inside cabin that lacked some of the amenities of the previous cabin. Temporarily moved to a suite and later rejected offer to accommodate in another cabin due to lack of hanging space for C2's clothes. Moved back to original cabin but noise continued to cause distress. Disembarked in Hawaii 28 days into trip, and spent some time there at their own cost before returning home.	£3500	£4000 (C1) and £4500 (C2)	£3861.31 (Diminution) £4412 (C1) (Enjoyment) £4964.54 (C2) (Enjoyment)
Crosby v Fleetwood Travel (18/10/06) [2007] CLY 2127	14 days	£3,620 (RPI £4440.10)	C booked holiday for himself and family in Egypt but a terrorist attack led to the cancellation of flights. Alternative holiday was not of equivalent standard. C had to pay £1600 more for a three star hotel, an additional supplement had to be paid and diving (which had been a specific requirement) 15 miles from accommodation. Hotel was overcrowded and prevented family from enjoying facilities.	£1600	£250 pp (£1000)	£1962.48 (Diminution) £1226.55 (Enjoyment)

Case	Length of Holiday	Cost	Complaint	Damages: Diminution in Value	Damages: Loss of Enjoyment	RPI	
Stainsby v Balkan Holidays Ltd (29/9/05) [2006] CLY 1992	14 days	£718 (RPI £913.95)	Honeymoon in Bulgaria. Two star hotel with no lift. Room dirty and damp. Allocated room on 4th floor despite request to be on lower floors due to pregnancy. Eventually given room on lower floors but incredibly noisy. Alternative hotel offered at extra cost of £422 but construction works meant it was noisy and disruptive. Food of poor standard so additional cost of eating out.		£1000 for both loss of bargain and loss of enjoyment	£1272.92	
Cherry v Malta Bargain Ltd (5/5/05) [2005] CLY 1978	7 days	£1848 (RPI £2365.83)	Holiday for family of six. Rooms dirty, bedding stained. Offered new hotel but unsuitable for family. On third day allocated to another hotel which was suitable. Claimed that first 3 days of holiday ruined.	£198	£450 (25 pp p/day)	£253.48 (Diminution)	£576.09 (Enjoyment)
Samuels v My Travel Tour Operators Ltd (27/2/04) [2005] CLY 1979	14 days	£3778 (RPI £5052.41)	Luxury honeymoon in Mauritius. Rated four star. Woken by construction every day, and continued into the night. No alternative accommodation found and C had to move out at his own cost.	£3778	£1000	£5052.41 (Diminution)	£1337.32 (Enjoyment)

Case	Length of Holiday	Cost	Complaint	Damages: Diminution in Value	Damages: Loss of Enjoyment	RPI
Dickson v Thompson Holidays (20/10/03) [2004] CLY 1877		c. £1000 (RPI c. £1346.11)	Holiday in Spain for C, husband and son. Advertised as being on beach and suitable for families. Brochure depicted a pool at the front of the hotel and beach immediately across the road. C subsequently told that there may be works that might cause a disturbance, but then was told later that the works were taking place some distance from hotel and would not cause disturbance. On arrival found that beach opposite hotel like building site and unusable. Works caused disturbance in terms of noise and dust night and day. View obscured by lorries and machines on beach, unable to use balcony or open patio doors, use the pool or eating facilities.	£660	£750 (£250 for each family member).	£888.43 (Diminution); £1009.58 (Enjoyment)

Case	Length of Holiday	Cost	Complaint	Damages: Diminution in Value	Damages: Loss of Enjoyment	RPI
Richards v Goldtrail Travel Ltd (15/9/03) [2004] CLY 1880	14 days	£2195 (RPI £2956.33)	C and four travelling companions booked apartment in Turkey. No room when arrived. Taken to another hotel for the first night. Then taken back to the apartments the next day and told to use small staff room as no other rooms available. Although checked that English food provided at apartments, was really only suited to Turkish tastes. C also had concerns about food hygiene. Had been no hot water during evenings, frequent power cuts and telephone in C's room did not work.	£1317	£3400	£1773.80 (Diminution) £4579.29 (Enjoyment)
Dale v Golden Sun Holidays Ltd (12/02/2003)	14	£1300 (RPI £1782.15)	Holiday for C and his family. Two studio apartments allocated completely unsuitable. Below ground, dark, dirty, infested with ants and cockroaches. Door handle to one was broken, cooking facilities inadequate, cooking utensils were rusty and unusable. Pool and showers surrounding it were dirty. Alternative accommodation provided for wife and daughter just as dirty. D and his son not moved.	£975	£750	£1336.61 (Diminution) £1028.17 (Enjoyment)

Case	Length of Holiday	Cost	Complaint	Damages: Diminution in Value	Damages: Loss of Enjoyment	RPI
Thompson v Airtours Holidays Ltd (No 2) (17/10/01) [2002] CLY 2323	7		Holiday in Portugal described as a 'Winter Sun' holiday. Hotel described as four star and listed a number of facilities. C made request for quiet room but the room overlooked busy and noisy dual carriageway (increasing at night) and situation exacerbated by the arrival of noisy guests. A number of outdoor facilities closed and C's room had no heating and was damp and cold. No alternative accommodation offered.	£300 (for misleading nature of brochure)	£550 (£300 for C and £250 for wife)	£423.06 £775.62 (Enjoyment)
Buhus-Orwin v Costa Smeralda Holidays Ltd (16/8/01) [2001] CLY 4279	14		Luxury holiday in Sardinia promised to be 'opulent luxury in a dramatic landscape and a beautiful villa with private garden and swimming pool'. Was infested with rats. Eventually offered smaller accommodation with only communal pool and no private garden. No compensation offered. Alternative accommodation declined and C and family returned home.	Entire cost of the holiday	£2000	£2825.29

Case	Length of Holiday	Cost	Complaint	Damages: Diminution in Value	Damages: Loss of Enjoyment	RPI
Coughlan v Thomson Holidays Ltd (20/3/01) [2001] CLY 4276	14	£1320 (RPI £1884.18)	C and wife booked 14 day 'gold' package holiday in Majorca. Flight delayed but C and wife not informed until just before midnight. Offered hotel but would have had to wait for taxi, drive one hour and be back at 7.30 am next day so offer refused. Offered blankets that never materialised so spent night in freezing and uncomfortable conditions. First two days of holiday ruined.	No separate award	£550 (£40 paid from separate insurance policy taken into account).	£785.08
Curry v Magic Travel Group (Holidays) Ltd (2/1/01) [2001] CLY 4278	14	£894 pp (RPI £1284.31 pp)	Holiday in Spain. Hotel rated 'platinum' in brochure and described as of high standard and quality. C asked for quiet room at time of booking but was given room at top of kitchen and next to restaurant. Noise until 12.30 am, and started again at 6 am. Offered room in another hotel 10km away but would have to have paid additional costs. Flew home instead.	Total cost of holiday	£225 each (£450)	£646.46

Case	Length of Holiday	Cost	Complaint	Damages: Diminution in Value	Damages: Loss of Enjoyment	RPI
McSharry v Lloyds TSB Bank plc (5/10/00) [2000] CLY 4037			C booked holiday accommodation in the shape of five bed villa using credit card issued by D. Villa had not been cleaned following previous tenants. Dirty crockery, cutlery, utensils and kitchen facilities. Disposal unit blocked. Guests spent first 2 days cleaning. Venue had been chosen because of indoor pool which was unusable. Claimant upset by regular presence of cleaners and workmen who had come to try and repair and treat pool and the pool furniture that was mouldy and damp. Garage was also damp and untidy.	Total cost of holiday	£750	£1074.30

Case	Length of Holiday	Cost	Complaint	Damages: Diminution in Value	Damages: Loss of Enjoyment	RPI
Milne-Williamson v Thomson Holidays Ltd (14/5/99) [1999] CLY 3827		£732 (RPI £1086.51)	C booked family holiday in Menorca at 4T rated hotel. Less than a day before departing, advised that was overbooked and alternative resort offered. Alternative unacceptable and 3T hotel eventually agreed. D paid £100 towards cost of holiday and £200 compensation for late alternation. The new resort offered 'better' resorts and 'ideal' for families. C disappointed as only one plug socket in room, long queues for lifts, items had to be paid in cash, beach was rocky, entertainment poor, food tasteless and room infected with ants. Sought to go home but this would have involved waiting at the airport with young child for unknown period of time.	£0	£150	£222.64
Thompson v Airtour Holidays Ltd (3/3/1999) [1999] CLY 3819			Five star hotel booked in Luxor. Sought quiet sunny holiday by pool. Paid additional sums for view of the Nile. Extensive work being carried out at hotel with continuous noise from 6.30 am to 1.30 am. Room with view of Nile not available.	Two thirds of the cost of the holiday.	£500 each	£748.93 each

Case	Length of Holiday	Cost	Complaint	Damages: Diminution in Value	Damages: Loss of Enjoyment	RPI
Davis v Thompson Holidays Ltd (18/2/99) [1999] CLY 3826	11 days	£889.90 (RPI £1336.21)	Holiday in Majorca. Delay at airport for 12 hours. Hotel overbooked and C and her husband were given a room in a nearby hotel for one night, and thereafter a room in a different resort that catered mostly to German tourists. The World Cup was on and they found the more 'cosmopolitan resort intimidating and unpleasant'.	No separate award.	£250 each	£375.38
Martin v Travel Promotions Ltd (9/2/99) [1999] CLY 3821		£795 pp (RPI £1193.71)	Cs were scheduled to return from holiday from India on 17 April. Lived in Menorca and had booked flight from UK to Menorca on 18th April. On 16th, due to get internal flight to Bombay from Delhi and thereafter connect with UK bound flight. Internal flight delayed and missed UK bound flight. C sought assurances that booked on alternative flight on the 18th but by time assurances given, C had booked first class seats on same flight. This arrived in the UK in sufficient time for the connection with the Menorca flight to be made.	No separate award.	£250 each	£375.38

CHAPTER 10

PLEADINGS

10.1 PARTICULARS OF CLAIM – TOUR OPERATOR CLAIM – ACCIDENT CLAIM

IN THE LOCAL COUNTY COURT   Claim No 3LO0001

BETWEEN:

JAMES KIRK

Claimant

–and–

SUNNYSIDE HOLIDAYS LIMITED

Defendant

PARTICULARS OF CLAIM

---

1.   Pursuant to a contract entered into with the Defendant evidenced by the booking reference ZZ54321 ('the contract') the Defendant agreed to organise and supply to the Claimant and six other persons (collectively, 'the travel party') a package holiday to Turkey between 21 July 2009 and 10 August 2009 ('the holiday').

2.   There were, amongst others, the following pre-arranged components of the said package:

(a)   return flights from Cardiff airport to Antalya airport;
(b)   all-inclusive accommodation at the Slippery Inn ('the hotel') in Antalya, Turkey for the duration of the holiday.

3.   The Package Travel, Package Holidays and Package Tours Regulations 1992 ('the Regulations') applied to the contract which was for the supply of a package within the meaning of regulation 2 of the Regulations.

4.   Further, within the meaning of the Regulations:

(a) the Defendant was the organiser and/or retailer of the holiday and was the 'other party to the contract';
(b) the Claimant and the other members of the travel party were each a 'consumer' and/or 'beneficiary';
(c) the owners and managers of the hotel, their employees, servants and agents were 'suppliers' of the Defendant within the meaning of regulation 15.

5. There were the following express or implied terms of the holiday contract, pursuant to regulation 15(1) and (2) of the Regulations and/or by section 13 of the Supply of Goods and Services Act 1982 and/or at common law:

(a) the Defendant would exercise such skill and care as could reasonably be expected of an experienced tour operator in relation to the selection and monitoring of all accommodation, services and facilities which formed part of the holiday;
(b) the Defendant, its suppliers, employees, agents and servants would exercise reasonable skill and care in relation to the provision of the accommodation, services, facilities and amenities that formed part of the holiday;
(c) the hotel would be of a reasonable standard, reasonably safe and would comply with all applicable local safety standards and regulations;
(d) the Defendant would check that all applicable local safety regulations, practices, standards and customs had been complied with;
(e) the hotel, including its services, operations and facilities would not be such that, irrespective of the applicable standards and/or regulations, no reasonable holidaymaker would agree to take a holiday there.

6. Further, and in any event, by regulation 15(1) and 15(2) of the Regulations, the Defendant is liable to the Claimant for any loss and damage caused by the improper performance of the contract by its suppliers, including the hotel.

7. The hotel's facilities included a restaurant providing buffet style self-service. On the evening of 1 August 2009, the Claimant was in the said restaurant for dinner. As the Claimant was walking from his table to the self-service display, he slipped and fell on liquid which had been left accumulated on the floor. The accident occurred in the vicinity of an area in the restaurant where drinks are served and where trolleys containing trays with items cleared from tables (including drinks) were deposited ('the accident location'). The Claimant was not aware of the presence of the clear liquid on the floor prior to his fall. As a result of the foregoing, the Claimant suffered personal injury, loss and damage, as more fully set out hereinafter.

8. The abovementioned accident was caused by the negligence of the Defendant, its suppliers, employees, agents or servants and/or by breach of the abovementioned express and/or implied terms of the holiday contract, which breach constituted improper performance of the holiday contract by the Defendant, its suppliers, employees, agents or servants pursuant to regulation 15(1) of the Regulations.

PARTICULARS OF IMPROPER PERFORMANCE

(a) Caused or permitted the accident location to become and/or remain wet and slippery and accordingly unsafe to be traversed by the Claimant;

(b) Failed to dry or mop up the liquid on the floor of the accident location, whether adequately or in time, or at all;

(c) Failed to warn the Claimant of the presence of the liquid on the floor of the accident location, whether by the display of a warning sign or otherwise;

(d) Failed to inspect the accident location, whether adequately, regularly, in time, or at all;

(e) Failed to have or the institute, monitor or enforce any or any adequate system for the inspection and/or cleaning and/or drying of the accident location;

(f) Failed to cordon-off or prevent access to the accident location, at a time when it was unsafe to use for the reasons given above;

(g) Caused the Claimant to encounter a trap;

(h) Failed in all the circumstances to exercise any or any reasonable skill and care for the Claimant's health and safety;

(i) Failed to exercise such skill and care as could reasonably be expected or an experienced tour operator in relation to the selection and monitoring of all accommodation, services, facilities and suppliers which formed part of the holiday;

(j) Provided hotel accommodation which was so unsafe that no reasonable holidaymaker would agree to go on holiday there;

(k) Failed to comply with its duty to check that all applicable local safety standards had been observed and complied with.

9. Further, the Claimant will establish that the material particulars of fault constituted acts or omissions which fell below the standard of care established or evidenced by the safety standards, practices and/or customs applicable at the material time in the material locality

10. As a result of the above matters, the Claimant, who was born on 2 May 1942, suffered pain, injury, loss and damage.

PARTICULARS OF PERSONAL INJURY

[ ]

PARTICULARS OF LOSS AND DAMAGE

A schedule of special damages is served herewith.

PARTICULARS OF LOSS OF ENJOYMENT

The holiday which was intended as a family celebration following the 25th wedding anniversary of the Claimant and her husband was ruined. The family derived none of the enjoyment which they had anticipated and took part in none of the pre-booked activities or entertainments.

11.   Further, the Claimant claims interest pursuant to section 69 of the County Courts Act 1984 on the amount found due to him. In particular the Claimant claims a rate of 2% of general damages from the date of service of proceedings until judgment or sooner payment and on special damages at the full special account rate from the date on which losses were incurred; alternatively at such rate and for such period as the Court thinks fit.

12.   The Claimant's claim for general damages for pain, suffering and loss of amenity exceeds £1,000. The total value of the claim is not presently expected to exceed £50,000.

AND the Claimant claims:

(1)   Damages.
(2)   Interest as aforesaid.

A.   LAWYER

10.2   PARTICULARS OF CLAIM – PACKAGE TRAVEL – GASTRIC ILLNESS

IN THE NOMANSLAND COUNTY COURT   Claim No

BETWEEN:

SAM O'NELLA

Claimant

–and–

OWN RISK HOLIDAYS LIMITED

Defendant

PARTICULARS OF CLAIM

---

1.   At all material times the Defendant carried on business organising and supplying holidays to customers.

2.   By a contract made by or for the benefit of the Claimant under booking reference 123456, 'the contract', the Defendant agreed to supply the Claimant and her fiancé with a package holiday incorporating flights and all-inclusive accommodation at the Ells Bells Beach resort in St Lucia, 'the hotel', between 16 and 30 May 2010 for a total price of £5,000.

3.   As the Defendant and the hotel knew, the holiday incorporated the Claimant's wedding, which was booked to take place at the hotel on 25 May 2010.

4.   The contract was for a package holiday, the Claimant was a consumer, the hotel its servants and agents were suppliers and the Defendant was the other party to the contract within the meaning of the Package Travel, Package Holidays and Package Tours Regulations 1992, 'the Regulations'.

5.   The following were express and/or implied terms or warranties of the contract by virtue of the Defendant's booking conditions, Regulation 6 of the Regulations, sections 4 and 13 of the Supply of Goods and Services Act 1982 and the Defendant's duty to ensure that:

(1)   The Defendant would exercise the reasonable care and skill to be expected of an experienced tour operator in the selection and monitoring of accommodation allocated to the Claimant, in this case the hotel.

(2)   All services and facilities provided under the contract would be provided to a reasonable standard.

(3)   Food and drink provided for the Claimant at the hotel would be of satisfactory quality and safe for human consumption.

(4)   The hotel would exercise reasonable skill and care in the storage, preparation and service of food and drink to guests including the Claimant. In particular food especially poultry products would be stored correctly, cooked thoroughly, kept hot (if intended to be eaten hot), kept chilled (if intended to be eaten cold), and would be free from harmful bacteria including salmonella.

(5)   There was an adequate system for the regular inspection and/or monitoring of standards of hygiene and cleanliness in the hotel.

6.   Further, by virtue of Regulation 15 of the Regulations the Defendant is liable to the Claimant for the proper performance of the obligations under the contract, irrespective of whether such obligations were to be supplied by the Defendant or by other suppliers of services including the hotel.

7.   For the avoidance of doubt, breach of any of the terms set out at paragraph 5 above would amount to improper performance of the contract.

8.   During the course of her holiday on around 20 May 2010 the Claimant contracted salmonella poisoning having eaten until that time exclusively at the hotel. Her illness was contracted as a result of eating contaminated food (probably chicken or egg products) supplied by the hotel. She suffered personal injury, loss and damage as set out further below.

9.   The said injury loss and damage sustained by the Claimant was caused by the Defendant's breach of the said express or implied terms or warranties of the contract and/or by the negligence of the Defendant and the hotel. There was no proper performance of the holiday contract, the food supplied for the Claimant's consumption was not of satisfactory quality or safe for her to eat and the hotel its servants and agents were negligent whilst in the course of their duties. In the premises the Defendant is liable for the Claimant's claims pursuant to the terms of the holiday contract, alternatively pursuant to Regulation 15 of the Regulations.

(1)   Food and drink at the hotel was not of a satisfactory quality or safe for the Claimant's consumption. The Claimant contracted salmonella having eaten only at the hotel prior to falling ill.

(2)   The hotel did not institute and maintain and the Defendant did not enforce adequate standards of hygiene and of food storage,

preparation or service. Had adequate standards been maintained it speaks for itself that the Claimant would not have contracted salmonella.

(3)   Food was frequently served buffet-style outside and was left exposed to the environment for prolonged periods.

(4)   The restaurant area in the hotel was often grubby, with tables that were not cleared between diners and sometimes inadequately washed crockery, cutlery, glasses and utensils.

(5)   Food appeared to be reheated and foodstuffs (particularly meat) appeared to be recycled for subsequent meals.

(6)   Hot food was poured directly on top of cooling dishes of the same kind and stirred in.

(7)   Food (including raw food) was not kept adequately covered and was frequently infested with flies.

(8)   Food was not thoroughly and adequately heated and kept at a suitable temperature before being served for consumption. Hot meals in the buffets were invariably inadequately heated.

(9)   Food intended to be served cold was served lukewarm.

(10) Cats and monkeys were on occasion seen in the dining areas of the hotels. The monkeys were frequently seen urinating on the bar and tables.

(11) Food at risk of containing or transmitting salmonella bacteria (including in particular poultry products) was undercooked or cross contaminated, with the result that the Claimant contracted salmonella after consuming it.

(12) The Claimant was exposed to a foreseeable and avoidable risk of illness.

10.   By reason of the matters aforesaid, the Claimant suffered personal injury, loss and damage.

PARTICULARS OF PERSONAL INJURY

[   ]

PARTICULARS OF LOSS AND DAMAGE

A schedule of loss and damage is annexed.

11.   The Claimant suffered distress and anxiety both for herself and for her fiancé/husband. Their wedding and honeymoon was ruined. They each lost the enjoyment of their holidays. The holiday was of little or no benefit to them. Accordingly the Claimant claims damages for loss of enjoyment and diminution of value.

12.   Further the Claimant claims interest pursuant to section 69 of the County Courts Act 1984 on such sums as may be found due to her. In particular she claims interest until judgment or sooner payment on general damages at a rate of 2% per annum from date of service of proceedings and on special damages at the full special account rate from

the date on which such losses were incurred; alternatively at such rate and for such period as the Court may think fit.

13.   The Claimant's claim in respect of general damages for pain, suffering and loss of amenity exceeds £1,000. The Claimant's claim overall is not expected to exceed £25,000.

AND the Claimant claims:

(1)   Damages not exceeding £25,000.
(2)   Interest as aforesaid.

F ATCAT

10.3   PARTICULARS OF CLAIM – CHOICE OF LAW
ROME II – SKIING COLLISION CLAIM

IN THE TOYTOWN COUNTY COURT   Claim No 3TO0003

BETWEEN:

P PIGG

Claimant

–and–

S SHEEP

Defendant

PARTICULARS OF CLAIM

---

1.   On around 14 February 2012 at about 2pm the Claimant was skiing down a blue run known as 'Avalanche' in the ski resort of Chamonix in France. The Defendant was skiing down the same run at high speed. He was uphill of the Claimant. He skied into collision with the Claimant from behind, causing her injury, loss and damage as set out below.

2.   The provisions of Regulation (EC) No 864/2007 of the European Parliament and Council of 11 July 2007 on the law applicable to non-contractual obligations, 'Rome II' govern the Claimant's claim herein. Pursuant to Article 4.2, the law applicable to the claim is English law because the Claimant and the Defendant both had their common habitual residence in England at the time of the accident.

3.   In the alternative the tort is manifestly more closely connected with England and so English law applies to the claim pursuant to Article 4.3 of Rome II. In particular, both the Claimant and the Defendant are British and were and are both domiciled and resident in England. The Defendant was temporarily on holiday in France at the time of the accident and, although she was temporarily living there and working on a seasonal contract due to expire in April 2012, the Claimant had no permanent or lasting connection with France either.

4.   The accident was caused by the negligence of the Defendant in that he:

PARTICULARS OF NEGLIGENCE
(a)   Skied into collision with the Claimant from behind.
(b)   Failed to accord priority to the Claimant who was downhill of him.
(c)   Failed to notice or heed the presence of the Claimant on the hill below him.

(d)   Failed to stop, slow, turn or otherwise take any reasonable steps to avoid the Claimant.

(e)   Failed to notice or heed the signs warning that two runs overlapped and warning skiers such as the Defendant to slow down because of the danger.

(f)   Failed adequately to control his skis.

(g)   Skied too fast for the prevailing conditions, including the presence of the Claimant ahead of him.

(h)   Failed generally to adhere to the Rules for the Conduct of Skiers and Snowboarders of the International Ski Federation. In particular he:

  (i)   Failed to show respect for the Claimant but rather endangered her.

  (ii)   Failed to stay in control and skied into her from behind.

  (iii)   Failed to adapt his speed to the prevailing conditions, in particular the fact that another run joined the run down which he was skiing.

  (iv)   Failed to choose a route that did not endanger the Claimant ahead of him.

(i)   Otherwise failed in all the circumstances to ski with the reasonable skill and care expected of him under English law; alternatively under French law.

5.   By reason of the matters aforesaid the Claimant suffered personal injury, loss and damage as set out below.

PARTICULARS OF PERSONAL INJURY
[   ]
PARTICULARS OF LOSS AND DAMAGE

A preliminary schedule of loss and damage is annexed.

6.   Further the Claimant seeks interest on such damages as she may be awarded pursuant to section 69 of the County Courts Act 1984; alternatively pursuant to French law. In particular the Claimant claims interest to judgment or sooner payment on general damages at 2 per cent per annum from the date of service of the claim, and on special damages at half the special account rate from the date of the accident; alternatively at such rate and for such period as the Court may think fit.

7.   The Claimant's claim for general damages for pain, suffering and loss of amenity exceeds £1,000. Her claim overall is expected to exceed £25,000.

AND the Claimant claims:

(1)   Damages exceeding £25,000.

(2) Interest pursuant to section 69 of the County Courts Act 1984 as aforesaid; alternatively pursuant to French law.

H HORSE

10.4   DEFENCE – GASTRIC ILLNESS – PACKAGE TRAVEL – GROUP CLAIM – REG 15 DEFENCES – LOCAL STANDARDS

IN THE HIGH COURT OF JUSTICE   Claim No

QUEEN'S BENCH DIVISION

BETWEEN:

A PILL & 45 OTHERS

Claimant

–and–

LOWCOST HOLIDAYS LIMITED

Defendant

DEFENCE

---

1.   Paragraph 1 of the Particulars of Claim is admitted.

2.   As to the relevant paragraphs of the Particulars of Claim, it is admitted that numerous Claimants were supplied with package holidays incorporating all inclusive board and accommodation at the Hellonearth Holiday Hotel in Turkey. The Claimants are each required to prove that they were parties to or benefited from contracts entered into with the Defendant.

3.   As to paragraph X of the Particulars of Claim, the Hotel was a sizeable 4 star resort accommodating around 3,000 guests at a time in around 1,000 rooms. It was owned and operated by an independent third party and not by the Defendant. There were five swimming pools, some three restaurants and snack bars on site together with two main kitchens and various bars. Some 40,000 guests stayed at the Hotel between 1 June and 31 October 2010.

4.   It is admitted that the Defendant advertised the Hotel in various promotional literature. The Claimants are each required to prove what promotional material they saw prior to booking their holidays. Save as aforesaid, the [relevant parts of] the Particulars of Claim are not admitted.

5.   All holidays booked with the Defendant were subject to the Defendant's booking conditions. Those booking conditions set out the entirety of the Defendant's obligations to the Claimants. It is admitted that the terms pleaded formed part of those booking conditions. The Defendant will refer to the booking conditions at trial for their full meaning and effect.

6.   Further, it is admitted that, subject to the statutory defences set out at Regulation 15(2) and particularised below, the Defendant is liable to the consumer pursuant to Regulation 15(1) of the Regulations for the proper performance of the obligations under the respective holiday contracts, irrespective of whether such obligations were to be performed by the Defendant or by other suppliers of services such as the Hotel.

7.   Those obligations were limited in that they did not extend to failures in the performance of the holiday contracts which were attributable to:

(a)   the Claimants;
(b)   third parties unconnected with the provision of services under the contracts and which were unforeseeable or unavoidable; and/or
(c)   unusual and unforeseeable circumstances beyond the control of the Defendant, the consequences of which could not have been avoided even if all due care had been exercised, or an event which the Defendant or the Hotel, even with all due care, could not foresee or forestall.

8.   For the avoidance of doubt, whilst no admissions are made as to the relevance or applicability of the laws and regulations set out in the material part of the Particulars of Claim, it is for the Claimants to prove what relevant health and safety standards applied in Turkey at the relevant time.

9.   Further and for the avoidance of doubt:

(a)   It is expressly denied that the Defendant owed the Claimants a strict duty to ensure that food and drink was 'safe to consume' or 'fit' for human consumption (whatever those terms might mean) or was otherwise free from bacteria that might cause illness.

   (i)   The Defendant's duty under the holiday contracts was to exercise reasonable skill and care. It did not warrant that tourists would not fall ill on holiday.
   (ii)   The imposition of strict liability in the context of a package holiday overseas is inconsistent with the binding authority in *Hone v Going Places Leisure Travel Ltd* [2001] EWCA Civ 947.

(b)   It is expressly denied that the Defendant was under a duty pursuant to warn holidaymakers of 'known significant previous or continuing episodes of illness at the hotel'.

   (i)   Such a term would be so vague and meaningless as to be embarrassing and entirely unenforceable.
   (ii)   In any event, the contraction of gastric illness during the course of a holiday is such a well-known risk of overseas travel that the Defendant was under no duty specifically to warn guests of

this; nor would any warning of illness (given that the Hotel was at no stage implicated in the same) prior to the Claimants' respective holidays reasonably have caused any of the Claimants to cancel or defer their holidays.

10. Save as aforesaid, the relevant paragraphs of the Particulars of Claim are denied. The Defendant's obligations were contained in the booking conditions and as set out above and there is no room to imply additional obligations.

11. Paragraph [X] of the Particulars of Claim is denied. The Defendant owed duties in contract and not in tort.

12. As to paragraphs [XX to YY] of the Particulars of Claim, at no stage was the Hotel implicated in any episode of gastric illness suffered by the Claimants or any other guests. It is admitted that some of the Claimants reported gastric illness and other complaints during their holidays. Many did not. Others reported alleged illness to the Defendant's representatives but declined to attend a doctor for a free medical consultation. None of those who gave a stool sample for testing whilst in Turkey were diagnosed with any bacterial pathogen or protozoan organism causative of illness. The Claimants were all free to travel outside the Hotel and many would have done so. They are each of them individually put to proof as to when, where and under what circumstances they fell ill, as well as the means by which their illness was transmitted to them. Further, they are each required to prove the steps taken to mitigate the consequences of any illness they may allege by seeking the appropriate medical attention at the Hotel or local hospital.

13. Gastric illness is a common feature of overseas travel. The possible causes of gastric illness are numerous. Whilst there may have been guests at the hotel suffering from gastric illness at various stages between May and October 2010, it is denied that the Hotel was in any way implicated in the contraction of illness of any of the guests.

14. It is denied that the Defendant by itself or its suppliers were in breach of contract as alleged or at all. It is denied that any duty was owed by the Defendant in tort or by way of statutory duty, and further denied that the Defendant, the Hotel or their respective servants or agents were negligent or in breach of statutory duty as pleaded or otherwise. There was no improper performance of the holiday contracts. There was no misrepresentation. There was no failure of consideration. Standards at the Hotel, including standards of maintenance, cleanliness, hygiene and food preparation, were of a good standard given the Hotel's rating as a 4 star establishment and its location in Turkey, and were in any event reasonable in all the circumstances. The Defendant, the Hotel, its management and staff exercised reasonable care and skill in the provision

of facilities and services. Thousands of guests stayed at the Hotel without complaint or illness between May and October 2010. Further:

(a) It is for the Claimants to prove the specific local standards which applied to the services and facilities provided by the Hotel and that there was any breach thereof causative of the alleged illnesses.

(b) It is inherently unlikely that the Claimants would have eaten undercooked or lukewarm food (particularly chicken or eggs), food infested with flies, food that had been sitting out for hours, food which they perceived to be recycled, used inadequately washed utensils and the like.

(c) To the best of the Defendant's knowledge, no guest who reported illness to the medical professionals at the Hotel and who gave a stool sample for analysis was diagnosed with salmonella. Nor, for the avoidance of doubt, were any of the Hotel staff.

(d) The Hotel implemented a good food hygiene system which adhered to HACCP principles. Its health and hygiene procedures were monitored by its own quality staff with responsibility for maintaining health, safety and hygiene. Which included:

(e) Independent food hygiene testing.

(f) The Hotel operated a reasonable system of cleaning and disinfection of all parts of the Hotel and used reputable sub-contractors.

(g) The Hotel implemented and observed prevention of the spread of infection procedures.

(h) Staff were properly trained in and implemented hygienic methods of food and drink preparation.

(i) Additional cleaning and sanitisation measures were introduced during the summer season by way of a reasonable response to complaints of illness and to prevent the spread of infection.

(j) Food temperatures for storage and buffet display were regularly checked and were consistently maintained at an appropriate level, particularly given the quick rotation of food.

(k) Food samples were regularly subjected to testing.

(l) The Hotel was the subject of a health and safety audit.

(m) The Defendant had a suitable and effective system of sickness monitoring in place at the Hotel.

(n) Specifically as to sub paragraph (o), gastric illness is a common feature of overseas travel, particularly to warmer climates such as Turkey. A small proportion of guests at the Hotel reported illness and the Hotel was at no stage implicated as the cause of any 'outbreak' of gastric illness. The Defendant was not reasonably required to pass any additional information about the Hotel to the Claimants. Nor would any further (accurate) information reasonably have caused any of the Claimants to cancel their holidays.

15. Further, it is expressly denied that the Claimants or any of them can rely upon their alleged illness as evidence of the negligence of the Defendant or the Hotel. There are numerous potential causes of gastric

illness whilst on holiday which are not attributable to negligence. Negligence cannot in any event be inferred on the part of the Hotel given its location in Turkey.

16.   Further or alternatively it is denied that any of the alleged breaches were causative of the Claimants' alleged illnesses. Paragraphs 12 to 15 above are repeated. Further:

(a)   Some Claimants report early onset of illness after their arrival at the Hotel, such that it is likely that they had contracted illness before arrival at the Hotel.

(b)   Claimants had freedom to eat and travel outside the Hotel (and many would have done so, including on excursions), suggesting obvious potential sources of infection unrelated to the resort.

(c)   The overwhelming majority of the Claimants did not test positive for any bacterial agent which might have caused the alleged symptoms.

(d)   The stronger likelihood is that genuine incidents of sickness and diarrhoea which those Claimants who did not return a stool sample testing positive for salmonella may prove they contracted whilst in the Hotel were airborne and viral in origin and contracted without fault on the part of the Hotel or the Defendant. This was the conclusion of the local hospital, which did not encounter a single stool sample testing positive for bacterial infection of all those who reported illness to the Hotel.

(e)   Reports of illness among family members and guests staying in close proximity to each other with communal swimming pools and eating areas suggests that infections were being passed by guests to other guests without fault on the part of the Hotel or the Defendant.

(f)   Guests on all-inclusive packages were inclined to over indulge on sun, food and drink (including alcohol) during their holidays, as well as changing their diets. This frequently caused illness.

(g)   Guests travelled to the Hotel from other parts of the world potentially bringing illness with them without fault on the part of the Hotel or the Defendant.

(h)   Deficiencies in the public health infrastructure and other environmental and community factors could cause illness without fault on the part of the Hotel or the Defendant.

(i)   Numerous guests reported illness but declined to avail themselves of free consultations with medical professionals at the Hotel or local hospital and/or declined to give stool samples for analysis. This is strongly suggestive that any reports of illness were not genuine or too minor to amount to compensatable damage.

(j)   It is a common feature of these claims that guests will encourage other guests to complain. Some guests reported that other guests were scaremongering or encouraging people to report illness.

17.   Further and in any event if, which is denied, the Claimants and any of them contracted gastrointestinal infections whilst at the resort, these were events which the Hotel or the Defendant could not foresee or forestall even with all due care (which in fact they each exercised) within the meaning of Regulation 15(2)(c)(ii) of the Regulations. Further the Defendant relies on the provisions of Regulation 15(2)(c)(i) in that any failures were due to unusual and unforeseeable circumstances beyond the Defendant's control. The Defendant repeats the matters set out above.

18.   In the premises it is denied that the Defendant is liable to the Claimants as alleged or at all.

19.   Further or in the alternative, if and to the extent that any Claimants suffered personal injury and illness, the same was caused or contributed to by their own negligence in that they:

PARTICULARS OF CONTRIBUTORY NEGLIGENCE

(a)   Consumed food or drink adversely affected in the various ways alleged in the Particulars of Claim.

(b)   Ate or drank too much or spent too much time in the sun, sea or swimming pools.

(c)   Failed to take any or adequate care for their own personal hygiene in particular as regards washing hands and using hygienic gel and anti bacterial wipes.

(d)   Failing to go to the bathroom, or failing to take children to the bathroom, with sufficient frequency but instead excreting faeces in the swimming pools.

(e)   Mixed with others who were ill.

(f)   Ate or drank outside the Hotel.

(g)   Failed to follow the reasonable travel tips given by the Defendant or otherwise to conduct themselves as reasonable travellers.

(h)   Otherwise failed in the circumstances to take reasonable care for their own safety.

20.   Save that the conclusions of Professor Biased are denied for the reasons set out above, the Defendant is unable to admit or deny and has no knowledge of the facts and matters contained in the relevant paragraphs of the Particulars of Claim. The Defendant will serve counter schedules in due course following disclosure.

21.   Further, numerous Claimants failed to take reasonable steps to mitigate their loss in that they did not seek medical attention whilst on holiday. The Defendant reserves the right to contend that any symptoms would have been less severe and less prolonged had they done so.

22.   As to the material pleading of the Particulars of Claim, a contingent right to interest is admitted pursuant to section 35A of the Senior Courts Act 1981 at such rates and for such period as the Court may think fit. The

appropriate rate for special damages is half the special account rate from time to time prevailing from the date of onset of illness.

23.   Save as is otherwise expressly referred to above, the Particulars of Claim are denied. The Claimants and each of them are required to prove all matters on which they will seek to rely.

10.5 PARTICULARS OF CLAIM – FRENCH LAW DIRECT ACTION AGAINST AN INSURER

IN THE RANDOM COUNTY COURT   Claim No 3RA0004

BETWEEN:

ANDREW ACCIDENT

Claimant

–and–

(1) ERIC BERNARD

(2) LUX ASSURANCE IARD SA

(a company incorporated under the laws of the Republic of France)

Defendants

PARTICULARS OF CLAIM

---

1.   At all material times:

(a)   The Claimant was and is an individual domiciled in England.

(b)   The First Defendant was an individual domiciled in France who provided ski instruction to members of the public in the Chamonix ski resort in France.

(c)   The Second Defendant was an insurance company domiciled in and incorporated under the laws of the Republic of France providing liability insurance pursuant to a policy of insurance to the First Defendant in respect of his liability for ski instruction provided to members of the public in the Chamonix region of France.

2.   On around 14 February 2011 the Claimant was on holiday in France skiing in the Chamonix ski resort.

3.   Prior to arriving in the resort the Claimant had purchased six lessons of ski instruction which were provided by the First Defendant.

4.   The provisions of Regulation (EC) No 864/2007 of the European Parliament and Council of 11 July 2007 on the law applicable to non-contractual obligations, 'Rome II' govern the Claimant's claim herein. Pursuant to Article 4.1 thereof and/or Article 4.1 of Schedule I of the Contracts (Applicable Law) Act 1990 the law applicable to the issues in the claim against all of the Defendants is French law.

5.   There was a contract under French law between the Claimant and the First Defendant in respect of the ski instruction provided to the

Claimant, an express alternatively implied term of which was that the First Defendant would exercise the reasonable care and skill expected of them by the laws, regulations, standards and practices of France in the provision of ski instruction to members of the public such as the Claimant.

6.   Further or alternatively the First Defendant owed the Claimant a duty of care under French law to the same effect. The Claimant will plead particulars of French law further following receipt of expert evidence in French law.

7.   The Claimant commenced ski lessons on 12 February. He was registered as a beginner and placed in the group which was led and instructed by the First Defendant.

8.   On 12 and 13 February 2011 the Claimant received a total of around 4 hours of ski instruction from the First Defendant. The first lesson was spent at the bottom of one of the main slopes close to the main ski lift. The second lesson was spent on the nursery slopes.

9.   On 14 February 2011 the Claimant's group were led down one nursery run and then taken to the blue (intermediate) run which he believes was known as the Eauneau piste. This started off with a shallow drop before entering a steep multi drop section where the run was some 5 metres wide, bordered on the left by a snow wall and on the right by a vertical drop.

10.   The First Defendant warned the Claimant and the rest of the group to keep clear of both sides of the run.

11.   Within moments of embarking on his descent the Claimant lost control of his skis and fell over, sustaining severe injuries to his left leg together with loss and damage as set out below.

12.   The Claimant fell because the run was beyond his level of skill, competence and experience. It was too narrow to enable him to make use of his limited ability to turn and snowplough safely.

13.   The accident was caused by the failure on the part of the First Defendant to exercise the reasonable skill and care expected of them under French law in the provision of ski instruction to the Claimant, in that he:

PARTICULARS OF NEGLIGENCE OR BREACH OF DUTY OF THE FIRST DEFENDANT

(a) Caused or permitted the Claimant to descend a run that was too difficult for his level of skill, competence and experience. In particular, it was too narrow to permit effective use of snow plough turns (which was all the Claimant could do, as the First Defendant knew or ought to have known), it was steep and it was icy.

(b) Selected a run that was inappropriate for a class of beginners on their third lesson, and in any event was inappropriate for the Claimant's group.

(c) Failed to provide the Claimant with the instruction needed to enable him to navigate the run safely.

(d) Failed to advise or instruct the Claimant how to descend whilst at the same time avoiding both sides of the run. This limited the Claimant's ability to do snow plough turns and led to him losing control.

(e) Failed to give the Claimant any or adequate supervision.

(f) Failed to give the Claimant any or adequate instructions as to how to descend safely other than by skiing. The Claimant would have tried an alternative method of descending in preference to skiing.

(g) Failed to require the Claimant to bring his ski poles to the lesson to assist his descent and in fact expressly informed the Claimant that he would not need them.

(h) Put the Claimant under undue pressure to attempt the run and further, to do so at a speed with which he was uncomfortable. The First Defendant stressed to the Claimant on at least two occasions that he had to 'hurry' or 'hurry up'.

(i) Exposed the Claimant to an obvious danger and a foreseeable risk of injury.

(j) Failed to exercise reasonable care for the safety of the Claimant whilst under his supervision and control.

(k) Otherwise failed in all the circumstances to comply with the relevant laws, regulations, standards and practices applicable in France.

14. In the premises the First Defendant is liable to the Claimant for the injury, loss and damage he sustained as a result of his accident aforesaid.

15. The Claimant has a direct right of action in respect of the accident against the Third Defendant under French law pursuant inter alia to the provisions of the French Insurance Code by virtue of the fact that it is liable to indemnify the First Defendant, against the injury, loss and damage caused to the Claimant as a result of the accident aforesaid. The Claimant repeats paragraphs 8 to 14 above. The Third Defendant is accordingly liable under French law to compensate the Claimant for the personal injury, loss and damage he sustained in the accident.

16. By reason of the matters aforesaid the Claimant suffered personal injury, loss and damage as set out below.

PARTICULARS OF PERSONAL INJURY
[   ]
PARTICULARS OF LOSS AND DAMAGE

A preliminary schedule of loss and damage is annexed.

17.   Further the Claimant seeks interest on such damages as he may be awarded pursuant to section 69 of the County Courts Act 1984 at such rate and for such period as the Court may think fit; alternatively pursuant to French law.

18.   The Claimant's claim for general damages for pain, suffering and loss of amenity exceeds £1,000. His claim overall exceeds £50,000.

AND the Claimant claims:

(1)   Damages in excess of £50,000 of which general damages for pain, suffering and loss of amenity exceed £1,000.
(2)   Interest pursuant to section 69 of the County Courts Act 1984; alternatively pursuant to French law as aforesaid.

A P Leader

APPENDIX 1

PACKAGE TRAVEL REGULATIONS 1992

Package Travel, Package Holidays and Package Tours Regulations 1992/3288

(version 1 of 1)

Made:	22 December 1992
Coming into force:	23 December 1992

Whereas the Secretary of State is a Minister designated[1] – for the purposes of section 2(2) of the European Communities Act 1972 in relation to measures relating to consumer protection as regards package travel, package holidays and package tours;

And whereas a draft of these Regulations has been approved by a resolution of each House of Parliament pursuant to section 2(2) of and paragraph 2(2) of Schedule 2 to that Act;

Now, therefore the Secretary of State in exercise of the powers conferred on him by section 2(2) of that Act hereby makes the following Regulations:

1 – Citation and commencement

These Regulations may be cited as the Package Travel, Package Holidays and Package Tours Regulations 1992 and shall come into force on the day after the day on which they are made.

2 – Interpretation

(1) In these Regulations –

"brochure" means any brochure in which packages are offered for sale;

"contract" means the agreement linking the consumer to the organiser or to the retailer, or to both, as the case may be;

"the Directive" means Council Directive 90/314/EEC on package travel, package holidays and package tours;

["member State" means a member State of the European Community or another State in the European Economic Area;][2]

---

[1]   SI 1991/755.
[2]   Definition inserted by Package Travel, Package Holidays and Package Tours (Amendment) Regulations 1995/1648, reg 2(a) (24June 1995).

"offer" includes an invitation to treat whether by means of advertising or otherwise, and cognate expressions shall be construed accordingly;

"organiser" means the person who, otherwise than occasionally, organises packages and sells or offers them for sale, whether directly or through a retailer;

"the other party to the contract" means the party, other than the consumer, to the contract, that is, the organiser or the retailer, or both, as the case may be;

"package" means the pre-arranged combination of at least two of the following components when sold or offered for sale at an inclusive price and when the service covers a period of more than twenty-four hours or includes overnight accommodation:

(a)   transport;
(b)   accommodation;
(c)   other tourist services not ancillary to transport or accommodation and accounting for a significant proportion of the package,

and

     (i)   the submission of separate accounts for different components shall not cause the arrangements to be other than a package;
    (ii)   the fact that a combination is arranged at the request of the consumer and in accordance with his specific instructions (whether modified or not) shall not of itself cause it to be treated as other than pre-arranged;

and

"retailer" means the person who sells or offers for sale the package put together by the organiser.

(2) In the definition of "contract" in paragraph (1) above, "consumer" means the person who takes or agrees to take the package ("the principal contractor") and elsewhere in these Regulations "consumer" means, as the context requires, the principal contractor, any person on whose behalf the principal contractor agrees to purchase the package ("the other beneficiaries") or any person to whom the principal contractor or any of the other beneficiaries transfers the package ("the transferee").

3 – Application of Regulations

(1) These Regulations apply to packages sold or offered for sale in the territory of the United Kingdom.

(2) Regulations 4 to 15 apply to packages so sold or offered for sale on or after 31st December 1992.

(3) Regulations 16 to 22 apply to contracts which, in whole or part, remain to be performed on 31st December 1992.

4 – Descriptive matter relating to packages must not be misleading

(1) No organiser or retailer shall supply to a consumer any descriptive matter concerning a package, the price of a package or any other conditions applying to the contract which contains any misleading information.

(2) If an organiser or retailer is in breach of paragraph (1) he shall be liable to compensate the consumer for any loss which the consumer suffers in consequence.

5 – Requirements as to brochures

(1) Subject to paragraph (4) below, no organiser shall make available a brochure to a possible consumer unless it indicates in a legible, comprehensible and accurate manner the price and adequate information about the matters specified in Schedule 1 to these Regulations in respect of the packages offered for sale in the brochure to the extent that those matters are relevant to the packages so offered.

(2) Subject to paragraph (4) below, no retailer shall make available to a possible consumer a brochure which he knows or has reasonable cause to believe does not comply with the requirements of paragraph (1).

(3) An organiser who contravenes paragraph (1) of this regulation and a retailer who contravenes paragraph (2) thereof shall be guilty of an offence and liable:

(a) on summary conviction, to a fine not exceeding level 5 on the standard scale; and
(b) on conviction on indictment, to a fine.

(4) Where a brochure was first made available to consumers generally before 31st December 1992 no liability shall arise under this regulation in respect of an identical brochure being made available to a consumer at any time.

6 – Circumstances in which particulars in brochure are to be binding

(1) Subject to paragraphs (2) and (3) of this regulation, the particulars in the brochure (whether or not they are required by regulation 5(1) above to be included in the brochure) shall constitute implied warranties (or, as regards Scotland, implied terms) for the purposes of any contract to which the particulars relate.

(2) Paragraph (1) of this regulation does not apply –

(a) in relation to information required to be included by virtue of paragraph 9 of Schedule 1 to these Regulations; or
(b) where the brochure contains an express statement that changes may be made in the particulars contained in it before a contract is concluded and changes in the particulars so contained are clearly communicated to the consumer before a contract is concluded.

(3) Paragraph (1) of this regulation does not apply when the consumer and the other party to the contract agree after the contract has been made that the particulars in the brochure, or some of those particulars, should not form part of the contract.

7 – Information to be provided before contract is concluded

(1) Before a contract is concluded, the other party to the contract shall provide the intending consumer with the information specified in paragraph (2) below in writing or in some other appropriate form.

(2) The information referred to in paragraph (1) is:

(a)   general information about passport and visa requirements which apply to [nationals of the member State or States concerned][3] who purchase the package in question, including information about the length of time it is likely to take to obtain the appropriate passports and visas;
(b)   information about health formalities required for the journey and the stay; and
(c)   the arrangements for security for the money paid over and (where applicable) for the repatriation of the consumer in the event of insolvency.

(3) If the intending consumer is not provided with the information required by paragraph (1) in accordance with that paragraph the other party to the contract shall be guilty of an offence and liable:–

(a)   on summary conviction, to a fine not exceeding level 5 on the standard scale; and
(b)   on conviction on indictment, to a fine.

8 – Information to be provided in good time

(1) The other party to the contract shall in good time before the start of the journey provide the consumer with the information specified in paragraph (2) below in writing or in some other appropriate form.

(2) The information referred to in paragraph (1) is the following:

(a)   the times and places of intermediate stops and transport connections and particulars of the place to be occupied by the traveller (for example, cabin or berth on ship, sleeper compartment on train);
(b)   the name, address and telephone number –

   (i)   of the representative of the other party to the contract in the locality where the consumer is to stay,
          or, if there is no such representative,
   (ii)   of an agency in that locality on whose assistance a consumer in difficulty would be able to call,

---

[3]   Words substituted by Package Travel, Package Holidays and Package Tours (Amendment) Regulations 1998/1208, reg 5 (30 June 1998).

or, if there is no such representative or agency, a telephone number or other information which will enable the consumer to contact the other party to the contract during the stay; and

(c)   in the case of a journey or stay abroad by a child under the age of 16 on the day when the journey or stay is due to start, information enabling direct contact to be made with the child or the person responsible at the place where he is to stay; and

(d)   except where the consumer is required as a term of the contract to take out an insurance policy in order to cover the cost of cancellation by the consumer or the cost of assistance, including repatriation, in the event of accident or illness, information about an insurance policy which the consumer may, if he wishes, take out in respect of the risk of those costs being incurred.

(3) If the consumer is not provided with the information required by paragraph (1) in accordance with that paragraph the other party to the contract shall be guilty of an offence and liable:

(a)   on summary conviction, to a fine not exceeding level 5 on the standard scale; and

(b)   on conviction on indictment, to a fine.

9 – Contents and form of contract

(1) The other party to the contract shall ensure that –

(a)   depending on the nature of the package being purchased, the contract contains at least the elements specified in Schedule 2 to these Regulations;

(b)   subject to paragraph (2) below, all the terms of the contract are set out in writing or such other form as is comprehensible and accessible to the consumer and are communicated to the consumer before the contract is made; and

(c)   a written copy of these terms is supplied to the consumer.

(2) Paragraph (1)(b) above does not apply when the interval between the time when the consumer approaches the other party to the contract with a view to entering into a contract and the time of departure under the proposed contract is so short that it is impracticable to comply with the sub-paragraph.

(3) It is an implied condition (or, as regards Scotland, an implied term) of the contract that the other party to the contract complies with the provisions of paragraph (1).

(4) In Scotland, any breach of the condition implied by paragraph (3) above shall be deemed to be a material breach justifying rescission of the contract.

10 – Transfer of bookings

(1) In every contract there is an implied term that where the consumer is prevented from proceeding with the package the consumer may transfer his booking to a person who satisfies all the conditions applicable to the package, provided that the

consumer gives reasonable notice to the other party to the contract of his intention to transfer before the date when departure is due to take place.

(2) Where a transfer is made in accordance with the implied term set out in paragraph (1) above, the transferor and the transferee shall be jointly and severally liable to the other party to the contract for payment of the price of the package (or, if part of the price has been paid, for payment of the balance) and for any additional costs arising from such transfer.

11 – Price revision

(1) Any term in a contract to the effect that the prices laid down in the contract may be revised shall be void and of no effect unless the contract provides for the possibility of upward or downward revision and satisfies the conditions laid down in paragraph (2) below.

(2) The conditions mentioned in paragraph (1) are that –

(a)   the contract states precisely how the revised price is to be calculated;
(b)   the contract provides that price revisions are to be made solely to allow for variations in:

(i)   transportation costs, including the cost of fuel,
(ii)   dues, taxes or fees chargeable for services such as landing taxes or embarkation or disembarkation fees at ports and airports, or
(iii)   the exchange rates applied to the particular package; and

(3) Notwithstanding any terms of a contract,

(i)   no price increase may be made in a specified period which may not be less than 30 days before the departure date stipulated; and
(ii)   as against an individual consumer liable under the contract, no price increase may be made in respect of variations which would produce an increase of less than 2%, or such greater percentage as the contract may specify, ("non-eligible variations") and that the non-eligible variations shall be left out of account in the calculation.

12 – Significant alterations to essential terms

In every contract there are implied terms to the effect that–

(a)   where the organiser is constrained before the departure to alter significantly an essential term of the contract, such as the price (so far as regulation 11 permits him to do so), he will notify the consumer as quickly as possible in order to enable him to take appropriate decisions and in particular to withdraw from the contract without penalty or to accept a rider to the contract specifying the alterations made and their impact on the price; and
(b)   the consumer will inform the organiser or the retailer of his decision as soon as possible.

13 – Withdrawal by consumer pursuant to regulation 12 and cancellation by organiser

(1) The terms set out in paragraphs (2) and (3) below are implied in every contract and apply where the consumer withdraws from the contract pursuant to the term in it implied by virtue of regulation 12(a), or where the organiser, for any reason other than the fault of the consumer, cancels the package before the agreed date of departure.

(2) The consumer is entitled–

(a) to take a substitute package of equivalent or superior quality if the other party to the contract is able to offer him such a substitute; or

(b) to take a substitute package of lower quality if the other party to the contract is able to offer him one and to recover from the organiser the difference in price between the price of the package purchased and that of the substitute package; or

(c) to have repaid to him as soon as possible all the monies paid by him under the contract.

(3) The consumer is entitled, if appropriate, to be compensated by the organiser for non-performance of the contract except where–

(a) the package is cancelled because the number of persons who agree to take it is less than the minimum number required and the consumer is informed of the cancellation, in writing, within the period indicated in the description of the package; or

(b) the package is cancelled by reason of unusual and unforeseeable circumstances beyond the control of the party by whom this exception is pleaded, the consequences of which could not have been avoided even if all due care had been exercised.

(4) Overbooking shall not be regarded as a circumstance falling within the provisions of sub-paragraph (b) of paragraph (3) above.

14 – Significant proportion of services not provided

(1) The terms set out in paragraphs (2) and (3) below are implied in every contract and apply where, after departure, a significant proportion of the services contracted for is not provided or the organiser becomes aware that he will be unable to procure a significant proportion of the services to be provided.

(2) The organiser will make suitable alternative arrangements, at no extra cost to the consumer, for the continuation of the package and will, where appropriate, compensate the consumer for the difference between the services to be supplied under the contract and those supplied.

(3) If it is impossible to make arrangements as described in paragraph (2), or these are not accepted by the consumer for good reasons, the organiser will, where appropriate, provide the consumer with equivalent transport back to the place of departure or to another place to which the consumer has agreed and will, where appropriate, compensate the consumer.

15 – Liability of other party to the contract for proper performance of obligations under contract

(1) The other party to the contract is liable to the consumer for the proper performance of the obligations under the contract, irrespective of whether such obligations are to be performed by that other party or by other suppliers of services but this shall not affect any remedy or right of action which that other party may have against those other suppliers of services.

(2) The other party to the contract is liable to the consumer for any damage caused to him by the failure to perform the contract or the improper performance of the contract unless the failure or the improper performance is due neither to any fault of that other party nor to that of another supplier of services, because –

(a)   the failures which occur in the performance of the contract are attributable to the consumer;

(b)   such failures are attributable to a third party unconnected with the provision of the services contracted for, and are unforeseeable or unavoidable; or

(c)   such failures are due to –

  (i)   unusual and unforeseeable circumstances beyond the control of the party by whom this exception is pleaded, the consequences of which could not have been avoided even if all due care had been exercised; or

  (ii) an event which the other party to the contract or the supplier of services, even with all due care, could not foresee or forestall.

(3) In the case of damage arising from the non-performance or improper performance of the services involved in the package, the contract may provide for compensation to be limited in accordance with the international conventions which govern such services.

(4) In the case of damage other than personal injury resulting from the non-performance or improper performance of the services involved in the package, the contract may include a term limiting the amount of compensation which will be paid to the consumer, provided that the limitation is not unreasonable.

(5) Without prejudice to paragraph (3) and paragraph (4) above, liability under paragraphs (1) and (2) above cannot be excluded by any contractual term.

(6) The terms set out in paragraphs (7) and (8) below are implied in every contract.

(7) In the circumstances described in paragraph (2)(b) and (c) of this regulation, the other party to the contract will give prompt assistance to a consumer in difficulty.

(8) If the consumer complains about a defect in the performance of the contract, the other party to the contract, or his local representative, if there is one, will make prompt efforts to find appropriate solutions.

(9) The contract must clearly and explicitly oblige the consumer to communicate at the earliest opportunity, in writing or any other appropriate form, to the supplier of the services concerned and to the other party to the contract any failure which he perceives at the place where the services concerned are supplied.

16 – Security in event of insolvency – requirements and offences

(1) The other party to the contract shall at all times be able to provide sufficient evidence of security for the refund of money paid over and for the repatriation of the consumer in the event of insolvency.

(2) Without prejudice to paragraph (1) above, and subject to paragraph (4) below, save to the extent that –

(a)   the package is covered by measures adopted or retained by the member State where he is established for the purpose of implementing Article 7 of the Directive; or
(b)   the package is one in respect of which he is required to hold a licence under the Civil Aviation (Air Travel Organisers' Licensing) Regulations 1972 or the package is one that is covered by the arrangements he has entered into for the purposes of those Regulations,

the other party to the contract shall at least ensure that there are in force arrangements as described in regulations 17, 18, 19 or 20 or, if that party is acting otherwise than in the course of business, as described in any of those regulations or in regulation 21.

(3) Any person who contravenes paragraph (1) or (2) of this regulation shall be guilty of an offence and liable:

(a)   on summary conviction to a fine not exceeding level 5 on the standard scale; and
(b)   on conviction on indictment, to a fine.

(4) A person shall not be guilty of an offence under paragraph (3) above by reason only of the fact that arrangements such as are mentioned in paragraph (2) above are not in force in respect of any period before 1 April 1993 unless money paid over is not refunded when it is due or the consumer is not repatriated in the event of insolvency.

(5) For the purposes of regulations 17 to 21 below a contract shall be treated as having been fully performed if the package or, as the case may be, the part of the package has been completed irrespective of whether the obligations under the contract have been properly performed for the purposes of regulation 15.

17 – Bonding

(1) The other party to the contract shall ensure that a bond is entered into by an authorised institution under which the institution binds itself to pay to an

approved body of which that other party is a member a sum calculated in accordance with paragraph (3) below in the event of the insolvency of that other party.

(2) Any bond entered into pursuant to paragraph (1) above shall not be expressed to be in force for a period exceeding eighteen months.

(3) The sum referred to in paragraph (1) above shall be such sum as may reasonably be expected to enable all monies paid over by consumers under or in contemplation of contracts for relevant packages which have not been fully performed to be repaid and shall not in any event be a sum which is less than the minimum sum calculated in accordance with paragraph (4) below.

(4) The minimum sum for the purposes of paragraph (3) above shall be a sum which represents:–

(a)   not less than 25% of all the payments which the other party to the contract estimates that he will receive under or in contemplation of contracts for relevant packages in the twelve month period from the date of entry into force of the bond referred to in paragraph (1) above; or

(b)   the maximum amount of all the payments which the other party to the contract expects to hold at any one time, in respect of contracts which have not been fully performed,

whichever sum is the smaller.

(5) Before a bond is entered into pursuant to paragraph (1) above, the other party to the contract shall inform the approved body of which he is a member of the minimum sum which he proposes for the purposes of paragraphs (3) and (4) above and it shall be the duty of the approved body to consider whether such sum is sufficient for the purpose mentioned in paragraph (3) and, if it does not consider that this is the case, it shall be the duty of the approved body so to inform the other party to the contract and to inform him of the sum which, in the opinion of the approved body, is sufficient for that purpose.

(6) Where an approved body has informed the other party to the contract of a sum pursuant to paragraph (5) above, the minimum sum for the purposes of paragraphs (3) and (4) above shall be that sum.

(7) In this regulation –

"approved body" means a body which is for the time being approved by the Secretary of State for the purposes of this regulation;

"authorised institution" means a person authorised under the law of a member State [, of the Channel Islands or of the Isle of Man][4] to carry on the business of entering into bonds of the kind required by this regulation.

---

[4]   Words inserted by Package Travel, Package Holidays and Package Tours (Amendment) Regulations 1995/1648, reg 2(b) (24 June 1995).

18 – Bonding where approved body has reserve fund or insurance

(1) The other party to the contract shall ensure that a bond is entered into by an authorised institution, under which the institution agrees to pay to an approved body of which that other party is a member a sum calculated in accordance with paragraph (3) below in the event of the insolvency of that other party.

(2) Any bond entered into pursuant to paragraph (1) above shall not be expressed to be in force for a period exceeding eighteen months.

(3) The sum referred to in paragraph (1) above shall be such sum as may be specified by the approved body as representing the lesser of –

(a)   the maximum amount of all the payments which the other party to the contract expects to hold at any one time in respect of contracts which have not been fully performed; or

(b)   the minimum sum calculated in accordance with paragraph (4) below.

(4) The minimum sum for the purposes of paragraph (3) above shall be a sum which represents not less than 10% of all the payments which the other party to the contract estimates that he will receive under or in contemplation of contracts for relevant packages in the twelve month period from the date of entry referred to in paragraph (1) above.

(5) In this regulation "approved body" means a body which is for the time being approved by the Secretary of State for the purposes of this regulation and no such approval shall be given unless the conditions mentioned in paragraph (6) below are satisfied in relation to it.

(6) A body may not be approved for the purposes of this regulation unless–

(a)   it has a reserve fund or insurance cover with an insurer authorised in respect of such business in a member State [, the Channel Islands or the Isle of Man][5] of an amount in each case which is designed to enable all monies paid over to a member of the body of consumers under or in contemplation of contracts for relevant packages which have not been fully performed to be repaid to those consumers in the event of the insolvency of the member; and

(b)   where it has a reserve fund, it agrees that the fund will be held by persons and in a manner approved by the Secretary of State.

(7) In this regulation, authorised institution has the meaning given to that expression by paragraph (7) of regulation 17.

19 – Insurance

(1) The other party to the contract shall have insurance under one or more appropriate policies with an insurer authorised in respect of such business in a member State under which the insurer agrees to indemnify consumers, who shall

---

[5]   Words inserted by Package Travel, Package Holidays and Package Tours (Amendment) Regulations 1995/1648, reg 2(c) (24 June 1995).

be insured persons under the policy, against the loss of money paid over by them under or in contemplation of contracts for packages in the event of the insolvency of the contractor.

(2) The other party to the contract shall ensure that it is a term of every contract with a consumer that the consumer acquires the benefit of a policy of a kind mentioned in paragraph (1) above in the event of the insolvency of the other party to the contract.

(3) In this regulation:

"appropriate policy" means one which does not contain a condition which provides (in whatever terms) that no liability shall arise under the policy, or that any liability so arising shall cease: (i) in the event of some specified thing being done or omitted to be done after the happening of the event giving rise to a claim under the policy;

(ii)   in the event of the policy holder not making payments under or in connection with other policies; or

(iii)   unless the policy holder keeps specified records or provides the insurer with or makes available to him information therefrom.

20 – Monies in trust

(1) The other party to the contract shall ensure that all monies paid over by a consumer under or in contemplation of a contract for a relevant package are held in the United Kingdom by a person as trustee for the consumer until the contract has been fully performed or any sum of money paid by the consumer in respect of the contract has been repaid to him or has been forfeited on cancellation by the consumer.

(2) The costs of administering the trust mentioned in paragraph (1) above shall be paid for by the other party to the contract.

(3) Any interest which is earned on the monies held by the trustee pursuant to paragraph (1) shall be held for the other party to the contract and shall be payable to him on demand.

(4) Where there is produced to the trustee a statement signed by the other party to the contract to the effect that –

(a)   a contract for a package the price of which is specified in that statement has been fully performed;

(b)   the other party to the contract has repaid to the consumer a sum of money specified in that statement which the consumer had paid in respect of a contract for a package; or

(c)   the consumer has on cancellation forfeited a sum of money specified in that statement which he had paid in respect of a contract for a relevant package,

the trustee shall (subject to paragraph (5) below) release to the other party to the contract the sum specified in the statement.

(5) Where the trustee considers it appropriate to do so, he may require the other party to the contract to provide further information or evidence of the matters mentioned in sub-paragraph (a), (b) or (c) of paragraph (4) above before he releases any sum to that other party pursuant to that paragraph.

(6) Subject to paragraph (7) below, in the event of the insolvency of the other party to the contract the monies held in trust by the trustee pursuant to paragraph (1) of this regulation shall be applied to meet the claims of consumers who are creditors of that other party in respect of contracts for packages in respect of which the arrangements were established and which have not been fully performed and, if there is a surplus after those claims have been met, it shall form part of the estate of that insolvent other party for the purposes of insolvency law.

(7) If the monies held in trust by the trustee pursuant to paragraph (1) of this regulation are insufficient to meet the claims of consumers as described in paragraph (6), payments to those consumers shall be made by the trustee on a pari passu basis.

21 – Monies in trust where other party to contract is acting otherwise than in the course of business

(1) The other party to the contract shall ensure that all monies paid over by a consumer under or in contemplation of a contract for a relevant package are held in the United Kingdom by a person as trustee for the consumer for the purpose of paying for the consumer's package.

(2) The costs of administering the trust mentioned in paragraph (1) shall be paid for out of the monies held in trust and the interest earned on those monies.

(3) Where there is produced to the trustee a statement signed by the other party to the contract to the effect that –

(a) the consumer has previously paid over a sum of money specified in that statement in respect of a contract for a package and that sum is required for the purpose of paying for a component (or part of a component) of the package;
(b) the consumer has previously paid over a sum of money specified in that statement in respect of a contract for a package and the other party to the contract has paid that sum in respect of a component (or part of a component) of the package;
(c) the consumer requires the repayment to him of a sum of money specified in that statement which was previously paid over by the consumer in respect of a contract for a package; or
(d) the consumer has on cancellation forfeited a sum of money specified in that statement which he had paid in respect of a contract for a package,

the trustee shall (subject to paragraph (4) below) release to the other party to the contract the sum specified in the statement.

(4) Where the trustee considers it appropriate to do so, he may require the other party to the contract to provide further information or evidence of the matters

mentioned in sub-paragraph (a), (b), (c) or (d) of paragraph (3) above before he releases to that other party any sum from the monies held in trust for the consumer.

(5) Subject to paragraph (6) below, in the event of the insolvency of the other party to the contract and of contracts for packages not being fully performed (whether before or after the insolvency) the monies held in trust by the trustee pursuant to paragraph (1) of this regulation shall be applied to meet the claims of consumers who are creditors of that other party in respect of amounts paid over by them and remaining in the trust fund after deductions have been made in respect of amounts released to that other party pursuant to paragraph (3) and, if there is a surplus after those claims have been met, it shall be divided amongst those consumers pro rata.

(6) If the monies held in trust by the trustee pursuant to paragraph (1) of this regulation are insufficient to meet the claims of consumers as described in paragraph (5) above, payments to those consumers shall be made by the trustee on a pari passu basis.

(7) Any sums remaining after all the packages in respect of which the arrangements were established have been fully performed shall be dealt with as provided in the arrangements or, in default of such provision, may be paid to the other party to the contract.

22 – Offences arising from breach of regulations 20 and 21

(1) If the other party to the contract makes a false statement under paragraph (4) of regulation 20 or paragraph (3) of regulation 21 he shall be guilty of an offence.

(2) If the other party to the contract applies monies released to him on the basis of a statement made by him under regulation 21(3)(a) or (c) for a purpose other than that mentioned in the statement he shall be guilty of an offence.

(3) If the other party to the contract is guilty of an offence under paragraph (1) or (2) of this regulation shall be liable –

(a)   on summary conviction to a fine not exceeding level 5 on the standard scale; and
(b)   on conviction on indictment, to a fine.

23 – Enforcement

Schedule 3 to these Regulations (which makes provision about the enforcement of regulations 5, 7, 8, 16 and 22 of these Regulations) shall have effect.

24 – Due diligence defence

(1) Subject to the following provisions of this regulation, in proceedings against any person for an offence under regulation 5, 7, 8, 16 or 22 of these Regulations, it shall be a defence for that person to show that he took all reasonable steps and exercised all due diligence to avoid committing the offence.

(2) Where in any proceedings against any person for such an offence the defence provided by paragraph (1) above involves an allegation that the commission of the offence was due –

(a)   to the act or default of another; or
(b)   to reliance on information given by another,

that person shall not, without the leave of the court, be entitled to rely on the defence unless, not less than seven clear days before the hearing of the proceedings, or, in Scotland, the trial diet, he has served a notice under paragraph (3) below on the person bringing the proceedings.

(3) A notice under this paragraph shall give such information identifying or assisting in the identification of the person who committed the act or default or gave the information as is in the possession of the person serving the notice at the time he serves it.

(4) It is hereby declared that a person shall not be entitled to rely on the defence provided by paragraph (1) above by reason of his reliance on information supplied by another, unless he shows that it was reasonable in all the circumstances for him to have relied on the information, having regard in particular –

(a)   to the steps which he took, and those which might reasonably have been taken, for the purpose of verifying the information; and
(b)   to whether he had any reason to disbelieve the information.

25 – Liability of persons other than principal offender

(1) Where the commission by any person of an offence under regulation 5, 7, 8, 16 or 22 of these Regulations is due to an act or default committed by some other person in the course of any business of his, the other person shall be guilty of the offence and may be proceeded against and punished by virtue of this paragraph whether or not proceedings are taken against the first-mentioned person.

(2) Where a body corporate is guilty of an offence under any of the provisions mentioned in paragraph (1) above (including where it is so guilty by virtue of the said paragraph (1)) in respect of any act or default which is shown to have been committed with the consent or connivance of, or to be attributable to any neglect on the part of, any director, manager, secretary or other similar officer of the body corporate or any person who was purporting to act in any such capacity he, as well as the body corporate, shall be guilty of that offence and shall be liable to be proceeded against and punished accordingly.

(3) Where the affairs of a body corporate are managed by its members, paragraph (2) above shall apply in relation to the acts and defaults of a member in connection with his functions of management as if he were a director of the body corporate.

(4) Where an offence under any of the provisions mentioned in paragraph (1) above committed in Scotland by a Scottish partnership is proved to have been committed with the consent or connivance of, or to be attributable to neglect on

the part of, a partner, he (as well as the partnership) is guilty of the offence and liable to be proceeded against and punished accordingly.

(5) On proceedings for an offence under regulation 5 by virtue of paragraph (1) above committed by the making available of a brochure it shall be a defence for the person charged to prove that he is a person whose business it is to publish or arrange for the publication of brochures and that he received the brochure for publication in the ordinary course of business and did not know and had no reason to suspect that its publication would amount to an offence under these Regulations.

26 – Prosecution time limit

(1) No proceedings for an offence under regulation 5, 7, 8, 16 or 22 of these Regulations or under paragraphs 5(3), 6 or 7 of Schedule 3 thereto shall be commenced after –

(a)   the end of the period of three years beginning within the date of the commission of the offence; or
(b)   the end of the period of one year beginning with the date of the discovery of the offence by the prosecutor,

whichever is the earlier.

(2) For the purposes of this regulation a certificate signed by or on behalf of the prosecutor and stating the date on which the offence was discovered by him shall be conclusive evidence of that fact; and a certificate stating that matter and purporting to be so signed shall be treated as so signed unless the contrary is proved.

(3) In relation to proceedings in Scotland, subsection (3) of section 331 of the Criminal Procedure (Scotland) Act 1975 (date of commencement of proceedings) shall apply for the purposes of this regulation as it applies for the purposes of that section.

27 – Saving for civil consequences

No contract shall be void or unenforceable, and no right of action in civil proceedings in respect of any loss shall arise, by reason only of the commission of an offence under regulations 5, 7, 8, 16 or 22 of these Regulations.

28 – Terms implied in contract

Where it is provided in these Regulations that a term (whether so described or whether described as a condition or warranty) is implied in the contract it is so implied irrespective of the law which governs the contract.

Denton of Wakefield
Parliamentary Under-Secretary of State,
Department of Trade and Industry

22 December 1992

Schedule 1

Information to be included (in addition to the price) in brochures where relevant to packages offered

This version in force from: **December 23, 1992** to **present**

1.

The destination and the means, characteristics and categories of transport used.

2.

The type of accommodation, its location, category or degree of comfort and its main features and, where the accommodation is to be provided in a member State, its approval or tourist classification under the rules of that member State.

3.

The meals which are included in the package.

4.

The itinerary.

5.

General information about passport and visa requirements which apply for [nationals of the member State or States in which the brochure is made available][6] and health formalities required for the journey and the stay.

6.

Either the monetary amount or the percentage of the price which is to be paid on account and the timetable for payment of the balance.

7.

Whether a minimum number of persons is required for the package to take place and, if so, the deadline for informing the consumer in the event of cancellation.

---

[6]   Words substituted by Package Travel, Package Holidays and Package Tours (Amendment) Regulations 1998/1208, reg 4 (30 June 1998).

8.

The arrangements (if any) which apply if consumers are delayed at the outward or homeward points of departure.

9.

The arrangements for security for money paid over and for the repatriation of the consumer in the event of insolvency.

Schedule 2

Elements to be included in the contract if relevant to the particular package

This version in force from: **December 23, 1992** to **present**

1.

The travel destination(s) and, where periods of stay are involved, the relevant periods, with dates.

2.

The means, characteristics and categories of transport to be used and the dates, times and points of departure and return.

3.

Where the package includes accommodation, its location, its tourist category or degree of comfort, its main features and, where the accommodation is to be provided in a member State, its compliance with the rules of that member State.

4.

The meals which are included in the package.

5.

Whether a minimum number of persons is required for the package to take place and, if so, the deadline for informing the consumer in the event of cancellation.

6.

The itinerary.

7.

Visits, excursions or other services which are included in the total price agreed for the package.

8.

The name and address of the organiser, the retailer and, where appropriate, the insurer.

9.

The price of the package, if the price may be revised in accordance with the term which may be included in the contract under regulation 11, an indication of the possibility of such price revisions, and an indication of any dues, taxes or fees chargeable for certain services (landing, embarkation or disembarkation fees at ports and airports and tourist taxes) where such costs are not included in the package.

10.

The payment schedule and method of payment.

11.

Special requirements which the consumer has communicated to the organiser or retailer when making the booking and which both have accepted.

12.

The periods within which the consumer must make any complaint about the failure to perform or the inadequate performance of the contract.

Schedule 3

ENFORCEMENT

This version in force from: **December 23, 1992** to **present**

1 – Enforcement authority

(1) Every local weights and measures authority in Great Britain shall be an enforcement authority for the purposes of regulations 5, 7, 8, 16 and 22 of these Regulations ("the relevant regulations"), and it shall be the duty of each such authority to enforce those provisions within their area.

(2) The Department of Economic Development in Northern Ireland shall be an enforcement authority for the purposes of the relevant regulations, and it shall be the duty of the Department to enforce those provisions within Northern Ireland.

Repealed on: June 20, 2003

[...]⁷

3 – Powers of officers of enforcement authority

(1) If a duly authorised officer of an enforcement authority has reasonable grounds for suspecting that an offence has been committed under any of the relevant regulations, he may –

(a)   require a person whom he believes on reasonable grounds to be engaged in the organisation or retailing of packages to produce any book or document relating to the activity and take copies of it or any entry in it, or

(b)   require such a person to produce in a visible and legible documentary form any information so relating which is contained in a computer, and take copies of it,

for the purpose of ascertaining whether such an offence has been committed.

(2) Such an officer may inspect any goods for the purpose of ascertaining whether such an offence has been committed.

(3) If such an officer has reasonable grounds for believing that any documents or goods may be required as evidence in proceedings for such an offence, he may seize and detain them.

(4) An officer seizing any documents or goods in the exercise of his power under sub-paragraph (3) above shall inform the person from whom they are seized.

(5) The powers of an officer under this paragraph may be exercised by him only at a reasonable hour and on production (if required) of his credentials.

(6) Nothing in this paragraph –

(a)   requires a person to produce a document if he would be entitled to refuse to produce it in proceedings in a court on the ground that it is the subject of legal professional privilege or, in Scotland, that it contains a confidential communication made by or to an advocate or a solicitor in that capacity; or

(b)   authorises the taking possession of a document which is in the possession of a person who would be so entitled.

4 –

(1) A duly authorised officer of an enforcement authority may, at a reasonable hour and on production (if required) of his credentials, enter any premises for the purpose of ascertaining whether an offence under any of the relevant regulations has been committed.

(2) If a justice of the peace, or in Scotland a justice of the peace or a sheriff, is satisfied –

---

⁷   Revoked by Enterprise Act 2002 (Part 8 Notice to OFT of Intended Prosecution Specified Enactments, Revocation and Transitional Provision) Order 2003/1376, art 3 (20 June 2003).

(a)   that any relevant books, documents or goods are on, or that any relevant information contained in a computer is available from, any premises, and that production or inspection is likely to disclose the commission of an offence under the relevant regulations; or

(b)   that any such an offence has been, is being or is about to be committed on any premises.

and that any of the conditions specified in sub-paragraph (3) below is met, he may be warrant under his hand authorise an officer of an enforcement authority to enter the premises, if need be by force.

(3) The conditions referred to in sub-paragraph (2) above are –

(a)   that admission to the premises has been or is likely to be refused and that notice of intention to apply for a warrant under that sub-paragraph has been given to the occupier;

(b)   that an application for admission, or the giving of such a notice, would defeat the object of the entry;

(c)   that the premises are unoccupied; and

(d)   that the occupier is temporarily absent and it might defeat the object of the entry to await his return.

(4) In sub-paragraph (2) above "relevant", in relation to books, documents, goods or information, means books, documents, goods or information which, under paragraph 3 above, a duly authorised officer may require to be produced or may inspect.

(5) A warrant under sub-paragraph (2) above may be issued only if –

(a)   in England and Wales, the justice of the peace is satisfied as required by that sub-paragraph by written information on oath;

(b)   in Scotland, the justice of the peace or sheriff is so satisfied by evidence on oath; or

(c)   in Northern Ireland, the justice of the peace is so satisfied by complaint on oath.

(6) A warrant under sub-paragraph (2) above shall continue in force for a period of one month.

(7) An officer entering any premises by virtue of this paragraph may take with him such other persons as may appear to him necessary.

(8) On leaving premises which he has entered by virtue of a warrant under sub-paragraph (2) above, an officer shall, if the premises are unoccupied or the occupier is temporarily absent, leave the premises as effectively secured against trespassers as he found them.

(9) In this paragraph "premises" includes any place (including any vehicle, ship or aircraft) except premises used only as a dwelling.

5 – Obstruction of officers

(1) A person who–

(a)   intentionally obstructs an officer of an enforcement authority acting in pursuance of this Schedule;
(b)   without reasonable excuse fails to comply with a requirement made of him by such an officer under paragraph 3(1) above; or
(c)   without reasonable excuse fails to give an officer of an enforcement authority acting in pursuance of this Schedule any other assistance or information which the officer may reasonably require of him for the purpose of the performance of the officer's functions under this Schedule,

shall be guilty of an offence.

(2) A person guilty of an offence under sub-paragraph (1) above shall be liable on summary conviction to a fine not exceeding level 5 on the standard scale.

(3) If a person, in giving any such information as is mentioned in sub-paragraph (1)(c) above, –

(a)   makes a statement which he knows is false in a material particular; or
(b)   recklessly makes a statement which is false in a material particular,

he shall be guilty of an offence.

(4) A person guilty of an offence under sub-paragraph (3) above shall be liable –

(a)   on summary conviction, to a fine not exceeding level 5 on the standard scale; and
(b)   on conviction on indictment, to a fine.

6 – Impersonation of officers

(1) If a person who is not a duly authorised officer of an enforcement authority purports to act as such under this Schedule he shall be guilty of an offence.

(2) A person guilty of an offence under sub-paragraph (1) above shall be liable –

(a)   on summary conviction, to a fine not exceeding level 5 on the standard scale; and
(b)   on conviction on indictment, to a fine.

Repealed on: June 20, 2003

[...][8]

8 – Privilege against self-incrimination

---

[8]   Revoked by Enterprise Act 2002 (Part 9 Restrictions on Disclosure of Information) (Amendment and Specification) Order 2003/1400, Sch 5, para 1 (20 June 2003).

Nothing in this Schedule requires a person to answer any question or give any information if to do so might incriminate him.

Explanatory Note

These Regulations implement Council Directive 90/314/EEC on package travel, package holidays, and package tours (OJ No. L158, 13 June 1990, p 59).

The Regulations control the sale and performance of packages sold or offered for sale in the UK. Packages are defined as the pre-arranged combination of at least two of the following when sold or offered for sale at an inclusive price and when the service covers a period of 24 hours or more or includes overnight accommodation:

- transport;
- accommodation;
- other tourist services not ancillary to transport or accommodation and accounting for a significant proportion of the package.

The Regulations set out what information must be given to the consumer before the contract is concluded (including information to be in brochures, where one is published) and information which must be given to the consumer before the package starts. They lay down terms which must be included in the contract and prescribe the circumstances in which price revisions may be made. They provide that the other party to the contract (ie the organiser and/or retailer, as the case may be) should be strictly liable to the consumer for the proper performance of the obligations under the contract, irrespective of whether such obligations are to be provided by that other party or by other suppliers of services. They also provide that the other party to the contract shall provide sufficient evidence of security for the refund of money paid over and for the repatriation of the consumer in the event of insolvency.

The Regulations will be enforced by local weights and measures authorities in Great Britain and by the Department of Economic Development in Northern Ireland.

APPENDIX 2

EC JUDGMENTS REGULATION 44/2001 ('BRUSSELS I')

COUNCIL REGULATION (EC) No 44/2001

of 22 December 2000

on jurisdiction and the recognition and enforcement of judgments in civil and commercial matters

THE COUNCIL OF THE EUROPEAN UNION,

Having regard to the Treaty establishing the European Community, and in particular Article 61(c) and Article 67(1) thereof,

Having regard to the proposal from the Commission,[1]

Having regard to the opinion of the European Parliament,[2]

Having regard to the opinion of the Economic and Social Committee,[3]

Whereas:

(1) The Community has set itself the objective of maintaining and developing an area of freedom, security and justice, in which the free movement of persons is ensured. In order to establish progressively such an area, the Community should adopt, amongst other things, the measures relating to judicial cooperation in civil matters which are necessary for the sound operation of the internal market.

(2) Certain differences between national rules governing jurisdiction and recognition of judgments hamper the sound operation of the internal market. Provisions to unify the rules of conflict of jurisdiction in civil and commercial matters and to simplify the formalities with a view to rapid and simple recognition and enforcement of judgments from Member States bound by this Regulation are essential.

(3) This area is within the field of judicial cooperation in civil matters within the meaning of Article 65 of the Treaty.

(4) In accordance with the principles of subsidiarity and proportionality as set out in Article 5 of the Treaty, the objectives of this Regulation cannot be sufficiently achieved by the Member States and can therefore be better achieved by the Community. This Regulation confines itself to the minimum required in order to achieve those objectives and does not go beyond what is necessary for that purpose.

---

[1]   OJ C 376, 28.12.1999, p 1.
[2]   Opinion delivered on 21 September 2000 (not yet published in the Official Journal).
[3]   OJ C 117, 26.4.2000, p 6.

(5) On 27 September 1968 the Member States, acting under Article 293, fourth indent, of the Treaty, concluded the Brussels Convention on Jurisdiction and the Enforcement of Judgments in Civil and Commercial Matters, as amended by Conventions on the Accession of the New Member States to that Convention (hereinafter referred to as the 'Brussels Convention').[4] On 16 September 1988 Member States and EFTA States concluded the Lugano Convention on Jurisdiction and the Enforcement of Judgments in Civil and Commercial Matters, which is a parallel Convention to the 1968 Brussels Convention. Work has been undertaken for the revision of those Conventions, and the Council has approved the content of the revised texts. Continuity in the results achieved in that revision should be ensured.

(6) In order to attain the objective of free movement of judgments in civil and commercial matters, it is necessary and appropriate that the rules governing jurisdiction and the recognition and enforcement of judgments be governed by a Community legal instrument which is binding and directly applicable.

(7) The scope of this Regulation must cover all the main civil and commercial matters apart from certain well-defined matters.

(8) There must be a link between proceedings to which this Regulation applies and the territory of the Member States bound by this Regulation. Accordingly common rules on jurisdiction should, in principle, apply when the defendant is domiciled in one of those Member States.

(9) A defendant not domiciled in a Member State is in general subject to national rules of jurisdiction applicable in the territory of the Member State of the court seised, and a defendant domiciled in a Member State not bound by this Regulation must remain subject to the Brussels Convention.

(10) For the purposes of the free movement of judgments, judgments given in a Member State bound by this Regulation should be recognised and enforced in another Member State bound by this Regulation, even if the judgment debtor is domiciled in a third State.

(11) The rules of jurisdiction must be highly predictable and founded on the principle that jurisdiction is generally based on the defendant's domicile and jurisdiction must always be available on this ground save in a few well-defined situations in which the subject-matter of the litigation or the autonomy of the parties warrants a different linking factor. The domicile of a legal person must be defined autonomously so as to make the common rules more transparent and avoid conflicts of jurisdiction.

(12) In addition to the defendant's domicile, there should be alternative grounds of jurisdiction based on a close link between the court and the action or in order to facilitate the sound administration of justice.

---

[4]   OJ L 299, 31.12.1972, p 32. OJ L 304, 30.10.1978, p 1. OJ L 388, 31.12.1982, p 1. OJ L 285, 3.10.1989, p 1. OJ C 15, 15.1.1997, p 1. For a consolidated text, see OJ C 27, 26.1.1998, p 1.

(13) In relation to insurance, consumer contracts and employment, the weaker party should be protected by rules of jurisdiction more favourable to his interests than the general rules provide for.

(14) The autonomy of the parties to a contract, other than an insurance, consumer or employment contract, where only limited autonomy to determine the courts having jurisdiction is allowed. must be respected subject to the exclusive grounds of jurisdiction laid down in this Regulation.

(15) In the interests of the harmonious administration of justice it is necessary to minimise the possibility of concurrent proceedings and to ensure that irreconcilable judgments will not be given in two Member States. There must be a clear and effective mechanism for resolving cases of *lis pendens* and related actions and for obviating problems flowing from national differences as to the determination of the time when a case is regarded as pending. For the purposes of this Regulation that time should be defined autonomously.

(16) Mutual trust in the administration of justice in the Community justifies judgments given in a Member State being recognised automatically without the need for any procedure except in cases of dispute.

(17) By virtue of the same principle of mutual trust, the procedure for making enforceable in one Member State a judgment given in another must be efficient and rapid. To that end, the declaration that a judgment is enforceable should be issued virtually automatically after purely formal checks of the documents supplied, without there being any possibility for the court to raise of its own motion any of the grounds for non-enforcement provided for by this Regulation.

(18) However, respect for the rights of the defence means that the defendant should be able to appeal in an adversarial procedure, against the declaration of enforceability, if he considers one of the grounds for non-enforcement to be present. Redress procedures should also be available to the claimant where his application for a declaration of enforceability has been rejected.

(19) Continuity between the Brussels Convention and this Regulation should be ensured, and transitional provisions should be laid down to that end. The same need for continuity applies as regards the interpretation of the Brussels Convention by the Court of Justice of the European Communities and the 1971 Protocol[5] should remain applicable also to cases already pending when this Regulation enters into force.

(20) The United Kingdom and Ireland, in accordance with Article 3 of the Protocol on the position of the United Kingdom and Ireland annexed to the Treaty on European Union and to the Treaty establishing the European Community, have given notice of their wish to take part in the adoption and application of this Regulation.

(21) Denmark, in accordance with Articles 1 and 2 of the Protocol on the position of Denmark annexed to the Treaty on European Union and to the Treaty

---

[5]   OJ L 204, 2.8.1975, p. 28. OJ L 304, 30.10.1978, p. 1. OJ L 388, 31.12.1982, p. 1. OJ L 285, 3.10.1989, p. 1. OJ C 15, 15.1.1997, p. 1. For a consolidated text see OJ C 27, 26.1.1998, p. 28.

establishing the European Community, is not participating in the adoption of this Regulation, and is therefore not bound by it nor subject to its application.

(22) Since the Brussels Convention remains in force in relations between Denmark and the Member States that are bound by this Regulation, both the Convention and the 1971 Protocol continue to apply between Denmark and the Member States bound by this Regulation.

(23) The Brussels Convention also continues to apply to the territories of the Member States which fall within the territorial scope of that Convention and which are excluded from this Regulation pursuant to Article 299 of the Treaty.

(24) Likewise for the sake of consistency, this Regulation should not affect rules governing jurisdiction and the recognition of judgments contained in specific Community instruments.

(25) Respect for international commitments entered into by the Member States means that this Regulation should not affect conventions relating to specific matters to which the Member States are parties.

(26) The necessary flexibility should be provided for in the basic rules of this Regulation in order to take account of the specific procedural rules of certain Member States. Certain provisions of the Protocol annexed to the Brussels Convention should accordingly be incorporated in this Regulation.

(27) In order to allow a harmonious transition in certain areas which were the subject of special provisions in the Protocol annexed to the Brussels Convention, this Regulation lays down, for a transitional period, provisions taking into consideration the specific situation in certain Member States.

(28) No later than five years after entry into force of this Regulation the Commission will present a report on its application and, if need be, submit proposals for adaptations.

(29) The Commission will have to adjust Annexes I to IV on the rules of national jurisdiction, the courts or competent authorities and redress procedures available on the basis of the amendments forwarded by the Member State concerned; amendments made to Annexes V and VI should be adopted in accordance with Council Decision 1999/468/EC of 28 June 1999 laying down the procedures for the exercise of implementing powers conferred on the Commission,[6]

HAS ADOPTED THIS REGULATION:

CHAPTER I

SCOPE

Article 1

---

[6]   OJ L 184, 17.7.1999, p 23.

1. This Regulation shall apply in civil and commercial matters whatever the nature of the court or tribunal. It shall not extend, in particular, to revenue, customs or administrative matters.

2. The Regulation shall not apply to:

(a) the status or legal capacity of natural persons, rights in property arising out of a matrimonial relationship, wills and succession;
(b) bankruptcy, proceedings relating to the winding-up of insolvent companies or other legal persons, judicial arrangements, compositions and analogous proceedings;
(c) social security;
(d) arbitration.

3. In this Regulation, the term 'Member State' shall mean Member States with the exception of Denmark.

CHAPTER II

JURISDICTION

Section 1

General provisions

Article 2

1. Subject to this Regulation, persons domiciled in a Member State shall, whatever their nationality, be sued in the courts of that Member State.

2. Persons who are not nationals of the Member State in which they are domiciled shall be governed by the rules of jurisdiction applicable to nationals of that State.

Article 3

1. Persons domiciled in a Member State may be sued in the courts of another Member State only by virtue of the rules set out in Sections 2 to 7 of this Chapter.

2. In particular the rules of national jurisdiction set out in Annex I shall not be applicable as against them.

Article 4

1. If the defendant is not domiciled in a Member State, the jurisdiction of the courts of each Member State shall, subject to Articles 22 and 23, be determined by the law of that Member State.

2. As against such a defendant, any person domiciled in a Member State may, whatever his nationality, avail himself in that State of the rules of jurisdiction there in force, and in particular those specified in Annex I, in the same way as the nationals of that State.

Section 2

Special jurisdiction

Article 5

A person domiciled in a Member State may, in another Member State, be sued:

1.   (a) in matters relating to a contract, in the courts for the place of performance of the obligation in question;

(b)   for the purpose of this provision and unless otherwise agreed, the place of performance of the obligation in question shall be:

–   in the case of the sale of goods, the place in a Member State where, under the contract, the goods were delivered or should have been delivered,

–   in the case of the provision of services, the place in a Member State where, under the contract, the services were provided or should have been provided,

(c)   if subparagraph (b) does not apply then subparagraph (a) applies;

2.   in matters relating to maintenance, in the courts for the place where the maintenance creditor is domiciled or habitually resident or, if the matter is ancillary to proceedings concerning the status of a person, in the court which, according to its own law, has jurisdiction to entertain those proceedings, unless that jurisdiction is based solely on the nationality of one of the parties;

3.   in matters relating to tort, delict or quasi-delict, in the courts for the place where the harmful event occurred or may occur;

4.   as regards a civil claim for damages or restitution which is based on an act giving rise to criminal proceedings, in the court seised of those proceedings, to the extent that that court has jurisdiction under its own law to entertain civil proceedings;

5.   as regards a dispute arising out of the operations of a branch, agency or other establishment, in the courts for the place in which the branch, agency or other establishment is situated;

6.   as settlor, trustee or beneficiary of a trust created by the operation of a statute, or by a written instrument, or created orally and evidenced in writing, in the courts of the Member State in which the trust is domiciled;

7.   as regards a dispute concerning the payment of remuneration claimed in respect of the salvage of a cargo or freight, in the court under the authority of which the cargo or freight in question:

(a)   has been arrested to secure such payment, or
(b)   could have been so arrested, but bail or other security has been given;

provided that this provision shall apply only if it is claimed that the defendant has an interest in the cargo or freight or had such an interest at the time of salvage.

Article 6

A person domiciled in a Member State may also be sued:

1.   where he is one of a number of defendants, in the courts for the place where any one of them is domiciled, provided the claims are so closely connected that it is expedient to hear and determine them together to avoid the risk of irreconcilable judgments resulting from separate proceedings;

2.   as a third party in an action on a warranty or guarantee or in any other third party proceedings, in the court seised of the original proceedings, unless these were instituted solely with the object of removing him from the jurisdiction of the court which would be competent in his case;

3.   on a counter-claim arising from the same contract or facts on which the original claim was based, in the court in which the original claim is pending;

4.   in matters relating to a contract, if the action may be combined with an action against the same defendant in matters relating to rights in rem in immovable property, in the court of the Member State in which the property is situated.

Article 7

Where by virtue of this Regulation a court of a Member State has jurisdiction in actions relating to liability from the use or operation of a ship, that court, or any other court substituted for this purpose by the internal law of that Member State, shall also have jurisdiction over claims for limitation of such liability.

Section 3

Jurisdiction in matters relating to insurance

Article 8

In matters relating to insurance, jurisdiction shall be determined by this Section, without prejudice to Article 4 and point 5 of Article 5.

Article 9

1.   An insurer domiciled in a Member State may be sued:

(a)   in the courts of the Member State where he is domiciled, or
(b)   in another Member State, in the case of actions brought by the policyholder, the insured or a beneficiary, in the courts for the place where the plaintiff is domiciled,
(c)   if he is a co-insurer, in the courts of a Member State in which proceedings are brought against the leading insurer.

2.   An insurer who is not domiciled in a Member State but has a branch, agency or other establishment in one of the Member States shall, in disputes arising out of the operations of the branch, agency or establishment, be deemed to be domiciled in that Member State.

Article 10

In respect of liability insurance or insurance of immovable property, the insurer may in addition be sued in the courts for the place where the harmful event occurred. The same applies if movable and immovable property are covered by the same insurance policy and both are adversely affected by the same contingency.

Article 11

1.   In respect of liability insurance, the insurer may also, if the law of the court permits it, be joined in proceedings which the injured party has brought against the insured.

2.   Articles 8, 9 and 10 shall apply to actions brought by the injured party directly against the insurer, where such direct actions are permitted.

3.   If the law governing such direct actions provides that the policyholder or the insured may be joined as a party to the action, the same court shall have jurisdiction over them.

Article 12

1.   Without prejudice to Article 11(3), an insurer may bring proceedings only in the courts of the Member State in which the defendant is domiciled, irrespective of whether he is the policyholder, the insured or a beneficiary.

2.   The provisions of this Section shall not affect the right to bring a counter-claim in the court in which, in accordance with this Section, the original claim is pending.

Article 13

The provisions of this Section may be departed from only by an agreement:

1.   which is entered into after the dispute has arisen, or

2.   which allows the policyholder, the insured or a beneficiary to bring proceedings in courts other than those indicated in this Section, or

3.   which is concluded between a policyholder and an insurer, both of whom are at the time of conclusion of the contract domiciled or habitually resident in the same Member State, and which has the effect of conferring jurisdiction on the courts of that State even if the harmful event were to occur abroad, provided that such an agreement is not contrary to the law of that State, or

4.   which is concluded with a policyholder who is not domiciled in a Member State, except in so far as the insurance is compulsory or relates to immovable property in a Member State, or

5.   which relates to a contract of insurance in so far as it covers one or more of the risks set out in Article 14.

Article 14

The following are the risks referred to in Article 13(5):

1. any loss of or damage to:

(a) seagoing ships, installations situated offshore or on the high seas, or aircraft, arising from perils which relate to their use for commercial purposes;
(b) goods in transit other than passengers' baggage where the transit consists of or includes carriage by such ships or aircraft;

2. any liability, other than for bodily injury to passengers or loss of or damage to their baggage:

(a) arising out of the use or operation of ships, installations or aircraft as referred to in point 1(a) in so far as, in respect of the latter, the law of the Member State in which such aircraft are registered does not prohibit agreements on jurisdiction regarding insurance of such risks;
(b) for loss or damage caused by goods in transit as described in point 1(b);

3. any financial loss connected with the use or operation of ships, installations or aircraft as referred to in point 1(a), in particular loss of freight or charter-hire;

4. any risk or interest connected with any of those referred to in points 1 to 3;

5. notwithstanding points 1 to 4, all 'large risks' as defined in Council Directive 73/239/EEC[7] as amended by Council Directives 88/357/EEC[8] and 90/618/EEC,[9] as they may be amended.

---

[7] OJ L 228, 16.8.1973, p 3. Directive as last amended by Directive 2000/26/EC of the European Parliament and of the Council (OJ L 181, 20.7.2000, p 65).
[8] OJ L 172, 4.7.1988, p 1. Directive as last amended by Directive 2000/26/EC.
[9] OJ L 330, 29.11.1990, p 44.

Section 4

Jurisdiction over consumer contracts

Article 15

1.   In matters relating to a contract concluded by a person, the consumer, for a purpose which can be regarded as being outside his trade or profession, jurisdiction shall be determined by this Section, without prejudice to Article 4 and point 5 of Article 5, if:

(a)   it is a contract for the sale of goods on instalment credit terms; or
(b)   it is a contract for a loan repayable by instalments, or for any other form of credit, made to finance the sale of goods; or
(c)   in all other cases, the contract has been concluded with a person who pursues commercial or professional activities in the Member State of the consumer's domicile or, by any means, directs such activities to that Member State or to several States including that Member State, and the contract falls within the scope of such activities.

2.   Where a consumer enters into a contract with a party who is not domiciled in the Member State but has a branch, agency or other establishment in one of the Member States, that party shall, in disputes arising out of the operations of the branch, agency or establishment, be deemed to be domiciled in that State.

3.   This Section shall not apply to a contract of transport other than a contract which, for an inclusive price, provides for a combination of travel and accommodation.

Article 16

1.   A consumer may bring proceedings against the other party to a contract either in the courts of the Member State in which that party is domiciled or in the courts for the place where the consumer is domiciled.

2.   Proceedings may be brought against a consumer by the other party to the contract only in the courts of the Member State in which the consumer is domiciled.

3.   This Article shall not affect the right to bring a counter-claim in the court in which, in accordance with this Section, the original claim is pending.

Article 17

The provisions of this Section may be departed from only by an agreement:

1.   which is entered into after the dispute has arisen; or

2.   which allows the consumer to bring proceedings in courts other than those indicated in this Section; or

3.   which is entered into by the consumer and the other party to the contract, both of whom are at the time of conclusion of the contract domiciled or

habitually resident in the same Member State, and which confers jurisdiction on the courts of that Member State, provided that such an agreement is not contrary to the law of that Member State.

Section 5

Jurisdiction over individual contracts of employment

Article 18

1.   In matters relating to individual contracts of employment, jurisdiction shall be determined by this Section, without prejudice to Article 4 and point 5 of Article 5.

2.   Where an employee enters into an individual contract of employment with an employer who is not domiciled in a Member State but has a branch, agency or other establishment in one of the Member States, the employer shall, in disputes arising out of the operations of the branch, agency or establishment, be deemed to be domiciled in that Member State.

Article 19

An employer domiciled in a Member State may be sued:

1.   in the courts of the Member State where he is domiciled; or

2.   in another Member State:

(a)   in the courts for the place where the employee habitually carries out his work or in the courts for the last place where he did so, or
(b)   if the employee does not or did not habitually carry out his work in any one country, in the courts for the place where the business which engaged the employee is or was situated.

Article 20

1.   An employer may bring proceedings only in the courts of the Member State in which the employee is domiciled.

2.   The provisions of this Section shall not affect the right to bring a counter-claim in the court in which, in accordance with this Section, the original claim is pending.

Article 21

The provisions of this Section may be departed from only by an agreement on jurisdiction:

1.   which is entered into after the dispute has arisen; or

2.   which allows the employee to bring proceedings in courts other than those indicated in this Section.

Section 6

Exclusive jurisdiction

Article 22

The following courts shall have exclusive jurisdiction, regardless of domicile:

1.   in proceedings which have as their object rights in rem in immovable property or tenancies of immovable property, the courts of the Member State in which the property is situated.

However, in proceedings which have as their object tenancies of immovable property concluded for temporary private use for a maximum period of six consecutive months, the courts of the Member State in which the defendant is domiciled shall also have jurisdiction, provided that the tenant is a natural person and that the landlord and the tenant are domiciled in the same Member State;

2.   in proceedings which have as their object the validity of the constitution, the nullity or the dissolution of companies or other legal persons or associations of natural or legal persons, or of the validity of the decisions of their organs, the courts of the Member State in which the company, legal person or association has its seat. In order to determine that seat, the court shall apply its rules of private international law;

3.   in proceedings which have as their object the validity of entries in public registers, the courts of the Member State in which the register is kept;

4.   in proceedings concerned with the registration or validity of patents, trade marks, designs, or other similar rights required to be deposited or registered, the courts of the Member State in which the deposit or registration has been applied for, has taken place or is under the terms of a Community instrument or an international convention deemed to have taken place. Without prejudice to the jurisdiction of the European Patent Office under the Convention on the Grant of European Patents, signed at Munich on 5 October 1973, the courts of each Member State shall have exclusive jurisdiction, regardless of domicile, in proceedings concerned with the registration or validity of any European patent granted for that State;

5.   in proceedings concerned with the enforcement of judgments, the courts of the Member State in which the judgment has been or is to be enforced.

Section 7

Prorogation of jurisdiction

Article 23

1.   If the parties, one or more of whom is domiciled in a Member State, have agreed that a court or the courts of a Member State are to have jurisdiction to settle any disputes which have arisen or which may arise in connection with a particular legal relationship, that court or those courts shall have jurisdiction. Such jurisdiction shall be exclusive unless the parties have agreed otherwise. Such an agreement conferring jurisdiction shall be either:

(a)   in writing or evidenced in writing; or
(b)   in a form which accords with practices which the parties have established between themselves; or
(c)   in international trade or commerce, in a form which accords with a usage of which the parties are or ought to have been aware and which in such trade or commerce is widely known to, and regularly observed by, parties to contracts of the type involved in the particular trade or commerce concerned.

2.   Any communication by electronic means which provides a durable record of the agreement shall be equivalent to 'writing'.

3.   Where such an agreement is concluded by parties, none of whom is domiciled in a Member State, the courts of other Member States shall have no jurisdiction over their disputes unless the court or courts chosen have declined jurisdiction.

4.   The court or courts of a Member State on which a trust instrument has conferred jurisdiction shall have exclusive jurisdiction in any proceedings brought against a settlor, trustee or beneficiary, if relations between these persons or their rights or obligations under the trust are involved.

5.   Agreements or provisions of a trust instrument conferring jurisdiction shall have no legal force if they are contrary to Articles 13, 17 or 21, or if the courts whose jurisdiction they purport to exclude have exclusive jurisdiction by virtue of Article 22.

Article 24

Apart from jurisdiction derived from other provisions of this Regulation, a court of a Member State before which a defendant enters an appearance shall have jurisdiction. This rule shall not apply where appearance was entered to contest the jurisdiction, or where another court has exclusive jurisdiction by virtue of Article 22.

Section 8

Examination as to jurisdiction and admissibility

Article 25

Where a court of a Member State is seised of a claim which is principally concerned with a matter over which the courts of another Member State have exclusive jurisdiction by virtue of Article 22, it shall declare of its own motion that it has no jurisdiction.

Article 26

1.   Where a defendant domiciled in one Member State is sued in a court of another Member State and does not enter an appearance, the court shall declare of its own motion that it has no jurisdiction unless its jurisdiction is derived from the provisions of this Regulation.

2. The court shall stay the proceedings so long as it is not shown that the defendant has been able to receive the document instituting the proceedings or an equivalent document in sufficient time to enable him to arrange for his defence, or that all necessary steps have been taken to this end.

3. Article 19 of Council Regulation (EC) No 1348/2000 of 29 May 2000 on the service in the Member States of judicial and extrajudicial documents in civil or commercial matters[10] shall apply instead of the provisions of paragraph 2 if the document instituting the proceedings or an equivalent document had to be transmitted from one Member State to another pursuant to this Regulation.

4. Where the provisions of Regulation (EC) No 1348/2000 are not applicable, Article 15 of the Hague Convention of 15 November 1965 on the Service Abroad of Judicial and Extrajudicial Documents in Civil or Commercial Matters shall apply if the document instituting the proceedings or an equivalent document had to be transmitted pursuant to that Convention.

Section 9

Lis pendens – related actions

Article 27

1. Where proceedings involving the same cause of action and between the same parties are brought in the courts of different Member States, any court other than the court first seised shall of its own motion stay its proceedings until such time as the jurisdiction of the court first seised is established.

2. Where the jurisdiction of the court first seised is established, any court other than the court first seised shall decline jurisdiction in favour of that court.

Article 28

1. Where related actions are pending in the courts of different Member States, any court other than the court first seised may stay its proceedings.

2. Where these actions are pending at first instance, any court other than the court first seised may also, on the application of one of the parties, decline jurisdiction if the court first seised has jurisdiction over the actions in question and its law permits the consolidation thereof.

3. For the purposes of this Article, actions are deemed to be related where they are so closely connected that it is expedient to hear and determine them together to avoid the risk of irreconcilable judgments resulting from separate proceedings.

Article 29

Where actions come within the exclusive jurisdiction of several courts, any court other than the court first seised shall decline jurisdiction in favour of that court.

Article 30

---

[10] OJ L 160, 30.6.2000, p 37.

For the purposes of this Section, a court shall be deemed to be seised:

1.   at the time when the document instituting the proceedings or an equivalent document is lodged with the court, provided that the plaintiff has not subsequently failed to take the steps he was required to take to have service effected on the defendant, or

2.   if the document has to be served before being lodged with the court, at the time when it is received by the authority responsible for service, provided that the plaintiff has not subsequently failed to take the steps he was required to take to have the document lodged with the court.

Section 10

Provisional, including protective, measures

Article 31

Application may be made to the courts of a Member State for such provisional, including protective, measures as may be available under the law of that State, even if, under this Regulation, the courts of another Member State have jurisdiction as to the substance of the matter.

CHAPTER III

RECOGNITION AND ENFORCEMENT

Article 32

For the purposes of this Regulation, 'judgment' means any judgment given by a court or tribunal of a Member State, whatever the judgment may be called, including a decree, order, decision or writ of execution, as well as the determination of costs or expenses by an officer of the court.

Section 1

Recognition

Article 33

1.   A judgment given in a Member State shall be recognised in the other Member States without any special procedure being required.

2.   Any interested party who raises the recognition of a judgment as the principal issue in a dispute may, in accordance with the procedures provided for in Sections 2 and 3 of this Chapter, apply for a decision that the judgment be recognised.

3.   If the outcome of proceedings in a court of a Member State depends on the determination of an incidental question of recognition that court shall have jurisdiction over that question.

Article 34

A judgment shall not be recognised:

1.   if such recognition is manifestly contrary to public policy in the Member State in which recognition is sought;

2.   where it was given in default of appearance, if the defendant was not served with the document which instituted the proceedings or with an equivalent document in sufficient time and in such a way as to enable him to arrange for his defence, unless the defendant failed to commence proceedings to challenge the judgment when it was possible for him to do so;

3.   if it is irreconcilable with a judgment given in a dispute between the same parties in the Member State in which recognition is sought;

4.   if it is irreconcilable with an earlier judgment given in another Member State or in a third State involving the same cause of action and between the same parties, provided that the earlier judgment fulfils the conditions necessary for its recognition in the Member State addressed.

Article 35

1.   Moreover, a judgment shall not be recognised if it conflicts with Sections 3, 4 or 6 of Chapter II, or in a case provided for in Article 72.

2.   In its examination of the grounds of jurisdiction referred to in the foregoing paragraph, the court or authority applied to shall be bound by the findings of fact on which the court of the Member State of origin based its jurisdiction.

3.   Subject to the paragraph 1, the jurisdiction of the court of the Member State of origin may not be reviewed. The test of public policy referred to in point 1 of Article 34 may not be applied to the rules relating to jurisdiction.

Article 36

Under no circumstances may a foreign judgment be reviewed as to its substance.

Article 37

1.   A court of a Member State in which recognition is sought of a judgment given in another Member State may stay the proceedings if an ordinary appeal against the judgment has been lodged.

2.   A court of a Member State in which recognition is sought of a judgment given in Ireland or the United Kingdom may stay the proceedings if enforcement is suspended in the State of origin, by reason of an appeal.

Section 2

Enforcement

Article 38

1.   A judgment given in a Member State and enforceable in that State shall be enforced in another Member State when, on the application of any interested party, it has been declared enforceable there.

2.   However, in the United Kingdom, such a judgment shall be enforced in England and Wales, in Scotland, or in Northern Ireland when, on the application of any interested party, it has been registered for enforcement in that part of the United Kingdom.

Article 39

1.   The application shall be submitted to the court or competent authority indicated in the list in Annex II.

2.   The local jurisdiction shall be determined by reference to the place of domicile of the party against whom enforcement is sought, or to the place of enforcement.

Article 40

1.   The procedure for making the application shall be governed by the law of the Member State in which enforcement is sought.

2.   The applicant must give an address for service of process within the area of jurisdiction of the court applied to. However, if the law of the Member State in which enforcement is sought does not provide for the furnishing of such an address, the applicant shall appoint a representative ad litem.

3.   The documents referred to in Article 53 shall be attached to the application.

Article 41

The judgment shall be declared enforceable immediately on completion of the formalities in Article 53 without any review under Articles 34 and 35. The party against whom enforcement is sought shall not at this stage of the proceedings be entitled to make any submissions on the application.

Article 42

1.   The decision on the application for a declaration of enforceability shall forthwith be brought to the notice of the applicant in accordance with the procedure laid down by the law of the Member State in which enforcement is sought.

2.   The declaration of enforceability shall be served on the party against whom enforcement is sought, accompanied by the judgment, if not already served on that party.

Article 43

1.   The decision on the application for a declaration of enforceability may be appealed against by either party.

2.   The appeal is to be lodged with the court indicated in the list in Annex III.

3.   The appeal shall be dealt with in accordance with the rules governing procedure in contradictory matters.

4.   If the party against whom enforcement is sought fails to appear before the appellate court in proceedings concerning an appeal brought by the applicant, Article 26(2) to (4) shall apply even where the party against whom enforcement is sought is not domiciled in any of the Member States.

5.   An appeal against the declaration of enforceability is to be lodged within one month of service thereof. If the party against whom enforcement is sought is domiciled in a Member State other than that in which the declaration of enforceability was given, the time for appealing shall be two months and shall run from the date of service, either on him in person or at his residence. No extension of time may be granted on account of distance.

Article 44

The judgment given on the appeal may be contested only by the appeal referred to in Annex IV.

Article 45

1.   The court with which an appeal is lodged under Article 43 or Article 44 shall refuse or revoke a declaration of enforceability only on one of the grounds specified in Articles 34 and 35. It shall give its decision without delay.

2.   Under no circumstances may the foreign judgment be reviewed as to its substance.

Article 46

1.   The court with which an appeal is lodged under Article 43 or Article 44 may, on the application of the party against whom enforcement is sought, stay the proceedings if an ordinary appeal has been lodged against the judgment in the Member State of origin or if the time for such an appeal has not yet expired; in the latter case, the court may specify the time within which such an appeal is to be lodged.

2.   Where the judgment was given in Ireland or the United Kingdom, any form of appeal available in the Member State of origin shall be treated as an ordinary appeal for the purposes of paragraph 1.

3.   The court may also make enforcement conditional on the provision of such security as it shall determine.

Article 47

1.   When a judgment must be recognised in accordance with this Regulation, nothing shall prevent the applicant from availing himself of provisional, including protective, measures in accordance with the law of the Member State requested without a declaration of enforceability under Article 41 being required.

2.   The declaration of enforceability shall carry with it the power to proceed to any protective measures.

3.   During the time specified for an appeal pursuant to Article 43(5) against the declaration of enforceability and until any such appeal has been determined, no measures of enforcement may be taken other than protective measures against the property of the party against whom enforcement is sought.

Article 48

1.   Where a foreign judgment has been given in respect of several matters and the declaration of enforceability cannot be given for all of them, the court or competent authority shall give it for one or more of them.

2.   An applicant may request a declaration of enforceability limited to parts of a judgment.

Article 49

A foreign judgment which orders a periodic payment by way of a penalty shall be enforceable in the Member State in which enforcement is sought only if the amount of the payment has been finally determined by the courts of the Member State of origin.

Article 50

An applicant who, in the Member State of origin has benefited from complete or partial legal aid or exemption from costs or expenses, shall be entitled, in the procedure provided for in this Section, to benefit from the most favourable legal aid or the most extensive exemption from costs or expenses provided for by the law of the Member State addressed.

Article 51

No security, bond or deposit, however described, shall be required of a party who in one Member State applies for enforcement of a judgment given in another Member State on the ground that he is a foreign national or that he is not domiciled or resident in the State in which enforcement is sought.

Article 52

In proceedings for the issue of a declaration of enforceability, no charge, duty or fee calculated by reference to the value of the matter at issue may be levied in the Member State in which enforcement is sought.

Section 3

Common provisions

Article 53

1.   A party seeking recognition or applying for a declaration of enforceability shall produce a copy of the judgment which satisfies the conditions necessary to establish its authenticity.

2.   A party applying for a declaration of enforceability shall also produce the certificate referred to in Article 54, without prejudice to Article 55.

Article 54

The court or competent authority of a Member State where a judgment was given shall issue, at the request of any interested party, a certificate using the standard form in Annex V to this Regulation.

Article 55

1.   If the certificate referred to in Article 54 is not produced, the court or competent authority may specify a time for its production or accept an equivalent document or, if it considers that it has sufficient information before it, dispense with its production.

2.   If the court or competent authority so requires, a translation of the documents shall be produced. The translation shall be certified by a person qualified to do so in one of the Member States.

Article 56

No legalisation or other similar formality shall be required in respect of the documents referred to in Article 53 or Article 55(2), or in respect of a document appointing a representative ad litem.

CHAPTER IV
AUTHENTIC INSTRUMENTS AND COURT SETTLEMENTS
Article 57

1.   A document which has been formally drawn up or registered as an authentic instrument and is enforceable in one Member State shall, in another Member State, be declared enforceable there, on application made in accordance with the procedures provided for in Articles 38, et seq. The court with which an appeal is lodged under Article 43 or Article 44 shall refuse or revoke a declaration of enforceability only if enforcement of the instrument is manifestly contrary to public policy in the Member State addressed.

2.   Arrangements relating to maintenance obligations concluded with administrative authorities or authenticated by them shall also be regarded as authentic instruments within the meaning of paragraph 1.

3.   The instrument produced must satisfy the conditions necessary to establish its authenticity in the Member State of origin.

4.   Section 3 of Chapter III shall apply as appropriate. The competent authority of a Member State where an authentic instrument was drawn up or registered shall issue, at the request of any interested party, a certificate using the standard form in Annex VI to this Regulation.

Article 58

A settlement which has been approved by a court in the course of proceedings and is enforceable in the Member State in which it was concluded shall be enforceable in the State addressed under the same conditions as authentic instruments. The court or competent authority of a Member State where a court settlement was approved shall issue, at the request of any interested party, a certificate using the standard form in Annex V to this Regulation.

CHAPTER V
GENERAL PROVISIONS
Article 59

1.   In order to determine whether a party is domiciled in the Member State whose courts are seised of a matter, the court shall apply its internal law.

2.   If a party is not domiciled in the Member State whose courts are seised of the matter, then, in order to determine whether the party is domiciled in another Member State, the court shall apply the law of that Member State.

Article 60

1. For the purposes of this Regulation, a company or other legal person or association of natural or legal persons is domiciled at the place where it has its:

(a)   statutory seat, or
(b)   central administration, or
(c)   principal place of business.

2. For the purposes of the United Kingdom and Ireland 'statutory seat' means the registered office or, where there is no such office anywhere, the place of incorporation or, where there is no such place anywhere, the place under the law of which the formation took place.

3. In order to determine whether a trust is domiciled in the Member State whose courts are seised of the matter, the court shall apply its rules of private international law.

Article 61

Without prejudice to any more favourable provisions of national laws, persons domiciled in a Member State who are being prosecuted in the criminal courts of another Member State of which they are not nationals for an offence which was not intentionally committed may be defended by persons qualified to do so, even if they do not appear in person. However, the court seised of the matter may order appearance in person; in the case of failure to appear, a judgment given in the civil action without the person concerned having had the opportunity to arrange for his defence need not be recognised or enforced in the other Member States.

Article 62

In Sweden, in summary proceedings concerning orders to pay (betalningsforelig-gande) and assistance (handrickning), the expression 'court' includes the 'Swedish enforcement service' (kronofogdemyndighet).

Article 63

1. A person domiciled in the territory of the Grand Duchy of Luxembourg and sued in the court of another Member State pursuant to Article 5(1) may refuse to submit to the jurisdiction of that court if the final place of delivery of the goods or provision of the services is in Luxembourg.

2. Where, under paragraph 1, the final place of delivery of the goods or provision of the services is in Luxembourg, any agreement conferring jurisdiction must, in order to be valid, be accepted in writing or evidenced in writing within the meaning of Article 23(1)(a).

3. The provisions of this Article shall not apply to contracts for the provision of financial services.

4. The provisions of this Article shall apply for a period of six years from entry into force of this Regulation.

Article 64

1. In proceedings involving a dispute between the master and a member of the crew of a seagoing ship registered in Greece or in Portugal, concerning remuneration or other conditions of service, a court in a Member State shall establish whether the diplomatic or consular officer responsible for the ship has been notified of the dispute. It may act as soon as that officer has been notified.

2. The provisions of this Article shall apply for a period of six years from entry into force of this Regulation.

Article 65

1. The jurisdiction specified in Article 6(2), and Article 11 in actions on a warranty of guarantee or in any other third party proceedings may not be resorted to in Germany and Austria. Any person domiciled in another Member State may be sued in the courts:

(a)   of Germany, pursuant to Articles 68 and 72 to 74 of the Code of Civil Procedure (Zivilprozessordnung) concerning third-party notices,
(b)   of Austria, pursuant to Article 21 of the Code of Civil Procedure (Zivilprozessordnung) concerning third-party notices.

2.   Judgments given in other Member States by virtue of Article 6(2), or Article 11 shall be recognised and enforced in Germany and Austria in accordance with Chapter III. Any effects which judgments given in these States may have on third parties by application of the provisions in paragraph 1 shall also be recognised in the other Member States.

CHAPTER VI

TRANSITIONAL PROVISIONS

Article 66

1. This Regulation shall apply only to legal proceedings instituted and to documents formally drawn up or registered as authentic instruments after the entry into force thereof.

2. However, if the proceedings in the Member State of origin were instituted before the entry into force of this Regulation, judgments given after that date shall be recognised and enforced in accordance with Chapter III,

(a)   if the proceedings in the Member State of origin were instituted after the entry into force of the Brussels or the Lugano Convention both in the Member State or origin and in the Member State addressed;

(b)   in all other cases, if jurisdiction was founded upon rules which accorded with those provided for either in Chapter II or in a convention concluded between the Member State of origin and the Member State addressed which was in force when the proceedings were instituted.

CHAPTER VII

RELATIONS WITH OTHER INSTRUMENTS

Article 67

This Regulation shall not prejudice the application of provisions governing jurisdiction and the recognition and enforcement of judgments in specific matters which are contained in Community instruments or in national legislation harmonised pursuant to such instruments.

Article 68

1. This Regulation shall, as between the Member States, supersede the Brussels Convention, except as regards the territories of the Member States which fall within the territorial scope of that Convention and which are excluded from this Regulation pursuant to Article 299 of the Treaty.

2. In so far as this Regulation replaces the provisions of the Brussels Convention between Member States, any reference to the Convention shall be understood as a reference to this Regulation.

Article 69

Subject to Article 66(2) and Article 70, this Regulation shall, as between Member States, supersede the following conventions and treaty concluded between two or more of them:

– the Convention between Belgium and France on Jurisdiction and the Validity and Enforcement of Judgments, Arbitration Awards and Authentic Instruments, signed at Paris on 8 July 1899,
– the Convention between Belgium and the Netherlands on Jurisdiction, Bankruptcy, and the Validity and Enforcement of Judgments, Arbitration Awards and Authentic Instruments, signed at Brussels on 28 March 1925,
– the Convention between France and Italy on the Enforcement of Judgments in Civil and Commercial Matters, signed at Rome on 3 June 1930,
– the Convention between Germany and Italy on the Recognition and Enforcement of Judgments in Civil and Commercial Matters, signed at Rome on 9 March 1936,
– the Convention between Belgium and Austria on the Reciprocal Recognition and Enforcement of Judgments and Authentic Instruments relating to Maintenance Obligations, signed at Vienna on 25 October 1957,
– the Convention between Germany and Belgium on the Mutual Recognition and Enforcement of Judgments, Arbitration Awards and Authentic Instruments in Civil and Commercial Matters, signed at Bonn on 30 June 1958,
– the Convention between the Netherlands and Italy on the Recognition and Enforcement of Judgments in Civil and Commercial Matters, signed at Rome on 17 April 1959,
– the Convention between Germany and Austria on the Reciprocal Recognition and Enforcement of Judgments, Settlements and Authentic Instruments in Civil and Commercial Matters, signed at Vienna on 6 June 1959,
– the Convention between Belgium and Austria on the Reciprocal Recognition and Enforcement of Judgments. Arbitral Awards and Authentic Instruments in Civil and Commercial Matters, signed at Vienna on 16 June 1959,
– the Convention between Greece and Germany for the Reciprocal Recognition and Enforcement of Judgments, Settlements and Authentic Instruments in Civil and Commercial Matters, signed in Athens on 4 November 1961,
– the Convention between Belgium and Italy on the Recognition and Enforcement of Judgments and other Enforceable Instruments in Civil and Commercial Matters, signed at Rome on 6 April 1962,
– the Convention between the Netherlands and Germany on the Mutual Recognition and Enforcement of Judgments and Other Enforceable Instruments in Civil and Commercial Matters, signed at The Hague on 30 August 1962, the Convention between the Netherlands and Austria on the Reciprocal Recognition and Enforcement of Judgments and Authentic Instruments in Civil and Commercial Matters, signed at The Hague on 6 February 1963,
– the Convention between France and Austria on the Recognition and Enforcement of Judgments and Authentic Instruments in Civil and Commercial Matters, signed at Vienna on 15 July 1966,
– the Convention between Spain and France on the Recognition and Enforcement of Judgment Arbitration Awards in Civil and Commercial Matters, signed at Paris on 28 May 1969,

- the Convention between Luxembourg and Austria on the Recognition and Enforcement of Judgments and Authentic Instruments in Civil and Commercial Matters, signed at Luxembourg on 29 July 1971,
- the Convention between Italy and Austria on the Recognition and Enforcement of Judgments in Civil and Commercial Matters, of Judicial Settlements and of Authentic Instruments, signed at Rome on 16 November 1971,
- the Convention between Spain and Italy regarding Legal Aid and the Recognition and Enforcement of Judgments in Civil and Commercial Matters, signed at Madrid on 22 May 1973,
- the Convention between Finland, Iceland, Norway, Sweden and Denmark on the Recognition and Enforcement of Judgments in Civil Matters, signed at Copenhagen on 11 October 1977,
- the Convention between Austria and Sweden on the Recognition and Enforcement of Judgments in Civil Matters, signed at Stockholm on 16 September 1982,
- the Convention between Spain and the Federal Republic of Germany on the Recognition and Enforcement of Judgments, Settlements and Enforceable Authentic Instruments in Civil and Commercial Matters, signed at Bonn on 14 November 1983,
- the Convention between Austria and Spain on the Recognition and Enforcement of Judgments, Settlements and Enforceable Authentic Instruments in Civil and Commercial Matters, signed at Vienna on 17 February 1984,
- the Convention between Finland and Austria on the Recognition and Enforcement of Judgments in Civil Matters, signed at Vienna on 17 November 1986, and
- the Treaty between Belgium, the Netherlands and Luxembourg in Jurisdiction, Bankruptcy, and the Validity and Enforcement of Judgments, Arbitration Awards and Authentic Instruments, signed at Brussels on 24 November 1961, in so far as it is in force.

Article 70

1.   The Treaty and the Conventions referred to in Article 69 shall continue to have effect in relation to matters to which this Regulation does not apply.

2.   They shall continue to have effect in respect of judgments given and documents formally drawn up or registered as authentic instruments before the entry into force of this Regulation.

Article 71

1.   This Regulation shall not affect any conventions to which the Member States are parties and which in relation to particular matters, govern jurisdiction or the recognition or enforcement of judgments.

2.   With a view to its uniform interpretation, paragraph 1 shall be applied in the following manner:

(a)   this Regulation shall not prevent a court of a Member State, which is a party to a convention on a particular matter, from assuming jurisdiction in accordance with that convention, even where the defendant is domiciled in another Member State which is not a party to that convention. The court hearing the action shall, in any event, apply Article 26 of this Regulation;

(b) judgments given in a Member State by a court in the exercise of jurisdiction provided for in a convention on a particular matter shall be recognised and enforced in the other Member States in accordance with this Regulation.

Where a convention on a particular matter to which both the Member State of origin and the Member State addressed are parties lays down conditions for the recognition or enforcement of judgments, those conditions shall apply. In any event, the provisions of this Regulation which concern the procedure for recognition and enforcement of judgments may be applied.

Article 72

This Regulation shall not affect agreements by which Member States undertook, prior to the entry into force of this Regulation pursuant to Article 59 of the Brussels Convention, not to recognise judgments given, in particular in other Contracting States to that Convention, against defendants domiciled or habitually resident in a third country where, in cases provided for in Article 4 of that Convention, the judgment could only be founded on a ground of jurisdiction

CHAPTER VIII
FINAL PROVISIONS
Article 73

No later than five years after the entry into force of this Regulation, the Commission shall present to the European Parliament, the Council and the Economic and Social Committee a report on the application of this Regulation. The report shall be accompanied, if need be, by proposals for adaptations to this Regulation.

Article 74

1. The Member States shall notify the Commission of the texts amending the lists set out in Annexes I to IV. The Commission shall adapt the Annexes concerned accordingly.

2. The updating or technical adjustment of the forms, specimens of which appear in Annexes V and VI, shall be adopted in accordance with the advisory procedure referred to in Article 75(2).

Article 75

1. The Commission shall be assisted by a committee.

2. Where reference is made to this paragraph, Articles 3 and 7 of Decision 1999/468/EC shall apply.

3. The Committee shall adopt its rules of procedure.

Article 76

This Regulation shall enter into force on 1 March 2002.

This Regulation is binding in its entirety and directly applicable in the Member States in accordance with the Treaty establishing the European Community.

Done at Brussels, 22 December 2000.

For the Council
The President
C. PIERRET

ANNEX I

Rules of jurisdiction referred to in Article 3(2) and Article 4(2)

The rules of jurisdiction referred to in Article 3(2) and Article 4(2) are the following:

– in Belgium: Article 15 of the Civil Code (*Code civil/Burgerlijk Wetboek*) and Article 638 of the Judicial Code (*Code judiciaire/Gerechtelijk Wetboek*);
– in Germany: Article 23 of the Code of Civil Procedure (*Zivilprozessordnung*), in Greece, Article 40 of the Code of Civil Procedure (KwDlKa; IoAlTlKt; LlKovo)ia;);
– in France: Articles 14 and 15 of the Civil Code (*Code civil*),
– in Ireland: the rules which enable jurisdiction to be founded on the document instituting the proceedings having been served on the defendant during his temporary presence in Ireland,
– in Italy: Articles 3 and 4 of Act 218 of 31 May 1995,
– in Luxembourg: Articles 14 and 15 of the Civil Code (*Code civil*),
– in the Netherlands: Articles 126(3) and 127 of the Code of Civil Procedure (*Wetboek van Burgerlijke Rechtsvordering*),
– in Austria: Article 99 of the Court Jurisdiction Act (*Jurisdiktionsnorm*),
– in Portugal: Articles 65 and 65A of the Code of Civil Procedure (*Código de Processo Civil*) and Article 11 of the Code of Labour Procedure (*Código de Processo de Trabalho*),
– in Finland: the second, third and fourth sentences of the first paragraph of Section 1 of Chapter 10 of the Code of Judicial Procedure (*oikeudenkiymiskaari/rittegangsbalken*),
– in Sweden: the first sentence of the first paragraph of Section 3 of Chapter 10 of the Code of Judicial Procedure (*rittegangsbalken*),
– in the United Kingdom: rules which enable jurisdiction to be founded on:

(a) the document instituting the proceedings having been served on the defendant during his temporary presence in the United Kingdom; or
(b) the presence within the United Kingdom of property belonging to the defendant; or
(c) the seizure by the plaintiff of property situated in the United Kingdom.

ANNEX II

The courts or competent authorities to which the application referred to in Article 39 may be submitted are the following:

- in Belgium, the '*tribunal de premiere instance*' or 'rechtbank van eerste aanleg' or' 'rstinstanzliches Gericht',
- in Germany, the presiding judge of a chamber of the '*Landgericht*',
- in Greece, the 'Movo)dA:; IpWToDlKdio',
- in Spain, the '*Juzgado de Primera Instancia*',
- in France, the presiding judge of the '*tribunal de grande instance*',
- in Ireland, the High Court,
- in Italy, the '*Corte d'appello*',
- in Luxembourg, the presiding judge of the '*tribunal d'arrondissement*',
- in the Netherlands, the presiding judge of the '*arrondissementsrechtbank*';
- in Austria, the '*Bezirksgericht*',
- in Portugal, the '*Tribunal de Comarca*',
- in Finland, the '*kirijioikeus/tingsritt*',
- in Sweden, the '*Svea hovritt*',
- in the United Kingdom:

    (a)   in England and Wales, the High Court of Justice, or in the case of a maintenance judgment, the Magistrate's Court on transmission by the Secretary of State;

    (b)   in Scotland, the Court of Session, or in the case of a maintenance judgment, the Sheriff Court on transmission by the Secretary of State;

    (c)   in Northern Ireland, the High Court of Justice, or in the case of a maintenance judgment, the Magistrate's Court on transmission by the Secretary of State;

    (d)   in Gibraltar, the Supreme Court of Gibraltar, or in the case of a maintenance judgment, the Magistrates' Court on transmission by the Attorney General of Gibraltar.

ANNEX III

The courts with which appeals referred to in Article 43(2) may be lodged are the following:

–   in Belgium,

   (a)   as regards appeal by the defendant: the *'tribunal de première instance'* or *'rechtbank van eerste aanleg'* or *'erstinstanzliches Gericht'*,
   (b)   as regards appeal by the applicant: the *'Cour d'appel'* or *'hof van beroep'*,

–   in the Federal Republic of Germany, the *'Oberlandesgericht'*,
–   in Greece, the *'EedTdio'*,
–   in Spain, the *'Audiencia Provincial'*,
–   in France, the *'cour d'appel'*,
–   in Ireland, the High Court,
–   in Italy, the *'corte d'appello'*,
–   in Luxembourg, the *'Cour supérieure de Justice'* sitting as a court of civil appeal,
–   in the Netherlands:

   (a)   for the defendant: the *'arrondissementsrechtbank'*,
   (b)   for the applicant: the *'gerechtshof'*,

–   in Austria, the *'Bezirksgericht'*,
–   in Portugal, the *'Tribunal de Relação'*,
–   in Finland, the *'hovioikeus/hovritt'*,
–   in Sweden, the *'Svea hovritt'*,
–   in the United Kingdom:

   (a)   in England and Wales, the High Court of Justice, or in the case of a maintenance judgment, the Magistrate's Court;
   (b)   in Scotland, the Court of Session, or in the case of a maintenance judgment, the Sheriff Court;
   (c)   in Northern Ireland, the High Court of Justice, or in the case of a maintenance judgment, the Magistrate's Court;
   (d)   in Gibraltar, the Supreme Court of Gibraltar, or in the case of a maintenance judgment, the Magistrates' Court.

ANNEX IV

The appeals which may be lodged pursuant to Article 44 are the following

- in Belgium, Greece, Spain, France, Italy, Luxembourg and the Netherlands, an appeal in cassation,
- in Germany, a *'Rechtsbeschwerde'*,
- in Ireland, an appeal on a point of law to the Supreme Court,
- in Austria, a *'Revisionsrekurs'*,
- in Portugal, an appeal on a point of law,
- in Finland, an appeal to the *'korkein oikeus/hogsta domstolen'*,
- in Sweden, an appeal to the *'Hogsta domstolen'*,
- in the United Kingdom, a single further appeal on a point of law.

ANNEX V

Certificate referred to in Articles 54 and 58 of the Regulation on judgments and court settlements

(English, ingles, anglais, inglese, . . .)

1. Member State of origin

2. Court or competent authority issuing the certificate

2.1.   Name
2.2.   Address
2.3.   Tel./fax/e-mail

3. Court which delivered the judgment/approved the court settlement (*)

3.1.   Type of court
3.2.   Place of court

4. Judgment/court settlement (*)

4.1.   Date
4.2.   Reference number
4.3.   The parties to the judgment/court settlement (*)

    4.3.1.   Name(s) of plaintiff(s)
    4.3.2.   Name(s) of defendant(s)
    4.3.3.   Name(s) of other party(ies), if any

4.4.   Date of service of the document instituting the proceedings where judgment was given in default of appearance
4.5.   Text of the judgment/court settlement (*) as annexed to this certificate

5. Names of parties to whom legal aid has been granted

The judgment/court settlement (*) is enforceable in the Member State of origin (Articles 38 and 58 of the Regulation) against:

Name:

Done at .... date ....

Signature and/or stamp ....

ANNEX VI

Certificate referred to in Article 57(4) of the Regulation on authentic instruments

(English, ingles, anglais, inglese, . . .)

1. Member State of origin

2. Competent authority issuing the certificate

2.1. Name
2.2. Address
2.3. Tel./fax/e-mail

3. Authority which has given authenticity to the instrument

3.1. Authority involved in the drawing up of the authentic instrument (if applicable)

    3.1.1. Name and designation of authority
    3.1.2. Place of authority

3.2. Authority which has registered the authentic instrument (if applicable)

    3.2.1. Type of authority
    3.2.2. Place of authority

4. Authentic instrument

    4.1. Description of the instrument
    4.2. Date

        4.2.1. on which the instrument was drawn up
        4.2.2. if different: on which the instrument was registered

4.3. Reference number
4.4. Parties to the instrument

    4.4.1. Name of the creditor
    4.4.2. Name of the debtor

5. Text of the enforceable obligation as annexed to this certificate

The authentic instrument is enforceable against the debtor in the Member State of origin (Article 57(1) of the Regulation)

Done at .... date ....

Signature and/or stamp ....

APPENDIX 3

EC REGULATION 864/2007 ('ROME II')

REGULATION (EC) No 864/2007 OF THE EUROPEAN PARLIAMENT AND OF THE COUNCIL

of 11 July 2007

on the law applicable to non-contractual obligations (Rome II)

THE EUROPEAN PARLIAMENT AND THE COUNCIL OF THE EUROPEAN UNION,

Having regard to the Treaty establishing the European Community, and in particular Articles 61(c) and 67 thereof,

Having regard to the proposal from the Commission,

Having regard to the opinion of the European Economic and Social Committee,[1]

Acting in accordance with the procedure laid down in Article 251 of the Treaty in the light of the joint text approved by the Conciliation Committee on 25 June 2007,[2]

Whereas:

(1) The Community has set itself the objective of maintaining and developing an area of freedom, security and justice. For the progressive establishment of such an area, the Community is to adopt measures relating to judicial cooperation in civil matters with a cross-border impact to the extent necessary for the proper functioning of the internal market.

(2) According to Article 65(b) of the Treaty, these measures are to include those promoting the compatibility of the rules applicable in the Member States concerning the conflict of laws and of jurisdiction.

(3) The European Council meeting in Tampere on 15 and 16 October 1999 endorsed the principle of mutual recognition of judgments and other decisions of judicial authorities as the cornerstone of judicial cooperation in civil matters and invited the Council and the Commission to adopt a programme of measures to implement the principle of mutual recognition.

---

[1] OJ C 241, 28.9.2004, p. 1.

[2] Opinion of the European Parliament of 6 July 2005 (OJ C 157 E, 6.7.2006, p. 371), Council Common Position of 25 September 2006 (OJ C 289 E, 28.11.2006, p. 68) and Position of the European Parliament of 18 January 2007 (not yet published in the Official Journal). European Parliament Legislative Resolution of 10 July 2007 and Council Decision of 28 June 2007.

(4) On 30 November 2000, the Council adopted a joint Commission and Council programme of measures for implementation of the principle of mutual recognition of decisions in civil and commercial matters.[3] The programme identifies measures relating to the harmonisation of conflict-of-law rules as those facilitating the mutual recognition of judgments.

(5) The Hague Programme,[4] adopted by the European Council on 5 November 2004, called for work to be pursued actively on the rules of conflict of laws regarding non-contractual obligations (Rome II).

(6) The proper functioning of the internal market creates a need, in order to improve the predictability of the outcome of litigation, certainty as to the law applicable and the free movement of judgments, for the conflict-of-law rules in the Member States to designate the same national law irrespective of the country of the court in which an action is brought.

(7) The substantive scope and the provisions of this Regulation should be consistent with Council Regulation (EC) No 44/2001 of 22 December 2000 on jurisdiction and the recognition and enforcement of judgments in civil and commercial matters[5] (Brussels I) and the instruments dealing with the law applicable to contractual obligations.

(8) This Regulation should apply irrespective of the nature of the court or tribunal seised.

(9) Claims arising out of *acta iure imperii* should include claims against officials who act on behalf of the State and liability for acts of public authorities, including liability of publicly appointed office-holders. Therefore, these matters should be excluded from the scope of this Regulation.

(10) Family relationships should cover parentage, marriage, affinity and collateral relatives. The reference in Article 1(2) to relationships having comparable effects to marriage and other family relationships should be interpreted in accordance with the law of the Member State in which the court is seised.

(11) The concept of a non-contractual obligation varies from one Member State to another. Therefore for the purposes of this Regulation non-contractual obligation should be understood as an autonomous concept. The conflict-of law rules set out in this Regulation should also cover non-contractual obligations arising out of strict liability.

(12) The law applicable should also govern the question of the capacity to incur liability in tort/delict.

(13) Uniform rules applied irrespective of the law they designate may avert the risk of distortions of competition between Community litigants.

---

[3]   OJ C 12, 15.1.2001, p. 1.
[4]   OJ C 53, 3.3.2005, p. 1.
[5]   OJ L 12, 16.1.2001, p. 1. Regulation as last amended by Regulation(EC) No 1791/2006 (OJ L 363, 20.12.2006, p. 1).

(14) The requirement of legal certainty and the need to do justice in individual cases are essential elements of an area of justice. This Regulation provides for the connecting factors which are the most appropriate to achieve these objectives. Therefore, this Regulation provides for a general rule but also for specific rules and, in certain provisions, for an 'escape clause' which allows a departure from these rules where it is clear from all the circumstances of the case that the tort/delict is manifestly more closely connected with another country. This set of rules thus creates a flexible framework of conflict-of-law rules. Equally, it enables the court seised to treat individual cases in an appropriate manner.

(15) The principle of the *lex loci delicti commissi* is the basic solution for non-contractual obligations in virtually all the Member States, but the practical application of the principle where the component factors of the case are spread over several countries varies. This situation engenders uncertainty as to the law applicable.

(16) Uniform rules should enhance the foreseeability of court decisions and ensure a reasonable balance between the interests of the person claimed to be liable and the person who has sustained damage. A connection with the country where the direct damage occurred (*lex loci damni*) strikes a fair balance between the interests of the person claimed to be liable and the person sustaining the damage, and also reflects the modern approach to civil liability and the development of systems of strict liability.

(17) The law applicable should be determined on the basis of where the damage occurs, regardless of the country or countries in which the indirect consequences could occur. Accordingly, in cases of personal injury or damage to property, the country in which the damage occurs should be the country where the injury was sustained or the property was damaged respectively.

(18) The general rule in this Regulation should be the *lex loci damni* provided for in Article 4(1). Article 4(2) should be seen as an exception to this general principle, creating a special connection where the parties have their habitual residence in the same country. Article 4(3) should be understood as an 'escape clause' from Article 4(1) and (2), where it is clear from all the circumstances of the case that the tort/delict is manifestly more closely connected with another country.

(19) Specific rules should be laid down for special torts/delicts where the general rule does not allow a reasonable balance to be struck between the interests at stake.

(20) The conflict-of-law rule in matters of product liability should meet the objectives of fairly spreading the risks inherent in a modern high-technology society, protecting consumers' health, stimulating innovation, securing undistorted competition and facilitating trade. Creation of a cascade system of connecting factors, together with a foreseeability clause, is a balanced solution in regard to these objectives. The first element to be taken into account is the law of the country in which the person sustaining the damage had his or her habitual residence when the damage occurred, if the product was marketed in that country. The other elements of the cascade are triggered if the product was not marketed

in that country, without prejudice to Article 4(2) and to the possibility of a manifestly closer connection to another country.

(21) The special rule in Article 6 is not an exception to the general rule in Article 4(1) but rather a clarification of it. In matters of unfair competition, the conflict-of-law rule should protect competitors, consumers and the general public and ensure that the market economy functions properly. The connection to the law of the country where competitive relations or the collective interests of consumers are, or are likely to be, affected generally satisfies these objectives.

(22) The non-contractual obligations arising out of restrictions of competition in Article 6(3) should cover infringements of both national and Community competition law. The law applicable to such non-contractual obligations should be the law of the country where the market is, or is likely to be, affected. In cases where the market is, or is likely to be, affected in more than one country, the claimant should be able in certain circumstances to choose to base his or her claim on the law of the court seised.

(23) For the purposes of this Regulation, the concept of restriction of competition should cover prohibitions on agreements between undertakings, decisions by associations of undertakings and concerted practices which have as their object or effect the prevention, restriction or distortion of competition within a Member State or within the internal market, as well as prohibitions on the abuse of a dominant position within a Member State or within the internal market, where such agreements, decisions, concerted practices or abuses are prohibited by Articles 81 and 82 of the Treaty or by the law of a Member State.

(24) 'Environmental damage' should be understood as meaning adverse change in a natural resource, such as water, land or air, impairment of a function performed by that resource for the benefit of another natural resource or the public, or impairment of the variability among living organisms.

(25) Regarding environmental damage, Article 174 of the Treaty, which provides that there should be a high level of protection based on the precautionary principle and the principle that preventive action should be taken, the principle of priority for corrective action at source and the principle that the polluter pays, fully justifies the use of the principle of discriminating in favour of the person sustaining the damage. The question of when the person seeking compensation can make the choice of the law applicable should be determined in accordance with the law of the Member State in which the court is seised.

(26) Regarding infringements of intellectual property rights, the universally acknowledged principle of the *lex loci protectionis* should be preserved. For the purposes of this Regulation, the term 'intellectual property rights' should be interpreted as meaning, for instance, copyright, related rights, the *sui generis* right for the protection of databases and industrial property rights.

(27) The exact concept of industrial action, such as strike action or lock-out, varies from one Member State to another and is governed by each Member State's internal rules. Therefore, this Regulation assumes as a general principle that the

law of the country where the industrial action was taken should apply, with the aim of protecting the rights and obligations of workers and employers.

(28) The special rule on industrial action in Article 9 is without prejudice to the conditions relating to the exercise of such action in accordance with national law and without prejudice to the legal status of trade unions or of the representative organisations of workers as provided for in the law of the Member States.

(29) Provision should be made for special rules where damage is caused by an act other than a tort/delict, such as unjust enrichment, *negotiorum gestio* and *culpa in contrahendo*.

(30) *Culpa in contrahendo* for the purposes of this Regulation is an autonomous concept and should not necessarily be interpreted within the meaning of national law. It should include the violation of the duty of disclosure and the breakdown of contractual negotiations. Article 12 covers only non-contractual obligations presenting a direct link with the dealings prior to the conclusion of a contract. This means that if, while a contract is being negotiated, a person suffers personal injury, Article 4 or other relevant provisions of this Regulation should apply.

(31) To respect the principle of party autonomy and to enhance legal certainty, the parties should be allowed to make a choice as to the law applicable to a non-contractual obligation. This choice should be expressed or demonstrated with reasonable certainty by the circumstances of the case. Where establishing the existence of the agreement, the court has to respect the intentions of the parties. Protection should be given to weaker parties by imposing certain conditions on the choice.

(32) Considerations of public interest justify giving the courts of the Member States the possibility, in exceptional circumstances, of applying exceptions based on public policy and overriding mandatory provisions. In particular, the application of a provision of the law designated by this Regulation which would have the effect of causing noncompensatory exemplary or punitive damages of an excessive nature to be awarded may, depending on the circumstances of the case and the legal order of the Member State of the court seised, be regarded as being contrary to the public policy (*ordre public*) of the forum.

(33) According to the current national rules on compensation awarded to victims of road traffic accidents, when quantifying damages for personal injury in cases in which the accident takes place in a State other than that of the habitual residence of the victim, the court seised should take into account all the relevant actual circumstances of the specific victim, including in particular the actual losses and costs of after-care and medical attention.

(34) In order to strike a reasonable balance between the parties, account must be taken, in so far as appropriate, of the rules of safety and conduct in operation in the country in which the harmful act was committed, even where the non-contractual obligation is governed by the law of another country. The term 'rules of safety and conduct' should be interpreted as referring to all regulations having any relation to safety and conduct, including, for example, road safety rules in the case of an accident.

(35) A situation where conflict-of-law rules are dispersed among several instruments and where there are differences between those rules should be avoided. This Regulation, however, does not exclude the possibility of inclusion of conflict-of-law rules relating to noncontractual obligations in provisions of Community law with regard to particular matters. This Regulation should not prejudice the application of other instruments laying down provisions designed to contribute to the proper functioning of the internal market in so far as they cannot be applied in conjunction with the law designated by the rules of this Regulation. The application of provisions of the applicable law designated by the rules of this Regulation should not restrict the free movement of goods and services as regulated by Community instruments, such as Directive 2000/31/EC of the European Parliament and of the Council of 8 June 2000 on certain legal aspects of information society services, in particular electronic commerce, in the Internal Market (Directive on electronic commerce).[6]

(36) Respect for international commitments entered into by the Member States means that this Regulation should not affect international conventions to which one or more Member States are parties at the time this Regulation is adopted. To make the rules more accessible, the Commission should publish the list of the relevant conventions in the *Official Journal of the European Union* on the basis of information supplied by the Member States.

(37) The Commission will make a proposal to the European Parliament and the Council concerning the procedures and conditions according to which Member States would be entitled to negotiate and conclude on their own behalf agreements with third countries in individual and exceptional cases, concerning sectoral matters, containing provisions on the law applicable to non-contractual obligations.

(38) Since the objective of this Regulation cannot be sufficiently achieved by the Member States, and can therefore, by reason of the scale and effects of this Regulation, be better achieved at Community level, the Community may adopt measures, in accordance with the principle of subsidiarity set out in Article 5 of the Treaty. In accordance with the principle of proportionality set out in that Article, this Regulation does not go beyond what is necessary to attain that objective.

(39) In accordance with Article 3 of the Protocol on the position of the United Kingdom and Ireland annexed to the Treaty on European Union and to the Treaty establishing the European Community, the United Kingdom and Ireland are taking part in the adoption and application of this Regulation.

(40) In accordance with Articles 1 and 2 of the Protocol on the position of Denmark, annexed to the Treaty on European Union and to the Treaty establishing the European Community, Denmark does not take part in the adoption of this Regulation, and is not bound by it or subject to its application,

HAVE ADOPTED THIS REGULATION:

---

[6]   OJ L 178, 17.7.2000, p. 1.

CHAPTER I
SCOPE

Article 1

Scope

1. This Regulation shall apply, in situations involving a conflict of laws, to non-contractual obligations in civil and commercial matters. It shall not apply, in particular, to revenue, customs or administrative matters or to the liability of the State for acts and omissions in the exercise of State authority (*acta iure imperii*).

2. The following shall be excluded from the scope of this Regulation:

(a) non-contractual obligations arising out of family relationships and relationships deemed by the law applicable to such relationships to have comparable effects including maintenance obligations;

(b) non-contractual obligations arising out of matrimonial property regimes, property regimes of relationships deemed by the law applicable to such relationships to have comparable effects to marriage, and wills and succession;

(c) non-contractual obligations arising under bills of exchange, cheques and promissory notes and other negotiable instruments to the extent that the obligations under such other negotiable instruments arise out of their negotiable character;

(d) non-contractual obligations arising out of the law of companies and other bodies corporate or unincorporated regarding matters such as the creation, by registration or otherwise, legal capacity, internal organisation or winding-up of companies and other bodies corporate or unincorporated, the personal liability of officers and members as such for the obligations of the company or body and the personal liability of auditors to a company or to its members in the statutory audits of accounting documents;

(e) non-contractual obligations arising out of the relations between the settlors, trustees and beneficiaries of a trust created voluntarily;

(f) non-contractual obligations arising out of nuclear damage;

(g) non-contractual obligations arising out of violations of privacy and rights relating to personality, including defamation.

3. This Regulation shall not apply to evidence and procedure, without prejudice to Articles 21 and 22.

4. For the purposes of this Regulation, 'Member State' shall mean any Member State other than Denmark.

Article 2

Non-contractual obligations

1. For the purposes of this Regulation, damage shall cover any consequence arising out of tort/delict, unjust enrichment, *negotiorum gestio* or *culpa in contrahendo*.

2. This Regulation shall apply also to non-contractual obligations that are likely to arise.

3. Any reference in this Regulation to:

(a)   an event giving rise to damage shall include events giving rise to damage that are likely to occur; and
(b)   damage shall include damage that is likely to occur.

Article 3
Universal application

Any law specified by this Regulation shall be applied whether or not it is the law of a Member State.

CHAPTER II
TORTS/DELICTS

Article 4
General rule

1. Unless otherwise provided for in this Regulation, the law applicable to a non-contractual obligation arising out of a tort/delict shall be the law of the country in which the damage occurs irrespective of the country in which the event giving rise to the damage occurred and irrespective of the country or countries in which the indirect consequences of that event occur.

2. However, where the person claimed to be liable and the person sustaining damage both have their habitual residence in the same country at the time when the damage occurs, the law of that country shall apply.

3. Where it is clear from all the circumstances of the case that the tort/delict is manifestly more closely connected with a country other than that indicated in paragraphs 1 or 2, the law of that other country shall apply. A manifestly closer connection with another country might be based in particular on a preexisting relationship between the parties, such as a contract, that is closely connected with the tort/delict in question.

Article 5
Product liability

1. Without prejudice to Article 4(2), the law applicable to a non-contractual obligation arising out of damage caused by a product shall be:

(a)   the law of the country in which the person sustaining the damage had his or her habitual residence when the damage occurred, if the product was marketed in that country; or, failing that,
(b)   the law of the country in which the product was acquired, if the product was marketed in that country; or, failing that,

(c) the law of the country in which the damage occurred, if the product was marketed in that country. However, the law applicable shall be the law of the country in which the person claimed to be liable is habitually resident if he or she could not reasonably foresee the marketing of the product, or a product of the same type, in the country the law of which is applicable under (a), (b) or (c).

2. Where it is clear from all the circumstances of the case that the tort/delict is manifestly more closely connected with a country other than that indicated in paragraph 1, the law of that other country shall apply. A manifestly closer connection with another country might be based in particular on a pre-existing relationship between the parties, such as a contract, that is closely connected with the tort/delict in question.

Article 6

Unfair competition and acts restricting free competition

1. The law applicable to a non-contractual obligation arising out of an act of unfair competition shall be the law of the country where competitive relations or the collective interests of consumers are, or are likely to be, affected.

2. Where an act of unfair competition affects exclusively the interests of a specific competitor, Article 4 shall apply.

3.(a) The law applicable to a non-contractual obligation arising out of a restriction of competition shall be the law of the country where the market is, or is likely to be, affected.

(b) When the market is, or is likely to be, affected in more than one country, the person seeking compensation for damage who sues in the court of the domicile of the defendant, may instead choose to base his or her claim on the law of the court seised, provided that the market in that Member State is amongst those directly and substantially affected by the restriction of competition out of which the non-contractual obligation on which the claim is based arises; where the claimant sues, in accordance with the applicable rules on jurisdiction, more than one defendant in that court, he or she can only choose to base his or her claim on the law of that court if the restriction of competition on which the claim against each of these defendants relies directly and substantially affects also the market in the Member State of that court.

4. The law applicable under this Article may not be derogated from by an agreement pursuant to Article 14.

Article 7

Environmental damage

The law applicable to a non-contractual obligation arising out of environmental damage or damage sustained by persons or property as a result of such damage shall be the law determined pursuant to Article 4(1), unless the person seeking compensation for damage chooses to base his or her claim on the law of the country in which the event giving rise to the damage occurred.

Article 8

Infringement of intellectual property rights

1. The law applicable to a non-contractual obligation arising from an infringement of an intellectual property right shall be the law of the country for which protection is claimed.

2. In the case of a non-contractual obligation arising from an infringement of a unitary Community intellectual property right, the law applicable shall, for any question that is not governed by the relevant Community instrument, be the law of the country in which the act of infringement was committed.

3. The law applicable under this Article may not be derogated from by an agreement pursuant to Article 14.

Article 9

Industrial action

Without prejudice to Article 4(2), the law applicable to a noncontractual obligation in respect of the liability of a person in the capacity of a worker or an employer or the organisations representing their professional interests for damages caused by an industrial action, pending or carried out, shall be the law of the country where the action is to be, or has been, taken.

CHAPTER III

UNJUST ENRICHMENT, *NEGOTIORUM GESTIO* AND *CULPA IN CONTRAHENDO*

Article 10

Unjust enrichment

1. If a non-contractual obligation arising out of unjust enrichment, including payment of amounts wrongly received, concerns a relationship existing between the parties, such as one arising out of a contract or a tort/delict, that is closely connected with that unjust enrichment, it shall be governed by the law that governs that relationship.

2. Where the law applicable cannot be determined on the basis of paragraph 1 and the parties have their habitual residence in the same country when the event giving rise to unjust enrichment occurs, the law of that country shall apply.

3. Where the law applicable cannot be determined on the basis of paragraphs 1 or 2, it shall be the law of the country in which the unjust enrichment took place.

4. Where it is clear from all the circumstances of the case that the non-contractual obligation arising out of unjust enrichment is manifestly more closely connected with a country other than that indicated in paragraphs 1, 2 and 3, the law of that other country shall apply.

Article 11
Negotiorum gestio

1. If a non-contractual obligation arising out of an act performed without due authority in connection with the affairs of another person concerns a relationship existing between the parties, such as one arising out of a contract or a tort/delict, that is closely connected with that non-contractual obligation, it shall be governed by the law that governs that relationship.

2. Where the law applicable cannot be determined on the basis of paragraph 1, and the parties have their habitual residence in the same country when the event giving rise to the damage occurs, the law of that country shall apply.

3. Where the law applicable cannot be determined on the basis of paragraphs 1 or 2, it shall be the law of the country in which the act was performed.

4. Where it is clear from all the circumstances of the case that the non-contractual obligation arising out of an act performed without due authority in connection with the affairs of another person is manifestly more closely connected with a country other than that indicated in paragraphs 1, 2 and 3, the law of that other country shall apply.

Article 12
Culpa in contrahendo

1. The law applicable to a non-contractual obligation arising out of dealings prior to the conclusion of a contract, regardless of whether the contract was actually concluded or not, shall be the law that applies to the contract or that would have been applicable to it had it been entered into.

2. Where the law applicable cannot be determined on the basis of paragraph 1, it shall be:

(a) the law of the country in which the damage occurs, irrespective of the country in which the event giving rise to the damage occurred and irrespective of the country or countries in which the indirect consequences of that event occurred; or

(b) where the parties have their habitual residence in the same country at the time when the event giving rise to the damage occurs, the law of that country; or

(c) where it is clear from all the circumstances of the case that the non-contractual obligation arising out of dealings prior to the conclusion of a contract is manifestly more closely connected with a country other than that indicated in points (a) and (b), the law of that other country.

Article 13
Applicability of Article 8

For the purposes of this Chapter, Article 8 shall apply to noncontractual obligations arising from an infringement of an intellectual property right.

CHAPTER IV
FREEDOM OF CHOICE

Article 14

Freedom of choice

1. The parties may agree to submit non-contractual obligations to the law of their choice:

(a) by an agreement entered into after the event giving rise to the damage occurred; or
(b) where all the parties are pursuing a commercial activity, also by an agreement freely negotiated before the event giving rise to the damage occurred. The choice shall be expressed or demonstrated with reasonable certainty by the circumstances of the case and shall not prejudice the rights of third parties.

2. Where all the elements relevant to the situation at the time when the event giving rise to the damage occurs are located in a country other than the country whose law has been chosen, the choice of the parties shall not prejudice the application of provisions of the law of that other country which cannot be derogated from by agreement.

3. Where all the elements relevant to the situation at the time when the event giving rise to the damage occurs are located in one or more of the Member States, the parties' choice of the law applicable other than that of a Member State shall not prejudice the application of provisions of Community law, where appropriate as implemented in the Member State of the forum, which cannot be derogated from by agreement.

CHAPTER V
COMMON RULES

Article 15

Scope of the law applicable

The law applicable to non-contractual obligations under this Regulation shall govern in particular:

(a) the basis and extent of liability, including the determination of persons who may be held liable for acts performed by them;
(b) the grounds for exemption from liability, any limitation of liability and any division of liability;
(c) the existence, the nature and the assessment of damage or the remedy claimed;
(d) within the limits of powers conferred on the court by its procedural law, the measures which a court may take to prevent or terminate injury or damage or to ensure the provision of compensation;
(e) the question whether a right to claim damages or a remedy may be transferred, including by inheritance;

(f)   persons entitled to compensation for damage sustained personally;
(g)   liability for the acts of another person;
(h)   the manner in which an obligation may be extinguished and rules of prescription and limitation, including rules relating to the commencement, interruption and suspension of a period of prescription or limitation.

Article 16

Overriding mandatory provisions8

Nothing in this Regulation shall restrict the application of the provisions of the law of the forum in a situation where they are mandatory irrespective of the law otherwise applicable to the non-contractual obligation.

Article 17

Rules of safety and conduct

In assessing the conduct of the person claimed to be liable, account shall be taken, as a matter of fact and in so far as is appropriate, of the rules of safety and conduct which were in force at the place and time of the event giving rise to the liability.

Article 18

Direct action against the insurer of the person liable

The person having suffered damage may bring his or her claim directly against the insurer of the person liable to provide compensation if the law applicable to the non-contractual obligation or the law applicable to the insurance contract so provides.

Article 19

Subrogation

Where a person (the creditor) has a non-contractual claim upon another (the debtor), and a third person has a duty to satisfy the creditor, or has in fact satisfied the creditor in discharge of that duty, the law which governs the third person's duty to satisfy the creditor shall determine whether, and the extent to which, the third person is entitled to exercise against the debtor the rights which the creditor had against the debtor under the law governing their relationship.

Article 20

Multiple liability

If a creditor has a claim against several debtors who are liable for the same claim, and one of the debtors has already satisfied the claim in whole or in part, the question of that debtor's right to demand compensation from the other debtors shall be governed by the law applicable to that debtor's non-contractual obligation towards the creditor.

Article 21

Formal validity

A unilateral act intended to have legal effect and relating to a non-contractual obligation shall be formally valid if it satisfies the formal requirements of the law governing the noncontractual obligation in question or the law of the country in which the act is performed.

Article 22

Burden of proof

1. The law governing a non-contractual obligation under this Regulation shall apply to the extent that, in matters of noncontractual obligations, it contains rules which raise presumptions of law or determine the burden of proof.

2. Acts intended to have legal effect may be proved by any mode of proof recognised by the law of the forum or by any of the laws referred to in Article 21 under which that act is formally valid, provided that such mode of proof can be administered by the forum.

CHAPTER VI

OTHER PROVISIONS

Article 23

Habitual residence

1. For the purposes of this Regulation, the habitual residence of companies and other bodies, corporate or unincorporated, shall be the place of central administration. Where the event giving rise to the damage occurs, or the damage arises, in the course of operation of a branch, agency or any other establishment, the place where the branch, agency or any other establishment is located shall be treated as the place of habitual residence.

2. For the purposes of this Regulation, the habitual residence of a natural person acting in the course of his or her business activity shall be his or her principal place of business.

Article 24

Exclusion of renvoi

The application of the law of any country specified by this Regulation means the application of the rules of law in force in that country other than its rules of private international law.

Article 25

States with more than one legal system

1. Where a State comprises several territorial units, each of which has its own rules of law in respect of non-contractual obligations, each territorial unit shall be considered as a country for the purposes of identifying the law applicable under this Regulation.

2. A Member State within which different territorial units have their own rules of law in respect of non-contractual obligations shall not be required to apply this Regulation to conflicts solely between the laws of such units.

Article 26

Public policy of the forum

The application of a provision of the law of any country specified by this Regulation may be refused only if such application is manifestly incompatible with the public policy (*ordre public*) of the forum.

Article 27

Relationship with other provisions of Community law

This Regulation shall not prejudice the application of provisions of Community law which, in relation to particular matters, lay down conflict-of-law rules relating to non-contractual obligations.

Article 28

Relationship with existing international conventions

1. This Regulation shall not prejudice the application of international conventions to which one or more Member States are parties at the time when this Regulation is adopted and which lay down conflict-of-law rules relating to non-contractual obligations.

2. However, this Regulation shall, as between Member States, take precedence over conventions concluded exclusively between two or more of them in so far as such conventions concern matters governed by this Regulation.

CHAPTER VII
FINAL PROVISIONS

Article 29

List of conventions

1. By 11 July 2008, Member States shall notify the Commission of the conventions referred to in Article 28(1). After that date, Member States shall notify the Commission of all denunciations of such conventions.

2. The Commission shall publish in the *Official Journal of the European Union* within six months of receipt:

(i)   a list of the conventions referred to in paragraph 1;
(ii)   the denunciations referred to in paragraph 1.

Article 30

Review clause

1. Not later than 20 August 2011, the Commission shall submit to the European Parliament, the Council and the European Economic and Social Committee a report on the application of this Regulation. If necessary, the report shall be accompanied by proposals to adapt this Regulation. The report shall include:

(i)   a study on the effects of the way in which foreign law is treated in the different jurisdictions and on the extent to which courts in the Member States apply foreign law in practice pursuant to this Regulation;
(ii)   a study on the effects of Article 28 of this Regulation with respect to the Hague Convention of 4 May 1971 on the law applicable to traffic accidents.

2. Not later than 31 December 2008, the Commission shall submit to the European Parliament, the Council and the European Economic and Social Committee a study on the situation in the field of the law applicable to non-contractual obligations arising out of violations of privacy and rights relating to personality, taking into account rules relating to freedom of the press and freedom of expression in the media, and conflict-of-law issues related to Directive 95/46/EC of the European Parliament and of the Council of 24 October 1995 on the protection of individuals with regard to the processing of personal data and on the free movement of such data.[7]

Article 31

Application in time

This Regulation shall apply to events giving rise to damage which occur after its entry into force.

Article 32

Date of application

---

[7]   OJ L 281, 23.11.1995, p 31.

This Regulation shall apply from 11 January 2009, except for Article 29, which shall apply from 11 July 2008.

This Regulation shall be binding in its entirety and directly applicable in the Member States in accordance with the Treaty establishing the European Community.

Done at Strasbourg, 11 July 2007.

<table>
<tr><td align="center">*For the European Parliament*</td><td align="center">*For the Council*</td></tr>
<tr><td align="center">*The President*</td><td align="center">*The President*</td></tr>
<tr><td align="center">H.-G. PÖTTERING</td><td align="center">M. LOBO ANTUNES</td></tr>
</table>

Commission Statement on the review clause (Article 30)

The Commission, following the invitation by the European Parliament and the Council in the frame of Article 30 of the 'Rome II' Regulation, will submit, not later than December 2008, a study on the situation in the field of the law applicable to non-contractual obligations arising out of violations of privacy and rights relating to personality. The Commission will take into consideration all aspects of the situation and take appropriate measures if necessary.

Commission Statement on road accidents

The Commission, being aware of the different practices followed in the Member States as regards the level of compensation awarded to victims of road traffic accidents, is prepared to examine the specific problems resulting for EU residents involved in road traffic accidents in a Member State other than the Member State of their habitual residence. To that end the Commission will make available to the European Parliament and to the Council, before the end of 2008, a study on all options, including insurance aspects, for improving the position of cross-border victims, which would pave the way for a Green Paper.

Commission Statement on the treatment of foreign law

The Commission, being aware of the different practices followed in the Member States as regards the treatment of foreign law, will publish at the latest four years after the entry into force of the 'Rome II' Regulation and in any event as soon as it is available a horizontal study on the application of foreign law in civil and commercial matters by the courts of the Member States, having regard to the aims of the Hague Programme. It is also prepared to take appropriate measures if necessary.

APPENDIX 4

EC REGULATION 593/2008 ('ROME I')

REGULATION (EC) No 593/2008 OF THE EUROPEAN PARLIAMENT AND OF THE COUNCIL

of 17 June 2008

on the law applicable to contractual obligations (Rome I)

THE EUROPEAN PARLIAMENT AND THE COUNCIL OF THE EUROPEAN UNION,

Having regard to the Treaty establishing the European Community, and in particular Article 61(c) and the second indent of Article 67(5) thereof,

Having regard to the proposal from the Commission,

Having regard to the opinion of the European Economic and

Social Committee (¹),

Acting in accordance with the procedure laid down in Article 251 of the Treaty (²),

Whereas:

(1) The Community has set itself the objective of maintaining and developing an area of freedom, security and justice. For the progressive establishment of such an area, the Community is to adopt measures relating to judicial cooperation in civil matters with a cross-border impact to the extent necessary for the proper functioning of the internal market.

(2) According to Article 65, point (b) of the Treaty, these measures are to include those promoting the compatibility of the rules applicable in the Member States concerning the conflict of laws and of jurisdiction.

(3) The European Council meeting in Tampere on 15 and 16 October 1999 endorsed the principle of mutual recognition of judgments and other decisions of judicial authorities as the cornerstone of judicial cooperation in civil matters and invited the Council and the Commission to adopt a programme of measures to implement that principle.

---

¹ OJ C 318, 23.12.2006, p. 56.
² Opinion of the European Parliament of 29 November 2007 (not yet published in the Official Journal) and Council Decision of 5 June 2008.

(4) On 30 November 2000 the Council adopted a joint Commission and Council programme of measures for implementation of the principle of mutual recognition of decisions in civil and commercial matters (³). The programme identifies measures relating to the harmonisation of conflict-of-law rules as those facilitating the mutual recognition of judgments.

(5) The Hague Programme (⁴), adopted by the European Council on 5 November 2004, called for work to be pursued actively on the conflict-of-law rules regarding contractual obligations (Rome I).

(6) The proper functioning of the internal market creates a need, in order to improve the predictability of the outcome of litigation, certainty as to the law applicable and the free movement of judgments, for the conflict-of-law rules in the Member States to designate the same national law irrespective of the country of the court in which an action is brought.

(7) The substantive scope and the provisions of this Regulation should be consistent with Council Regulation (EC) No 44/ 2001 of 22 December 2000 on jurisdiction and the recognition and enforcement of judgments in civil and commercial matters (⁵) (Brussels I) and Regulation (EC) No 864/2007 of the European Parliament and of the Council of 11 July 2007 on the law applicable to non-contractual obligations (Rome II) (⁶).

(8) Family relationships should cover parentage, marriage, affinity and collateral relatives. The reference in Article 1(2) to relationships having comparable effects to marriage and other family relationships should be interpreted in accordance with the law of the Member State in which the court is seised.

(9) Obligations under bills of exchange, cheques and promissory notes and other negotiable instruments should also cover bills of lading to the extent that the obligations under the bill of lading arise out of its negotiable character.

(10) Obligations arising out of dealings prior to the conclusion of the contract are covered by Article 12 of Regulation (EC) No 864/2007. Such obligations should therefore be excluded from the scope of this Regulation.

(11) The parties' freedom to choose the applicable law should be one of the cornerstones of the system of conflict-of-law rules in matters of contractual obligations.

(12) An agreement between the parties to confer on one or more courts or tribunals of a Member State exclusive jurisdiction to determine disputes under the contract should be one of the factors to be taken into account in determining whether a choice of law has been clearly demonstrated.

---

³　　OJ C 12, 15.1.2001, p. 1.
⁴　　OJ C 53, 3.3.2005, p. 1.
⁵　　OJ L 12, 16.1.2001, p. 1. Regulation as last amended by Regulation (EC) No 1791/2006 (OJ L 363, 20.12.2006, p. 1).
⁶　　OJ L 199, 31.7.2007, p. 40.

(13) This Regulation does not preclude parties from incorporating by reference into their contract a non-State body of law or an international convention.

(14) Should the Community adopt, in an appropriate legal instrument, rules of substantive contract law, including standard terms and conditions, such instrument may provide that the parties may choose to apply those rules.

(15) Where a choice of law is made and all other elements relevant to the situation are located in a country other than the country whose law has been chosen, the choice of law should not prejudice the application of provisions of the law of that country which cannot be derogated from by agreement. This rule should apply whether or not the choice of law was accompanied by a choice of court or tribunal. Whereas no substantial change is intended as compared with Article 3(3) of the 1980 Convention on the Law Applicable to Contractual Obligations (7) (the Rome Convention), the wording of this Regulation is aligned as far as possible with Article 14 of Regulation (EC) No 864/2007.

(16) To contribute to the general objective of this Regulation, legal certainty in the European judicial area, the conflict-of-law rules should be highly foreseeable. The courts should, however, retain a degree of discretion to determine the law that is most closely connected to the situation.

(17) As far as the applicable law in the absence of choice is concerned, the concept of 'provision of services' and 'sale of goods' should be interpreted in the same way as when applying Article 5 of Regulation (EC) No 44/2001 in so far as sale of goods and provision of services are covered by that Regulation. Although franchise and distribution contracts are contracts for services, they are the subject of specific rules.

(18) As far as the applicable law in the absence of choice is concerned, multilateral systems should be those in which trading is conducted, such as regulated markets and multilateral trading facilities as referred to in Article 4 of Directive 2004/39/EC of the European Parliament and of the Council of 21 April 2004 on markets in financial instruments (8), regardless of whether or not they rely on a central counterparty.

(19) Where there has been no choice of law, the applicable law should be determined in accordance with the rule specified for the particular type of contract. Where the contract cannot be categorised as being one of the specified types or where its elements fall within more than one of the specified types, it should be governed by the law of the country where the party required to effect the characteristic performance of the contract has his habitual residence. In the case of a contract consisting of a bundle of rights and obligations capable of being categorised as falling within more than one of the specified types of contract, the characteristic performance of the contract should be determined having regard to its centre of gravity.

---

7   OJ C 334, 30.12.2005, p. 1.
8   OJ L 145, 30.4.2004, p. 1. Directive as last amended by Directive 2008/10/EC (OJ L 76, 19.3.2008, p. 33).

(20) Where the contract is manifestly more closely connected with a country other than that indicated in Article 4(1) or (2), an escape clause should provide that the law of that other country is to apply. In order to determine that country, account should be taken, inter alia, of whether the contract in question has a very close relationship with another contract or contracts.

(21) In the absence of choice, where the applicable law cannot be determined either on the basis of the fact that the contract can be categorised as one of the specified types or as being the law of the country of habitual residence of the party required to effect the characteristic performance of the contract, the contract should be governed by the law of the country with which it is most closely connected. In order to determine that country, account should be taken, inter alia, of whether the contract in question has a very close relationship with another contract or contracts.

(22) As regards the interpretation of contracts for the carriage of goods, no change in substance is intended with respect to Article 4(4), third sentence, of the Rome Convention. Consequently, single-voyage charter parties and other contracts the main purpose of which is the carriage of goods should be treated as contracts for the carriage of goods. For the purposes of this Regulation, the term 'consignor' should refer to any person who enters into a contract of carriage with the carrier and the term 'the carrier' should refer to the party to the contract who undertakes to carry the goods, whether or not he performs the carriage himself.

(23) As regards contracts concluded with parties regarded as being weaker, those parties should be protected by conflict-of-law rules that are more favourable to their interests than the general rules.

(24) With more specific reference to consumer contracts, the conflict-of-law rule should make it possible to cut the cost of settling disputes concerning what are commonly relatively small claims and to take account of the development of distance-selling techniques. Consistency with Regulation (EC) No 44/2001 requires both that there be a reference to the concept of directed activity as a condition for applying the consumer protection rule and that the concept be interpreted harmoniously in Regulation (EC) No 44/2001 and this Regulation, bearing in mind that a joint declaration by the Council and the Commission on Article 15 of Regulation (EC) No 44/2001 states that 'for Article 15(1)(c) to be applicable it is not sufficient for an undertaking to target its activities at the Member State of the consumer's residence, or at a number of Member States including that Member State; a contract must also be concluded within the framework of its activities'. The declaration also states that 'the mere fact that an Internet site is accessible is not sufficient for Article 15 to be applicable, although a factor will be that this Internet site solicits the conclusion of distance contracts and that a contract has actually been concluded at a distance, by whatever means. In this respect, the language or currency which a website uses does not constitute a relevant factor.'

(25) Consumers should be protected by such rules of the country of their habitual residence that cannot be derogated from by agreement, provided that the consumer contract has been concluded as a result of the professional pursuing his commercial or professional activities in that particular country. The same protection should be guaranteed if the professional, while not pursuing his

commercial or professional activities in the country where the consumer has his habitual residence, directs his activities by any means to that country or to several countries, including that country, and the contract is concluded as a result of such activities.

(26) For the purposes of this Regulation, financial services such as investment services and activities and ancillary services provided by a professional to a consumer, as referred to in sections A and B of Annex I to Directive 2004/39/EC, and contracts for the sale of units in collective investment undertakings, whether or not covered by Council Directive 85/611/EEC of 20 December 1985 on the coordination of laws, regulations and administrative provisions relating to undertakings for collective investment in transferable securities (UCITS) (⁹), should be subject to Article 6 of this Regulation. Consequently, when a reference is made to terms and conditions governing the issuance or offer to the public of transferable securities or to the subscription and redemption of units in collective investment undertakings, that reference should include all aspects binding the issuer or the offeror to the consumer, but should not include those aspects involving the provision of financial services.

(27) Various exceptions should be made to the general conflict-of-law rule for consumer contracts. Under one such exception the general rule should not apply to contracts relating to rights in rem in immovable property or tenancies of such property unless the contract relates to the right to use immovable property on a timeshare basis within the meaning of Directive 94/47/EC of the European Parliament and of the Council of 26 October 1994 on the protection of purchasers in respect of certain aspects of contracts relating to the purchase of the right to use immovable properties on a timeshare basis (¹⁰).

(28) It is important to ensure that rights and obligations which constitute a financial instrument are not covered by the general rule applicable to consumer contracts, as that could lead to different laws being applicable to each of the instruments issued, therefore changing their nature and preventing their fungible trading and offering. Likewise, whenever such instruments are issued or offered, the contractual relationship established between the issuer or the offeror and the consumer should not necessarily be subject to the mandatory application of the law of the country of habitual residence of the consumer, as there is a need to ensure uniformity in the terms and conditions of an issuance or an offer. The same rationale should apply with regard to the multilateral systems covered by Article 4(1)(h), in respect of which it should be ensured that the law of the country of habitual residence of the consumer will not interfere with the rules applicable to contracts concluded within those systems or with the operator of such systems.

(29) For the purposes of this Regulation, references to rights and obligations constituting the terms and conditions governing the issuance, offers to the public or public take-over bids of transferable securities and references to the subscription and redemption of units in collective investment undertakings should include the terms governing, inter alia, the allocation of securities or units, rights in the event of over-subscription, withdrawal rights and similar matters in the context of the offer as well as those matters referred to in Articles 10, 11, 12 and

---

⁹   OJ L 375, 31.12.1985, p. 3. Directive as last amended by Directive 2008/18/EC of the European Parliament and of the Council (OJ L 76, 19.3.2008, p. 42).

¹⁰   OJ L 280, 29.10.1994, p. 83.

13, thus ensuring that all relevant contractual aspects of an offer binding the issuer or the offeror to the consumer are governed by a single law.

(30) For the purposes of this Regulation, financial instruments and transferable securities are those instruments referred to in Article 4 of Directive 2004/39/EC.

(31) Nothing in this Regulation should prejudice the operation of a formal arrangement designated as a system under Article 2(a) of Directive 98/26/EC of the European Parliament and of the Council of 19 May 1998 on settlement finality in payment and securities settlement systems ([11]).

(32) Owing to the particular nature of contracts of carriage and insurance contracts, specific provisions should ensure an adequate level of protection of passengers and policy holders. Therefore, Article 6 should not apply in the context of those particular contracts.

(33) Where an insurance contract not covering a large risk covers more than one risk, at least one of which is situated in a Member State and at least one of which is situated in a third country, the special rules on insurance contracts in this Regulation should apply only to the risk or risks situated in the relevant Member State or Member States.

(34) The rule on individual employment contracts should not prejudice the application of the overriding mandatory provisions of the country to which a worker is posted in accordance with Directive 96/71/EC of the European Parliament and of the Council of 16 December 1996 concerning the posting of workers in the framework of the provision of services ([12]).

(35) Employees should not be deprived of the protection afforded to them by provisions which cannot be derogated from by agreement or which can only be derogated from to their benefit.

(36) As regards individual employment contracts, work carried out in another country should be regarded as temporary if the employee is expected to resume working in the country of origin after carrying out his tasks abroad. The conclusion of a new contract of employment with the original employer or an employer belonging to the same group of companies as the original employer should not preclude the employee from being regarded as carrying out his work in another country temporarily.

(37) Considerations of public interest justify giving the courts of the Member States the possibility, in exceptional circumstances, of applying exceptions based on public policy and overriding mandatory provisions. The concept of 'overriding mandatory provisions' should be distinguished from the expression 'provisions which cannot be derogated from by agreement' and should be construed more restrictively.

---

[11]   OJ L 166, 11.6.1998, p. 45.
[12]   OJ L 18, 21.1.1997, p. 1.

(38) In the context of voluntary assignment, the term 'relationship' should make it clear that Article 14(1) also applies to the property aspects of an assignment, as between assignor and assignee, in legal orders where such aspects are treated separately from the aspects under the law of obligations. However, the term 'relationship' should not be understood as relating to any relationship that may exist between assignor and assignee. In particular, it should not cover preliminary questions as regards a voluntary assignment or a contractual subrogation. The term should be strictly limited to the aspects which are directly relevant to the voluntary assignment or contractual subrogation in question.

(39) For the sake of legal certainty there should be a clear definition of habitual residence, in particular for companies and other bodies, corporate or unincorporated. Unlike Article 60(1) of Regulation (EC) No 44/2001, which establishes three criteria, the conflict-of-law rule should proceed on the basis of a single criterion; otherwise, the parties would be unable to foresee the law applicable to their situation.

(40) A situation where conflict-of-law rules are dispersed among several instruments and where there are differences between those rules should be avoided. This Regulation, however, should not exclude the possibility of inclusion of conflict-of-law rules relating to contractual obligations in provisions of Community law with regard to particular matters.

This Regulation should not prejudice the application of other instruments laying down provisions designed to contribute to the proper functioning of the internal market application of provisions of the applicable law designated by the rules of this Regulation should not restrict the free movement of goods and services as regulated by Community instruments, such as Directive 2000/31/EC of the European Parliament and of the Council of 8 June 2000 on certain legal aspects of information society services, in particular electronic commerce, in the Internal Market (Directive on electronic commerce) ([13]).

(41) Respect for international commitments entered into by the Member States means that this Regulation should not affect international conventions to which one or more Member States are parties at the time when this Regulation is adopted. To make the rules more accessible, the Commission should publish the list of the relevant conventions in the Official Journal of the European Union on the basis of information supplied by the Member States.

(42) The Commission will make a proposal to the European Parliament and to the Council concerning the procedures and conditions according to which Member States would be entitled to negotiate and conclude, on their own behalf, agreements with third countries in individual and exceptional cases, concerning sectoral matters and containing provisions on the law applicable to contractual obligations.

(43) Since the objective of this Regulation cannot be sufficiently achieved by the Member States and can therefore, by reason of the scale and effects of this Regulation, be better achieved at Community level, the Community may adopt measures, in accordance with the principle of subsidiarity as set out in Article 5 of

---

[13]   OJ L 178, 17.7.2000, p. 1.

the Treaty. In accordance with the principle of proportionality, as set out in that Article, this Regulation does not go beyond what is necessary to attain its objective.

(44) In accordance with Article 3 of the Protocol on the position of the United Kingdom and Ireland, annexed to the Treaty on European Union and to the Treaty establishing the European Community, Ireland has notified its wish to take part in the adoption and application of the present Regulation.

(45) In accordance with Articles 1 and 2 of the Protocol on the position of the United Kingdom and Ireland, annexed to the Treaty on European Union and to the Treaty establishing the European Community, and without prejudice to Article 4 of the said Protocol, the United Kingdom is not taking part in the adoption of this Regulation and is not bound by it or subject to its application.

(46) In accordance with Articles 1 and 2 of the Protocol on the position of Denmark, annexed to the Treaty on European Union and to the Treaty establishing the European Community, Denmark is not taking part in the adoption of this Regulation and is not bound by it or subject to its application,

HAVE ADOPTED THIS REGULATION:

CHAPTER I
SCOPE

Article 1
Material scope

1. This Regulation shall apply, in situations involving a conflict of laws, to contractual obligations in civil and commercial matters.

It shall not apply, in particular, to revenue, customs or administrative matters.

2. The following shall be excluded from the scope of this Regulation:

(a) questions involving the status or legal capacity of natural persons, without prejudice to Article 13;
(b) obligations arising out of family relationships and relationships deemed by the law applicable to such relationships to have comparable effects, including maintenance obligations;
(c) obligations arising out of matrimonial property regimes, property regimes of relationships deemed by the law applicable to such relationships to have comparable effects to marriage, and wills and succession;
(d) obligations arising under bills of exchange, cheques and promissory notes and other negotiable instruments to the extent that the obligations under such other negotiable instruments arise out of their negotiable character;
(e) arbitration agreements and agreements on the choice of court;
(f) questions governed by the law of companies and other bodies, corporate or unincorporated, such as the creation, by registration or otherwise, legal capacity, internal organisation or winding-up of companies and other

bodies, corporate or unincorporated, and the personal liability of officers and members as such for the obligations of the company or body;

(g) the question whether an agent is able to bind a principal, or an organ to bind a company or other body corporate or unincorporated, in relation to a third party;

(h) the constitution of trusts and the relationship between settlors, trustees and beneficiaries;

(i) obligations arising out of dealings prior to the conclusion of a contract;

(j) insurance contracts arising out of operations carried out by organisations other than undertakings referred to in Article 2 of Directive 2002/83/EC of the European Parliament and of the Council of 5 November 2002 concerning life assurance ([14]) the object of which is to provide benefits for employed or self-employed persons belonging to an undertaking or group of undertakings, or to a trade or group of trades, in the event of death or survival or of discontinuance or curtailment of activity, or of sickness related to work or accidents at work.

3. This Regulation shall not apply to evidence and procedure, without prejudice to Article 18.

4. In this Regulation, the term 'Member State' shall mean Member States to which this Regulation applies. However, in Article 3(4) and Article 7 the term shall mean all the Member States.

Article 2

Universal application

Any law specified by this Regulation shall be applied whether or not it is the law of a Member State.

CHAPTER II

UNIFORM RULES

Article 3

Freedom of choice

1. A contract shall be governed by the law chosen by the parties. The choice shall be made expressly or clearly demonstrated by the terms of the contract or the circumstances of the case. By their choice the parties can select the law applicable to the whole or to part only of the contract.

2. The parties may at any time agree to subject the contract to a law other than that which previously governed it, whether as a result of an earlier choice made under this Article or of other provisions of this Regulation. Any change in the law to be applied that is made after the conclusion of the contract shall not prejudice its formal validity under Article 11 or adversely affect the rights of third parties.

---

[14] OJ L 345, 19.12.2002, p. 1. Directive as last amended by Directive 2008/19/EC (OJ L 76, 19.3.2008, p. 44).

3. Where all other elements relevant to the situation at the time of the choice are located in a country other than the country whose law has been chosen, the choice of the parties shall not prejudice the application of provisions of the law of that other country which cannot be derogated from by agreement.

4. Where all other elements relevant to the situation at the time of the choice are located in one or more Member States, the parties' choice of applicable law other than that of a Member State shall not prejudice the application of provisions of Community law, where appropriate as implemented in the Member State of the forum, which cannot be derogated from by agreement.

5. The existence and validity of the consent of the parties as to the choice of the applicable law shall be determined in accordance with the provisions of Articles 10, 11 and 13.

Article 4

Applicable law in the absence of choice

1. To the extent that the law applicable to the contract has not been chosen in accordance with Article 3 and without prejudice to Articles 5 to 8, the law governing the contract shall be determined as follows:

(a) a contract for the sale of goods shall be governed by the law of the country where the seller has his habitual residence;

(b) a contract for the provision of services shall be governed by the law of the country where the service provider has his habitual residence;

(c) a contract relating to a right in rem in immovable property or to a tenancy of immovable property shall be governed by the law of the country where the property is situated;

(d) notwithstanding point (c), a tenancy of immovable property concluded for temporary private use for a period of no more than six consecutive months shall be governed by the law of the country where the landlord has his habitual residence, provided that the tenant is a natural person and has his habitual residence in the same country;

(e) a franchise contract shall be governed by the law of the country where the franchisee has his habitual residence;

(f) a distribution contract shall be governed by the law of the country where the distributor has his habitual residence;

(g) a contract for the sale of goods by auction shall be governed by the law of the country where the auction takes place, if such a place can be determined;

(h) a contract concluded within a multilateral system which brings together or facilitates the bringing together of multiple third-party buying and selling interests in financial instruments, as defined by Article 4(1), point (17) of Directive 2004/39/EC, in accordance with non-discretionary rules and governed by a single law, shall be governed by that law.

2. Where the contract is not covered by paragraph 1 or where the elements of the contract would be covered by more than one of points (a) to (h) of paragraph 1, the contract shall be governed by the law of the country where the party required to effect the characteristic performance of the contract has his habitual residence.

3. Where it is clear from all the circumstances of the case that the contract is manifestly more closely connected with a country other than that indicated in paragraphs 1 or 2, the law of that other country shall apply.

4. Where the law applicable cannot be determined pursuant to paragraphs 1 or 2, the contract shall be governed by the law of the country with which it is most closely connected.

Article 5

Contracts of carriage

1. To the extent that the law applicable to a contract for the carriage of goods has not been chosen in accordance with Article 3, the law applicable shall be the law of the country of habitual residence of the carrier, provided that the place of receipt or the place of delivery or the habitual residence of the consignor is also situated in that country. If those requirements are not met, the law of the country where the place of delivery as agreed by the parties is situated shall apply.

2. To the extent that the law applicable to a contract for the carriage of passengers has not been chosen by the parties in accordance with the second subparagraph, the law applicable shall be the law of the country where the passenger has his habitual residence, provided that either the place of departure or the place of destination is situated in that country. If these requirements are not met, the law of the country where the carrier has his habitual residence shall apply.

The parties may choose as the law applicable to a contract for the carriage of passengers in accordance with Article 3 only the law of the country where:

(a)   the passenger has his habitual residence; or
(b)   the carrier has his habitual residence; or
(c)   the carrier has his place of central administration; or
(d)   the place of departure is situated; or
(e)   the place of destination is situated.

3. Where it is clear from all the circumstances of the case that the contract, in the absence of a choice of law, is manifestly more closely connected with a country other than that indicated in paragraphs 1 or 2, the law of that other country shall apply.

Article 6

Consumer contracts

1. Without prejudice to Articles 5 and 7, a contract concluded by a natural person for a purpose which can be regarded as being outside his trade or profession (the consumer) with another person acting in the exercise of his trade or profession (the professional) shall be governed by the law of the country where the consumer has his habitual residence, provided that the professional:

(a)   pursues his commercial or professional activities in the country where the consumer has his habitual residence, or
(b)   by any means, directs such activities to that country or to several countries including that country,

and the contract falls within the scope of such activities.

2. Notwithstanding paragraph 1, the parties may choose the law applicable to a contract which fulfils the requirements of paragraph 1, in accordance with Article 3. Such a choice may not, however, have the result of depriving the consumer of the protection afforded to him by provisions that cannot be derogated from by agreement by virtue of the law which, in the absence of choice, would have been applicable on the basis of paragraph 1.

3. If the requirements in points (a) or (b) of paragraph 1 are not fulfilled, the law applicable to a contract between a consumer and a professional shall be determined pursuant to Articles 3 and 4.

4. Paragraphs 1 and 2 shall not apply to:

(a)   a contract for the supply of services where the services are to be supplied to the consumer exclusively in a country other than that in which he has his habitual residence;

(b)   a contract of carriage other than a contract relating to package travel within the meaning of Council Directive 90/314/EEC of 13 June 1990 on package travel, package holidays and package tours ([15]);

(c)   a contract relating to a right in rem in immovable property or a tenancy of immovable property other than a contract relating to the right to use immovable properties on a timeshare basis within the meaning of Directive 94/47/EC;

(d)   rights and obligations which constitute a financial instrument and rights and obligations constituting the terms and conditions governing the issuance or offer to the public and public take-over bids of transferable securities, and the subscription and redemption of units in collective investment undertakings in so far as these activities do not constitute provision of a financial service;

(e)   a contract concluded within the type of system falling within the scope of Article 4(1)(h).

Article 7

Insurance contracts

1. This Article shall apply to contracts referred to in paragraph 2, whether or not the risk covered is situated in a Member State, and to all other insurance contracts covering risks situated inside the territory of the Member States. It shall not apply to reinsurance contracts.

2. An insurance contract covering a large risk as defined in Article 5(d) of the First Council Directive 73/239/EEC of 24 July 1973 on the coordination of laws, regulations and administrative provisions relating to the taking-up and pursuit of the business of direct insurance other than life assurance ([16]) shall be governed by the law chosen by the parties in accordance with Article 3 of this Regulation.

---

[15]   OJ L 158, 23.6.1990, p. 59.
[16]   OJ L 228, 16.8.1973, p. 3. Directive as last amended by Directive 2005/68/EC of the European Parliament and of the Council (OJ L 323, 9.12.2005, p. 1).

To the extent that the applicable law has not been chosen by the parties, the insurance contract shall be governed by the law of the country where the insurer has his habitual residence. Where it is clear from all the circumstances of the case that the contract is manifestly more closely connected with another country, the law of that other country shall apply.

3. In the case of an insurance contract other than a contract falling within paragraph 2, only the following laws may be chosen by the parties in accordance with Article 3:

(a)   the law of any Member State where the risk is situated at the time of conclusion of the contract;

(b)   the law of the country where the policy holder has his habitual residence;

(c)   in the case of life assurance, the law of the Member State of which the policy holder is a national;

(d)   for insurance contracts covering risks limited to events occurring in one Member State other than the Member State where the risk is situated, the law of that Member State;

(e)   where the policy holder of a contract falling under this paragraph pursues a commercial or industrial activity or a liberal profession and the insurance contract covers two or more risks which relate to those activities and are situated in different Member States, the law of any of the Member States concerned or the law of the country of habitual residence of the policy holder.

Where, in the cases set out in points (a), (b) or (e), the Member States referred to grant greater freedom of choice of the law applicable to the insurance contract, the parties may take advantage of that freedom.

To the extent that the law applicable has not been chosen by the parties in accordance with this paragraph, such a contract shall be governed by the law of the Member State in which the risk is situated at the time of conclusion of the contract.

4. The following additional rules shall apply to insurance contracts covering risks for which a Member State imposes an obligation to take out insurance:

(a)   the insurance contract shall not satisfy the obligation to take out insurance unless it complies with the specific provisions relating to that insurance laid down by the Member State that imposes the obligation. Where the law of the Member State in which the risk is situated and the law of the Member State imposing the obligation to take out insurance contradict each other, the latter shall prevail;

(b)   by way of derogation from paragraphs 2 and 3, a Member State may lay down that the insurance contract shall be governed by the law of the Member State that imposes the obligation to take out insurance.

5. For the purposes of paragraph 3, third subparagraph, and paragraph 4, where the contract covers risks situated in more than one Member State, the contract shall be considered as constituting several contracts each relating to only one Member State.

6. For the purposes of this Article, the country in which the risk is situated shall be determined in accordance with Article 2(d) of the Second Council Directive 88/357/EEC of 22 June 1988 on the coordination of laws, regulations and administrative provisions relating to direct insurance other than life assurance and laying down provisions to facilitate the effective exercise of freedom to provide services ([17]) and, in the case of life assurance, the country in which the risk is situated shall be the country of the commitment within the meaning of Article 1(1) (g) of Directive 2002/83/EC.

Article 8

Individual employment contracts

1. An individual employment contract shall be governed by the law chosen by the parties in accordance with Article 3. Such a choice of law may not, however, have the result of depriving the employee of the protection afforded to him by provisions that cannot be derogated from by agreement under the law that, in the absence of choice, would have been applicable pursuant to paragraphs 2, 3 and 4 of this Article.

2. To the extent that the law applicable to the individual employment contract has not been chosen by the parties, the contract shall be governed by the law of the country in which or, failing that, from which the employee habitually carries out his work in performance of the contract. The country where the work is habitually carried out shall not be deemed to have changed if he is temporarily employed in another country.

3. Where the law applicable cannot be determined pursuant to paragraph 2, the contract shall be governed by the law of the country where the place of business through which the employee was engaged is situated.

4. Where it appears from the circumstances as a whole that the contract is more closely connected with a country other than that indicated in paragraphs 2 or 3, the law of that other country shall apply.

Article 9

Overriding mandatory provisions

1. Overriding mandatory provisions are provisions the respect for which is regarded as crucial by a country for safeguarding its public interests, such as its political, social or economic organisation, to such an extent that they are applicable to any situation falling within their scope, irrespective of the law otherwise applicable to the contract under this Regulation.

2. Nothing in this Regulation shall restrict the application of the overriding mandatory provisions of the law of the forum.

3. Effect may be given to the overriding mandatory provisions of the law of the country where the obligations arising out of the contract have to be or have been

---

[17]   OJ L 172, 4.7.1988, p. 1. Directive as last amended by Directive 2005/14/EC of the European Parliament and of the Council (OJ L 149, 11.6.2005, p. 14).

performed, in so far as those overriding mandatory provisions render the performance of the contract unlawful. In considering whether to give effect to those provisions, regard shall be had to their nature and purpose and to the consequences of their application or non-application.

Article 10
Consent and material validity

1. The existence and validity of a contract, or of any term of a contract, shall be determined by the law which would govern it under this Regulation if the contract or term were valid.

2. Nevertheless, a party, in order to establish that he did not consent, may rely upon the law of the country in which he has his habitual residence if it appears from the circumstances that it would not be reasonable to determine the effect of his conduct in accordance with the law specified in paragraph 1.

Article 11

Formal validity

1. A contract concluded between persons who, or whose agents, are in the same country at the time of its conclusion is formally valid if it satisfies the formal requirements of the law which governs it in substance under this Regulation or of the law of the country where it is concluded.

2. A contract concluded between persons who, or whose agents, are in different countries at the time of its conclusion is formally valid if it satisfies the formal requirements of the law which governs it in substance under this Regulation, or of the law of either of the countries where either of the parties or their agent is present at the time of conclusion, or of the law of the country where either of the parties had his habitual residence at that time.

3. A unilateral act intended to have legal effect relating to an existing or contemplated contract is formally valid if it satisfies the formal requirements of the law which governs or would govern the contract in substance under this Regulation, or of the law of the country where the act was done, or of the law of the country where the person by whom it was done had his habitual residence at that time.

4. Paragraphs 1, 2 and 3 of this Article shall not apply to contracts that fall within the scope of Article 6. The form of such contracts shall be governed by the law of the country where the consumer has his habitual residence.

5. Notwithstanding paragraphs 1 to 4, a contract the subject matter of which is a right in rem in immovable property or a tenancy of immovable property shall be subject to the requirements of form of the law of the country where the property is situated if by that law:

(a)   those requirements are imposed irrespective of the country where the contract is concluded and irrespective of the law governing the contract; and

(b)   those requirements cannot be derogated from by agreement.

Article 12

Scope of the law applicable

1. The law applicable to a contract by virtue of this Regulation shall govern in particular:

(a)   interpretation;

(b)   performance;

(c)   within the limits of the powers conferred on the court by its procedural law, the consequences of a total or partial breach of obligations, including the assessment of damages in so far as it is governed by rules of law;

(d)   the various ways of extinguishing obligations, and prescription and limitation of actions;

(e)   the consequences of nullity of the contract.

2. In relation to the manner of performance and the steps to be taken in the event of defective performance, regard shall be had to the law of the country in which performance takes place.

Article 13

Incapacity

In a contract concluded between persons who are in the same country, a natural person who would have capacity under the law of that country may invoke his incapacity resulting from the law of another country, only if the other party to the contract was aware of that incapacity at the time of the conclusion of the contract or was not aware thereof as a result of negligence.

Article 14

Voluntary assignment and contractual subrogation

1. The relationship between assignor and assignee under a voluntary assignment or contractual subrogation of a claim against another person (the debtor) shall be governed by the law that applies to the contract between the assignor and assignee under this Regulation.

2. The law governing the assigned or subrogated claim shall determine its assignability, the relationship between the assignee and the debtor, the conditions under which the assignment or subrogation can be invoked against the debtor and whether the debtor's obligations have been discharged.

3. The concept of assignment in this Article includes outright transfers of claims, transfers of claims by way of security and pledges or other security rights over claims.

Article 15

Legal subrogation

Where a person (the creditor) has a contractual claim against another (the debtor) and a third person has a duty to satisfy the creditor, or has in fact satisfied the creditor in discharge of that duty, the law which governs the third person's duty to satisfy the creditor shall determine whether and to what extent the third person is entitled to exercise against the debtor the rights which the creditor had against the debtor under the law governing their relationship.

Article 16

Multiple liability

If a creditor has a claim against several debtors who are liable for the same claim, and one of the debtors has already satisfied the claim in whole or in part, the law governing the debtor's obligation towards the creditor also governs the debtor's right to claim recourse from the other debtors. The other debtors may rely on the defences they had against the creditor to the extent allowed by the law governing their obligations towards the creditor.

Article 17

Set-off

Where the right to set-off is not agreed by the parties, set-off shall be governed by the law applicable to the claim against which the right to set-off is asserted.

Article 18

Burden of proof

1. The law governing a contractual obligation under this Regulation shall apply to the extent that, in matters of contractual obligations, it contains rules which raise presumptions of law or determine the burden of proof.

2. A contract or an act intended to have legal effect may be proved by any mode of proof recognised by the law of the forum or by any of the laws referred to in Article 11 under which that contract or act is formally valid, provided that such mode of proof can be administered by the forum.

CHAPTER III

OTHER PROVISIONS

Article 19

Habitual residence

1. For the purposes of this Regulation, the habitual residence of companies and other bodies, corporate or unincorporated, shall be the place of central administration.

The habitual residence of a natural person acting in the course of his business activity shall be his principal place of business.

2. Where the contract is concluded in the course of the operations of a branch, agency or any other establishment, or if, under the contract, performance is the responsibility of such a branch, agency or establishment, the place where the branch, agency or any other establishment is located shall be treated as the place of habitual residence.

3. For the purposes of determining the habitual residence, the relevant point in time shall be the time of the conclusion of the contract.

Article 20

Exclusion of renvoi

The application of the law of any country specified by this Regulation means the application of the rules of law in force in that country other than its rules of private international law, unless provided otherwise in this Regulation.

Article 21

Public policy of the forum

The application of a provision of the law of any country specified by this Regulation may be refused only if such application is manifestly incompatible with the public policy (ordre public) of the forum.

Article 22

States with more than one legal system

1. Where a State comprises several territorial units, each of which has its own rules of law in respect of contractual obligations, each territorial unit shall be considered as a country for the purposes of identifying the law applicable under this Regulation.

2. A Member State where different territorial units have their own rules of law in respect of contractual obligations shall not be required to apply this Regulation to conflicts solely between the laws of such units.

Article 23

Relationship with other provisions of Community law

With the exception of Article 7, this Regulation shall not prejudice the application of provisions of Community law which, in relation to particular matters, lay down conflict-of-law rules relating to contractual obligations.

Article 24

Relationship with the Rome Convention

1. This Regulation shall replace the Rome Convention in the Member States, except as regards the territories of the Member States which fall within the territorial scope of that Convention and to which this Regulation does not apply pursuant to Article 299 of the Treaty.

2. In so far as this Regulation replaces the provisions of the Rome Convention, any reference to that Convention shall be understood as a reference to this Regulation.

Article 25

Relationship with existing international conventions

1. This Regulation shall not prejudice the application of international conventions to which one or more Member States are parties at the time when this Regulation is adopted and which lay down conflict-of-law rules relating to contractual obligations.

2. However, this Regulation shall, as between Member States, take precedence over conventions concluded exclusively between two or more of them in so far as such conventions concern matters governed by this Regulation.

Article 26

List of Conventions

1. By 17 June 2009, Member States shall notify the Commission of the conventions referred to in Article 25(1). After that date, Member States shall notify the Commission of all denunciations of such conventions.

2. Within six months of receipt of the notifications referred to in paragraph 1, the Commission shall publish in the Official Journal of the European Union:

(a)   a list of the conventions referred to in paragraph 1;
(b)   the denunciations referred to in paragraph 1.

Article 27

Review clause

1. By 17 June 2013, the Commission shall submit to the European Parliament, the Council and the European Economic and Social Committee a report on the application of this Regulation. If appropriate, the report shall be accompanied by proposals to amend this Regulation. The report shall include:

(a)   a study on the law applicable to insurance contracts and an assessment of the impact of the provisions to be introduced, if any; and
(b)   an evaluation on the application of Article 6, in particular as regards the coherence of Community law in the field of consumer protection.

2. By 17 June 2010, the Commission shall submit to the European Parliament, the Council and the European Economic and Social Committee a report on the question of the effectiveness of an assignment or subrogation of a claim against third parties and the priority of the assigned or subrogated claim over a right of another person. The report shall be accompanied, if appropriate, by a proposal to amend this Regulation and an assessment of the impact of the provisions to be introduced.

Article 28

Application in time

This Regulation shall apply to contracts concluded after 17 December 2009.

CHAPTER IV

FINAL PROVISIONS

Article 29

Entry into force and application

This Regulation shall enter into force on the 20th day following its publication in the Official Journal of the European Union.

It shall apply from 17 December 2009 except for Article 26 which shall apply from 17 June 2009.

This Regulation shall be binding in its entirety and directly applicable in the Member States in accordance with the Treaty establishing the European Community.

Done at Strasbourg, 17 June 2008.

For the European Parliament	*For the Council*
The President	*The President*
H.-G. PÖTTERING	J. LENARČIČ

APPENDIX 5

EC REGULATION 392/2009 ('THE 2002 ATHENS CONVENTION')

Schedule 6

CONVENTION RELATING TO THE CARRIAGE OF PASSENGERS AND THEIR LUGGAGE BY SEA

Part I

TEXT OF CONVENTION

This version in force from: **January 1, 1996** to **present**

ARTICLE 1

Definitions

In this Convention the following expressions have the meaning hereby assigned to them:

1.

(a) "carrier" means a person by or on behalf of whom a contract of carriage has been concluded, whether the carriage is actually performed by him or by a performing carrier;

(b) "performing carrier" means a person other than the carrier, being the owner, charterer or operator of a ship, who actually performs the whole or a part of the carriage;

2.

"contract of carriage" means a contract made by or on behalf of a carrier for the carriage by sea of a passenger or of a passenger and his luggage, as the case may be;

3.

"ship" means only a seagoing vessel, excluding an air-cushion vehicle;

4.

"passenger" means any person carried in a ship,

(a) under a contract of carriage, or

(b) who, with the consent of the carrier, is accompanying a vehicle or live animals which are covered by a contract for the carriage of goods not governed by this Convention;

5.

"luggage" means any article or vehicle carried by the carrier under a contract of carriage, excluding:

(a) articles and vehicles carried under a charter party, bill of lading or other contract primarily concerned with the carriage of goods, and
(b) live animals;

6.

"cabin luggage" means luggage which the passenger has in his cabin or is otherwise in his possession, custody or control. Except for the application of paragraph 8 of this Article and Article 8, cabin luggage includes luggage which the passenger has in or on his vehicle.

7.

"loss of or damage to luggage" includes pecuniary loss resulting from the luggage not having been re-delivered to the passenger within a reasonable time after the arrival of the ship on which the luggage has been or should have been carried, but does not include delays resulting from labour disputes;

8.

"carriage" covers the following periods:

(a) with regard to the passenger and his cabin luggage, the period during which the passenger and/or his cabin luggage are on board the ship or in the course of embarkation or disembarkation, and the period during which the passenger and his cabin luggage are transported by water from land to the ship or vice versa, if the cost of such transport is included in the fare or if the vessel used for the purpose of auxiliary transport has been put at the disposal of the passenger by the carrier. However, with regard to the passenger, carriage does not include the period during which he is in a marine terminal or station or on a quay or in or on any other port installation;
(b) with regard to cabin luggage, also the period during which the passenger is in a marine terminal or station or on a quay or in or on any other port installation if that luggage has been taken over by the carrier or his servant or agent and has not been re-delivered to the passenger;
(c) with regard to other luggage which is not cabin luggage, the period from the time of its taking over by the carrier or his servant or agent onshore or on board until the time of its re-delivery by the carrier or his servant or agent;

9.

"international carriage" means any carriage in which, according to the contract of carriage, the place of departure and the place of destination are situated in two different States, or in a single State if, according to the contract of carriage or the scheduled itinerary, there is an intermediate port of call in another State.

ARTICLE 2

Application

1.

This Convention shall apply to any international carriage if:

(a) the ship is flying the flag of or is registered in a State Party to this Convention, or
(b) the contract of carriage has been made in a State Party to this Convention, or
(c) the place of departure or destination, according to the contract of carriage, is in a State Party to this Convention.

2.

Notwithstanding paragraph 1 of this Article, this Convention shall not apply when the carriage is subject, under any other international convention concerning the carriage of passengers or luggage by another mode of transport, to a civil liability regime under the provisions of such convention, in so far as those provisions have mandatory application to carriage by sea.

ARTICLE 3

Liability of the carrier

1.

The carrier shall be liable for the damage suffered as a result of the death of or personal injury to a passenger and the loss of or damage to luggage if the incident which caused the damage so suffered occurred in the course of the carriage and was due to the fault or neglect of the carrier or of his servants or agents acting within the scope of their employment.

2.

The burden of proving that the incident which caused the loss or damage occurred in the course of the carriage, and the extent of the loss or damage, shall lie with the claimant.

3.

Fault or neglect of the carrier or of his servants or agents acting within the scope of their employment shall be presumed, unless the contrary is proved, if the death of or personal injury to the passenger or the loss of or damage to cabin luggage arose from or in connection with the shipwreck, collision, stranding, explosion or fire, or defect in the ship. In respect of loss of or damage to other luggage, such fault or neglect shall be presumed, unless the contrary is proved, irrespective of the nature of the incident which caused the loss or damage. In all other cases the burden of proving fault or neglect shall lie with the claimant.

ARTICLE 4

Performing carrier

1.

If the performance of the carriage or part thereof has been entrusted to a performing carrier, the carrier shall nevertheless remain liable for the entire carriage according to the provisions of this Convention. In addition, the performing carrier shall be subject and entitled to the provisions of this Convention for the part of the carriage performed by him.

2.

The carrier shall, in relation to the carriage performed by the performing carrier, be liable for the acts and omissions of the performing carrier and of his servants and agents acting within the scope of their employment.

3.

Any special agreement under which the carrier assumes obligations not imposed by this Convention or any waiver of rights conferred by this Convention shall affect the performing carrier only if agreed by him expressly and in writing.

4.

Where and to the extent that both the carrier and the performing carrier are liable, their liability shall be joint and several.

5.

Nothing in this Article shall prejudice any right of recourse as between the carrier and the performing carrier.

ARTICLE 5

Valuables

The carrier shall not be liable for the loss of or damage to monies, negotiable securities, gold, silverware, jewellery, ornaments, works of art, or other valuables, except where such valuables have been deposited with the carrier for the agreed purpose of safe-keeping in which case the carrier shall be liable up to the limit provided for in paragraph 3 of Article 8 unless a higher limit is agreed upon in accordance with paragraph 1 of Article 10.

ARTICLE 6

Contributory fault

If the carrier proves that the death of or personal injury to a passenger or the loss of or damage to his luggage was caused or contributed to by the fault or neglect of the passenger, the court seized of the case may exonerate the carrier wholly or partly from his liability in accordance with the provisions of the law of that court.

ARTICLE 7

Limit of liability for personal injury

1.

The liability of the carrier for the death of or personal injury to a passenger shall in no case exceed 46,666 units of account per carriage. Where in accordance with the law of the court seized of the case damages are awarded in the form of periodical income payments, the equivalent capital value of those payments shall not exceed the said limit.

2.

Notwithstanding paragraph 1 of this Article, the national law of any State Party to this Convention may fix, as far as carriers who are nationals of such State are concerned, a higher *per capita* limit of liability.

ARTICLE 8

Limit of liability for loss of or damage to luggage

1.

The liability of the carrier for the loss of or damage to cabin luggage shall in no case exceed 833 units of account per passenger, per carriage.

2.

The liability of the carrier for the loss of or damage to vehicles including all luggage carried in or on the vehicle shall in no case exceed 3,333 units of account per vehicle, per carriage.

3.

The liability of the carrier for the loss of or damage to luggage other than that mentioned in paragraphs 1 and 2 of this Article shall in no case exceed 1,200 units of account per passenger, per carriage.

4.

The carrier and the passenger may agree that the liability of the carrier shall be subject to a deduction not exceeding 117 units of account in the case of damage to a vehicle and not exceeding 13 units of account per passenger in the case of loss of or damage to other luggage, such sum to be deducted from the loss or damage.

ARTICLE 9

Unit of account and conversion

The Unit of Account mentioned in this Convention is the special drawing right as defined by the International Monetary Fund. The amounts mentioned in Articles 7 and 8 shall be converted into the national currency of the State of the court seized of the case on the basis of the value of that currency on the date of the judgment or the date agreed upon by the Parties.

ARTICLE 10

Supplementary provisions on limits of liability

1.

The carrier and the passenger may agree, expressly and in writing, to higher limits of liability than those prescribed in Articles 7 and 8.

2.

Interest on damages and legal costs shall not be included in the limits of liability prescribed in Articles 7 and 8.

ARTICLE 11

Defences and limits for carriers' servants

If an action is brought against a servant or agent of the carrier or of the performing carrier arising out of damage covered by this Convention, such servant or agent, if he proves that he acted within the scope of his employment, shall be entitled to avail himself of the defences and limits of liability which the carrier or the performing carrier is entitled to invoke under this Convention.

ARTICLE 12

Aggregation of claims

1.

Where the limits of liability prescribed in Articles 7 and 8 take effect, they shall apply to the aggregate of the amounts recoverable in all claims arising out of the death of or personal injury to any one passenger or the loss of or damage to his luggage.

2.

In relation to the carriage performed by a performing carrier, the aggregate of the amounts recoverable from the carrier and the performing carrier and from their servants and agents acting within the scope of their employment shall not exceed the highest amount which could be awarded against either the carrier or the performing carrier under this Convention, but none of the persons mentioned shall be liable for a sum in excess of the limit applicable to him.

3.

In any case where a servant or agent of the carrier or of the performing carrier is entitled under Article 11 of this Convention to avail himself of the limits of liability prescribed in Articles 7 and 8, the aggregate of the amounts recoverable from the carrier, or the performing carrier as the case may be, and from that servant or agent, shall not exceed those limits.

ARTICLE 13

Loss of right to limit liability

1.

The carrier shall not be entitled to the benefit of the limits of liability prescribed in Articles 7 and 8 and paragraph 1 of Article 10 if it is proved that the damage resulted from an act or omission of the carrier done with the intent to cause such damage, or recklessly and with knowledge that such damage would probably result.

2.

The servant or agent of the carrier or of the performing carrier shall not be entitled to the benefit of those limits if it is proved that the damage resulted from an act or omission of that servant or agent done with the intent to cause such damage, or recklessly and with knowledge that such damage would probably result.

ARTICLE 14

Basis for claims

No action for damages for the death of or personal injury to a passenger, or for the loss of or damage to luggage, shall be brought against a carrier or performing carrier otherwise than in accordance with this Convention.

ARTICLE 15

Notice of loss or damage to luggage

1.

The passenger shall give written notice to the carrier or his agent:

(a)   in the case of apparent damage to luggage:

   (i)   for cabin luggage, before or at the time of disembarkation of the passenger;
   (ii) for all other luggage, before or at the time of its re-delivery;

(b)   in the case of damage to luggage which is not apparent, or loss of luggage, within 15 days from the date of disembarkation or re-delivery or from the time when such re-delivery should have taken place.

2.

If the passenger fails to comply with this Article, he shall be presumed, unless the contrary is proved, to have received the luggage undamaged.

3.

The notice in writing need not be given if the condition of the luggage has at the time of its receipt been the subject of joint survey or inspection.

ARTICLE 16
Time-bar for actions

1.

Any action for damages arising out of the death of or personal injury to a passenger or for the loss of or damage to luggage shall be time-barred after a period of two years.

2.

The limitation period shall be calculated as follows:

(a)   in the case of personal injury, from the date of disembarkation of the passenger;

(b)   in the case of death occurring during carriage, from the date when the passenger should have disembarked, and in the case of personal injury occurring during carriage and resulting in the death of the passenger after disembarkation, from the date of death, provided that this period shall not exceed three years from the date of disembarkation;

(c)   in the case of loss of or damage to luggage, from the date of disembarkation or from the date when disembarkation should have taken place, whichever is later.

3.

The law of the court seized of the case shall govern the grounds of suspension and interruption of limitation periods, but in no case shall an action under this Convention be brought after the expiration of a period of three years from the date of disembarkation of the passenger or from the date when disembarkation should have taken place, whichever is later.

4.

Notwithstanding paragraphs 1, 2 and 3 of this Article, the period of limitation may be extended by a declaration of the carrier or by agreement of the parties after the cause of action has arisen. The declaration or agreement shall be in writing.

ARTICLE 17

Competent jurisdiction

1.

An action arising under this Convention shall, at the option of the claimant, be brought before one of the courts listed below, provided that the court is located in a State Party to this Convention:

(a) the court of the place of permanent residence or principal place of business of the defendant, or

(b) the court of the place of departure or that of the destination according to the contract of carriage, or

(c) a court of the State of the domicile or permanent residence of the claimant, if the defendant has a place of business and is subject to jurisdiction in that State, or

(d) a court of the State where the contract of carriage was made, if the defendant has a place of business and is subject to jurisdiction in that State.

2.

After the occurrence of the incident which has caused the damage, the parties may agree that the claim for damages shall be submitted to any jurisdiction or to arbitration.

ARTICLE 18

Invalidity of contractual provisions

Any contractual provision concluded before the occurrence of the incident which has caused the death of or personal injury to a passenger or the loss of or damage to his luggage, purporting to relieve the carrier of his liability towards the passenger or to prescribe a lower limit of liability than that fixed in this Convention except as provided in paragraph 4 of Article 8, and any such provision purporting to shift the burden of proof which rests on the carrier, or having the effect of restricting the option specified in paragraph 1 of Article 17, shall be null and void, but the nullity of that provision shall not render void the contract of carriage which shall remain subject to the provisions of this Convention.

ARTICLE 19

Other conventions on limitation of liability

This Convention shall not modify the rights or duties of the carrier, the performing carrier, and their servants or agents provided for in international conventions relating to the limitation of liability of owners of seagoing ships.

ARTICLE 20

Nuclear damage

No liability shall arise under this Convention for damage caused by a nuclear incident:

(a) if the operator of a nuclear installation is liable to such damage under either the Paris Convention of 29 July 1960 on Third Party Liability in the Field of Nuclear Energy as amended by its Additional Protocol of 28 January 1964, or the Vienna Convention of 21 May 1963 on Civil Liability for Nuclear Damage, or

(b) if the operator of a nuclear installation is liable for such damage by virtue of a national law governing the liability for such damage, provided that such law is in all respects as favourable to persons who may suffer damage as either the Paris or the Vienna Conventions.

ARTICLE 21

Commercial carriage by public authorities

This Convention shall apply to commercial carriage undertaken by States or Public Authorities under contracts of carriage within the meaning of Article 1.

ARTICLE 22

Revision and amendment[1]

ARTICLE 23

Amendment of limits

1.

Without prejudice to the provisions of Article 22, the special procedure in this Article shall apply solely for the purposes of amending the limits set out in Article 3(1), Article 4*bis*(1), Article 7(1) and Article 8 of the Convention as revised by this Protocol.

2.

Upon the request of at least one half, but in no case less than six, of the States Parties to this Protocol, any proposal to amend the limits, including the deductibles, specified in Article 3(1), Article 4*bis*(1), Article 7(1) and Article 8 of the Convention as revised by this Protocol shall be circulated by the Secretary General to all Members of the Organisation and to all States Parties.

3.

Any amendment proposed and circulated as above shall be submitted to the Legal Committee of the Organisation (hereinafter referred to as 'the Legal Committee') for consideration at a date at least six months after the date of its circulation.

---

[1]   Not reproduced.

4.

All States Parties to the Convention as revised by this Protocol, whether or not Members of the Organisation, shall be entitled to participate in the proceedings of the Legal Committee for the consideration and adoption of amendments.

5.

Amendments shall be adopted by a two thirds majority of the States Parties to the Convention as revised by this Protocol present and voting in the Legal Committee expanded as provided for in paragraph 4, on condition that at least one half of the States Parties to the Convention as revised by this Protocol shall be present at the time of voting.

6.

When acting on a proposal to amend the limits, the Legal Committee shall take into account the experience of incidents and, in particular, the amount of damage resulting therefrom, changes in the monetary values and the effect of the proposed amendment on the cost of insurance.

7.

(a) No amendment of the limits under this Article may be considered less than five years from the date on which this Protocol was opened for signature nor less than five years from the date of entry into force of a previous amendment under this Article.

(b) No limit may be increased so as to exceed an amount which corresponds to the limit laid down in the Convention as revised by this Protocol increased by six per cent per year calculated on a compound basis from the date on which this Protocol was opened for signature.

(c) No limit may be increased so as to exceed an amount which corresponds to the limit laid down in the Convention as revised by this Protocol multiplied by three.

8.

Any amendment adopted in accordance with paragraph 5 shall be notified by the Organisation to all States Parties. The amendment shall be deemed to have been accepted at the end of a period of 18 months after the date of notification, unless within that period not less than one fourth of the States that were States Parties at the time of the adoption of the amendment have communicated to the Secretary General that they do not accept the amendment, in which case the amendment is rejected and shall have no effect.

9.

An amendment deemed to have been accepted in accordance with paragraph 8 shall enter into force 18 months after its acceptance.

10.

All States Parties shall be bound by the amendment, unless they denounce this Protocol in accordance with Article 21, paragraphs 1 and 2 at least six months before the amendment enters into force. Such denunciation shall take effect when the amendment enters into force.

11.

When an amendment has been adopted but the 18 month period for its acceptance has not yet expired, a State which becomes a State Party during that period shall be bound by the amendment if it enters into force. A State which becomes a State Party after that period shall be bound by an amendment which has been accepted in accordance with paragraph 8. In the cases referred to in this paragraph, a State becomes bound by an amendment when that amendment enters into force, or when this Protocol enters into force for that State, if later.

ANNEX TO ATHENS CONVENTION

CERTIFICATE OF INSURANCE OR OTHER FINANCIAL SECURITY IN RESPECT OF LIABILITY FOR THE DEATH OF AND PERSONAL INJURY TO PASSENGERS

Issued in accordance with the provisions of Article 4*bis* of the Athens Convention relating to the Carriage of Passengers and their Luggage by Sea, 2002

[Table not reproduced]

This is to certify that there is in force in respect of the abovenamed ship a policy of insurance or other financial security satisfying the requirements of Article 4*bis* of the Athens Convention relating to the Carriage of Passengers and their Luggage by Sea, 2002.

Type of security ....

Duration of security ....

Name and address of the insurer(s) and/or guarantor(s)

Name ....

Address ....

This certificate is valid until ....

Issued or certified by the Government of ....

(Full designation of the State)

OR

The following text should be used when a State Party avails itself of Article 4*bis*, paragraph 3:

The present certificate is issued under the authority of the Government of .... (full designation of the State) by .... (name of institution or organisation)

At ....   On ....
              (Place)   (Date)

                                                      ....
                                                      (Signature and title of issuing or
                                                      certifying official)

Explanatory notes:

1. If desired, the designation of the State may include a reference to the competent public authority of the country where the Certificate is issued.
2. If the total amount of security has been furnished by more than one source, the amount of each of them should be indicated.
3. If security is furnished in several forms, these should be enumerated.
4. The entry 'Duration of Security' must stipulate the date on which such security takes effect.
5. The entry 'Address' of the insurer(s) and/or guarantor(s) must indicate the principal place of business of the insurer(s) and/or guarantor(s). If appropriate, the place of business where the insurance or other security is established shall be indicated.

ANNEX II

Extract From the IMO Reservation and Guidelines for Implementation of THE ATHENS Convention, adopted by the Legal Committee of the INTERNATIONAL MARITIME ORGANISATION on 19 October 2006

IMO RESERVATION AND GUIDELINES FOR IMPLEMENTATION OF THE ATHENS CONVENTION

Reservation

1. The Athens Convention should be ratified with the following reservation or a declaration to the same effect:

'[1.1.]   Reservation in connection with the ratification by the Government of . . . of the Athens Convention relating to the Carriage of Passengers and their Luggage by Sea, 2002 (the Convention)

Limitation of liability of carriers, etc.

[1.2.]   The Government of . . . reserves the right to and undertakes to limit liability under paragraph 1 or 2 of Article 3 of the Convention, if any, in respect of death of or personal injury to a passenger caused by any of the risks referred to in paragraph 2.2 of the IMO Guidelines for Implementation of the Athens Convention to the lower of the following amounts:

–   250 000 units of account in respect of each passenger on each distinct occasion,
    or
–   340 million units of account overall per ship on each distinct occasion.

[1.3.]   Furthermore, the Government of . . . reserves the right to and undertakes to apply the IMO Guidelines for Implementation of the Athens Convention paragraphs 2.1.1 and 2.2.2 *mutatis mutandis*, to such liabilities.

[1.4.]   The liability of the performing carrier pursuant to Article 4 of the Convention, the liability of the servants and agents of the carrier or the performing carrier pursuant to Article 11 of the Convention and the limit of the aggregate of the amounts recoverable pursuant to Article 12 of the Convention shall be limited in the same way.

[1.5.]   The reservation and undertaking in paragraph 1.2 will apply regardless of the basis of liability under paragraph 1 or 2 of Article 3 and notwithstanding anything to the contrary in Article 4 or 7 of the Convention; but this reservation and undertaking do not affect the operation of Articles 10 and 13.

Compulsory insurance and limitation of liability of insurers

[1.6.]   The Government of . . . reserves the right to and undertakes to limit the requirement under paragraph 1 of Article 4*bis* to maintain insurance or other financial security for death or personal injury to a passenger caused by any of the risks referred to in paragraph 2.2 of the IMO Guidelines for Implementation of the Athens Convention to the lower of the following amounts:

–   250 000 units of account in respect of each passenger on each distinct occasion,
    or
–   340 million units of account overall per ship on each distinct occasion.

[1.7.]   The Government of . . . reserves the right to and undertakes to limit the liability of the insurer or other person providing financial security under paragraph 10 of Article 4*bis*, for death or personal injury to a passenger caused by any of the risks referred to in paragraph 2.2 of the IMO Guidelines for Implementation of the Athens Convention, to a maximum limit of the amount of insurance or other financial security which the carrier is required to maintain under paragraph 1.6 of this reservation.

[1.8.]   The Government of . . . also reserves the right to and undertakes to apply the IMO Guidelines for Implementation of the Athens Convention including the application of the clauses referred to in paragraphs 2.1 and 2.2 in the Guidelines in all compulsory insurance under the Convention.

[1.9.]   The Government of . . . reserves the right to and undertakes to exempt the provider of insurance or other financial security under paragraph 1 of Article 4*bis* from any liability for which he has not undertaken to be liable.

Certification

[1.10.]   The Government of . . . reserves the right to and undertakes to issue insurance certificates under paragraph 2 of Article 4*bis* of the Convention so as:

–   to reflect the limitations of liability and the requirements for insurance cover referred to in paragraphs 1.2, 1.6, 1.7 and 1.9, and
–   to include such other limitations, requirements and exemptions as it finds that the insurance market conditions at the time of the issue of the certificate necessitate.

[1.11.]   The Government of . . . reserves the right to and undertakes to accept insurance certificates issued by other States Parties issued pursuant to a similar reservation.

[1.12.] All such limitations, requirements and exemptions will be clearly reflected in the Certificate issued or certified under paragraph 2 of Article 4*bis* of the Convention.

Relationship between this Reservation and the IMO Guidelines for Implementation of the Athens Convention

[1.13.] The rights retained by this reservation will be exercised with due regard to the IMO Guidelines for Implementation of the Athens Convention, or to any amendments thereto, with an aim to ensure uniformity. If a proposal to amend the IMO Guidelines for Implementation of the Athens Convention, including the limits, has been approved by the Legal Committee of the International Maritime Organisation, those amendments will apply as from the time determined by the Committee. This is without prejudice to the rules of international law regarding the right of a State to withdraw or amend its reservation.'

Guidelines

2. In the current state of the insurance market, State Parties should issue insurance certificates on the basis of one undertaking from an insurer covering war risks, and another insurer covering non war risks. Each insurer should only be liable for its part. The following rules should apply (the clauses referred to are set out in Appendix A):

2.1. Both war and non war insurance may be subject to the following clauses:

2.1.1. Institute Radioactive Contamination, Chemical, Biological, Bio-chemical and Electromagnetic Weapons Exclusion Clause (Institute clause No 370);

2.1.2. Institute Cyber Attack Exclusion Clause (Institute clause No 380);

2.1.3. the defences and limitations of a provider of compulsory financial security under the Convention as modified by these guidelines, in particular the limit of 250 000 units of account per passenger on each distinct occasion;

2.1.4. the proviso that the insurance shall only cover liabilities subject to the Convention as modified by these guidelines; and

2.1.5. the proviso that any amounts settled under the Convention shall serve to reduce the outstanding liability of the carrier and/or its insurer under Article 4*bis* of the Convention even if they are not paid by or claimed from the respective war or non war insurers.

2.2. War insurance shall cover liability, if any; for the loss suffered as a result of death or personal injury to passenger caused by:

– war, civil war, revolution, rebellion, insurrection, or civil strife arising there from, or any hostile act by or against a belligerent power,
– capture, seizure, arrest, restraint or detainment, and the consequences thereof or any attempt thereat,
– derelict mines, torpedoes, bombs or other derelict weapons of war,

– act of any terrorist or any person acting maliciously or from a political motive and any action taken to prevent or counter any such risk,
– confiscation and expropriation,

and may be subject to the following exemptions, limitations and requirements:

2.2.1.   War Automatic Termination and Exclusion Clause

2.2.2.   In the event the claims of individual passengers exceed in the aggregate the sum of 340 million units of account overall per ship on any distinct occasion, the carrier shall be entitled to invoke limitation of his liability in the amount of 340 million units of account, always provided that:

– this amount should be distributed amongst claimants in proportion to their established claims,
– the distribution of this amount may be made in one or more portions to claimants known at the time of the distribution, and
– the distribution of this amount may be made by the insurer, or by the Court or other competent authority seized by the insurer in any State Party in which legal proceedings are instituted in respect of claims allegedly covered by the insurance.
2.2.3.   30 days notice clause in cases not covered by 2.2.1.

2.3.   Non-war insurance should cover all perils subject to compulsory insurance other than those risks listed in 2.2, whether or not they are subject to exemptions, limitations or requirements in 2.1 and 2.2.

3.   An example of a set of insurance undertakings (Blue Cards) and an insurance certificate, all reflecting these guidelines, are included in Appendix B.

APPENDIX A

Clauses referred to in guidelines 2.1.1, 2.1.2 and 2.2.1

Institute Radioactive Contamination, Chemical, Biological, Bio-chemical and Electromagnetic Exclusion Clause (Cl. 370, 10/11/2003)

This clause shall be paramount and shall override anything contained in this insurance inconsistent therewith

1.   In no case shall this insurance cover loss damage liability or expense directly or indirectly caused by or contributed to by or arising from:

1.1.   ionising radiations from or contamination by radioactivity from any nuclear fuel or from any nuclear waste or from the combustion of nuclear fuel;

1.2.   the radioactive, toxic, explosive or other hazardous or contaminating properties of any nuclear installation, reactor or other nuclear assembly or nuclear component thereof;

1.3.   any weapon or device employing atomic or nuclear fission and/or fusion or other like reaction or radioactive force or matter;

1.4.   the radioactive, toxic, explosve or other hazardous or contaminating properties of any radioactive matter. The exclusion in this sub clause does not extend to radioactive isotopes, other than nuclear fuel, when such isotopes are being prepared, carried, stored, or used for commercial, agricultural, medical, scientific or other similar peaceful purposes;

1.5.   any chemical, biological, bio chemical, or electromagnetic weapon.

Institute Cyber Attack Exclusion Clause (Cl. 380, 10/11/03)

1.   Subject only to clause 10.2 below, in no case shall this insurance cover loss damage liability or expense directly or indirectly caused by or contributed to by or arising from the use or operation, as a means for inflicting harm, of any computer, computer system, computer software programme, malicious code, computer virus or process or any other electronic system.

2.   Where this clause is endorsed on policies covering risks of war, civil war, revolution, rebellion, insurrection, or civil strife arising therefrom, or any hostile act by or against a belligerent power, or terrorism or any person acting from a political motive, Clause 10.1 shall not operate to exclude losses (which would otherwise be covered) arising from the use of any computer, computer system or computer software programme or any other electronic system in the launch and/or guidance system and/or firing mechanism of any weapon or missile.

War Automatic Termination and Exclusion

1.1.   Automatic Termination of Cover

Whether or not such notice of cancellation has been given cover hereunder shall TERMINATE AUTOMATICALLY

1.1.1.   upon the outbreak of war (whether there be a declaration of war or not) between any of the following: United Kingdom, United States of America, France, the Russian Federation, the People's Republic of China;

1.1.2.   in respect of any vessel, in connection with which cover is granted hereunder, in the event of such vessel being requisitioned either for title or use.

1.2.   Five Powers War

This insurance excludes

1.2.1.   loss damage liability or expense arising from the outbreak of war (whether there be a declaration of war or not) between any of the following: United Kingdom, United States of America, France, the Russian Federation, the People's Republic of China;

1.2.2.   requisition either for title or use.

APPENDIX B

I. Examples of insurance undertakings (Blue Cards) referred to in guideline 3

Blue Card issued by War Insurer

Certificate furnished as evidence of insurance pursuant to Article 4*bis* of the Athens Convention relating to the Carriage of Passengers and their Luggage by Sea, 2002.

Name of Ship:
IMO Ship Identification Number:
Port of registry:
Name and Address of owner:

This is to certify that there is in force in respect of the above named ship while in the above ownership a policy of insurance satisfying the requirements of Article 4*bis* of the Athens Convention relating to the Carriage of Passengers and their Luggage by Sea, 2002, subject to all exceptions and limitations allowed for compulsory war insurance under the Convention and the implementation guidelines adopted by the Legal Committee of the International Maritime Organisation in October 2006, including in particular the following clauses: [Here the text of the Convention and the guidelines with appendices can be inserted to the extent desirable]

Period of insurance from: 20 February 2007
to: 20 February 2008

Provided always that the insurer may cancel this certificate by giving 30 days written notice to the above Authority whereupon the liability of the insurer hereunder shall cease as from the date of the expiry of the said period of notice but only as regards incidents arising thereafter.

Date:

This certificate has been issued by: War Risks, Inc

                                          [Address]

....   As agent only for *War Risks, Inc.*

Signature of insurer

Blue Card issued by Non-War Insurer

Certificate furnished as evidence of insurance pursuant to Article 4*bis* of the Athens Convention relating to the Carriage of Passengers and their Luggage by Sea, 2002

Name of Ship:
IMO Ship Identification Number:
Port of registry:
Name and Address of owner:

This is to certify that there is in force in respect of the above named ship while in the above ownership a policy of insurance satisfying the requirements of Article 4*bis* of the Athens Convention relating to the Carriage of Passengers and their Luggage by Sea, 2002, subject to all exceptions and limitations allowed for non-war insurers under the Convention and the implementation guidelines adopted by the Legal Committee of the International Maritime Organisation in October 2006, including in particular the following clauses: [Here the text of the Convention and the guidelines with appendices can be inserted to the extent desirable]

Period of insurance from: 20 February 2007
to: 20 February 2008

Provided always that the insurer may cancel this certificate by giving three months written notice to the above Authority whereupon the liability of the insurer hereunder shall cease as from the date of the expiry of the said period of notice but only as regards incidents arising thereafter.

Date:

This certificate has been issued by: PANDI P&I

                                      [Address]

....   As agent only for *PANDI P&I*

Signature of insurer

II. Model of certificate of insurance referred to in guideline 3

CERTIFICATE OF INSURANCE OR OTHER FINANCIAL SECURITY IN RESPECT OF LIABILITY FOR THE DEATH OF AND PERSONAL INJURY TO PASSENGERS

Issued in accordance with the provisions of Article 4*bis* of the Athens Convention relating to the Carriage of Passengers and their Luggage by Sea, 2002

[Table not reproduced]

This is to certify that there is in force in respect of the abovenamed ship a policy of insurance or other financial security satisfying the requirements of Article 4*bis* of the Athens Convention relating to the Carriage of Passengers and their Luggage by Sea, 2002.

Type of Security ....

Duration of Security ....

Name and address of the insurer(s) and/or guarantor(s)

The insurance cover hereby certified is split in one war insurance part and one non-war insurance part, pursuant to the implementation guidelines adopted by the Legal Committee of the International Maritime Organisation in October 2006. Each of these parts of the insurance cover is subject to all exceptions and limitations allowed under the Convention and the implementation guidelines. The insurers are not jointly and severally liable. The insurers are:

For war risks: War Risks, Inc., [address]

For non-war risks: Pandi P&I, [address]

This certificate is valid until ....

Issued or certified by the Government of ....

(Full designation of the State)

OR

The following text should be used when a State Party avails itself of Article 4*bis*, paragraph 3:

The present certificate is issued under the authority of the Government of .... (full designation of the State) by .... (name of institution or organisation)

At ....   On ....

            (Place)   (Date)

....

(Signature and title of issuing or certifying official)

Explanatory notes:

1. If desired, the designation of the State may include a reference to the competent public authority of the country where the certificate is issued.
2. If the total amount of security has been furnished by more than one source, the amount of each of them should be indicated.
3. If security is furnished in several forms, these should be enumerated.
4. The entry 'Duration of Security' must stipulate the date on which such security takes effect.
5. The entry 'Address' of the insurer(s) and/or guarantor(s) must indicate the principal place of business of the insurer(s) and/or guarantor(s). If appropriate, the place of business where the insurance or other security is established shall be indicated.

APPENDIX 6

MONTREAL CONVENTION 1999

Schedule 1B
CONVENTION FOR THE UNIFICATION OF CERTAIN RULES FOR INTERNATIONAL CARRIAGE BY AIR

This version in force from: **June 28, 2004** to **present**

[

THE STATES PARTIES TO THIS CONVENTION

RECOGNIZING the significant contribution of the Convention for the Unification of Certain Rules Relating to International Carriage by Air signed in Warsaw on 12th October 1929, hereinafter referred to as the "Warsaw Convention", and other related instruments to the harmonization of private international air law;

RECOGNIZING the need to modernize and consolidate the Warsaw Convention and related instruments;

RECOGNIZING the importance of ensuring protection of the interests of consumers in international carriage by air and the need for equitable compensation based on the principle of restitution;

REAFFIRMING the desirability of an orderly development of international air transport operations and the smooth flow of passengers, baggage and cargo in accordance with the principles and objectives of the Convention on International Civil Aviation, done at Chicago on 7 December 1944;

CONVINCED that collective State action for further harmonization and codification of certain rules governing international carriage by air through a new Convention is the most adequate means of achieving an equitable balance of interests;

HAVE AGREED AS FOLLOWS:

Chapter I GENERAL PROVISIONS

Article 1 – Scope of Application

1.

This Convention applies to all international carriage of persons, baggage or cargo performed by aircraft for reward. It applies equally to gratuitous carriage by aircraft performed by an air transport undertaking.

2.

For the purposes of this Convention, the expression *international carriage* means any carriage in which, according to the agreement between the parties, the place of departure and the place of destination, whether or not there be a break in the carriage or a transhipment, are situated either within the territories of two States Parties, or within the territory of a single State Party if there is an agreed stopping place within the territory of another State, even if that State is not a State Party. Carriage between two points within the territory of a single State Party without an agreed stopping place within the territory of another State is not international carriage for the purposes of this Convention.

3.

Carriage to be performed by several successive carriers is deemed, for the purposes of this Convention, to be one undivided carriage if it has been regarded by the parties as a single operation, whether it had been agreed upon under the form of a single contract or of a series of contracts, and it does not lose its international character merely because one contract or a series of contracts is to be performed entirely within the territory of the same State.

4.

This Convention applies also to carriage as set out in Chapter V, subject to the terms contained therein.

Article 2 – Carriage Performed by State and Carriage of Postal Items

1.

This Convention applies to carriage performed by the State or by legally constituted public bodies provided it falls within the conditions laid down in Article 1.

2.

In the carriage of postal items, the carrier shall be liable only to the relevant postal administration in accordance with the rules applicable to the relationship between the carriers and the postal administrations.

3.

Except as provided in paragraph 2 of this Article, the provisions of this Convention shall not apply to the carriage of postal items.

Chapter II DOCUMENTATION AND DUTIES OF THE PARTIES RELAT-ING TO THE CARRIAGE OF PASSENGERS, BAGGAGE AND CARGO

Article 3 – Passengers and Baggage

1.

In respect of carriage of passengers, an individual or collective document of carriage shall be delivered containing:

(a)   an indication of the places of departure and destination;
(b)   if the places of departure and destination are within the territory of a single State Party, one or more agreed stopping places being within the territory of another State, an indication of at least one such stopping place.

2.

Any other means which preserves the information indicated in paragraph 1 may be substituted for the delivery of the document referred to in that paragraph. If any such other means is used, the carrier shall offer to deliver to the passenger a written statement of the information so preserved.

3.

The carrier shall deliver to the passenger a baggage identification tag for each piece of checked baggage.

4.

The passenger shall be given written notice to the effect that where this Convention is applicable it governs and may limit the liability of carriers in respect of death or injury and for destruction or loss of, or damage to, baggage, and for delay.

5.

Non-compliance with the provisions of the foregoing paragraphs shall not affect the existence or the validity of the contract of carriage, which shall, nonetheless, be subject to the rules of this Convention including those relating to limitation of liability.

Article 4 – Cargo

1.

In respect of the carriage of cargo, an air waybill shall be delivered.

2.

Any other means which preserves a record of the carriage to be performed may be substituted for the delivery of an air waybill. If such other means are used, the carrier shall, if so requested by the consignor, deliver to the consignor a cargo receipt permitting identification of the consignment and access to the information contained in the record preserved by such other means.

Article 5 – Contents of Air Waybill or Cargo Receipt

The air waybill or the cargo receipt shall include:

(a)   an indication of the places of departure and destination;
(b)   if the places of departure and destination are within the territory of a single State Party, one or more agreed stopping places being within the territory of another State, an indication of at least one such stopping place; and
(c)   an indication of the weight of the consignment.

Article 6 – Document Relating to the Nature of the Cargo

The consignor may be required, if necessary to meet the formalities of customs, police and similar public authorities, to deliver a document indicating the nature of the cargo. This provision creates for the carrier no duty, obligation or liability resulting therefrom.

Article 7 – Description of Air Waybill

1.

The air waybill shall be made out by the consignor in three original parts.

2.

The first part shall be marked "for the carrier"; it shall be signed by the consignor. The second part shall be marked "for the consignee"; it shall be signed by the consignor and by the carrier. The third part shall be signed by the carrier who shall hand it to the consignor after the cargo has been accepted.

3.

The signature of the carrier and that of the consignor may be printed or stamped.

4.

If, at the request of the consignor, the carrier makes out the air waybill, the carrier shall be deemed, subject to proof to the contrary, to have done so on behalf of the consignor.

Article 8 – Documentation for Multiple Packages

When there is more than one package:

(a) the carrier of cargo has the right to require the consignor to make out separate air waybills;
(b) the consignor has the right to require the carrier to deliver separate cargo receipts when the other means referred to in paragraph 2 of Article 4 are used.

Article 9 – Non-compliance with Documentary Requirements

Non-compliance with the provisions of Articles 4 to 8 shall not affect the existence or the validity of the contract of carriage, which shall, nonetheless, be subject to the rules of this Convention including those relating to limitation of liability.

Article 10 – Responsibility for Particulars of Documentation

1.

The consignor is responsible for the correctness of the particulars and statements relating to the cargo inserted by it or on its behalf in the air waybill or furnished by it or on its behalf to the carrier for insertion in the cargo receipt or for insertion in the record preserved by the other means referred to in paragraph 2 of Article 4. The foregoing shall also apply where the person acting on behalf of the consignor is also the agent of the carrier.

2.

The consignor shall indemnify the carrier against all damage suffered by it, or by any other person to whom the carrier is liable, by reason of the irregularity, incorrectness or incompleteness of the particulars and statements furnished by the consignor or on its behalf.

3.

Subject to the provisions of paragraphs 1 and 2 of this Article, the carrier shall indemnify the consignor against all damage suffered by it, or by any other person to whom the consignor is liable, by reason of the irregularity, incorrectness or incompleteness of the particulars and statements inserted by the carrier or on its behalf in the cargo receipt or in the record preserved by the other means referred to in paragraph 2 of Article 4.

Article 11 – Evidentiary Value of Documentation

1.

The air waybill or the cargo receipt is prima facie evidence of the conclusion of the contract, of the acceptance of the cargo and of the conditions of carriage mentioned therein.

2.

Any statements in the air waybill or the cargo receipt relating to the weight, dimensions and packing of the cargo, as well as those relating to the number of packages, are prima facie evidence of the facts stated; those relating to the quantity, volume and condition of the cargo do not constitute evidence against the carrier except so far as they both have been, and are stated in the air waybill or the cargo receipt to have been, checked by it in the presence of the consignor, or relate to the apparent condition of the cargo.

Article 12 – Right of Disposition of Cargo

1.

Subject to its liability to carry out all its obligations under the contract of carriage, the consignor has the right to dispose of the cargo by withdrawing it at the airport of departure or destination, or by stopping it in the course of the journey on any landing, or by calling for it to be delivered at the place of destination or in the course of the journey to a person other than the consignee originally designated, or by requiring it to be returned to the airport of departure. The consignor must not exercise this right of disposition in such a way as to prejudice the carrier or other consignors and must reimburse any expenses occasioned by the exercise of this right.

2.

If it is impossible to carry out the instructions of the consignor, the carrier must so inform the consignor forthwith.

3.

If the carrier carries out the instructions of the consignor for the disposition of the cargo without requiring the production of the part of the air waybill or the cargo receipt delivered to the latter, the carrier will be liable, without prejudice to its right of recovery from the consignor, for any damage which may be caused thereby to any person who is lawfully in possession of that part of the air waybill or the cargo receipt.

4.

The right conferred on the consignor ceases at the moment when that of the consignee begins in accordance with Article 13. Nevertheless, if the consignee declines to accept the cargo, or cannot be communicated with, the consignor resumes its right of disposition.

Article 13 – Delivery of the Cargo

1.

Except when the consignor has exercised its right under Article 12, the consignee is entitled, on arrival of the cargo at the place of destination, to require the carrier to deliver the cargo to it, on payment of the charges due and on complying with the conditions of carriage.

2.

Unless it is otherwise agreed, it is the duty of the carrier to give notice to the consignee as soon as the cargo arrives.

3.

If the carrier admits the loss of the cargo, or if the cargo has not arrived at the expiration of seven days after the date on which it ought to have arrived, the consignee is entitled to enforce against the carrier the rights which flow from the contract of carriage.

Article 14 – Enforcement of the Rights of Consignor and Consignee

The consignor and the consignee can respectively enforce all the rights given to them by Articles 12 and 13, each in its own name, whether it is acting in its own interest or in the interest of another, provided that it carries out the obligations imposed by the contract of carriage.

Article 15 – Relations of Consignor and Consignee or Mutual Relations of Third Parties

1.

Articles 12, 13 and 14 do not affect either the relations of the consignor and the consignee with each other or the mutual relations of third parties whose rights are derived either from the consignor or from the consignee.

2.

The provisions of Articles 12, 13 and 14 can only be varied by express provision in the air waybill or the cargo receipt.

Article 16 – Formalities of Customs, Police or Other Public Authorities

1.

The consignor must furnish such information and such documents as are necessary to meet the formalities of customs, police and any other public authorities before the cargo can be delivered to the consignee. The consignor is liable to the carrier for any damage occasioned by the absence, insufficiency or irregularity of any such information or documents, unless the damage is due to the fault of the carrier, its servants or agents.

2.

The carrier is under no obligation to enquire into the correctness or sufficiency of such information or documents.

Chapter III LIABILITY OF THE CARRIER AND EXTENT OF COMPENSATION FOR DAMAGE

Article 17 – Death and Injury of Passengers – Damage to Baggage

1.

The carrier is liable for damage sustained in case of death or bodily injury of a passenger upon condition only that the accident which caused the death or injury took place on board the aircraft or in the course of any of the operations of embarking or disembarking.

2.

The carrier is liable for damage sustained in case of destruction or loss of, or of damage to, checked baggage upon condition only that the event which caused the destruction, loss or damage took place on board the aircraft or during any period within which the checked baggage was in the charge of the carrier. However, the carrier is not liable if and to the extent that the damage resulted from the inherent defect, quality or vice of the baggage. In the case of unchecked baggage, including personal items, the carrier is liable if the damage resulted from its fault or that of its servants or agents.

3.

If the carrier admits the loss of the checked baggage, or if the checked baggage has not arrived at the expiration of twenty-one days after the date on which it ought to have arrived, the passenger is entitled to enforce against the carrier the rights which flow from the contract of carriage.

4.

Unless otherwise specified, in this Convention the term "baggage" means both checked baggage and unchecked baggage.

Article 18 – Damage to Cargo

1.

The carrier is liable for damage sustained in the event of the destruction or loss of, or damage to, cargo upon condition only that the event which caused the damage so sustained took place during the carriage by air.

2.

However, the carrier is not liable if and to the extent it proves that the destruction, or loss of, or damage to, the cargo resulted from one or more of the following:

(a)   inherent defect, quality or vice of that cargo;
(b)   defective packing of that cargo performed by a person other than the carrier or its servants or agents;
(c)   an act of war or an armed conflict;
(d)   an act of public authority carried out in connection with the entry, exit or transit of the cargo.

3.

The carriage by air within the meaning of paragraph 1 of this Article comprises the period during which the cargo is in the charge of the carrier.

4.

The period of the carriage by air does not extend to any carriage by land, by sea or by inland waterway performed outside an airport. If, however, such carriage takes place in the performance of a contract for carriage by air, for the purpose of loading, delivery or transhipment, any damage is presumed, subject to proof to the contrary, to have been the result of an event which took place during the carriage by air. If a carrier, without the consent of the consignor, substitutes carriage by another mode of transport for the whole or part of a carriage intended by the agreement between the parties to be carriage by air, such carriage by another mode of transport is deemed to be within the period of carriage by air.

Article 19 – Delay

The carrier is liable for damage occasioned by delay in the carriage by air of passengers, baggage or cargo. Nevertheless, the carrier shall not be liable for damage occasioned by delay if it proves that it and its servants and agents took all measures that could reasonably be required to avoid the damage or that it was impossible for it or them to take such measures.

Article 20 – Exoneration

If the carrier proves that the damage was caused or contributed to by the negligence or other wrongful act or omission of the person claiming compensation, or the person from whom he or she derives his or her rights, the carrier shall be wholly or partly exonerated from its liability to the claimant to the extent that such negligence or wrongful act or omission caused or contributed to the damage. When by reason of death or injury of a passenger compensation is claimed by a person other than the passenger, the carrier shall likewise be wholly or partly exonerated from its liability to the extent that it proves that the damage was caused or contributed to by the negligence or other wrongful act or omission of that passenger. This Article applies to all the liability provisions in this Convention, including paragraph 1 of Article 21.

Article 21 – Compensation in Case of Death or Injury of Passengers

1.

For damages arising under paragraph 1 of Article 17 not exceeding 100,000 Special Drawing Rights for each passenger, the carrier shall not be able to exclude or limit its liability.

2.

The carrier shall not be liable for damages arising under paragraph 1 of Article 17 to the extent that they exceed for each passenger 100,000 Special Drawing Rights if the carrier proves that:

(a) such damage was not due to the negligence or other wrongful act or omission of the carrier or its servants or agents; or
(b) such damage was solely due to the negligence or other wrongful act or omission of a third party.

Article 22 – Limits of Liability in Relation to Delay, Baggage and Cargo

1.

In the case of damage caused by delay as specified in Article 19 in the carriage of persons, the liability of the carrier for each passenger is limited to 4,150 Special Drawing Rights.

2.

In the carriage of baggage, the liability of the carrier in the case of destruction, loss, damage or delay is limited to 1,000 Special Drawing Rights for each passenger unless the passenger has made, at the time when the checked baggage was handed over to the carrier, a special declaration of interest in delivery at destination and has paid a supplementary sum if the case so requires. In that case the carrier will be liable to pay a sum not exceeding the declared sum, unless it proves that the sum is greater than the passenger's actual interest in delivery at destination.

3.

In the carriage of cargo, the liability of the carrier in the case of destruction, loss, damage or delay is limited to a sum of 17 Special Drawing Rights per kilogramme, unless the consignor has made, at the time when the package was handed over to the carrier, a special declaration of interest in delivery at destination and has paid a supplementary sum if the case so requires. In that case the carrier will be liable to pay a sum not exceeding the declared sum, unless it proves that the sum is greater than the consignor's actual interest in delivery at destination.

4.

In the case of destruction, loss, damage or delay of part of the cargo, or of any object contained therein, the weight to be taken into consideration in determining the amount to which the carrier's liability is limited shall be only the total weight of the package or packages concerned. Nevertheless, when the destruction, loss, damage or delay of a part of the cargo, or of an object contained therein, affects the value of other packages covered by the same air waybill, or the same receipt or, if they were not issued, by the same record preserved by the other means referred to in paragraph 2 of Article 4, the total weight of such package or packages shall also be taken into consideration in determining the limit of liability.

5.

The foregoing provisions of paragraphs 1 and 2 of this Article shall not apply if it is proved that the damage resulted from an act or omission of the carrier, its servants or agents, done with intent to cause damage or recklessly and with knowledge that damage would probably result; provided that, in the case of such act or omission of a servant or agent, it is also proved that such servant or agent was acting within the scope of its employment.

6.

The limits prescribed in Article 21 and in this Article shall not prevent the court from awarding, in accordance with its own law, in addition, the whole or part of the court costs and of the other expenses of the litigation incurred by the plaintiff, including interest. The foregoing provision shall not apply if the amount of the damages awarded, excluding court costs and other expenses of the litigation, does not exceed the sum which the carrier has offered in writing to the plaintiff within a period of six months from the date of the occurrence causing the damage, or before the commencement of the action, if that is later.

Article 23 – Conversion of Monetary Units

1.

The sums mentioned in terms of Special Drawing Right in this Convention shall be deemed to refer to the Special Drawing Right as defined by the International Monetary Fund. Conversion of the sums into national currencies shall, in case of judicial proceedings, be made according to the value of such currencies in terms of the Special Drawing Right at the date of the judgement. The value of a national currency, in terms of the Special Drawing Right, of a State Party which is a Member of the International Monetary Fund, shall be calculated in accordance with the method of valuation applied by the International Monetary Fund, in effect at the date of the judgement, for its operations and transactions. The value of a national currency, in terms of the Special Drawing Right, of a State Party which is not a Member of the International Monetary Fund, shall be calculated in a manner determined by that State.

2.

Nevertheless, those States which are not Members of the International Monetary Fund and whose law does not permit the application of the provisions of paragraph 1 of this Article may, at the time of ratification or accession or at any time thereafter, declare that the limit of liability of the carrier prescribed in Article 21 is fixed at a sum of 1,500,000 monetary units per passenger in judicial proceedings in their territories; 62,500 monetary units per passenger with respect to paragraph 1 of Article 22; 15,000 monetary units per passenger with respect to paragraph 2 of Article 22; and 250 monetary units per kilogramme with respect to paragraph 3 of Article 22. This monetary unit corresponds to sixty-five and a half milligrammes of gold of millesimal fineness nine hundred. These sums may be converted into the national currency concerned in round figures. The conversion of these sums into national currency shall be made according to the law of the State concerned.

3.

The calculation mentioned in the last sentence of paragraph 1 of this Article and the conversion method mentioned in paragraph 2 of this Article shall be made in such manner as to express in the national currency of the State Party as far as possible the same real value for the amounts in Articles 21 and 22 as would result from the application of the first three sentences of paragraph 1 of this Article. States Parties shall communicate to the depositary the manner of calculation pursuant to paragraph 1 of this Article, or the result of the conversion in paragraph 2 of this Article as the case may be, when depositing an instrument of ratification, acceptance, approval of or accession to this Convention and whenever there is a change in either.

Article 24 – Review of Limits

1.

Without prejudice to the provisions of Article 25 of this Convention and subject to paragraph 2 below, the limits of liability prescribed in Articles 21, 22 and 23 shall be reviewed by the Depositary at five-year intervals, the first such review to take place at the end of the fifth year following the date of entry into force of this Convention, or if the Convention does not enter into force within five years of the date it is first open for signature, within the first year of its entry into force, by reference to an inflation factor which corresponds to the accumulated rate of inflation since the previous revision or in the first instance since the date of entry into force of the Convention. The measure of the rate of inflation to be used in determining the inflation factor shall be the weighted average of the annual rates of increase or decrease in the Consumer Price Indices of the States whose currencies comprise the Special Drawing Right mentioned in paragraph 1 of Article 23.

2.

If the review referred to in the preceding paragraph concludes that the inflation factor has exceeded 10 per cent, the Depositary shall notify States Parties of a revision of the limits of liability. Any such revision shall become effective six months after its notification to the States Parties. If within three months after its notification to the States Parties a majority of the States Parties register their disapproval, the revision shall not become effective and the Depositary shall refer the matter to a meeting of the States Parties. The Depositary shall immediately notify all States Parties of the coming into force of any revision.

3.

Notwithstanding paragraph 1 of this Article, the procedure referred to in paragraph 2 of this Article shall be applied at any time provided that one-third of the States Parties express a desire to that effect and upon condition that the inflation factor referred to in paragraph 1 has exceeded 30 per cent since the previous revision or since the date of entry into force of this Convention if there has been no previous revision. Subsequent reviews using the procedure described in paragraph 1 of this Article will take place at five-year intervals starting at the end of the fifth year following the date of the reviews under the present paragraph.

Article 25 – Stipulation on Limits

A carrier may stipulate that the contract of carriage shall be subject to higher limits of liability than those provided for in this Convention or to no limits of liability whatsoever.

Article 26 – Invalidity of Contractual Provisions

Any provision tending to relieve the carrier of liability or to fix a lower limit than that which is laid down in this Convention shall be null and void, but the nullity of any such provision does not involve the nullity of the whole contract, which shall remain subject to the provisions of this Convention.

Article 27 – Freedom to Contract

Nothing contained in this Convention shall prevent the carrier from refusing to enter into any contract of carriage, from waiving any defences available under the Convention, or from laying down conditions which do not conflict with the provisions of this Convention.

Article 28 – Advance Payments

In the case of aircraft accidents resulting in death or injury of passengers, the carrier shall, if required by its national law, make advance payments without delay to a natural person or persons who are entitled to claim compensation in order to meet the immediate economic needs of such persons. Such advance payments shall not constitute a recognition of liability and may be offset against any amounts subsequently paid as damages by the carrier.

Article 29 – Basis of Claims

In the carriage of passengers, baggage and cargo, any action for damages, however founded, whether under this Convention or in contract or in tort or otherwise, can only be brought subject to the conditions and such limits of liability as are set out in this Convention without prejudice to the question as to who are the persons who have the right to bring suit and what are their respective rights. In any such action, punitive, exemplary or any other non-compensatory damages shall not be recoverable.

Article 30 – Servants, Agents – Aggregation of Claims

1.

If an action is brought against a servant or agent of the carrier arising out of damage to which the Convention relates, such servant or agent, if they prove that they acted within the scope of their employment, shall be entitled to avail themselves of the conditions and limits of liability which the carrier itself is entitled to invoke under this Convention.

2.

The aggregate of the amounts recoverable from the carrier, its servants and agents, in that case, shall not exceed the said limits.

3.

Save in respect of the carriage of cargo, the provisions of paragraphs 1 and 2 of this Article shall not apply if it is proved that the damage resulted from an act or omission of the servant or agent done with intent to cause damage or recklessly and with knowledge that damage would probably result.

Article 31 – Timely Notice of Complaints

1.

Receipt by the person entitled to delivery of checked baggage or cargo without complaint is prima facie evidence that the same has been delivered in good condition and in accordance with the document of carriage or with the record preserved by the other means referred to in paragraph 2 of Article 3 and paragraph 2 of Article 4.

2.

In the case of damage, the person entitled to delivery must complain to the carrier forthwith after the discovery of the damage, and, at the latest, within seven days from the date of receipt in the case of checked baggage and fourteen days from the date of receipt in the case of cargo. In the case of delay, the complaint must be made at the latest within twenty-one days from the date on which the baggage or cargo have been placed at his or her disposal.

3.

Every complaint must be made in writing and given or dispatched within the times aforesaid.

4.

If no complaint is made within the times aforesaid, no action shall lie against the carrier, save in the case of fraud on its part.

Article 32 – Death of Person Liable

In the case of the death of the person liable, an action for damages lies in accordance with the terms of this Convention against those legally representing his or her estate.

Article 33 – Jurisdiction

1.

An action for damages must be brought, at the option of the plaintiff, in the territory of one of the States Parties, either before the court of the domicile of the carrier or of its principal place of business, or where it has a place of business through which the contract has beer. made or before the court at the place of destination.

2.

In respect of damage resulting from the death or injury of a passenger, an action may be brought before one of the courts mentioned in paragraph 1 of this Article, or in the territory of a State Party in which at the time of the accident the passenger has his or her principal anc. permanent residence and to or from which the carrier operates services for the carriage of passengers by air, either on its own aircraft, or on another carrier's aircraft pursuant to a commercial agreement, and in which that carrier conducts its business of carriage of passengers by air from premises leased or owned by the carrier itself or by another carrier with which it has a commercial agreement.

3.

For the purposes of paragraph 2,

(a) "commercial agreement" means an agreement, other than an agency agreement, made between carriers and relating to the provision of their joint services for carriage of passengers by air;

(b) "principal and permanent residence" means the one fixed and permanent abode of the passenger at the time of the accident. The nationality of the passenger shall not be the determining factor in this regard.

4.

Questions of procedure shall be governed by the law of the court seised of the case.

Article 34 – Arbitration

1.

Subject to the provisions of this Article, the parties to the contract of carriage for cargo may stipulate that any dispute relating to the liability of the carrier under this Convention shall be settled by arbitration. Such agreement shall be in writing.

2.

The arbitration proceedings shall, at the option of the claimant, take place within one of the jurisdictions referred to in Article 33.

3.

The arbitrator or arbitration tribunal shall apply the provisions of this Convention.

4.

The provisions of paragraphs 2 and 3 of this Article shall be deemed to be part of every arbitration clause or agreement, and any term of such clause or agreement which is inconsistent therewith shall be null and void.

Article 35 – Limitation of Actions

1.

The right to damages shall be extinguished if an action is not brought within a period of two years, reckoned from the date of arrival at the destination, or from the date on which the aircraft ought to have arrived, or from the date on which the carriage stopped.

2.

The method of calculating that period shall be determined by the law of the court seised of the case.

Article 36 – Successive Carriage

1.

In the case of carriage to be performed by various successive carriers and falling within the definition set out in paragraph 3 of Article 1, each carrier which accepts passengers, baggage or cargo is subject to the rules set out in this Convention and is deemed to be one of the parties to the contract of carriage in so far as the contract deals with that part of the carriage which is performed under its supervision.

2.

In the case of carriage of this nature, the passenger or any person entitled to compensation in respect of him or her can take action only against the carrier which performed the carriage during which the accident or the delay occurred, save in the case where, by express agreement, the first carrier has assumed liability for the whole journey.

3.

As regards baggage or cargo, the passenger or consignor will have a right of action against the first carrier, and the passenger or consignee who is entitled to delivery will have a right of action against the last carrier, and further, each may take action against the carrier which performed the carriage during which the destruction, loss, damage or delay took place. These carriers will be jointly and severally liable to the passenger or to the consignor or consignee.

Article 37 – Right of Recourse against Third Parties

Nothing in this Convention shall prejudice the question whether a person liable for damage in accordance with its provisions has a right of recourse against any other person.

Chapter IV COMBINED CARRIAGE

Article 38 – Combined Carriage

1.

In the case of combined carriage performed partly by air and partly by any other mode of carriage, the provisions of this Convention shall, subject to paragraph 4 of Article 18, apply only to the carriage by air, provided that the carriage by air falls within the terms of Article 1.

2.

Nothing in this Convention shall prevent the parties in the case of combined carriage from inserting in the document of air carriage conditions relating to other modes of carriage, provided that the provisions of this Convention are observed as regards the carriage by air.

Chapter V CARRIAGE BY AIR PERFORMED BY A PERSON OTHER THAN THE CONTRACTING CARRIER

Article 39 – Contracting Carrier – Actual Carrier

The provisions of this Chapter apply when a person (hereinafter referred to as "the contracting carrier") as a principal makes a contract governed by this Convention with a passenger or consignor or with a person acting on behalf of the passenger or consignor, and another person (hereinafter referred to as "the actual carrier") performs, by virtue of authority from the contracting carrier, the whole or part of the carriage, but is not with respect to such part a successive carrier within the meaning of this Convention. Such authority shall be presumed in the absence of proof to the contrary.

Article 40 – Respective Liability of Contracting and Actual Carriers

If an actual carrier performs the whole or part of carriage which, according to the contract referred to in Article 39, is governed by this Convention, both the contracting carrier and the actual carrier shall, except as otherwise provided in this Chapter, be subject to the rules of this Convention, the former for the whole of the carriage contemplated in the contract, the latter solely for the carriage which it performs.

Article 41 – Mutual Liability

1.

The acts and omissions of the actual carrier and of its servants and agents acting within the scope of their employment shall, in relation to the carriage performed by the actual carrier, be deemed to be also those of the contracting carrier.

2.

The acts and omissions of the contracting carrier and of its servants and agents acting within the scope of their employment shall, in relation to the carriage performed by the actual carrier, be deemed to be also those of the actual carrier. Nevertheless, no such act or omission shall subject the actual carrier to liability exceeding the amounts referred to in Articles 21, 22, 23 and 24. Any special agreement under which the contracting carrier assumes obligations not imposed by this Convention or any waiver of rights or defences conferred by this Convention or any special declaration of interest in delivery at destination contemplated in Article 22 shall not affect the actual carrier unless agreed to by it.

Article 42 – Addressee of Complaints and Instructions

Any complaint to be made or instruction to be given under this Convention to the carrier shall have the same effect whether addressed to the contracting carrier or to the actual carrier. Nevertheless, instructions referred to in Article 12 shall only be effective if addressed to the contracting carrier.

Article 43 – Servants and Agents

In relation to the carriage performed by the actual carrier, any servant or agent of that carrier or of the contracting carrier shall, if they prove that they acted within the scope of their employment, be entitled to avail themselves of the conditions and limits of liability which are applicable under this Convention to the carrier whose servant or agent they are, unless it is proved that they acted in a manner that prevents the limits of liability from being invoked in accordance with this Convention.

Article 44 – Aggregation of Damages

In relation to the carriage performed by the actual carrier, the aggregate of the amounts recoverable from that carrier and the contracting carrier, and from their servants and agents acting within the scope of their employment, shall not exceed the highest amount which could be awarded against either the contracting carrier or the actual carrier under this Convention, but none of the persons mentioned shall be liable for a sum in excess of the limit applicable to that person.

Article 45 – Addressee of Claims

In relation to the carriage performed by the actual carrier, an action for damages may be brought, at the option of the plaintiff, against that carrier or the contracting carrier, or against both together or separately. If the action is brought against only one of those carriers, that carrier shall have the right to require the other carrier to be joined in the proceedings, the procedure and effects being governed by the law of the court seised of the case.

Article 46 – Additional Jurisdiction

Any action for damages contemplated in Article 45 must be brought, at the option of the plaintiff, in the territory of one of the States Parties, either before a court in which an action may be brought against the contracting carrier, as provided in Article 33, or before the court having jurisdiction at the place where the actual carrier has its domicile or its principal place of business.

Article 47 – Invalidity of Contractual Provisions

Any contractual provision tending to relieve the contracting carrier or the actual carrier of liability under this Chapter or to fix a lower limit than that which is applicable according to this Chapter shall be null and void, but the nullity of any such provision does not involve the nullity of the whole contract, which shall remain subject to the provisions of this Chapter.

Article 48 – Mutual Relations of Contracting and Actual Carriers

Except as provided in Article 45, nothing in this Chapter shall affect the rights and obligations of the carriers between themselves, including any right of recourse or indemnification.

Chapter VI OTHER PROVISIONS

Article 49 – Mandatory Application

Any clause contained in the contract of carriage and all special agreements entered into before the damage occurred by which the parties purport to infringe the rules laid down by this Convention, whether by deciding the law to be applied, or by altering the rules as to jurisdiction, shall be null and void.

Article 50 – Insurance

States Parties shall require their carriers to maintain adequate insurance covering their liability under this Convention. A carrier may be required by the State Party into which it operates to furnish evidence that it maintains adequate insurance covering its liability under this Convention.

Article 51 – Carriage Performed in Extraordinary Circumstances

The provisions of Articles 3 to 5, 7 and 8 relating to the documentation of carriage shall not apply in the case of carriage performed in extraordinary circumstances outside the normal scope of a carrier's business.

Article 52 – Definition of Days

The expression "days" when used in this Convention means calendar days, not working days.

Chapter VII FINAL CLAUSES

Article 53 – Signature, Ratification and Entry into Force

2.

... For the purpose of this Convention, a "Regional Economic Integration Organisation" means any organisation which is constituted by sovereign States of a given region which has competence in respect of certain matters governed by this Convention and has been duly authorized to sign and to ratify, accept, approve or accede to this Convention. A reference to a "State Party" or "States Parties" in this Convention, otherwise than in paragraph 2 of Article 1, paragraph 1(b) of Article 3, paragraph (b) of Article 5, Articles 23, 33, 46 and paragraph (b) of Article 57, applies equally to a Regional Economic Integration Organisation. For the purpose of Article 24, the references to "a majority of the States Parties" and "one-third of the States Parties" shall not apply to a Regional Economic Integration Organisation.

Article 55 – Relationship with other Warsaw Convention Instruments

This Convention shall prevail over any rules which apply to international carriage by air:

1. between States Parties to this Convention by virtue of those States commonly being Party to:

(a) the Convention for the Unification of Certain Rules Relating to International Carriage by Air Signed at Warsaw on 12 October 1929 (hereinafter called the Warsaw Convention);

(b) the Protocol to Amend the Convention for the Unification of Certain Rules Relating to International Carriage by Air Signed at Warsaw on 12 October 1929, Done at The Hague on 28 September 1955 (hereinafter called The Hague Protocol);

(c) the Convention, Supplementary to the Warsaw Convention, for the Unification of Certain Rules Relating to International Carriage by Air Performed by a Person Other than the Contracting Carrier, signed at Guadalajara on 18 September 1961 (hereinafter called the Guadalajara Convention);

(d) the Protocol to Amend the Convention for the Unification of Certain Rules Relating to International Carriage by Air Signed at Warsaw on 12 October 1929 as Amended by the Protocol Done at The Hague on 28 September 1955 Signed at Guatemala City on 8 March 1971 (hereinafter called the Guatemala City Protocol);

(e) Additional Protocol Nos. 1 to 3 and Montreal Protocol No.4 to amend the Warsaw Convention as amended by The Hague Protocol or the Warsaw Convention as amended by both The Hague Protocol and the Guatemala City Protocol Signed at Montreal on 25 September 1975 (hereinafter called the Montreal Protocol); or

2. within the territory of any single State Party to this Convention by virtue of that State being Party to one or more of the instruments referred to in sub-paragraphs (a) to (e) above.

Article 57 – Reservations

No reservation may be made to this Convention except that a State Party may at any time declare by a notification addressed to the Depositary that this Convention shall not apply to:

(a) international carriage by air performed and operated directly by that State Party for non-commercial purposes in respect to its functions and duties as a sovereign State; and/or

(b) the carriage of persons, cargo and baggage for its military authorities on aircraft registered in or leased by that State Party, the whole capacity of which has been reserved by or on behalf of such authorities.

[Paragraphs 53 *(save for part of* paragraph 2*)*, 54 and 56 *and the concluding words of the Convention are not reproduced. They deal with signature, ratification, coming into force, denunciation and territorial extent where a State has more than one system of law*]

][1]

---

[1]   Added by Carriage by Air Acts (Implementation of the Montreal Convention 1999) Order 2002/263 Sch 1 para.1 (June 28, 2004 as specified in the London Gazette dated May 7, 2004)

INDEX

References are to paragraph numbers.